STUDY GUIDE

Jeannie Shearer-Gillmore
University of Western Ontario

Foundations of Microeconomics

Robin Bade

Michael Parkin
University of Western Ontario

Brian Lyons
Sheridan College

Toronto

© 2003 Pearson Education Canada Inc., Toronto, Ontario. *Study Guide, Foundations of Microeconomics* is published by Addison Wesley Longman, Inc., a division of Pearson Education, Needham Heights, MA. Copyright © 2003 by Addison Wesley Longman, Inc. This edition is authorized for sale in Canada only.

All rights reserved. This publication is protected by copyright, and permission should be obtained from the publisher prior to any prohibited reproduction, storage in a retrieval system, or transmission in any form or by any means, electronic, mechanical, photocopying, recording, or likewise. For information regarding permission, write to the Permissions Department.

We'd like to thank the original authors of the U.S. edition of the Study Guide:
- Thomas Meyer, *Patrick Henry Community College*
- Mark Rush, *University of Florida*

Study Guide multiple-choice questions authored by:
- Seema Ahmad, *Dutchess Community College*
- Sue Bartlett, *University of South Florida*
- Jack Chambless, *Valencia Community College*
- Paul Harris, *Camden County Community College*
- William Mosher, *Assumption College*
- Terry Sutton, *Southeast Missouri State University*

ISBN 0-201-79341-5

Executive Acquisitions Editor: Dave Ward
Projects Manager: Andrew Winton
Developmental Editor: Madhu Ranadive
Production Editor: Marisa D'Andrea
Production Coordinator: Deborah Starks

1 2 3 4 5   07 06 05 04 03

Printed and bound in Canada.

Table of Contents

Preface 1	Your Complete Learning Package	v
Preface 2	Your Course and Your Study Guide	ix

■Part 1 Introduction

Chapter 1	Getting Started	1
	Appendix: Making and Using Graphs	15
Chapter 2	The Canadian Economy	25
Chapter 3	The Economic Problem	39
Chapter 4	Demand and Supply	57

■Part 2 A Closer Look at Markets

Chapter 5	Elasticities of Demand and Supply	75
Chapter 6	Efficiency and Fairness of Markets	89

■Part 3 How Governments Influence the Economy

Chapter 7	Government Influences on Markets	107
Chapter 8	Externalities	125
Chapter 9	Public Goods and the Tax System	139

■Part 4 A Closer Look at Decision Makers

Chapter 10	Consumer Choice and Demand	153
	Appendix: Indifference Curves	169
Chapter 11	Production and Cost	175

■Part 5 Prices, Profits, and Industry Performance

Chapter 12	Perfect Competition	193
Chapter 13	Monopoly	209
Chapter 14	Monopolistic Competition and Oligopoly	227
Chapter 15	Regulation and Competition Law	243

■Part 6 How Incomes Are Determined

Chapter 16	Demand and Supply in Factor Markets	255
Chapter 17	Earnings Differences	271
Chapter 18	Inequality, Poverty, and Redistribution	287

■Part 7 Microeconomic Policy Issues

Chapter 19	International Trade	301
Chapter 20	Farms and Cities	317
Chapter 21	International Financial Markets	331

Your Complete Learning Package

YOUR *FOUNDATIONS* LEARNING TOOLS

■ **The Complete Package**

Your *Foundations of Microeconomics* package consists of:

- Textbook
- Study Guide
- *e*Foundations

And *e*Foundations consists of:

- *e*Text—the complete text online with animated figures and audio
- *e*Study Guide—the complete Study Guide online, with links to the *e*Text
- Foundations Interactive—Java tutorial and quiz software (also available on a CD)
- Web quiz—Multiple choice and true or false questions with instant feedback and links to the correct page in *e*Text.

■ **Checklist and Checkpoints: The Glue That Holds Your Tools Together**

Each chapter of your textbook opens with a Chapter Checklist that tells you what you'll be able to do when you've completed the chapter. The number of tasks varies from two to five and most often is three or four. Begin by reviewing this list thoughtfully and get a good sense of what you are about to learn.

Your Study Guide provides an Expanded Chapter Checklist that breaks down your tasks into detailed bite-size pieces. Use the Expanded Chapter Checklist to confirm that you have learned each one of the individual items.

Each part of a chapter in the textbook, Study Guide, and *e*Foundations is linked directly to a Checklist item to enable you to know exactly what you're studying and how it will enable you to accomplish your learning objective.

Each part of a chapter in the textbook ends with a Checkpoint—a page that offers you a practice problem to test your understanding of the key ideas of the part, a worked and illustrated solution to the practice problem, and a further (parallel) exercise. The Checkpoints enable you to review what you've read when it's fresh in your mind—the most effective and productive time to do so. The Checkpoints guide you in a step-by-step approach that takes the guesswork out of learning. The Study Guide reinforces each Checkpoint by providing a more detailed solution to the textbook practice problem and an additional practice problem. Use these if you're still not sure that you understand the topic.

The tutorials and quizzes in Foundations Interactive and the self-test questions in the Study Guide, Foundations Interactive, and Web quiz are all organized by Checkpoint. So that you know exactly where to go in your Study Guide and eFoundations, the Study Guide page numbers and eFoundations part numbers are listed at every textbook Checkpoint.

■ Practice Makes Perfect

As you study, distinguish between *practice* and *self-test*. Practice is part of the learning process—learning by doing. Self-test is a check. It shows you where you need to go back and reinforce your understanding, and it helps you build your confidence.

The Checkpoint practice problems and exercises, the Chapter Checkpoint exercises, and the quizzes in Foundations Interactive are designed for *practice*. The Study Guide, Foundations Interactive, and Web quiz are designed for *self testing*.

The table that follows shows you how the different tools help you practice and self-test. Take a look at it now and start thinking about which tools you think will be most useful to you.

■ Learn Your Learning Style

It is unlikely that you'll need to use all the tools that we've created all of the time. Try to discover how you learn best. Then exploit what you discover.

If you learn best by reading with a marker or pencil in your hand, you'll use the textbook and Study Guide more often than the other items. If you learn best by seeing the action, you'll often use the *e*Text and Foundations Interactive Demos with their animated graphics. If you learn best by hearing, you'll use the *e*Text audio explanations of the action in key figures. If you learn best by participating and acting, you'll often use the Action and Interactive Quiz in Foundations Interactive.

■ Tell Us What Works for *You*

Please tell us the tools that you find most helpful. And tell us what you think we can improve. You can email us at robin@econ100.com or michael.parkin@uwo.ca, or use the Office Hours in your Foundations Web site.

Robin Bade
Michael Parkin
Ontario, Canada
February, 2002

Your Learning Tools at a Glance

Activity	Print		eFoundations	
	Textbook	Study Guide	eText and eStudy Guide	Foundations Interactive
Getting into a chapter	Chapter opener—previews and places chapter in context	Chapter in perspective—a short summary of the core material		
	Chapter checklist tells you what you'll be able to do when you've completed the chapter	Expanded chapter checklist breaks down your tasks into detailed bite-size pieces		
Learning the material	Explanations; matched tables and figures; figures with numbered captions		eText has exactly the same content as the print textbook plus: dynamic figures and audio explanations	Fast track summarizes each topic. Textbook figures are interactive in Action and animated in Demo
	Key terms defined in text and in margin	Key terms list for review	Key terms with hyperlinks to definitions, examples, and related terms in both tools	
	Chapter checkpoint • Key points • Key terms list			
Practice makes perfect	Checkpoints • Practice problem • Exercise • Solution to practice problem	Checkpoints • Practice problem • Additional practice problem • Expanded solution to practice problem	eText practice problems, exercises and solutions; eStudy Guide additional practice problems and expanded solutions	Five question types in Interactive Quiz: • Fill in the blanks • True or False • Multiple Choice • Numeric • Complete the graph
	Chapter checkpoint exercises		Chapter checkpoint exercises link to external sites	
Self Test		Self Test: • Fill in the blanks • True or False • Multiple Choice • Complete the graph • Short Answer	eStudy Guide has the same content as the print Study Guide. Online quizzes with hyperlinks to eText for further review: • True or False • Multiple Choice	Self Test version of Interactive Quiz: • Fill in the blanks • True or False • Multiple Choice • Numeric • Complete the graph
Enrichment, Critical Thinking, and Applications	Eye On … • The Canadian economy • The global economy • The past			
	Economics in the News		Economics in the News hyperlinks to news article and related sites	

Your Course and Your Study Guide

INTRODUCTION

The goal of this Study Guide is to help you to understand the course material presented by your teacher and by your textbook. The Study Guide is just one of the tools that you will use to reach your peak performance on examinations. Using this Study Guide alone is not enough to guarantee that you will earn an A. To help you overcome the problems and difficulties that many students encounter, I have some general advice on how to study economics and some specific advice on how to use this Study Guide.

Economics is hard for many students because it studies familiar things in an unfamiliar way. Economics doesn't *describe* the economic world: it *explains* it. And to do so, economists make extensive use of *models* that are simpler than the world we live in. In an economic model, everything remains the same except for the tiny part of the world that we are trying to explain. We make assumptions about what people and businesses are trying to achieve. Then we figure out the decisions that people will make. This approach can be demanding. It feels unfamiliar to most students and requires practice.

It is not as easy to do well in economics on the basis of your raw intelligence and high-school knowledge as it is in many other courses. Many students are frustrated and puzzled that they are receiving As and Bs in their other courses but only a C or worse in economics. They have not recognized that economics is different and requires practice.

To avoid a frustrating visit to your instructor after your first exam, I suggest you do the following.

HOW TO STUDY ECONOMICS

■ **Don't rely solely on your high-school economics**

If you took high-school economics, you've already studied demand and supply, which your instructor will lecture on in the first few weeks. Don't be lulled into feeling that the course will be easy. Your high-school knowledge of economic concepts will be useful, but it will not be enough to guarantee high scores on exams. Your college instructor will demand more detailed knowledge of concepts and ask you to apply them in new circumstances.

■ **Keep up with the course material on a weekly basis**

Read the appropriate textbook chapter before your instructor lectures on it. You'll be amazed at how your instructor's teaching ability improves when you come to class prepared. After class, work the practice problems and exercise and Foundations Interactive quiz for practice. Then use the Study Guide quiz to test your understanding. Economics requires lots of practice and self testing.

■ Make a good set of notes

Good notes are vital to focus your studying. Writing the notes is more important than reading them! The note-writing process begins when you read the textbook *before* the lecture. Make an outline set of notes at that time. List all the key terms and be sure you know their definitions. Take the outline to class and fill in the details. After class, rewrite the notes clearly so that you can easily review them later. At this time, elaborate any items that your instructor emphasizes.

■ Use your instructor and/or teaching assistants for help

When you have questions or problems with course material, ask questions. Your instructor is here to help you learn. Instructors like to be asked questions. And there are no stupid questions! So try not to be shy. The personal contact that comes from one-on-one tutoring is rewarding for instructors as well as beneficial for you.

■ Form a study group

A useful way to motivate your studying and to learn economics is to discuss the course material and problems with other students. Explaining the answer to a question out loud is a very effective way of discovering how well you understand the question. When you answer a question only in your head, you often skip steps in the chain of reasoning without realizing it. When you are forced to explain your reasoning aloud, gaps and mistakes quickly appear, and you and your fellow group members can quickly correct your reasoning. The Checkpoint practice problems and exercises are extremely good study group material.

■ Work old exams intelligently

You can usually obtain old exam papers in your school library, from your instructor, or from students who have already taken the course. Past exams give you a feel for the style of question your instructor might ask, and working them under a time constraint helps you to pace yourself and do the exam in the allotted time. But remember that you are preparing for the *next* exam that your instructor will set, not the *last* one. You must *understand* the answer to each question. If you *memorize* answers, you are likely to fail. Every year, instructors hear students who tell them that this year's exam was much harder than last year's. In truth, it was the same paper with a few numbers and examples changed!

■ Use *All Your Tools*

The authors of your book, Robin Bade, Michael Parkin, and Brian Lyons, have created a rich array of learning tools that they describe in the preceding section, "Your Complete Learning Package." Make sure that you read this section and use *all* your tools! You should attempt to complete a chapter in the Study Guide only after you have read the corresponding textbook chapter and listened to your instructor lecture on the material.

HOW TO USE THE STUDY GUIDE

Each Study Guide chapter contains:

Chapter in Perspective

This first section is a short summary of the key material. It is designed to focus you quickly and precisely on the core material that you must master. You can use it to help you organize you own notes when you first read the textbook chapter. And you can use it before your exam to serve as a final check of the key concepts you have studied.

Expanded Chapter Checklist

A key point of the textbook is its use of Chapter Checklist and Checkpoints. Each Checklist item is explained in the textbook and is followed by a Checkpoint where you will work practice problems and exercises. The Study Guide repeats the Checklist learning objective and then breaks it down into a list of smaller objectives. Use this more detailed list to organize your study and for review. If you have mastered each of the detailed checklist objectives, you can be confident that you understand the material.

Key Terms

One aspect many students find difficult about economics is its vocabulary. To understand economics you must learn its vocabulary. The Study Guide lists the key terms in each chapter and gives the page in the textbook on which they are found. You can use this list to help you review for a test. Be sure that you can define each term and that you understand its definition.

After the Key Terms, the Study Guide is divided into topics that correspond to each Checkpoint in your text. At the beginning of each Checkpoint the learning objective is repeated. Always keep this objective in mind because it helps place the material in the Checkpoint into perspective.

Practice Problem

Each Checkpoint in the text contains a practice problem with answers. These practice problems are repeated in the Study Guide, but the explanations of the solutions are more detailed than in the textbook. Use these solutions to enhance your understanding of the topic.

Additional Practice Problem

After the original practice problem is explained, the Study Guide presents an additional practice problem. The additional practice problem either extends the original one or covers a related topic. Although the solution to the additional practice problem is given, try to solve it on your own first.

Following the additional practice problem is the Self Test. This section has fill in the blank, true or false, multiple choice, complete the graph, and short answer questions. The questions are designed to test your understanding of each topic.

Do the Self Test questions as if they were real exam questions, which means do them without looking at the answers. Struggling to work out the answers to a question that you find difficult is one of the most effective ways to learn. You will learn the most from right answers you had to struggle to work out and from your wrong answers and mistakes. Look at the answers, only after you have attempted all the questions in a Checkpoint. When you finally do check the answers, be sure to understand where you went wrong and why the answer given is correct.

Fill in the Blanks

Fill in the blank questions will help you with the economics vocabulary and allow you to check that you know the definitions of the key terms and how to use them. These questions will also help you review for a test because, once completed, they serve as a *very* brief list of the main points within a Checklist item.

True or False

Some instructors use true or false questions on exams or quizzes, so these questions can prove very valuable exam practice. The answers to the questions are given along with a textbook page reference. If you do not understand the answer, turn to the textbook and study the topic. Reviewing the textbook page at this time will enable you to improve your understanding and perhaps ensure that you will not miss a similar question on your exams.

Multiple Choice

Many exams contain multiple choice questions, so pay particular attention to these questions. The answers to each of these questions also contain a textbook page reference. If you have difficulty with a question, use this page reference to review the topic in the textbook and improve your understanding. Remember that multiple choice is not multiple guess. Work out the answer. Know why an incorrect option is incorrect.

Complete the Graph

The complete the graph questions allow you to practice using one of economists' major tools, graphs. If there are essay questions on your exams, it is a safe bet that you will be expected to use some graphs in your essay. Complete the graph questions are designed to ensure that you are well prepared to draw graphs correctly.

Use the graph in the Study Guide to answer the questions. Although the answer is given, do *not* look at it before you attempt to solve the problem. It is much too easy to deceive yourself into thinking that you understand the answer when you simply look at the question and then read the answer. Involve yourself in the material by answering the question and then looking at the answer. If you cannot answer the question or if you got the answer wrong, the Study Guide gives the textbook reference. Use the text and study the material!

Short Answer

The last set of questions are short answer questions. Approach them in the same way as you approach the other question types: Answer them before you look at the answers in the Study Guide. These questions make good discussion questions for your study group. Use them to check how well your study group members understand the topic. If your group disagrees about the answer, use the textbook page references to settle the disagreements and be sure that everyone has a solid grasp of the topic.

FINAL COMMENTS

This Study Guide could not have been written without the help of many people.

Robin Bade, Michael Parkin, and Brian Lyons have written an outstanding textbook. Their intense interest in their students and their dedication to producing the best learning package possible is inspirational. It was my privilege to be one of Michael Parkin's graduate students at the University of Western Ontario. I know from experience his outstanding pedagogical principles. And Robin Bade has taught me over the last six years that details are important and that we should always strive for excellence—a lesson we can use in all aspects of life, not just economics!

Mark Rush from the University of Florida provided the initial files upon which this Study Guide is based.

Jane McAndrew in the Economics Reference Centre at the University of Western Ontario has been extremely helpful in finding data for many of the questions in this Study Guide.

Richard Parkin produced all of the artwork and maintained a wonderful sense of humour when deadlines seem insurmountable.

My son Andy has been very supportive during the writing of this Study Guide. He seems to know just the right time that Mom needs a break and when Mom needs to give up an evening to do some extra work.

My husband Marvin has been almost as committed to this project as I have. He has willingly delayed family outings and rearranged his schedule to help me make deadlines. He also knows that a cup of tea at precisely the right moment is exactly what I need to keep going.

And finally my parents, Ve and Bill Shearer have shown a keen interest in this project from the start. My parents believe that if I set my mind to doing something, then the thing will be done. Thank you for your faith in me.

I have tried to make the Study Guide as helpful and useful as possible. Undoubtedly I have made some mistakes—mistakes that you might find. If you do find a mistake, please let me know so that I can correct any errors. If you have a question, suggestion, or comment, please contact me. My address follows, or you can e-mail me at

jeannie.gillmore@uwo.ca.

Jeannie Gillmore
Department of Economics
University of Western Ontario
London, Ontario
N6A 5C2
February, 2002.

Chapter 1
Getting Started

CHAPTER IN PERSPECTIVE

Chapter 1 defines economics, discusses the three major questions of microeconomics, and examines methods used by economists to study the economic world. In this chapter you will discover why even those who do not plan on becoming economists should learn the essential elements of this discipline.

- **Define economics, distinguish between microeconomics and macroeconomics, and explain the questions of microeconomics.**

Economic questions exist because of scarcity, the condition that human wants exceed the resources available to satisfy them. Economics is the social science that studies the choices that individuals, businesses, government, and entire societies make as they cope with scarcity. Microeconomics is the study of the choices that individuals and businesses make, the way these choices interact, and the influence that governments exert on these choices. Macroeconomics is the study of the aggregate (or total) effects on the national economy and the global economy of the choices that individuals, businesses, and governments make. The three major microeconomic questions are "*What* goods and services get produced and in what quantities?", "*How* are goods and services produced?", and "*For whom* are the various goods and services produced?"

- **Describe the work of economists as social scientists.**

Statements about "what *is*" are *positive* statements; statements about "what *ought to be*" are *normative* statements. Economists use observing and measuring, model building, and testing to develop their theories. An economic model simplifies reality by including only those features needed for the purpose at hand. *Ceteris paribus* is a Latin term that means "other things being equal" or "if all other relevant things remain the same." Correlation is the tendency for the values of two variables to move in a predictable and related way. The *post hoc* fallacy is the error of reasoning that a first event *causes* a second event because the first occurred before the second.

- **Explain five core ideas that define the economic way of thinking.**

The five core ideas that form the basis of all microeconomic models are: people make rational choices by comparing costs and benefits; cost is what you *must give up* to get something; benefit is what you gain when you get something and is measured by what you are *willing to give up* to get it; a rational choice is made on the margin; and people respond to incentives.

- **Explain why economics is worth studying.**

Studying economics provides understanding and expanded career opportunities. The costs of studying economics are forgone knowledge of some other subject and forgone leisure time.

EXPANDED CHAPTER CHECKLIST

When you have completed this chapter, you will be able to:

1 **Define economics, distinguish between microeconomics and macroeconomics, and explain the questions of microeconomics.**

- Define economics and explain the meaning of scarcity.
- Distinguish between macroeconomics and microeconomics and discuss the subjects each study.
- List and discuss the three major microeconomic questions.

2 **Describe the work of economists as social scientists.**

- Explain the difference between positive and normative statements.
- Describe the task of economic science.
- Define *ceteris paribus* and explain why it is used in economic models.
- Discuss the correlation between two variables.
- Define and give examples of the *post hoc* fallacy.

3 **Explain five core ideas that define the economic way of thinking.**

- Define rational choice and explain why a rational choice is made on the margin.
- Define opportunity cost and distinguish between an opportunity cost and a sunk cost.
- Define benefit.
- Define marginal cost and marginal benefit.
- Explain the role of incentives in making rational choices.

4 **Explain why economics is worth studying.**

- State two benefits from studying economics.
- State two costs of studying economics.

KEY TERMS

- Benefit (page 14)
- *Ceteris paribus* (page 10)
- Correlation (page 11)
- Economic model (page 9)
- Economic theory (page 9)
- Economics (page 5)
- Goods and services (page 6)
- Incentive (page 16)
- Macroeconomics (page 5)
- Margin (page 15)
- Marginal benefit (page 15)
- Marginal cost (page 15)
- Microeconomics (page 5)
- Opportunity cost (page 13)
- *Post hoc* fallacy (page 11)
- Rational choice (page 13)
- Scarcity (page 4)
- Sunk cost (page 14)

CHECKPOINT 1.1

■ **Define economics, distinguish between microeconomics and macroeconomics, and explain the questions of microeconomics.**

Practice Problems 1.1

1. Economics studies choices that arise from one fact. What is that fact?

2. Sort the following issues into microeconomic and macroeconomic issues:

a. More people are buying DVD players.

b. Unemployment in Canada is higher than it was last year.

c. Your local county opens a neighbourhood gym for teenagers.

2. Match the following headlines with the What, How, and For whom questions:

a. With more research, we will cure cancer.

b. A good education is the right of every child.

c. Will the government increase welfare benefits or cut income taxes?

Solution to Practice Problems 1.1

These practice problems use several definitions. You must know the distinction between microeconomics and macroeconomics, and understand the three major microeconomic questions.

Quick Review

- *Microeconomics* The study of the choices that individuals and businesses make, the interaction of these choices, and the influence that governments exert on these choices.

- *Macroeconomics* The study of the aggregate (or total) effects on the national economy and the global economy of the choices that individuals, businesses, and governments make.

- *What?* What goods and services get produced and in what quantities?

- *How?* How are goods and services produced?

- *For Whom?* For whom are the various goods and services produced?

1. **Economics studies choices that arise from one fact. What is that fact?**

The fact is scarcity. Our limited resources cannot meet our unlimited wants. Scarcity influences all of economics.

2. **Sort the following issues into microeconomic and macroeconomic issues:**

a. **More people are buying DVD players.**

Buying DVD players is a microeconomic issue because it deals with choices made by individuals.

b. **Unemployment in Canada is higher than it was last year.**

Canadian unemployment is a macroeconomic issue because it refers to the national economy.

c. **Your local county opens a neighbourhood gym for teenagers.**

Opening a neighbourhood gym for teenagers is a microeconomic issue because it deals with the interactions of the decisions of local government and individuals. It is not on a national, macroeconomic level.

3. **Match the following headlines with the What, How, and For whom questions:**

a. **With more research, we will cure cancer.**

The statement involves two of the three questions. First, we do not yet know how to cure cancer, so more research is a How question. Second, we could conduct research to find a cure for cancer or, say, a cure for diabetes, so a cure for cancer is a What question.

b. **A good education is the right of every child.**

Similar to part (a), this statement also involves two of the three questions. The production of good education instead of, say, more hospitals, is a What question. And "every child" receiving the education is a For whom question.

c. **Will the government increase welfare benefits or cut income taxes?**

An increase in welfare benefits or a cut in income taxes is a For whom question. Poor people receive the increased welfare benefits and workers would pay less tax and keep more of their incomes.

Additional Practice Problem 1.1a

Tell whether each product is a good or a service:
a. E.D. Smith strawberry jam
b. a dishwasher
c. a cup of coffee from Tim Horton's
d. a hair cut at your local salon
e. H&R Block completing your taxes
f. plywood purchased at Home Hardware

Solution to Additional Practice Problem 1.1a

a. E.D. Smith strawberry jam

E.D. Smith strawberry jam is a good.

b. a dishwasher

A dishwasher is a good.

c. a cup of coffee from Tim Horton's

A cup of coffee from Tim Horton's is a good.

d. a hair cut at your local salon

A hair cut at your local salon is a service.

e. H&R Block completing your taxes

H&R Block completing your taxes is a service.

f. plywood purchased at Home Hardware

Plywood purchased at Home Hardware is a good.

■ Self Test 1.1

Fill in the blanks

Economic questions arise because ____ (human wants; resources) exceed the ____ (human wants; resources) available to satisfy them. Faced with ____, people must make choices. ____ (Macroeconomics; Microeconomics) is the study of the choices of individuals and businesses, the interaction of these choices, and the influence that governments exert on these choices. The three major microeconomic questions are: ____, ____, ____.

True or false

1. Faced with scarcity we must make choices.
2. "Why are people buying more orange juice this winter than last winter?" is a macroeconomic question.
3. The subject of economics divides into two main parts, which are macroeconomics and microeconomics.
4. The three major questions of microeconomics are what, how, and why.

Multiple choice

1. The characteristic from which all economic problems arise is
a. political decisions.
b. providing a minimal standard of living for every person.
c. how to make a profit.
d. scarcity.

2. Scarcity results from the fact that
a. human wants exceed the resources available to satisfy them.
b. not all goals are desirable.
c. we cannot answer the major microeconomic questions.
d. the population keeps growing.

3. To economists, scarcity means that
a. limited wants cannot be satisfied by the unlimited resources.
b. a person looking for work is not able to find work.
c. the number of people without jobs rises when economic times are bad.
d. unlimited wants cannot be satisfied by the limited resources.

4. Which of the following is a microeconomic issue?
a. Why has unemployment risen nationwide?
b. Why has economic growth been rapid in China?
c. What is the impact on the quantity of regular coffee purchased if consumers' tastes change in favour of specialty coffee beverages?
d. All of the above are microeconomic issues.

5. The major microeconomic questions exist because
a. economic science hasn't yet determined the best answers.
b. we all live in a society with more than one person.
c. the federal government typically makes bad economic decisions.
d. of scarcity.

6. The question "Should we produce video tapes or DVDs?" is an example of a ____ question.
a. what
b. how
c. for whom
d. why

Short answer

1. Will there ever come a time without scarcity?
2. Explain the difference between microeconomics and macroeconomics.
3. What are the three major microeconomic questions? Give an example of each.

CHECKPOINT 1.2

■ **Describe the work of economists as social scientists.**

Practice Problems 1.2

1. Classify each of the following statements as positive or normative:
a. There is too much poverty in Canada.
b. More students would go to college if tuition were free.
c. An increase in the gas tax will cut pollution.
d. Cuts to health-care funding in Canada have been too deep.

2. Provide two examples of the *post hoc* fallacy.

Solution to Practice Problems 1.2

The key to whether a statement is positive or normative is whether the statement can be tested. If we can test the statement, it is positive; if we cannot test the statement, it is normative.

Quick Review

- *Positive statement* A positive statement tells what is currently believed about the way the world operates.
- *Normative statement* A normative statement tells what ought to be. It depends on values.
- *Post hoc* fallacy The error of reasoning that a first event *causes* a second event because the first occurred *before* the second.

a. **There is too much poverty in Canada.**

This statement cannot be tested. It depends on the values of the person making the statement. It is a normative statement.

b. **More students would go to college if tuition were free.**

This statement can be tested by giving students free tuition and then calculating the change in the number of students attending college. It is a positive statement.

c. **An increase in the gas tax will cut pollution.**

This statement can be tested by increasing the gas tax and then measuring the change in pollution. It is a positive statement.

d. **Cuts to health-care funding in Canada have been too deep.**

This statement cannot be tested. It depends on the values of the person making the statement. It is a normative statement.

2. **Provide two examples of the *post hoc* fallacy.**

Your examples will differ. The key is that the first event does not cause the second.

i) The Bay runs a sale on swimsuits in April and it is warm in June.

ii) I buy 100 shares of Bell Canada stock today and its price falls tomorrow.

Additional Practice Problem 1.2a

What is the relationship between *ceteris paribus*, a controlled experiment, and the approaches economists must take to test their theories?

Solution to Additional Practice Problem 1.2a

Ceteris paribus is a Latin term that means "if all other relevant things remain the same." Similar to other scientists, economists develop models that predict the effect of the change of one factor when all other factors remain the same. The model predicts the effect of a change in one factor, *ceteris paribus*. Laboratory sciences can conduct controlled experiments in which only the one factor under investigation changes. Economists cannot conduct such controlled experiments. So economists use: natural experiments, in which in the ordinary course of economic life, only one factor changes; statistical investigations, in which economists look for correlations; and, economic experiments, in which real subjects are placed in a decision-making situation and the influence of interest is varied to discover how the subjects respond to one factor at a time.

■ Self Test 1.2

Fill in the blanks

A statement that tells "what is" is a ____ (positive; normative) statement. A statement that tells "what ought to be" is a ____ (positive; normative) statement. An economic ____ (model; theory) simplifies the reality it describes. The process of building and testing models creates ____. The Latin term meaning "other things being equal" is ____ (*ceteris paribus*; *post hoc*).

True or false

1. The statement, "When more people volunteer in their communities, crime rates decrease" is a positive statement.

2. An economic model must include all the details about the real world.

3. A situation that arises in the ordinary course of economic life in which the one factor of interest is different and other things are equal is an economic experiment.

4. Assuming that one event causes another because the first occurs before the second is sound economic reasoning.

Multiple choice

1. A positive statement
   a. must always be right.
   b. cannot be tested.
   c. might be right or wrong.
   d. cannot be negative.

2. Which of the following is an example of a normative statement?
   a. If cars become more expensive, fewer people will buy them.
   b. Car prices should be affordable.
   c. If wages increase, firms will fire some workers.
   d. Cars emit pollution.

3. If an economic theory conflicts with actual data,
   a. it is a good theory.
   b. the model needs adjustment.
   c. it becomes an economic law.
   d. the subject matter must be normative.

4. The Latin term *ceteris paribus* means
   a. after this, therefore because of this.
   b. other things being equal.
   c. what is correct for the part is not correct for the whole.
   d. when one variable increases, the other variable decreases.

5. Economists are scientists and so want to construct and test economic models to help understand the economic world. Consequently, economists must use which of the following to construct economic models?
   a. natural experiments
   b. statistical investigations
   c. economic experiments
   d. all of the above

6. "The rooster crows every morning and then the sun comes out. Sunrise therefore, is caused by the rooster's crowing." This statement is a
   a. true statement.
   b. *post hoc* fallacy.
   c. normative statement.
   d. negative statement.

Short answer

1. Becky is writing an essay about the effectiveness of the law that requires all passengers in a car to use a seat belt. What might be a positive statement and a normative statement that she will include in her essay?

2. The task of economic science is broken into three steps. List these three steps.

CHECKPOINT 1.3

■ **Explain five core ideas that define the economic way of thinking.**

Practice Problem 1.3

Kate usually plays tennis for two hours a week and her grade on math tests is usually 70 percent. Last week, after playing two hours of tennis, Kate thought about playing for another hour. She decided to play another hour of tennis and cut her study time by one additional hour. But her grade on last week's math test was 60 percent.

a. What was Kate's opportunity cost of the third hour of tennis?
b. Given that Kate made the decision to play the third hour of tennis, what can you conclude about the comparison of her marginal benefit and marginal cost of the second hour of tennis?
c. Was Kate's decision to play the third hour of tennis rational?
d. Did Kate make her decision on the margin?

Solution to Practice Problem 1.3

This practice problem uses several ideas, including rational choice. To understand rational choice, you also need to understand marginal benefit and marginal cost because a rational choice compares the marginal benefit to the marginal cost.

Quick Review

- *Marginal cost* The cost that arises from a one-unit increase in an activity. The marginal cost of something is what you *must give up* to get *one more* unit of it.

- *Marginal benefit* The benefit that arises from a one-unit increase in an activity. The marginal benefit of something is *measured* by what you are *willing to give up* to get *one more* unit of it.

- *Rational choice* A choice that uses the available resources most effectively to satisfy the wants of the person making the choice.

a. **What was Kate's opportunity cost of the third hour of tennis?**

The opportunity cost of the third hour of tennis was the ten-percentage point drop on her math test grade because she cut her studying by one hour to play an additional hour of tennis. If Kate had not played tennis for the third hour, she would have studied and her grade would not have dropped.

b. **Given that Kate made the decision to play the third hour of tennis, what can you conclude about the comparison of her marginal benefit and marginal cost of the second hour of tennis?**

Kate chose to play the third hour of tennis, so the marginal benefit of the second hour of tennis was greater than the marginal cost of the second hour of tennis. If the marginal benefit of the second hour of tennis was not greater than the marginal cost of the second hour of tennis, Kate would have studied rather than played tennis in the third hour.

c. **Was Kate's decision to play the third hour of tennis rational?**

Kate's decision was rational if the marginal benefit of the third hour of playing tennis was greater than the marginal cost of the third hour of playing tennis.

d. **Did Kate make her decision on the margin?**

Kate's decision to play was made at the margin because she compared the cost and benefit of playing tennis for one additional hour.

Additional Practice Problem 1.3a

Tom over slept this morning and he may be late for work. When Tom reaches an intersection the traffic light turns yellow. Tom can (1) apply the brake, (2) accelerate and (hopefully) make the light, (3) drive through the parking lot on the corner to get around the light.

a. Analyze his choices on the margin.
b. Describe the outcome in terms of making a rational choice.

Solution to Additional Practice Problem 1.3a

a. **Analyze his choices on the margin.**

Braking preserves safety, order, and polite expectations, which are marginal benefits, while risking delay and the potential consequences of arriving late for work are marginal costs. Accelerating might get Tom to work on time, a marginal benefit, but is done at higher risk to self and others, a marginal cost. Cutting through the parking lot might reduce Tom's chances of getting fired, a marginal benefit, but if there is a police officer nearby, it might get him a ticket, a marginal cost.

b. **Describe the outcome in terms of making a rational choice.**

The choice Tom makes is rational if it is the strategy for which the marginal benefit exceeds the marginal cost.

■ Self Test 1.3

Fill in the blanks

A ____ (marginal; rational) choice uses the available resources most effectively to satisfy the wants of the person making the choice. The opportunity cost of an activity is ____ (all of the activities forgone; the highest-valued alternative forgone). The benefit of an activity is measured by what you ____ (are willing to; must) give up. A choice on the margin is made by comparing all the relevant alternatives ____ (incrementally; together). We make a rational choice when the marginal benefit of the activity ____ (exceeds or equals; is less than) the marginal cost.

True or false

1. Instead of attending her microeconomics class for two hours, Kim can play a game of tennis or watch a movie. For Kim the opportunity cost of attending class is forgoing the game of tennis *and* watching the movie.

2. Marginal cost is what you gain when you get one more unit of something.

3. A rational choice involves comparing the marginal benefit of an action to its marginal cost.

4. A change in marginal benefit or a change in marginal cost brings a change in the incentives that we face and leads us to change our actions.

Multiple choice

1. When people make rational choices, they

a. behave selfishly.
b. do not consider their emotions.
c. weigh the costs and benefits of their options and act to satisfy their wants.
d. are necessarily making the best decision.

2. Jamie has enough money to buy a Mountain Dew, or a Pepsi, or a bag of chips. He chooses to buy the Mountain Dew. The opportunity cost of the Mountain Dew is

a. the Pepsi and the bag of chips.
b. the Pepsi or the bag of chips, whichever is the highest-valued alternative forgone.
c. the Mountain Dew.
d. zero because he enjoys the Mountain Dew.

3. The benefit of something is

a. purely objective and measured in dollars.
b. how a person feels about something or the gain or pleasure that it brings.
c. the value of its sunk cost.
d. not measurable on the margin.

4. The cost of a one-unit increase in an activity

a. is the total one-unit cost.
b. is the marginal cost.
c. decreases as you do more of the activity.
d. Answers a and c are correct.

5. Marginal benefit

a. is the benefit from a one-unit increase in an activity.
b. means the benefit of some small activity.
c. is measured by what the person is willing to get.
d. All of the above answers are correct.

6. If the marginal benefit of the next slice of pizza exceeds the marginal cost, you will

a. eat the slice of pizza.
b. not eat the slice of pizza.
c. be unable to choose between eating or not eating.
d. eat half the slice.

Short answer

1. What is a sunk cost?
2. What is benefit and how is it measured?
3. What is a marginal cost? A marginal benefit? How do they relate to rational choice?

CHECKPOINT 1.4

■ **Explain why economics is worth studying.**

Practice Problem 1.4

A student is choosing between an economics course or a popular music course. List two opportunity costs and two benefits from taking the course in economics.

Solution to Practice Problem 1.4

This practice problem uses the idea of making a rational choice, which is a choice that uses the available resources most effectively to satisfy the wants of the person making the choice.

Quick Review

- *Opportunity cost* The opportunity cost of something is what you must give up to get it.

A student is choosing between an economics course or a popular music course. List two opportunity costs and two benefits from taking the course in economics.

The opportunity cost of taking the economics course is the forgone knowledge from the popular music course. If the popular music course does not involve as much time studying, forgone leisure is another opportunity cost.

Benefits from taking the economics course are knowledge gained from the class, a better understanding of the world, better problem-solving skills, and expanded career opportunities.

Additional Practice Problem 1.4a

What are the opportunity costs and benefits of using this *Study Guide*?

Solution to Additional Practice Problem 1.4a

The opportunity cost is the highest-valued activity, be it studying for another class, or sleeping, or some other activity, which is forgone because of the time spent using the *Study Guide*.

The benefits from the *Study Guide* are an enhanced understanding of the important topics in the book, which likely will lead to a higher grade in the class. Over a longer time horizon, an increased understanding might influence the future courses you take and lead to career benefits.

■ Self Test 1.4

Fill in the blanks

A better understanding of important issues is one of the ____ (benefits; costs) from studying economics. The cost of buying textbooks ____ (is; is not) an opportunity cost of studying economics rather than another subject.

True or false

1. Economics requires thinking abstractly about concrete issues.
2. Economics graduates are among the highest paid professionals.
3. The benefits of studying economics are forgone knowledge of some other subject.
4. Most students of economics do not go on to major in the subject.

Multiple choice

1. A benefit from studying economics is
   a. forgone knowledge of another subject.
   b. an understanding of many of today's events.
   c. increased leisure time.
   d. that you will become as rich as Mick Jagger.

2. Economics is a good major for a ____
   a. pre-med student.
   b. pre-law student.
   c. pre-MBA student.
   d. All of the above answers are correct.

3. On average, economics graduates earn less than ____ graduates and more than ____ graduates.
   a. engineering and computer science; commerce
   b. commerce; fine arts and humanities
   c. commerce; engineering and computer science
   d. fine arts and humanities; engineering and computer science

4. An opportunity cost of studying economics rather than another subject is the
   a. money you spent on textbooks and tuition.
   b. tuition you pay but not the expense of the textbooks you buy.
   c. the decreased leisure time from the choice of economics as a major.
   d. increased salary you might earn after you graduate.

5. Economics says that you should major in economics if
   a. your instructor tells you that the benefits from the major exceed the costs.
   b. you think the benefits from the major exceed the costs.
   c. you think you will make lots of money regardless of the costs.
   d. you are very good at memorization.

Short answer

1. What are the career benefits from taking economics courses?
2. Why do some students decide not to major in economics?

SELF TEST ANSWERS

■ CHECKPOINT 1.1

Fill in the blanks

Economic questions arise because <u>human wants</u> exceed the <u>resources</u> available to satisfy them. Faced with <u>scarcity</u>, people must make choices. <u>Microeconomics</u> is the study of the choices of individuals and businesses, the interaction of these choices, and the influence that governments exert on these choices. The three major microeconomic questions are: <u>what</u>, <u>how</u>, and <u>for whom</u>.

True or false

1. True; page 5
2. False; page 5
3. True; page 5
4. False; page 6

Multiple choice

1. d; page 4
2. a; page 4
3. d; page 4
4. c; page 5
5. d; page 6
6. a; page 6

Short answer

1. There will never be a time without scarcity because human wants are unlimited; page 4.
2. Microeconomics is the study of the choices that individuals and businesses make, the interaction of these choices, and the influence that governments exert on these choices. Macroeconomics is the study of the aggregate (or total) effects on the national economy and the global economy of the choices that individuals, businesses, and governments make; page 5.

3. The questions are "*What* goods and services get produced and in what quantities?", "*How* are goods and services produced?", and "*For whom* are the various goods and services produced?" An example of the "What" question is "Should more video tapes or DVDs be produced?" An example of the "How" question is "Should car washes use more people or more machinery to wash cars?" An example of the "For Whom" question is "Should college graduates earn higher incomes than high school graduates?" page 6.

■ CHECKPOINT 1.2

Fill in the blanks

A statement that tells "what is" is a <u>positive</u> statement. A statement that tells "what ought to be" is a <u>normative</u> statement. An economic <u>model</u> simplifies the reality it describes. The process of building and testing models creates <u>theories</u>. The Latin term meaning "other things being equal" is *<u>ceteris paribus</u>*.

True or false

1. True; page 8
2. False; page 9
3. False; page 11
4. False; page 11

Multiple choice

1. c; page 8
2. b; page 8
3. b; page 9
4. b; page 10
5. d; pages 11-12
6. b; page 11

Short answer

1. A positive statement is "People who obey the law and wear seat belts are involved in fewer road deaths." This statement can be tested. A

normative statement is "People should be free to choose whether to wear a seat belt or not." This statement cannot be tested; page 8.

2. The three steps are observing and measuring, model building, and testing; pages 8-9.

■ CHECKPOINT 1.3

Fill in the blanks

A <u>rational</u> choice uses the available resources most effectively to satisfy the wants of the person making the choice. The opportunity cost of an activity is <u>the highest-valued alternative forgone</u>. The benefit of an activity is measured by what you <u>are willing to</u> give up. A choice on the margin is made by comparing all the relevant alternatives <u>incrementally</u>. We make a rational choice when the marginal benefit of the activity <u>exceeds or equals</u> the marginal cost.

True or false

1. False; page 13
2. False; page 15
3. True; page 16
4. True; page 16

Multiple choice

1. c; page 13
2. b; page 13
3. b; page 14
4. b; page 15
5. a; page 15
6. a; page 16

Short answer

1. A sunk cost is a previously incurred and irreversible cost; page 14.

2. The benefit of something is the gain or pleasure that it brings. Economists measure the benefit of something by what a person is wiling to give up to get it; page 14.

3. Marginal cost is the cost that arises from a one-unit increase in an activity. The marginal cost of something is what you *must give up* to get *one more* unit of it. Marginal benefit is the benefit that arises from a one-unit increase in an activity. The marginal benefit of something is measured by what you are *willing to give up* to get *one more* unit of it. A rational choice is made by comparing the marginal cost and marginal benefit. If the marginal benefit of an activity exceeds or equals the marginal cost, the activity is undertaken; pages 15-16.

■ CHECKPOINT 1.4

Fill in the blanks

A better understanding of important issues is one of the <u>benefits</u> from studying economics. The cost of buying textbooks <u>is not</u> an opportunity cost of studying economics rather than another subject.

True or false

1. True; page 19
2. True; page 19
3. False; page 20
4. True; page 19

Multiple choice

1. b; page 18
2. d; page 19
3. a; page 19
4. c; page 20
5. b; page 20

Short answer

1. Economics courses stress thinking abstractly and logically about important subjects, which are valuable skills to possess. In addition, economics courses discuss many important economic concepts. A student's career benefits from the style of thought gained in

economics classes and from the economic concepts covered in the classes; pages 18-19.

2. There are students for whom the benefit of economics as a major is less than the cost. The costs might be high because the student does not enjoy economics or because the student finds the subject difficult. These students should not major in economics; page 20.

Chapter 1

Appendix: Making and Using Graphs

APPENDIX IN PERSPECTIVE

This appendix reviews the graphs used in your economics course.

■ **Making and using graphs.**

Graphs represent quantities as distances. The vertical axis is the y-axis and the horizontal axis is the x-axis. A scatter diagram is a graph of the value of one variable against the value of another variable. A time-series graph measures time along the x-axis and the variable or variables of interest along the y-axis. A cross-section graph shows the values of an economic variable for different groups in the population at a point in time. Graphs show the relationships among the variables in an economic model. Variables that move in the same direction have a positive or direct relationship. Variables that move in the opposite direction have a negative or inverse relationship. Some relationships have minimum or maximum points. The slope of a relationship is the change in the value of the variable measured on the y-axis divided by the change in the value of the variable measured on the x-axis. To graph a relationship among more than two variables, we use the *ceteris paribus* assumption and graph the relationship between two of the variables holding the other variables constant.

EXPANDED CHAPTER CHECKLIST

When you have completed this appendix, you will be able to:

1 Interpret a scatter diagram, time-series graph, and cross-section graph.

- Identify the x-axis, the y-axis, and the origin in a graph.
- Explain what is plotted and identify a scatter diagram, a time-series graph, and a cross-section graph.

2 Interpret the graphs used in economic models.

- Identify a positive or direct relationship between two variables.
- Identify a negative or inverse relationship between two variables.
- Identify a relationship that has a maximum or a minimum.
- Identify when variables are unrelated.

3 Define and calculate slope.

- Present the formula used to calculate the slope of a relationship and use it to calculate slope.

4 Graph relationships among more than two variables.

- Describe how the *ceteris paribus* assumption is used to allow us to illustrate the relationship among more than two variables.

KEY TERMS

- Cross-section graph (page 24)
- Direct relationship (page 26)
- Inverse relationship (page 27)
- Linear relationship (page 26)
- Negative relationship (page 27)
- Positive relationship (page 26)
- Scatter diagram (page 24)
- Slope (page 29)
- Time-series graph (page 24)
- Trend (page 24)

Year	Price (cents per litre)
1990	58.9
1991	59.2
1992	57.3
1993	54.2
1994	52.5
1995	53.8
1996	55.1
1997	56.0
1998	51.3
1999	56.2

■ FIGURE A1.1

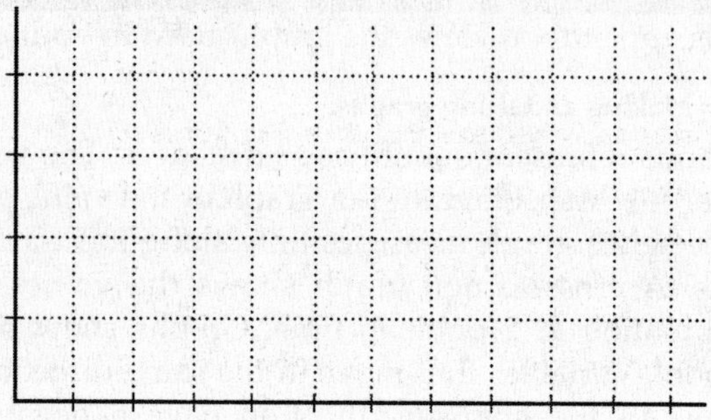

■ FIGURE A1.2

CHECKPOINT A1.1

■ Making and using graphs.

Additional Practice Problems A1.1

1. You have data on the average monthly rainfall and the monthly expenditure on umbrellas in Halifax. What sort of graph would be the best to reveal if any relationship exists between these variables?

2. The table in the next column shows the average price of a litre of gas in Ottawa for the decade of the 1990s. In Figure A1.1, label the axes and then plot these data. What type of graph are you creating? What is the trend of gas prices during this decade?

3. In Figure A1.2, draw a straight line that shows a positive relationship and another straight line that shows a negative relationship.

4. Figure A1.3 shows the relationship between the price of a paperback book and the quantity of paperback books a publisher is willing to sell. What is the slope of the line in Figure A1.3?

■ **FIGURE A1.3**

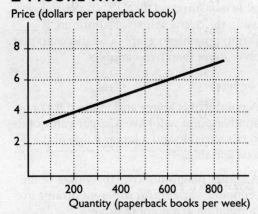

■ **FIGURE A1.4**

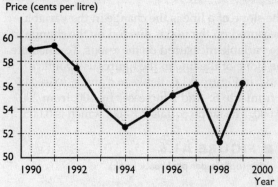

Solution to Additional Practice Problems A1.1

1. **You have data on the average monthly rainfall and the monthly expenditure on umbrellas in Halifax. What sort of graph would be the best to reveal if any relationship exists between these variables?**

A scatter diagram would be the best graph to use. A scatter diagram can plot the average monthly rainfall along the vertical axis (the y-axis) and the monthly expenditure on umbrellas along the horizontal axis (the x-axis).

2. **The table shows the average price of a litre of gas in Ottawa for the decade of the 1990s. In Figure A1.1, label the axes and then plot these data. What type of graph are you creating? What is the trend of gas prices during this decade?**

Figure A1.4 labels the axes and plots the data in the table. The graph is a time-series graph. The trend is negative because the price of gas has generally been decreasing during 1990s.

3. **In Figure A1.2, draw a straight line that shows a positive relationship and another straight line that shows a negative relationship.**

Figure A1.5 has two lines, one that shows a positive relationship and another that shows a negative relationship. Your figure might not show exactly these lines. The key point is that the line for the positive relationship slopes up as x increases along it and the line for the negative relationship slopes down as x increases along it.

■ **FIGURE A1.5**

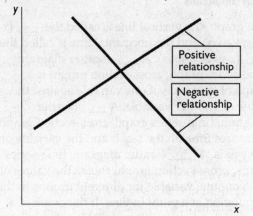

4. What is the slope of the line in Figure A1.3?

The slope of a line is the change in the variable measured on the y-axis divided by the change in the variable measured on the x-axis. To calculate the slope of the line in the figure, use points a and b in Figure A1.6. Between a and b, y rises by 2, from 4 to 6. And x increases by 400, from 200 to 600. The slope equals 2 ÷ 400, which is 0.005.

■ **FIGURE A1.6**

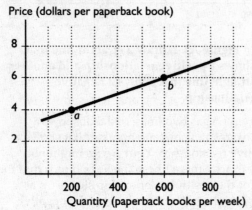

■ Self Test A1.1

Fill in the blanks

In a graph, the vertical line is called the ____ (x-axis; y-axis) and the horizontal line is called the ____ (x-axis; y-axis). A ____ (scatter diagram; time-series graph; cross-section graph) is a graph of the value of one variable against the value of another variable. A ____ (scatter diagram; time-series graph; cross-section graph) measures time on the x-axis and the variable on the y-axis. A ____ (scatter diagram; time-series graph; cross-section graph) shows the values of an economic variable for different groups in the population at a point in time. If the graph of a relationship between two variables slopes up to the right, the two variables have a ____ (positive; negative) relationship. If the graph between two variables is a vertical line, the two variables ____ (are; are not) related. The slope of a relationship is the change in the value of the variable measured on the ____ (x-axis; y-axis) divided by the change in the value of the variable measured on the ____ (x-axis; y-axis). By using the *ceteris paribus* assumption, it ____ (is; is not) possible to graph a relationship that involves more than two variables.

True or false

1. A point that is above and to the right of another point will have a larger value of the x-axis variable and a larger value of the y-axis variable.

2. A scatter diagram shows the values of an economic variable for different groups in a population at a point in time.

3. A time-series graph compares values of a variable for different groups at a single point in time.

4. A trend is a measure of the closeness of the points on a graph.

5. A positive relationship is always a linear relationship.

6. A relationship that starts out sloping upward and then slopes downward has a maximum.

7. A graph that shows a horizontal line indicates variables that are unrelated.

8. The slope of a relationship is calculated as the change in the value of the variable measured on the x-axis divided by the change in the value of the variable measured on the y-axis.

9. The slope at a point on a curve equals the slope of the straight line that touches the point and no other point on the curve.

Multiple choice

1. The best way to demonstrate how a variable changes from one year to the next is to use a
   a. scatter diagram.
   b. time-series graph.
   c. linear graph.
   d. cross-section graph.

2. To show the values of a variable for different groups in a population at a point in time, it is best to use a
   a. scatter diagram.
   b. time-series graph.
   c. linear graph.
   d. cross-section graph.

3. If whenever one variable increases, another variable also increases, then these two variables have a ____ relationship.
   a. positive
   b. negative
   c. inverse
   d. cross-sectional

4. A graph of the relationship between two variables is a line that slopes down to the right. These two variables have ____ relationship.
   a. a positive
   b. a direct
   c. a negative
   d. no

5. Two variables are unrelated if the relationship is illustrated by
   a. a vertical line.
   b. a 45° line.
   c. a horizontal line.
   d. Both (a) and (c) are correct.

6. Figure A1.7 shows the relationship between the price of rutabagas and the quantity purchased. Between points A and B, what is the slope of the line?
   a. 4
   b. 1
   c. 3
   d. –3

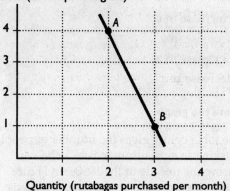

FIGURE A1.7
Price (dollars per kilogram)

7. In Figure A1.8 an increase in z leads to a
   a. movement up along one of the lines that shows the relationship between x and y.
   b. movement down along one of the lines that shows the relationship between x and y.
   c. rightward shift of the line that shows the relationship between x and y.
   d. leftward shift of the line that shows the relationship between x and y.

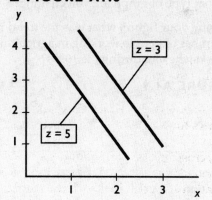

FIGURE A1.8

8. In Figure A1.8, *ceteris paribus*, an increase in x is associated with

   a. an increase in y.
   b. a decrease in y.
   c. an increase in z.
   d. a decrease in z.

Complete the graph

1. The table below gives the number of people working in agriculture in Saskatchewan during the decade of the 1990s. In Figure A1.9, measure time on the horizontal axis and the number of workers on the vertical axis, and then plot these data.

Year	Workers (thousands)
1990	83.0
1991	83.5
1992	81.6
1993	82.2
1994	75.3
1995	72.6
1996	71.4
1997	70.0
1998	71.6
1999	67.5

   a. What type of graph are you creating?
   b. Using your figure, what was the trend in the number of people working in agriculture in Saskatchewan during the 1990s?

   ■ **FIGURE A1.9**

   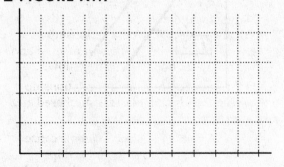

2. The table below gives the average annual value of the TSE composite index and the interest rate for the decade of the 1990s. In Figure A1.10, measure the interest rate along the x-axis and the TSE composite index along the y-axis. Then plot these data.

Year	Interest rate (percent per year)	TSE composite index
1990	10.9	3421
1991	9.8	3469
1992	8.8	3402
1993	7.8	3904
1994	8.6	4284
1995	8.3	4433
1996	7.5	5268
1997	6.4	6458
1998	5.5	6757
1999	5.7	7059

   a. What type of graph are you creating?
   b. What is the relationship between the interest rate and the TSE composite index that you see in your figure?

   ■ **FIGURE A1.10**

   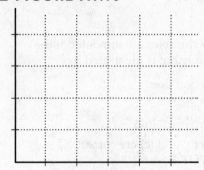

3. The number of sacks of premium cat food that cat lovers buy depends on the price of a sack of cat food. The relationship is given in the table. In Figure A1.11, plot this relationship, putting the price on the vertical axis and the quantity on the horizontal axis.

Price (dollars per sack of cat food)	Quantity (sacks of cat food per month)
1	10,000
2	8,000
3	7,000
4	4,000

a. If the price of a sack of cat food is $2, how many sacks are purchased?

b. If the price of a sack of cat food is $3, how many sacks are purchased?

c. Is the relationship between the price and the quantity positive or negative?

■ FIGURE A1.11

4. In Figure A1.12, label the maximum and minimum points.

■ FIGURE A1.12

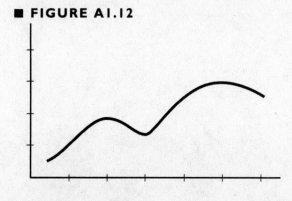

5. In Figure A1.13, draw a line through point A with a slope of 2. Label the line "1." Draw another line through point A with a slope of –2. Label this line "2."

■ FIGURE A1.13

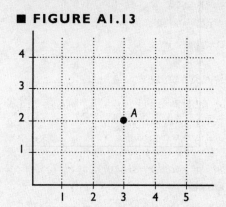

6. Bobby says that he buys fewer compact discs when the price of a compact disc is higher. Bobby also says that he will buy more compact discs after he graduates and his income is higher. The table below shows the number of compact discs Bobby buys in a month at different prices when his income is low and when his income is high.

Price (dollars per compact disc)	Quantity of compact discs purchased, low income	Quantity of compact discs purchased, high income
11	4	5
12	3	4
13	1	3
14	0	2

a. In Figure A1.14, put the price on the vertical axis and the quantity purchased on the horizontal axis. Show the relationship between the number of discs purchased and the price when Bobby's income is low.

b. On the same figure, draw the relationship between the number of discs purchased and the price when his income is high.

c. Does an increase in Bobby's income cause the curve that graphs the relationship between the price of a compact disc and the number purchased to shift rightward or leftward?

■ FIGURE A1.14

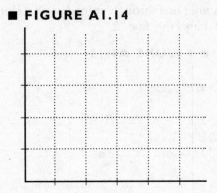

Short answer

1. What are the three types of graphs?
2. If two variables are positively related, will the slope of a graph of the two variables be positive or negative? If two variables are negatively related, will the slope of a graph of the two variables be positive or negative?
3. If a line slopes upward to the right, is its slope positive or negative? If a line slopes downward to the right, is its slope positive or negative?
4. In Figure A1.15, what is the slope of the curved line at point A? At point B?

■ FIGURE A1.15

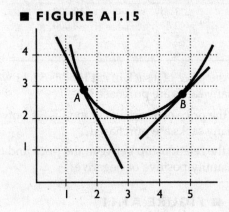

SELF TEST ANSWERS

■ CHECKPOINT A1.1

Fill in the blanks

In a graph, the vertical line is called the <u>y-axis</u> and the horizontal line is called the <u>x-axis</u>. A <u>scatter diagram</u> is a graph of the value of one variable against the value of another variable. A <u>time-series graph</u> measures time on the x-axis and the variable on the y-axis. <u>A cross-section graph</u> shows the values of an economic variable for different groups in the population at a point in time. If the graph of a relationship between two variables slopes up to the right, the two variables have a <u>positive</u> relationship. If the graph between two variables is a vertical line, the two variables <u>are not</u> related. The slope of a relationship is the change in the value of the variable measured on the <u>y-axis</u> divided by the change in the value of the variable measured on the <u>x-axis</u>. By using the *ceteris paribus* assumption, it <u>is</u> possible to graph a relationship that involves more than two variables.

True or false

1. True; page 23
2. False; page 24
3. False; page 24
4. False; page 24
5. False; page 26
6. True; page 28
7. True; page 28
8. False; page 29
9. True; page 29

Multiple choice

1. b; page 24
2. d; page 24
3. **a; page 26**
4. c; page 27
5. d; page 28
6. d; page 29
7. d; page 30
8. b; page 30

Complete the graph

1. Figure A1.16 plots the data.

■ **FIGURE A1.16**

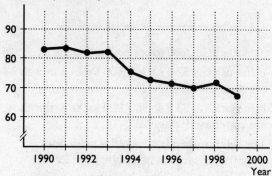

a. This is a time-series graph; page 24.
b. The trend is negative; page 24.

2. Figure A1.17 plots the data.

■ **FIGURE A1.17**

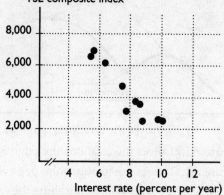

a. The figure is a scatter diagram; page 24.
b. The relationship between the interest rate and the TSE composite index is negative; page 27.

3. Figure A1.18 plots the relationship.

FIGURE A1.18

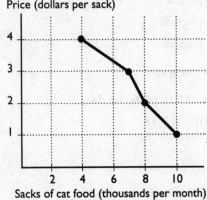

a. If the price is $2 a sack, 8,000 sacks a month are purchased; page 23.
b. If the price is $3 a sack, 7,000 sacks a month are purchased; page 23.
c. The relationship between the price and quantity of sacks is negative; page 27

4. Figure A1.19 labels the two maximum points and one minimum point; page 28.

FIGURE A1.19

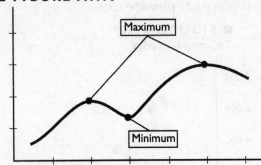

5. Figure A1.20 shows the two lines; page 29.
6a. Figure A1.21 plots the relationship; page 30.
b. Figure A1.21 plots the relationship; page 30.
c. An increase in Bobby's income shifts the curve that graphs the relationship between the price of a compact disc and the number purchased rightward; page 30.

FIGURE A1.20

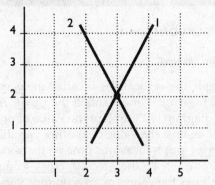

FIGURE A1.21

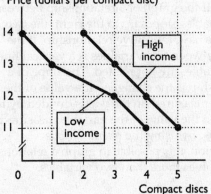

Short answer

1. The three types of graphs are scatter diagram, time-series graph, and cross-section graph; page 24.

2. If two variables are positively related, a graph of the relationship will have a positive slope. If two variables are negatively related, a graph of the relationship will have a negative slope; pages 26, 27, 29.

3. If a line slopes upward to the right, its slope is positive. If a line slopes downward to the right, its slope is negative; page 29.

4. The slope of a curved line at a point equals the slope of a straight line that touches that point and no other point on the curve. The slope of the curved line at point A is -2 and the slope of the curved line at point B is 1; page 29.

Chapter 2

The Canadian Economy

CHAPTER IN PERSPECTIVE

As in other countries, the economic activities of people in Canada answer the questions of what to produce, how much to produce, and for whom to produce. Chapter 2 explores these questions and develops the circular flow model to illustrate how the answers to these questions are determined.

■ Describe the patterns and changes in *what* goods and services are produced in Canada.

Shelter, transportation, and food are the items on which Canadians spend the largest share of their income. Over time, as incomes have increased, expenditure on necessities has taken a smaller percentage of income and expenditure on services has taken a larger percentage of income. We produce more services than goods. Machinery and equipment and automotive products are large categories of goods we buy from other countries.

■ Describe the patterns and changes in *how* goods and services are produced in Canada.

Goods and services are produced using the factors of production: land, labour, capital, and entrepreneurship. Land includes all the gifts of nature. Labour is the work time and work effort people devote to producing goods and services. Capital is the tools, instruments, machines, buildings, and other constructions that have been produced in the past and that businesses now use to produce goods and services. Entrepreneurship is the human resource that organizes labour, land, and capital.

■ Describe *for whom* goods and services are produced in Canada.

The functional distribution of income is the percentage distribution of income among the factors of production. In Canada, labour earns most of the income. The personal distribution of income is the percentage distribution of income among households. In Canada, the richest 20 percent of households earn about 46 percent of total income; the poorest 20 percent of households earn only about 4 percent of total income.

■ Use the circular flow model to show how households, firms, and governments interact to determine what, how, and for whom goods and services are produced.

The circular flow model shows that households provide factors of production and firms hire factors of production in factor markets and that households purchase goods and services and firms sell goods and services in goods markets. The federal government provides goods and services such as national defence and pays benefits to unemployed people and pensions to retired people. In the circular flow model, the government buys goods and services in goods markets. It makes transfers to firms and households and receives taxes from them. The federal government's largest payment is interest on the national debt and its largest source of receipts is personal income taxes. 25 percent of provincial and local governments' payments are for health care. 26 percent of provincial and local governments' receipts come from sales taxes and 20 percent come from personal income taxes.

EXPANDED CHAPTER CHECKLIST

When you have completed this chapter, you will be able to:

1 Describe the patterns and changes in *what* goods and services are produced in Canada.

- List the six largest items on which Canadians spend their incomes.
- Explain how consumption patterns have changed over time.
- List the largest categories of goods and services produced in Canada and the relative size of each.
- Describe the major categories of goods imported into Canada.

2 Describe the patterns and changes in *how* goods and services are produced in Canada.

- List the four factors of production
- Provide examples of what economists mean when they use the term "land."
- Give examples of renewable and nonrenewable resources.
- Define labour and human capital and explain what factors increase human capital.
- Define capital and explain why stocks and bonds are not capital goods.
- Define entrepreneurship.

3 Describe *for whom* goods and services are produced in Canada.

- List the type of income earned by each factor of production.
- Discuss the functional distribution of income and tell what factor earns most of the income in Canada.
- Discuss the personal distribution of income and categorize the amount of income earned by each 20 percent group of households.

4 Use the circular flow model to show how households, firms, and governments interact to determine what, how, and for whom goods and services are produced.

- Tell what is bought and sold in goods markets and in factor markets.
- Draw the circular flow between households and firms and between households, firms, and the government.
- Discuss the magnitude of the federal government's payments and receipts.
- Discuss the magnitudes of the provincial and local governments' payments and receipts.
- Define national debt.

KEY TERMS

- Capital (page 41)
- Circular flow model (page 46)
- Entrepreneurship (page 42)
- Factor markets (page 46)
- Factors of production (page 38)
- Firms (page 46)
- Functional distribution of income (page 44)
- Goods markets (page 46)
- Households (page 46)
- Human capital (page 40)
- Interest (page 44)
- Labour (page 40)
- Land (page 38)
- Market (page 46)
- National debt (page 50)
- Personal distribution of income (page 44)
- Profit (or loss) (page 44)
- Rent (page 44)
- Wages (page 44)

CHECKPOINT 2.1

■ **Describe the patterns and changes in *what* goods and services are produced in Canada.**

Practice Problems 2.1

1. On which goods and services do Canadians spend most of their incomes?
2. How have the goods and services on which Canadians spend most of their incomes changed between 1947 and 2000?

Solution to Practice Problems 2.1

These questions study trends and facts about the goods and services on which we spend our income.

1. On which goods and services do Canadians spend most of their incomes?

The six largest items of goods and services on which Canadians spend their income are shelter (27 percent of household expenditure), transportation (18 percent of household expenditure), food (16 percent of household expenditure), recreation (8 percent of household expenditure), household operations (6.4 percent of household expenditure) and clothing (6 percent of household expenditure). These six items account for 81.4 percent of Canadian household expenditure.

2. How have the goods and services on which Canadians spend most of their incomes changed between 1947 and 2000?

Over time, incomes have increased, and as they have done so, expenditure on the necessities of life has taken a smaller percentage of income and expenditure on services has taken a larger percentage of income.

For example, total expenditure on food has fallen from 27 percent of household expenditure in 1947 to 16 percent in 2000. But the amount that we spend on restaurant food has increased from 10 percent of total food expenditure in 1947 to nearly 30 percent of food expenditure in 2000.

Additional Practice Problem 2.1a

To which country does Canada export most of its output? Among consumer goods, what is Canada's largest import?

Solution to Additional Practice Problem 2.1a

Canada exports much of its output to the rest of the world, and exports mostly to the United States. Among consumer goods, automobiles are Canada's largest single import.

■ **Self Test 2.1**

Fill in the blanks

In Canada, the largest single category of expenditures is ____ (food; shelter; transportation) and the second largest is ____ (food; shelter; transportation). Between 1947 and 2000, as a percentage of total consumer spending, expenditure on food ____ (fell; rose). Canada produces ____ (more; fewer) services than goods.

True or false

1. In Canada, shelter and transportation are the two largest categories of household expenditure.
2. In Canada as incomes have increased, expenditure on services has taken a larger percentage of income.
3. Most of the goods and services that people in Canada buy are produced in Canada.
4. Canada produces more goods than services.

Multiple choice

1. Which of the following is the largest category of expenditure in Canada?
a. shelter
b. recreation
c. transportation
d. food

2. In Canada as incomes have increased, expenditure on necessities as a percentage of income has
a. risen more rapidly than has expenditure on services.
b. risen but less rapidly than has expenditure on services.
c. fallen.
d. not been affected.

3. In Canada as incomes have increased, expenditure on services as a percentage of income has
a. risen.
b. fallen.
c. not changed.
d. risen but in recent years has fallen dramatically.

4. Canada produces
a. more services than goods.
b. a smaller percentage of services now than in previous years.
c. wholesale trade and retail trade, which represent nearly 12 percent of the value of total production.
d. Both answers (a) and (c) are correct.

5. Most of the goods and services bought by people in Canada are produced
a. abroad and imported into the country.
b. by businesses located in Canada.
c. by the government.
d. by child labour.

6. Most of our manufactured imports, such as clothing, VCRs, toys, and sporting goods come from
a. Asia.
b. Australia.
c. Africa.
d. South America.

Short answer

1. Describe the goods and services produced in Canada today.
2. As incomes in Canada have increased, what has happened to expenditure on services?

CHECKPOINT 2.2

■ **Describe the patterns and changes in *how* goods and services are produced in Canada.**

Practice Problems 2.2

1. Name three different types of natural resources that Canada possesses in abundance.
2. Which energy resources will Canada run out of first? Which of Canada's proven reserves of gas, oil, and coal is the largest?
3. Classify each of the following as one of the four factors of production:
a. The St. Lawrence River.
b. School teachers.
c. A car-park attendant.
d. A robot owned by General Motors.
e. A cruise ship.

Solution to Practice Problems 2.2

The first two problems emphasize facts that will help shape your view of the Canadian economy and the nation's use of different resources.

Quick Review

- *Land* The "gifts of nature" or *natural resources*, that we use to produce goods and services.

1. Name three different types of natural resources that Canada possesses in abundance.

Canada has very large amounts of crude oil (300 billion barrels in the Alberta Tar Sands alone), fresh water (nearly 900,000 square kilometres of surface area), and forest land (over 4 million square kilometres).

2. Which energy resources will Canada run out of first? Which of Canada's proven reserves of gas, oil, and coal is the largest?

If actual reserves equal currently proven reserves, and the current growth rate of use persists, Canada will run out of natural gas first.

Canada's proven reserves of oil are larger than the proven reserves of natural gas and coal.

3. Classify each of the following as one of the four factors of production:

a. The St. Lawrence River.

The St. Lawrence River is a gift of nature and is classified as land.

b. School teachers.

School teachers are classified as labour.

c. A car-park attendant.

A car-park attendant is classified as labour.

d. A robot owned by General Motors.

A robot is used to produce other goods and services, so it is classified as capital.

e. A cruise ship.

A cruise ship is used to produce other goods and services, for example recreation, so it is classified as capital.

Additional Practice Problem 2.2a

What are the four factors of production?

Solution to Additional Practice Problem 2.2a

The four factors of production are land, labour, capital, and entrepreneurship.

Land is the "gifts of nature" or *natural resources*, that we use to produce goods and services.

Labour is the work time and work effort that people devote to producing goods and services.

Capital is the tools, instruments, machines, buildings, and other constructions that have been produced in the past and that businesses now use to produce goods and services.

Entrepreneurship is the human resource that organizes labour, land, and capital.

■ Self Test 2.2

Fill in the blanks

Productive resources are called ____ and are grouped into four categories: ____, ____, ____, and ____. In Canada, ____ (more; less) land is devoted to agricultural use than to urban use. The knowledge and skill that people obtain from education, on-the-job training, and work experience is called ____ (labour; human capital; human resources). Money, stocks, and bonds ____ (are; are not) productive resources.

True or false

1. In Canada between 1971 and 2001, built-up urban land increased from 16,000 square kilometres to more than 30,000 square kilometres.

2. Among natural gas, oil, and coal, the world's known resources of coal will last the greatest number of years.

3. There are more women than men in the Canadian labour force today.

4. Economists categorize money, stocks, and bonds as capital.

Multiple choice

1. Factors of production include
a. labour, capital, and entrepreneurship.
b. money, labour, land, and capital.
c. buyers and sellers.
d. land, labour, and markets.

2. Which of the following is classified as part of the "land" factor of production?
a. houses
b. commercial buildings
c. mineral resources
d. capital

3. Which of the following statements is true?
a. Almost 10 percent of Canada's land surface is water.
b. Less than 20 percent of Canada's land surface is forest land.
c. One-half of the Canadian population lives in the three largest cities.
d. 20 percent of Canada's population lives in 14 cities with populations that exceed 100,000.

4. Which of the following gifts of nature is non-renewable?
a. land surface
b. water
c. air
d. oil

5. _____ improves the quality of labour.
a. Capital
b. Entrepreneurship
c. Human capital
d. Financial capital

6. To an economist, the term "capital" includes
a. natural resources.
b. stocks, bonds, and money.
c. tools, machines, and buildings.
d. labour productivity.

Short answer

1. Describe how the surface area of Canada is used.
2. Describe the trend in the Canadian labour force between 1980 and 2000.
3. What is "capital"? Explain whether stocks, bonds, and money are capital.

CHECKPOINT 2.3

■ Describe *for whom* goods and services are produced in Canada.

Practice Problems 2.3

1. Distinguish between the functional distribution of income and the personal distribution of income.
2. How can wages account for 69 percent of all incomes when the 20 percent of households with the highest incomes receive 46 percent of total income?

Solution to Practice Problems 2.3

The distribution of income is a topic of interest to almost everyone, and this checkpoint gives you some basic facts about it. We will return to the topic in later chapters, so for now concentrate on learning the facts about the distribution of income.

Quick Review

- *Functional distribution of income* The percentage distribution of income among the factors of production.
- *Personal distribution of income* The percentage distribution of income among households.

1. Distinguish between the functional distribution of income and the personal distribution of income.

The two distributions of income differ in the groups into which they divide total income. The functional distribution of income is the percentage distribution of income among the factors of production. The personal distribution of income is the percentage distribution of income among households.

2. **How can wages account for 69 percent of all incomes when the 20 percent of households with the highest incomes receive 46 percent of total income?**

Many of the richest households earn much of their income from rent, interest, and profit, while most of the other 80 percent of households earn primarily wage income. And many of the richest 20 percent of households also earn high salaries.

Additional Practice Problem 2.3a

If income was distributed equally among households, what percentage of total income would the poorest 20 percent of households earn and what percentage would the richest 20 percent of households earn? How do those percentages compare with the actual Canadian personal distribution of income?

Solution to Additional Practice Problem 2.3a

If income was distributed equally, each household would earn the same income. The poorest 20 percent of households and the richest 20 percent of households would each earn 20 percent of total income. The actual personal distribution of income is far from equal, with the poorest 20 percent of households earning only about 4 percent of total income and the richest 20 percent of households earning 46 percent of total income.

■ Self Test 2.3

Fill in the blanks

____ (Interest; Rent) is paid for the use of land, ____ (profits; wages) are paid for the services of labour, ____ (interest; profit) is paid for the use of capital, and entrepreneurs receive a ____ (dividend; profit or incur a loss). The factor of production that earns the largest share of total income is ____ (labour; capital; entrepreneurship). The richest 20 percent of households earn about ____ (26; 46; 76) percent of total income.

True or false

1. The income earned by an entrepreneur is interest.

2. The functional distribution of income is the percentage distribution of income among the factors of production.

3. Among factors of production in Canada in 2000, labour earned the highest amount of income and capital earned the second highest.

4. In Canada in 2000, the richest 20 percent of households earned about 46 percent of total income and the other 80 percent earned about 54 percent of total income.

Multiple choice

1. Payments received by the factors of production
   a. are measured by the personal functional distribution of income.
   b. include rent, interest, wages, and profits.
   c. are always in cash.
   d. are mainly made to businesses.

2. Profit is earned by
   a. land.
   b. labour.
   c. capital.
   d. entrepreneurs.

3. Interest is paid for the use of
   a. land.
   b. labour.
   c. capital.
   d. entrepreneurial ability.

4. Which factor of production earns the largest share of total income?
   a. land
   b. labour
   c. capital
   d. entrepreneurship

5. Income in Canada is distributed such that the poorest 80 percent of households receive about ____ percent of total income.
   a. 69
   b. 54
   c. 46
   d. 10

6. About 46 percent of Canada's total income is earned by the _____ percent of households.
   a. poorest 20
   b. poorest 40
   c. richest 20
   d. richest 40

Short answer

1. What is the functional distribution of income?
2. What is the difference between the functional and the personal distribution of income?

CHECKPOINT 2.4

■ **Use the circular flow model to show how households, firms, and governments interact to determine what, how, and for whom goods and services are produced.**

Practice Problem 2.4

What are the real flows and money flows that run between households, firms, and government in the circular flow model?

Solution to Practice Problem 2.4

The circular flow model shows the interactions between firms, households, and the government in goods markets and in factor markets.

Quick Review

- *Circular flow model* A model of the economy that shows the circular flow of expenditure and incomes that result from decision makers' choices, and the way those choices interact to determine what, how, and for whom goods and services are produced.

What are the real flows and money flows that run between households, firms, and government in the circular flow model?

Start with the circular flow diagram, illustrated in Figure 2.1. The circular flow diagram illustrates the flows between households, firms, and the government. The real flows are in grey. They are the flows of the services of the factors of production through factor markets and the flows of goods and services through goods markets. In the goods market, households and the government buy goods and services from firms. In the factor markets, households provide land, labour, capital, and entrepreneurship to firms. The money flows are in black. The money flows are incomes earned by factors of production (rent, wages, interest, and profit or loss), expenditures made by households and the government on goods and services, and transfers from the government to households and firms and taxes from households and firms to the government.

■ **FIGURE 2.1**

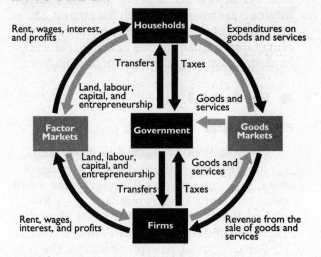

Additional Practice Problem 2.4a

In the circular flow, what is the relationship between the flow of expenditures into the goods markets from households and the government and the flow of revenue out of the goods markets to firms?

Solution to Additional Practice Problem 2.4a

The flow of expenditures into the goods markets—the funds that households and the government spend on the goods and services they purchase—equals the flow of revenue out of the goods markets.

■ Self Test 2.4

Fill in the blanks

The ____ (circular; economic) flow model shows the flow of expenditure and incomes. An arrangement that brings buyers and sellers together is a ____ (firm; household; market). A market in which goods and services are bought and sold is a ____ (goods; factor) market and a market in which factors of production are bought and sold is a ____ (goods; factor) market. In 2000, the federal government's receipts were equal to nearly ____ (20; 38; 75) percent of the total value of all the goods and services produced in Canada in that year. In 2000, local and provincial governments spent ____ (20; 38; 75) percent more than was spent by the federal government. ____ (Corporate; Personal) income taxes are the largest source of federal receipts. In 2000, transfers from the federal government provided ____ (12; 38; 75) percent of provincial receipts.

True or false

1. Firms own the factors of production.
2. A market is any arrangement where buyers and sellers meet face-to-face.
3. Old age security payments are made by provincial and local governments.
4. The largest part of the payments of provincial and local government is education.

Multiple choice

1. A market is
a. the physical place where goods are sold.
b. the physical place where goods and services are sold.
c. any arrangement that brings buyers and sellers together.
d. another name for a store such as a grocery store.

2. In the circular flow model,
a. only firms sell in markets.
b. only households buy from markets.
c. some firms sell and some firms buy.
d. both firms and households buy and sell in different markets.

3. In the circular flow model, ____ choose the quantities of goods and services to produce, and ____ choose the quantities of goods and services to buy.
a. households; firms
b. firms; households and the government
c. the government; firms
d. households; the government

4. In the circular flow model, the expenditures on goods and services flow in the
a. same direction as goods and services.
b. opposite direction as goods and services.
c. same direction as factor markets.
d. None of the above answers are correct.

5. The largest payment that the federal government makes is
a. unemployment benefits.
b. interest on the national debt.
c. transfers to provinces.
d. old age security.

6. The largest source of receipts for the federal government is
a. personal income taxes.
b. GST.
c. corporate income taxes.
d. lotteries.

Complete the graph

1. Figure 2.2 ignores the government and shows the flows into and out of households.

■ FIGURE 2.2

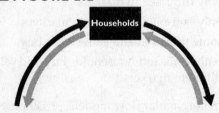

Label the flows and identify who they come from and who they go to.

2. Figure 2.3 ignores the government and shows the flows into and out of firms.

■ FIGURE 2.3

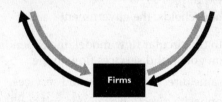

Label the flows and identify who they come from and who they go to.

■ FIGURE 2.4

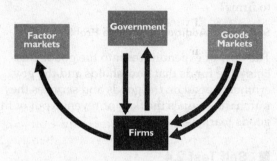

3. Figure 2.4 now includes the government and shows some of the flows into and out of firms. Label the flows.

Short answer

1. Ignoring taxes and transfer payments, what funds flow into firms and what funds flow out of firms?

2. In what markets do households earn their incomes? In what markets do households spend their income?

3. Compare the magnitude of the payments of local and provincial governments with the payments of the federal government in 2000.

4. Compare the amount of the federal government's spending on interest on the national debt to its spending on national defence and old age security.

SELF TEST ANSWERS

■ CHECKPOINT 2.1

Fill in the blanks

In Canada, the largest single category of expenditures is <u>shelter</u> and the second largest is <u>transportation</u>. Between 1947 and 2000, as a percentage of total consumer spending, expenditure on food <u>fell</u>. Canada produces <u>more</u> services than goods.

True or false

1. True; page 34
2. True; page 35
3. True; page 35
4. False; page 35

Multiple choice

1. a; page 34
2. c; page 35
3. a; page 35
4. d; page 35
5. b; page 35
6. a; page 36

Short answer

1. Today in Canada, 67 percent of what we produce is services and 33 percent is goods. The largest five service items produced in Canada are wholesale trade, health, retail trade, education, and financial services. Construction, motor vehicles, crude oil and natural gas, food, and electrical and electronic products are the largest five goods produced; page 35.

2. As incomes have increased, expenditure on the necessities of life has taken a smaller percentage of income and expenditure on services has taken a larger percentage of income; page 35.

■ CHECKPOINT 2.2

Fill in the blanks

Productive resources are called <u>factors of production</u> and are grouped into four categories: <u>land</u>, <u>labour</u>, <u>capital</u>, and <u>entrepreneurship</u>. In Canada, <u>more</u> land is devoted to agricultural use than to urban use. The knowledge and skill that people obtain from education, on-the-job training, and work experience is called <u>human capital</u>. Money, stocks, and bonds <u>are not</u> productive resources.

True or false

1. True; pages 38-39
2. True; page 39
3. False; page 40
4. False; page 41

Multiple choice

1. a; page 38
2. c; page 38
3. a; pages 38-39
4. d; page 39
5. c; page 40
6. c; page 41

Short answer

1. Canada covers 9.9 million square kilometres. Almost 10 percent of Canada's land surface is water, more than 30 percent is forest land, and more than 50 percent is wildland. In 2001, 650,000 square kilometres or 6.5 percent of the land was in agricultural use.

   People live on a very small proportion of Canada's land area. Between 1971 and 2001, built-up urban land increased from 16,000 square kilometres to more than 30,000 square kilometres; pages 38-39.

2. From 1980 to 2000, for every 10 men added to the labour force, more than 17 women were added, raising the proportion of the

labour force consisting of women from less than 40 percent to 46 percent. Over this period, women accounted for 63 percent of the growth of the labour force; page 40

3. Capital consists of the tools, instruments, machines, buildings, and other constructions that have been produced in the past and that businesses now use to produce goods and services. Stocks, bonds, and money are financial capital but are not capital; page 41.

■ CHECKPOINT 2.3

Fill in the blanks

Rent is paid for the use of land, wages are paid for the services of labour, interest is paid for the use of capital, and entrepreneurs receive a profit or incur a loss. The factor of production that earns the largest share of total income is labour. The richest 20 percent of households earn about 46 percent of total income.

True or false

1. False; page 44
2. True; page 44
3. True; page 44
4. True; page 44

Multiple choice

1. b; page 44
2. d; page 44
3. c; page 44
4. b; page 44
5. b; page 44
6. c; page 44

Short answer

1. The functional distribution of income is the percentage distribution of income among the factors of production; page 44.

2. The difference between the two income distributions is in how they divide total income. The functional distribution of income is the percentage distribution of income among the factors of production. The personal distribution of income is the percentage distribution of income among households; page 44.

■ CHECKPOINT 2.4

Fill in the blanks

The circular flow model shows the flow of expenditure and incomes. An arrangement that brings buyers and sellers together is a market. A market in which goods and services are bought and sold is a goods market and a market in which factors of production are bought and sold is a factor market. In 2000, the federal government's receipts were equal to nearly 20 percent of the total value of all the goods and services produced in Canada in that year. In 2000, local and provincial governments spent 75 percent more than was spent by the federal government. Personal income taxes are the largest source of federal receipts. In 2000, transfers from the federal government provided 12 percent of provincial receipts.

True or false

1. False; page 46
2. False; page 46
3. False; page 50
4. False; page 51

Multiple choice

1. c; page 46
2. d; page 46
3. b; pages 46, 49
4. b; page 47
5. b; page 50
6. a; page 50

Complete the graph

1. Figure 2.5 labels the flows.

■ FIGURE 2.5

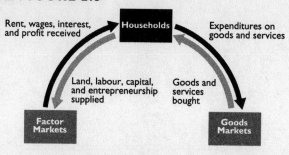

Rent, wages, interest, and profit (or loss) flow from factor markets while land, labour, capital, and entrepreneurship flow to factor markets. Expenditures on goods and services flow to goods markets and goods and services flow from goods markets; page 47

2. Figure 2.6 labels the flows.

■ FIGURE 2.6

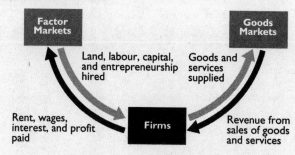

Revenue from the sale of goods and services flows into firms from goods markets and goods and services flow from firms to goods markets. Land, labour, capital, and entrepreneurship flow into firms from factor markets and rent, wages, interest, and profit (or loss) flow from firms to factor markets; page 47.

3. Figure 2.7 labels the flows into and out of firms; pages 47, 49.

■ FIGURE 2.7

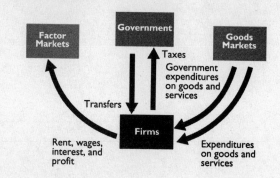

Short answer

1. Funds that flow into firms are household and government expenditures on goods and services. Funds that flow out of firms are payments for rent, wages, interest, and profit to households in exchange for the factors of production; pages 46, 47, 49.

2. Households earn their incomes by supplying factors of production in factor markets. Households spend their incomes on goods and services in goods markets; page 46.

3. In 2000, provincial and local governments spent about $257 billion—75 percent more than was spent by the federal government; page 48.

4. The federal government spends more on interest on the national debt than on national defence and old age security combined. In 2000, 27 percent of government payments was on interest on the national debt, while a total of 22 percent was spent on national defence and old age security; page 50.

38

Chapter 3
The Economic Problem

CHAPTER IN PERSPECTIVE

Chapter 3 studies the production possibilities frontier, *PPF*. The *PPF* shows how the opportunity cost of a good or service increases as more of the good or service is produced. The *PPF* also shows how societies and individuals gain by specializing according to comparative advantage.

■ **Use the production possibilities frontier to illustrate the economic problem.**

The production possibilities frontier is the boundary between the combinations of goods and services that can be produced and those that cannot be produced, given the available factors of production and the state of technology. A production point outside the *PPF* is unattainable. Points on and inside the *PPF* are attainable. When resources are fully employed, the economy produces at a point on the *PPF*. With unemployed resources, the economy produces at a point inside the *PPF*. As we move along the *PPF* producing more of one good, less of another good is produced. When we move from inside the *PPF* to a point on the *PPF* more of some goods and services can be produced without producing less of others—a free lunch.

■ **Calculate opportunity cost.**

Along the *PPF* all choices involve a tradeoff. The *PPF* enables us to calculate opportunity cost—how much of one good we have to give up to get an additional unit of another good. Along the *PPF*, the opportunity cost of the good on the *x*-axis is equal to the decrease in the good on the *y*-axis divided by the increase in the good on the *x*-axis. As more of a good is produced, its opportunity cost increases.

■ **Define efficiency and describe an efficient use of resources.**

Efficiency occurs when we produce the quantities of goods and services that people value most highly. Efficiency is achieved when the conditions of production efficiency and allocative efficiency are met. Production efficiency is a situation in which we cannot produce more of one good or service without producing less of some other good or service—production is at a point on the *PPF*. Allocative efficiency is the most highly valued combination of goods and services on the *PPF*.

■ **Explain how specialization and trade expand production possibilities.**

A person has a comparative advantage in an activity if he or she can perform the activity at a lower opportunity cost than someone else. People gain from specializing in the production of the good in which they have comparative advantage and then trading with others. Absolute advantage occurs when one person is more productive than another person in several or even all activities. A person can have an absolute advantage in all activities but cannot have a comparative advantage in all activities.

EXPANDED CHAPTER CHECKLIST

When you have completed this chapter, you will be able to:

1 Use the production possibilities frontier to illustrate the economic problem.

- Define the production possibilities frontier, *PPF*, and explain the relationship between the *PPF* and the available factors of production and the state of technology.
- State which production points are attainable and which are unattainable.
- Discuss production when resources are fully employed and when resources are unemployed.
- Discuss the difference between tradeoff and free lunch.

2 Calculate opportunity cost.

- Measure opportunity cost along the *PPF*.
- Describe how increasing opportunity cost is reflected in the shape of the *PPF*.

3 Define efficiency and describe an efficient use of resources.

- Define production efficiency and allocative efficiency.
- Use a marginal benefit curve and marginal cost curve to find the efficient use of resources.

4 Explain how specialization and trade expand production possibilities.

- Define comparative advantage and explain its relationship to the gains from trade.
- Determine which of two people will specialize in the production of a good.
- Define absolute advantage and explain why it is different from comparative advantage.

KEY TERMS

- Absolute advantage (page 75)
- Allocative efficiency (page 67)
- Comparative advantage (page 73)
- Efficiency (page 66)
- Production efficiency (page 66)
- Production possibilities frontier (page 56)
- Tradeoff (page 59)

CHECKPOINT 3.1

■ Use the production possibilities frontier to illustrate the economic problem.

Practice Problems 3.1

1. Robinson Crusoe, the pioneer of the television program *Survivor*, lived alone on a deserted island. He spent his day fishing and picking fruit. He varied the time spent on these two activities and kept a record of his production. The table shows the numbers that Crusoe wrote in the sand. Use these numbers to make Crusoe's *PPF* if he can work only 8 hours a day.

Hours	Fish (kilograms)		Fruit (kilograms)
0	0.0		0
1	4.0	or	8
2	7.5	or	15
3	10.5	or	21
4	13.0	or	26
5	15.0	or	30
6	16.5	or	33
7	17.5	or	35
8	18.0	or	36

2. Which combinations (in kilograms) are attainable and which are unattainable: (i) 10 fish and 30 fruit, (ii) 13 fish and 26 fruit, (iii) 20 fish and 21 fruit?

3. Which combinations (in kilograms) use all of Crusoe's available 8 hours a day: (i) 15 fish and 21 fruit, (ii) 7 fish and 30 fruit, (iii) 18 fish and 0 fruit?

4. Which combinations (in kilograms) provide Crusoe with a free lunch and which confront him with a tradeoff when he increases fruit by 1 kilogram: (i) 18 fish and 0 fruit, (ii) 15 fish and 15 fruit, (iii) 13 fish and 26 fruit?

Solution to Practice Problems 3.1

These Practice Problems involve the construction and interpretation of a production possibilities frontier.

Quick Review

- *Production possibilities frontier* The boundary between combinations of goods and services that can be produced and combinations that cannot be produced, given the available factors of production and the state of technology.
- *Unattainable points* Production points outside the *PPF* are unattainable.
- *Full employment* At full employment, the economy produces at a point on the *PPF*.
- *Unemployment* At production points inside the *PPF* some resources are unemployed.

1. **Make Crusoe's *PPF* if he can work only 8 hours a day.**

The table shows Crusoe's *PPF*.

Possibility	Fish (kilograms)		Fruit (kilograms)
A	0.0	and	36
B	4.0	and	35
C	7.5	and	33
D	10.5	and	30
E	13.0	and	26
F	15.0	and	21
G	16.5	and	15
H	17.5	and	8
I	18.0	and	0

To calculate the *PPF*, suppose that Crusoe puts all 8 hours into gathering fruit, so that he gathers 36 kilograms—row A. But there is no time left for fishing, so he gets 0 kilograms of fish. If he takes an hour off from gathering fruit, he gathers 35 kilograms of fruit and has an hour in which to fish, so he gets 4 kilograms of fish—row B. The rest of the *PPF* is constructed similarly.

2. **Which combinations (in kilograms) are attainable and which are unattainable: (i) 10 fish and 30 fruit, (ii) 13 fish and 26 fruit, (iii) 20 fish and 21 fruit?**

i) Row D shows that Crusoe can produce 10.5 fish and 30 fruit, so he can produce 10 fish and 30 fruit. So (i) is attainable.

ii) 13 fish and 26 fruit is on the production possibilities frontier—row E. So (ii) is attainable.

iii) 20 fish and 21 fruit is unattainable because when Crusoe spends the entire 8 hours fishing he can catch only 18 kilograms of fish—row I.

3. **Which combinations (in kilograms) use all of Crusoe's available 8 hours a day: (i) 15 fish and 21 fruit, (ii) 7 fish and 30 fruit, (iii) 18 fish and 0 fruit?**

i) If Crusoe spends enough time to pick 21 fruit, he can also catch 15 fish. This combination uses all his time and is on the *PPF*—row F.

ii) Row C shows that he can get 7.5 fish and 33 fruit if he works 8 hours, so combination (ii) does not require the full 8 hours. This combination is inside the *PPF*.

iii) Catching 18 fish takes 8 hours, leaving no time for picking fruit. So this combination uses all the 8 hours and is row I on the *PPF*.

4. **Which combinations (in kilograms) provide Crusoe with a free lunch and which confront him with a tradeoff when he increases fruit by 1 kilogram: (i) 18 fish and 0 fruit, (ii) 15 fish and 15 fruit, (iii) 13 fish and 26 fruit?**

i) 18 fish and 0 fruit is on the *PPF*—row *I*—so there is a tradeoff but no free lunch.

ii) The combination of 15 fish and 21 fruit is on the *PPF*—row *F*—so the combination of 15 fish and 15 fruit is inside the *PPF* and there is a free lunch.

iii) 13 fish and 26 fruit is on the *PPF*—row *E*—so there is a tradeoff but no free lunch.

Additional Practice Problem 3.1a

Use the *PPF* from Practice Problem 3.1. Can Crusoe gather 21 kilograms of fruit and catch 30 kilograms of fish? Explain your answer. Suppose that Crusoe discovers another fishing pond with more fish, so that he can catch twice as many fish as before. Now can Crusoe gather 21 kilograms of fruit and catch 30 kilograms of fish? Explain your answer.

Solution to Additional Practice Problem 3.1a

Initially, Crusoe cannot gather 21 kilograms of fruit and catch 30 kilograms of fish. This production point lies outside his *PPF* and is unattainable. He can gather 21 kilograms of fruit and 15 kilograms of fish—row F on his *PPF*. When Crusoe discovers the new pond, he doubles the quantity of fish he catches at each production point. He can now gather 21 kilograms of fruit and catch 30 kilograms of fish. The *PPF* depends on the factors of production available and when the factors of production increase, Crusoe's production possibilities change.

■ Self Test 3.1

Fill in the blanks

The ____ (production possibilities; consumption) frontier is the boundary between the combinations of goods and services that can and cannot be produced given the available ____ (goods; factors of production) and ____ (number of services; state of technology). Production points outside the *PPF* ____ (are unattainable; are attainable; represent a free lunch). Society has the possibility of a free lunch if production occurs ____ (inside; on; outside) the *PPF*. When resources are fully employed, we face a ____ (free lunch; tradeoff).

True or false

1. Our production capacity is limited by our available resources and by technology.
2. A point outside the production possibilities frontier is unattainable.
3. If all the factors of production are fully employed, the economy will produce at a point on the production possibilities frontier.
4. Moving from one point on the *PPF* to another point on the *PPF* illustrates a free lunch.

Multiple choice

1. A reason the production possibilities frontier exists is
   a. unlimited resources and technology.
   b. scarcity of resources.
   c. scarcity of resources and unlimited technology.
   d. unemployment.

2. The production possibilities frontier is a graph that shows the
   a. exact point of greatest efficiency for producing goods and services.
   b. combinations of goods and services that can be consumed.
   c. maximum combinations of goods and services that can be produced.
   d. minimum combinations of goods and services that can be produced.

3. The production possibilities frontier is a boundary that separates
   a. the combinations of goods that can be produced from the combinations of services.
   b. attainable combinations of goods and services that can be produced from unattainable combinations.
   c. equitable combinations of goods that can be produced from inequitable combinations.
   d. reasonable combinations of goods that can be consumed from unreasonable combinations.

4. Points inside the *PPF* are all
   a. unattainable and use fully employed resources.
   b. attainable and use fully employed resources.
   c. unattainable and have some unemployed resources.
   d. attainable and have some unemployed resources.

5. During a period of time with high unemployment, a country can increase the production of one good or service
   a. without decreasing the production of something else.
   b. but must decrease the production of something else.
   c. and must increase the production of something else.
   d. by using resources in the production process twice.

6. Moving along the production possibilities frontier itself illustrates
   a. the existence of tradeoffs.
   b. the existence of unemployment of factors of production.
   c. the benefits of free lunches.
   d. how free lunches can be exploited through trade.

Complete the graph

1. In Figure 3.1, draw a production possibilities frontier. Label the points that are attainable and unattainable. Label the points that have full employment and the points that have unemployment.

■ **FIGURE 3.1**
Computers (millions per year)

Food (tonnes per year)

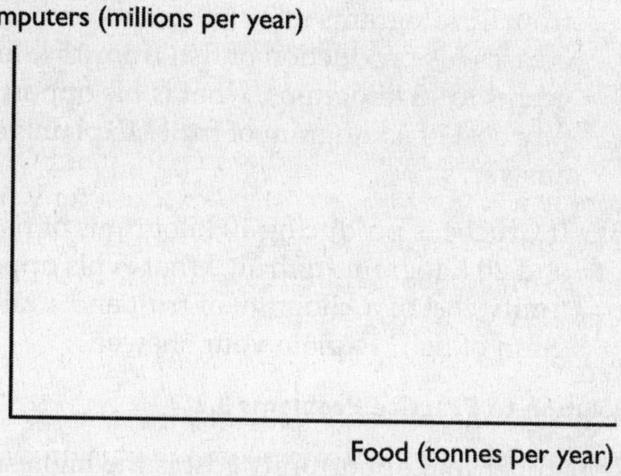

Short answer

1. What factors limit the amount of our production?
2. What is the relationship between unemployment and a free lunch? Between full employment and a tradeoff?

CHECKPOINT 3.2

■ **Calculate opportunity cost.**

Practice Problems 3.2

1. Use Robinson Crusoe's production possibilities shown in the table to calculate his opportunity cost of a kilogram of fish. Make a table that shows Crusoe's opportunity cost of a kilogram of fish as he increases the time he spends fishing and decreases the time he spends picking fruit.

Possibility	Fish (kilograms)		Fruit (kilograms)
A	0.0	and	36
B	4.0	and	35
C	7.5	and	33
D	10.5	and	30
E	13.0	and	26
F	15.0	and	21
G	16.5	and	15
H	17.5	and	8
I	18.0	and	0

2. If Crusoe increases his production of fruit from 21 kilograms to 26 kilograms and decreases his production of fish from 15 kilograms to 13 kilograms, what is his opportunity cost of a kilogram of fruit? Explain your answer.

3. If Crusoe is producing 10 kilograms of fish and 20 kilograms of fruit, what is his opportunity cost of a kilogram of fruit and a kilogram of fish? Explain your answer.

Solution to Practice Problems 3.2

Remember that opportunity cost is the highest-valued alternative forgone.

Quick Review

- *Opportunity cost is a ratio* Along a *PPF*, the opportunity cost of one good equals the quantity of the other good forgone divided by the increase in the quantity of the good.

1. **Make a table that shows Crusoe's opportunity cost of a kilogram of fish as he increases the time he spends fishing and decreases the time he spends picking fruit.**

The opportunity cost of a kilogram of fish is the decrease in fruit divided by the increase in fish as Crusoe moves along his *PPF*. If he increases his time fishing and moves from point *A* to point *B*, he gets 4 kilograms more fish (from 0 kilograms to 4 kilograms) and he picks 1 less kilogram of fruit (he picks 35 kilograms of fruit instead of 36 kilograms). The opportunity cost of 4 kilograms of fish is 1 kilogram of fruit. The opportunity cost of 1 kilogram of fish is (1 kilogram of fruit ÷ 4 kilograms of fish), which is 0.25 kilograms of fruit. The rest of the answers in the table are calculated similarly.

Move from	Increase in fish (kilograms)	Decrease in fruit (kilograms)	Opportunity cost of a kilogram fish (kilograms of fruit)
A to B	4.0	1	0.25
B to C	3.5	2	0.57
C to D	3.0	3	1.00
D to E	2.5	4	1.60
E to F	2.0	5	2.50
F to G	1.5	6	4.00
G to H	1.0	7	7.00
H to I	0.5	8	16.00

2. **If Crusoe increases his production of fruit from 21 kilograms to 26 kilograms and decreases his production of fish from 15 kilograms to 13 kilograms, what is his opportunity cost of a kilogram of fruit? Explain your answer.**

If he increases fruit production from 21 kilograms to 26 kilograms, he gains 5 kilograms of fruit. Production of fish decreases from 15 kilograms to 13 kilograms, a decrease of 2 kilograms. The 5 additional kilograms of fruit cost 2 kilograms of fish. The opportunity cost of 1 kilogram of fruit equals 2 kilograms of fish forgone divided by the gain of 5 kilograms of fruit, which is 2/5 kilograms of fish.

3. **If Crusoe is producing 10 kilograms of fish and 20 kilograms of fruit, what is his opportunity cost of a kilogram of fruit and a kilogram of fish? Explain your answer.**

This combination of fish and fruit lies inside his *PPF* so Crusoe enjoys a free lunch. He can gather more fruit without giving up fish and catch more fish without giving up fruit. His opportunity cost of fruit and of fish are zero.

Additional Practice Problem 3.2a

How does Crusoe's opportunity cost of a kilogram of fish change as he catches more fish?

Solution to Additional Practice Problem 3.2a

Crusoe's opportunity cost of a kilogram of fish increases as he catches more fish. In the table, as Crusoe moves from point *A* to point *B* and increases his quantity of fish from zero to 4 kilograms, the opportunity cost is only 0.25 kilograms of fruit per kilogram of fish. But as he catches more fish, the opportunity cost increases. For example, as he moves from point H to point I and increases his quantity of fish from 17.5 kilograms to 18 kilograms, the opportunity cost increases to 16.0 kilograms of fruit per kilogram of fish.

■ Self Test 3.2

Fill in the blanks

Along a production possibilities frontier, the opportunity cost of obtaining one more unit of a good is the amount of another good that is ____ (forgone; gained). The opportunity cost of a good is equal to the quantity of the other good forgone ____ (plus; divided by) the increase in the quantity of the good. As more of a good is produced, its opportunity cost ____ (decreases; increases).

True or false

1. Moving from one point on the PPF to another point on the PPF has no opportunity cost.

2. When we move along the PPF, the quantity of CDs increases by 2 and the quantity of DVDs decreases by 1, so the opportunity cost is 2 CDs minus 1 DVD.

3. The opportunity cost of a good increases as more of the good is produced.

4. Increasing opportunity costs are common.

Multiple choice

1. The opportunity cost of one more slice of pizza in terms of pop is the
   a. number of pizza slices we have to give up to get one extra pop.
   b. number of pops we have to give up to get one extra slice of pizza.
   c. total number of pops that we have divided by the total number of pizza slices that we have.
   d. total number of pizza slices that we have divided by the total number of pops that we have.

2. Moving between two points on a PPF, a country gains 6 automobiles and forgoes 3 trucks. The opportunity cost of 1 automobile is
   a. 3 trucks.
   b. 6 automobiles − 3 trucks.
   c. 2 trucks.
   d. ½ of a truck.

3. A country produces only cans of soup and pens. If the country produces on its PPF and increases the production of cans of soup, the opportunity cost of a
   a. can of soup is increasing.
   b. can of soup is decreasing.
   c. can of soup remains unchanged.
   d. pen is increasing.

4. The bowed-out shape of the PPF reflects
   a. different rates of unemployment.
   b. increasing availability of factors of production and improved technology.
   c. decreasing opportunity costs.
   d. increasing opportunity costs.

5. Moving along a country's *PPF*, a reason opportunity cost increases is that
   a. unemployment decreases as a country produces more and more of one good.
   b. unemployment increases as a country produces more and more of one good.
   c. technology declines as a country produces more and more of one good.
   d. some resources are better suited for producing one good rather than anther.

6. Increasing opportunity costs exist
   a. in the real world.
   b. as long as there is high unemployment.
   c. only in theory but not in real life.
   d. for a country but not for an individual.

Complete the graph

1. The table shows the production possibilities for a nation.

Production point	MP3 players (millions per year)		DVD players (millions per year)
A	4	and	0.0
B	3	and	3.0
C	2	and	4.0
D	1	and	4.7
E	0	and	5.0

   a. Placing MP3 players on the vertical axis, label the axes in Figure 3.2 and graph the production possibilities frontier.
   b. What is the opportunity cost of a DVD player when moving from point A to point B? B to C? C to D? D to E? How does the opportunity cost change as more DVD players are produced?

■ **FIGURE 3.2**

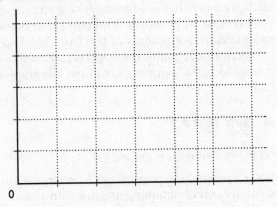

Short answer

1. What is the opportunity cost of increasing the production of a good while moving along a *PPF*? Why does this opportunity cost increase?
2. What does it mean for the opportunity cost to be a ratio?

CHECKPOINT 3.3

■ Define efficiency and describe an efficient use of resources.

Practice Problems 3.3

1. The table shows a nation's production possibilities of bananas and coffee.

Production point	Bananas (bunches)	Coffee (kilograms)
A	70	40
B	50	100
C	30	140
D	10	160

   Use the table to calculate the nation's marginal cost of a bunch of bananas. Draw the marginal cost curve.

2. Use the following data to draw the nation's marginal benefit curve for a bunch of bananas:

   i) When 20 bunches of bananas are available, people are willing to give up 3 kilograms of coffee to get an additional bunch of bananas.

ii) When 40 bunches of bananas are available, people are willing to give up 2 kilograms of coffee to get an additional bunch of bananas.

iii) When 60 bunches of bananas are available, people are willing to give up 1 kilogram of coffee to get an additional bunch of bananas.

3. Use the data in Practice Problems 1 and 2 to calculate the efficient use of the nation's resources.

Solution to Practice Problems 3.3

This Practice Problem uses marginal benefit and marginal cost to find the efficient use of resources.

Quick Review

- *Marginal benefit* The benefit that a person receives from consuming one more unit of a good or service.

- *Marginal cost* The opportunity cost of producing one more unit of a good or service.

- *Production efficiency* A situation in which we cannot produce more of one good or service without producing less of some other good or service—production is at a point *on* the PPF.

- *Allocative efficiency* The most highly valued combination of goods and services on the PPF.

1. **Use the table to calculate the nation's marginal cost of a bunch of bananas. Draw the marginal cost curve.**

The figure plots the marginal cost curve.

As you move from point D to point C along the PPF, the quantity of bananas increases from 10 bunches to 30 bunches, an increase of 20 bunches, and the quantity of coffee decreases from 160 kilograms to 140 kilograms, a decrease of 20 kilograms. So the opportunity cost of 1 bunch of bananas is 1 kilogram of coffee.

On the average, when the quantity of bananas increases from 10 bunches to 30 bunches, 1 bunch of bananas costs 1 kilogram of coffee. We graph this cost midway between 10 bunches and 30 bunches, at 20 bunches on the MC curve.

As you move from point C to point B along the PPF, the quantity of bananas increases from 30 bunches to 50 bunches, an increase of 20 bunches, and the quantity of coffee decreases from 140 kilograms to 100 kilograms, a decrease of 40 kilograms. So the opportunity cost of 1 bunch of bananas is 2 kilograms of coffee.

On the average, when the quantity of bananas increases from 30 bunches to 50 bunches, 1 bunch of bananas costs 2 kilograms of coffee. We graph this cost midway between 30 bunches and 50 bunches, at 40 bunches on the MC curve.

Similarly, as you move from point B to point A along the PPF, the quantity of bananas increases from 50 bunches to 70 bunches and the quantity of coffee decreases from 100 kilograms to 40 kilograms. So the opportunity cost of 1 bunch of bananas is 3 kilograms of coffee. We graph this cost midway between 50 bunches and 70 bunches, at 60 bunches on the MC curve.

2. **Draw the nation's marginal benefit curve for a bunch of bananas.**

The marginal benefit of a bunch of bananas is the amount of coffee people are willing to give up to get a bunch of bananas. The figure shows the MB curve, which graphs the data given in the problem.

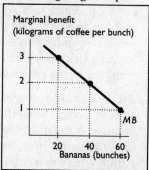

3. Use the data in Practice Problems 1 and 2 to calculate the efficient use of the nation's resources.

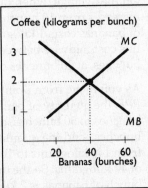

The figure shows the MC curve and the MB curve. The nation uses its resources efficiently when it produces 40 bunches of bananas at the intersection of the MC curve and the MB curve. From the PPF, when the nation produces 40 bunches of bananas, it also produces 120 kilograms of coffee.

All combinations on the PPF are combinations of production efficiency, so when the nation produces 40 bunches of bananas and 120 kilograms of coffee, it is achieving production efficiency. And this combination is also the combination of allocative efficiency because marginal benefit equals marginal cost.

Additional Practice Problem 3.3a

Explain the relationship between production efficiency and allocative efficiency.

Solution to Additional Practice Problem 3.3a

Production efficiency is a situation in which we cannot produce more of one good or service without producing less of some other good or service—production is at a point *on* the PPF. Allocative efficiency is the most highly valued combination of goods and services on the PPF.

All the combinations of goods on the PPF achieve production efficiency. But only one combination is the most highly valued. And the combination that is most highly valued is the combination where marginal benefit equals marginal cost.

■ Self Test 3.3

Fill in the blanks

____ (Production; Allocative) efficiency occurs at each combination of goods and services on the PPF. ____ (Production; Allocative) efficiency occurs when the economy produces the most highly valued combination of goods and services on the PPF. As more of a good is consumed, its marginal benefit ____ (increases; decreases), and as more of a good is produced, its marginal cost ____ (increases; decreases). Allocative efficiency occurs when the marginal benefit of a good is ____ (greater than; equal to; less than) the marginal cost of the good.

True or false

1. All combinations of goods and services on the production possibilities frontier are combinations of allocative efficiency.

2. The marginal benefit of a good increases as more of the good is consumed.

3. Marginal benefit is derived from the production possibilities frontier.

4. Resource use is efficient when we achieve production efficiency and allocative efficiency.

Multiple choice

1. Efficiency occurs when
   a. we produce the quantities of goods and services that people value most highly.
   b. all citizens have equal access to goods and services.
   c. the environment is protected at all cost.
   d. goods and services are free.

2. Production efficiency occurs
   a. anywhere inside or on the production possibilities frontier.
   b. when the total cost of production is minimized.
   c. at all points on the production possibilities frontier.
   d. at only one point on the production possibilities frontier.

3. Marginal benefit is the _____ one more unit of a good or service.
   a. benefit that a person receives from consuming
   b. additional efficiency from producing
   c. increase in profit from producing
   d. cost of producing

4. In general, the marginal cost curve
   a. has a positive slope.
   b. has a negative slope.
   c. is horizontal.
   d. is vertical.

5. For resource use to be efficient, when the marginal benefit of a slice of pizza exceeds the marginal cost,
   a. more slices of pizza should be produced.
   b. fewer slices of pizza should be produced
   c. no more slices of pizza should be produced.
   d. None of the above answers is correct.

6. Allocative efficiency is achieved when the marginal benefit of a good
   a. exceeds its marginal cost by as much as possible.
   b. exceeds its marginal cost but not by as much as possible.
   c. is less than its marginal cost.
   d. equals its marginal cost.

Complete the graph

1. Figure 3.3 shows a production possibilities frontier. Indicate on the *PPF* the combinations of production efficiency. Can you indicate the combination of allocative efficiency?

■ **FIGURE 3.3**
Computers (millions per year)

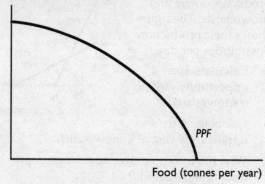

Food (tonnes per year)

2. In Figure 3.4, how many tractors are produced at the point of allocative efficiency?

■ **FIGURE 3.4**
Marginal benefit and marginal cost (T.V. sets per tractor)

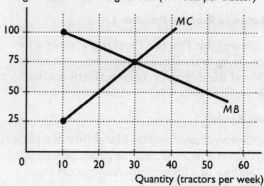

Quantity (tractors per week)

Short answer

1. Along a production possibilities frontier, to produce the first skateboard, 1 pair of roller blades must be forgone. To produce the second skateboard, 2 more pairs of roller blades must be forgone. Is the marginal cost of the second skate board 2 or 3 pairs of roller blades?

2. Is it possible to derive the marginal benefit schedule from the production possibilities frontier?

CHECKPOINT 3.4

■ **Explain how specialization and trade expand production possibilities.**

Practice Problem 3.4

Tony and Patty produce scooters and snowboards. The figure shows their production possibilities per day.

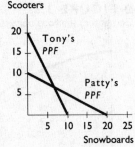

a. Calculate Tony's opportunity cost of a snowboard.
b. Calculate Patty's opportunity cost of a snowboard.
c. Who has a comparative advantage in producing snowboards?
d. Who has a comparative advantage in producing scooters?
e. If they specialize and trade, how many snowboards and scooters will they produce?

Solution to Practice Problem 3.4

To answer this Practice Problem, you need to know how to measure opportunity cost along a *PPF* and the definition of comparative advantage.

Quick Review

- *Comparative advantage* The ability of a person to perform an activity or produce a good or service at a lower opportunity cost than someone else.

a. Calculate Tony's opportunity cost of a snowboard.

In the figure Tony has a constant opportunity cost because the *PPF* is a straight line. If he uses all his resources to produce scooters he can make 20, and if he uses all his resources to produce snowboards, he can make 10. Each snowboard produced decreases his scooter production by 2. The opportunity cost of a snowboard is 2 scooters.

b. Calculate Patty's opportunity cost of a snowboard.

If Patty uses all her resources to produce scooters she can make 10, and if she uses all her resources to produce snowboards, she can make 20. Each snowboard produced decreases her scooter production by ½. The opportunity cost of a snowboard is ½ of a scooter.

c. Who has the comparative advantage in producing snowboards?

The opportunity cost of a snowboard for Patty is ½ of a scooter and for Tony is 2 scooters. Patty has a lower opportunity cost. Comparative advantage is the ability of a person to perform an activity or produce a good or service at a lower opportunity cost than someone else. So Patty has the comparative advantage in snowboards.

d. Who has the comparative advantage in producing scooters?

The opportunity cost of a scooter for Patty is 2 snowboards and the opportunity cost of a scooter for Tony is ½ of a snowboard. Tony has a lower opportunity cost and so he has the comparative advantage in scooters.

e. If they specialize and trade, how many snowboards and scooters will they produce?

Patty specializes in snowboards and Tony specializes in scooters. Patty can produce 20 snowboards and Tony can produce 20 scooters. A total of 20 snowboards and 20 scooters will be produced.

Additional Practice Problem 3.4a

Patty buys new equipment for scooter production that lets her produce 60 scooters a day. Should Patty and Tony specialize and trade?

Solution to Additional Practice Problem 3.4a

When Patty can produce 60 scooters a day, her opportunity cost of a scooter falls to 1/3 snowboards per scooter and her opportunity cost of a snowboard rises to 3 scooters per snowboard. Patty now has the comparative advantage in scooters and Tony in snowboards. Patty and Tony should still specialize and trade, only now Patty will specialize in scooters and Tony will specialize in snowboards.

■ Self Test 3.4

Fill in the blanks

A person has ____ (a comparative; an absolute) advantage in an activity if that person can perform the activity at a lower opportunity cost than someone else. If people specialize according to ____ (comparative; absolute) advantage and then trade, they can consume at a point ____ (outside; inside) their production possibilities frontiers. A person has ____ (a comparative; an absolute) advantage if she is more productive than someone else in several or even all activities. It ____ (is; is not) possible for someone to have a comparative advantage in all activities. It ____ (is; is not) possible for someone to have an absolute advantage in all activities.

True or false

1. Martin has an absolute advantage in an activity if he can perform the activity at a lower opportunity cost than someone else.
2. If Kevin can produce ice cream at a lower opportunity cost than Pat, Kevin has a comparative advantage in ice cream only if he produces more ice cream than Pat in an hour.
3. To achieve the gains from trade, a producer specializes in the product in which he or she has a comparative advantage and then trades with others.
4. Specialization and trade can make both producers better off even if one of them has an absolute advantage in producing all goods.

Multiple choice

1. Norman has a comparative advantage in the production of a good if he can produce
   a. more of all goods than another person.
   b. more of the good in which he has a comparative advantage than another person.
   c. the good in which he has a comparative advantage for a lower dollar cost than another person.
   d. that good at a lower opportunity cost than another person.

2. Bob produces baseballs and softballs. In one hour he produces 10 baseballs or 2 softballs. Bob's opportunity cost of producing 1 softball is
   a. 2 softballs.
   b. 10 baseballs.
   c. 5 baseballs.
   d. 1 baseball.

For the next three questions, use the following information: Scott and Cindy produce only tacos and pizzas. In one hour, Scott can produce 20 pizzas or 40 tacos and Cindy can produce 30 pizzas or 40 tacos.

3. Scott's opportunity cost of producing 1 taco is
   a. 1/2 of a pizza.
   b. 1 pizza.
   c. 2 pizzas.
   d. 20 pizzas.

4. Cindy's opportunity cost of producing 1 taco is
   a. 3/4 of a pizza.
   b. 1 pizza.
   c. 30 pizzas.
   d. 40 pizzas.

5. Based on the data given,
   a. Cindy has a comparative advantage in producing tacos.
   b. Scott has a comparative advantage in producing tacos.
   c. Cindy and Scott have the same comparative advantage when producing tacos.
   d. neither Cindy nor Scott has a comparative advantage when producing tacos.

6. In one hour John can produce 20 loaves of bread or 8 cakes. In one hour Phyllis can produce 30 loaves of bread or 15 cakes. Which of the following statements is true?
   a. Phyllis has a comparative advantage in producing bread.
   b. John has a comparative advantage in producing cakes.
   c. Phyllis has an absolute advantage in both goods.
   d. John has an absolute advantage in both goods.

Complete the graph

1. Figure 3.5 shows Mark's *PPF* and Sue's *PPF*.

   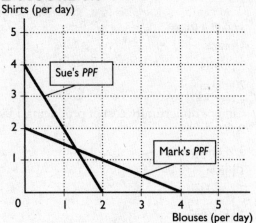

   ■ FIGURE 3.5

   a. Who has the comparative advantage in producing shirts and who has the comparative advantage in producing blouses?
   b. Who should specialize in producing blouses and who should specialize in producing shirts?
   c. If Mark and Sue specialize according to their comparative advantage, indicate the total production of shirts and blouses by putting a point in Figure 3.5 that shows total production. Label the point *A*.
   d. How does point *A* show the gains from trade?

Short answer

1. Why should people specialize according to their comparative advantage?
2. To achieve gains from trade, the opportunity costs of the trading partners must diverge. Why?
3. When it comes to trading one good for another, why is comparative advantage crucial and absolute advantage unimportant?

SELF TEST ANSWERS

■ CHECKPOINT 3.1

Fill in the blanks

The production possibilities frontier is the boundary between the combinations of goods and services that can and cannot be produced given the available factors of production and state of technology. Production points outside the *PPF* are unattainable. Society has the possibility of a free lunch if production occurs inside the *PPF*. When resources are fully employed we face a tradeoff.

True or false

1. True; page 56
2. True; page 58
3. True; pages 58-59
4. False; page 60

Multiple choice

1. b; page 56
2. c; page 56
3. b; page 58
4. d; pages 58-59
5. a; page 60
6. a; page 60

Complete the graph

1. Figure 3.6 shows a production possibilities frontier between computers and food and labels the points; page 58.

■ FIGURE 3.6
Computers (millions per year)

- Points outside the *PPF* are unattainable
- Points on the *PPF* are attainable and have full employment
- Points inside the *PPF* are attainable and have unemployed resources

Food (tonnes per year)

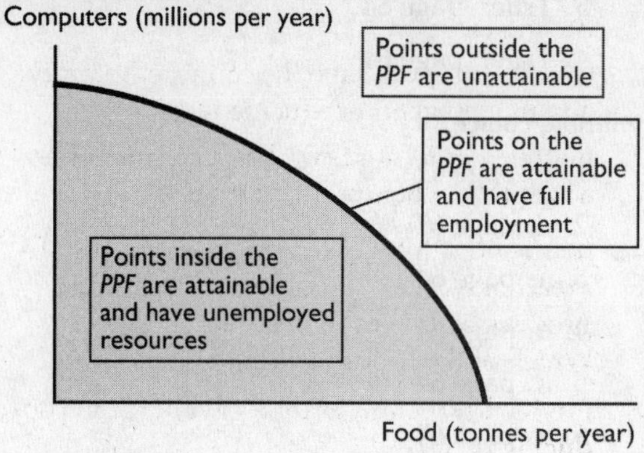

Short answer

1. The factors that limit the amount of our production are the available factors of production and the state of technology; page 56.

2. When a nation is producing at a point with unemployment, a free lunch is possible because the production of some goods and services can be increased without decreasing the production of anything else. When a nation is producing at full employment, it is on the *PPF* and an increase in the production of one good or service requires a tradeoff. If the production of one good or service is increased, the production of something else must be decreased; pages 59-60.

■ CHECKPOINT 3.2

Fill in the blanks

Along a production possibilities frontier, the opportunity cost of obtaining one more unit of a good is the amount of another good that is forgone. The opportunity cost is equal to the quantity of the other good forgone divided by the increase in the quantity of the good. As more of a good is produced, its opportunity cost increases.

True or false

1. False; page 62
2. False; page 63
3. True; page 64
4. True; page 64

Multiple choice

1. b; page 62
2. d; page 62
3. a; page 64
4. d; page 64
5. d; page 64
6. a; page 64

Complete the graph

1. a. Figure 3.7 illustrates the production possibilities frontier; page 62.

■ **FIGURE 3.7**

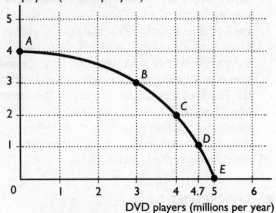

b. The opportunity cost of moving from point A to point B to is 0.33 MP3 players per DVD player; from B to C is 1.00 MP3 player per DVD player; from C to D is 1.43 MP3 players per DVD player; and, from D to E is 3.33 MP3 players per DVD player. The opportunity cost increases as more DVD players are produced; page 64.

Short answer

1. The opportunity cost of increasing production of one good is the production of some other good forgone. The opportunity cost increases because resources are not equally productive in all activities. When initially increasing the production of one good, resources that are well suited for its production are used. When still more of the good is produced, resources that are less well suited must be used. Because the resources are ill suited, more are necessary to increase the production of the first good, and the forgone amount of the other good increases; page 64.

2. The opportunity cost of a good is the amount of the other good forgone to gain an additional unit of the good. We divide the quantity of the other good forgone by the increase in the good. So opportunity cost is a ratio—the change in the quantity of one good divided by the change in the quantity of another good; pages 63-64.

■ **CHECKPOINT 3.3**

Fill in the blanks

<u>Production</u> efficiency occurs at each combination of goods and services on the *PPF*. <u>Allocative</u> efficiency occurs when the economy produces the most highly valued combination of goods and services on the *PPF*. As more of a good is consumed, its marginal benefit <u>decreases</u>, and as more of a good is produced, its marginal cost <u>increases</u>. Allocative efficiency occurs when the marginal benefit of a good is <u>equal to</u> the marginal cost of the good.

True or false

1. False; page 67
2. False; page 67
3. False page 68
4. True; page 70

Multiple choice

1. a; page 66
2. c; page 66
3. a; page 67
4. a; page 69
5. a; page 70
6. d; page 70

Complete the graph

1. Figure 3.8 labels the points on the *PPF* that are production efficient.

■ **FIGURE 3.8**
Computers (millions per year)

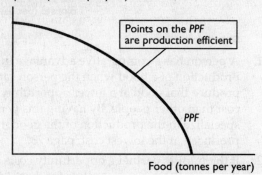

Food (tonnes per year)

Each combination of computers and food on the *PPF* is production efficient. Although the combination of allocative efficiency is a point on the *PPF*, it is not possible to determine that combination without additional information about the marginal benefit of the goods; page 67.

2. Allocative efficiency is the most highly valued combination of goods and services on the *PPF*. It is the combination where marginal cost equals marginal benefit. In Figure 3.9, allocative efficiency is achieved when 30 tractors a week are produced; pages 67, 70.

■ **FIGURE 3.9**
Marginal benefit and marginal cost (T.V. sets per tractor)

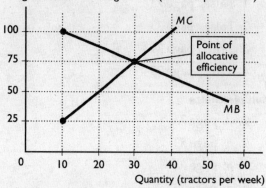

Short answer

1. The marginal cost of the second skateboard is 2 pairs of roller blades. Marginal cost is the opportunity cost of producing one more unit of a good or service. It is not the cost of all the units produced; page 69.

2. It is not possible to derive the marginal benefit schedule from the production possibilities frontier. The marginal benefit is the benefit that a person receives from consuming one more unit of a good or service. The production possibilities frontier does not give us any information about benefit. The production possibilities frontier is used to derive the marginal cost schedule; page 68, 69.

■ **CHECKPOINT 3.4**

Fill in the blanks

A person has <u>a comparative</u> advantage in an activity if that person can perform the activity at a lower opportunity cost than someone else. If people specialize according to <u>comparative</u> advantage and then trade, they can consume at a point <u>outside</u> their production possibilities frontiers. A person has <u>an absolute</u> advantage if she is more productive than someone else in several or even all activities. It <u>is not</u> possible for someone to have a comparative advantage in all activities. It <u>is</u> possible for someone to have an absolute advantage in all activities.

True or false

1. False; page 73
2. False; page 73
3. True; page 74
4. True; page 75

Multiple choice

1. d; page 73
2. c; page 73
3. a; page 73
4. a; page 73
5. b; page 73
6. c; page 75

Complete the graph

1. a. Sue has the comparative advantage in producing shirts. Her opportunity cost of a shirt is 1/2 of a blouse and Mark's opportunity cost of a shirt is 2 blouses. Mark has the comparative advantage in producing blouses. His opportunity cost of a blouse is 1/2 of a shirt and Sue's opportunity cost of a blouse is 2 shirts; page 73.

   b. Mark should specialize in producing blouses and Sue should specialize in producing shirts; page 74.

   c. Mark produces 4 blouses and Sue produces 4 shirts, so a total of 4 shirts and 4 blouses are produced. Figure 3.10 shows this production as point A; page 74.

   d. If the total production at point A is divided evenly, both Mark and Sue have 2 shirts and 2 blouses. When both were producing only for themselves, they could not produce 2 shirts and 2 blouses because this point is beyond both their *PPFs*. By specializing and trading, Mark and Sue get outside their *PPFs*; page 74.

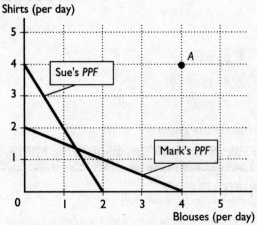

■ FIGURE 3.10

Short answer

1. A person has a comparative advantage in the production of a good when the person can produce that good at a lower opportunity cost than other people. By having this person specialize in the production of the good, it is produced at the lowest cost; page 73.

2. If the trading partners' opportunity costs are the same, there is no incentive for them to trade. For example, if two people produce gum and pop and both have the same opportunity cost of producing gum and pop, neither is willing to buy or sell to the other. Only when opportunity costs diverge will one person be willing to buy (the person with the higher opportunity cost) and the other willing to sell (the person with the lower opportunity cost); page 74.

3. People are willing to trade if they can obtain a good at a lower opportunity cost than what it cost them to produce. Even if a person has an absolute advantage in all goods, he does not have a comparative advantage in all goods. Comparative advantage determines who produces a good and who buys it; page 75.

Chapter 4: Demand and Supply

CHAPTER IN PERSPECTIVE

Chapter 4 studies the tools of demand and supply, which determine the quantities and prices of the goods and services produced and consumed and the quantities of the factors of production employed.

■ **Distinguish between quantity demanded and demand and explain what determines demand.**

The quantity demanded is the amount of any good, service, or resource that people are willing and able to buy during a specified period at a specified price. Demand is the relationship between the quantity demanded and the price of a good when all other influences on buying plans remain the same. The law of demand states that other things remaining the same, if the price of a good rises, the quantity demanded of that good decreases; and if the price of a good falls, the quantity demanded of that good increases. A demand curve is a graph of the relationship between the quantity demanded of a good and its price when all other influences on buying plans remain the same. A change in price leads to a *change in the quantity demanded* and a movement along the demand curve. Factors that *change demand* and shift the demand curve are: prices of related goods; income; expectations; number of buyers; and preferences.

■ **Distinguish between quantity supplied and supply and explain what determines supply.**

The quantity supplied is the amount of any good, service, or resource that people are willing and able to sell during a specified period at a specified price. Supply is the relationship between the quantity supplied and the price of a good when all other influences on selling plans remain the same. The law of supply states that other things remaining the same, if the price of a good rises, the quantity supplied of that good increases; and if the price of a good falls, the quantity supplied of that good decreases. A supply curve is a graph of the relationship between the quantity supplied of a good and its price when all other influences on selling plans remain the same. A change in price leads to a *change in the quantity supplied* and a movement along the supply curve. Factors that *change supply* and shift the supply curve are: prices of related goods; prices of resources and other inputs; expectations; number of sellers; and productivity.

■ **Explain how demand and supply determine price and quantity in a market and explain the effects of changes in demand and supply.**

The equilibrium price and equilibrium quantity occur when the quantity demanded equals the quantity supplied. An increase in demand raises the price and increases the quantity. An increase in supply lowers the price and increases the quantity. An increase in both demand and supply increases the quantity and the price might rise, fall, or not change. An increase in demand and a decrease in supply raises the price and the quantity might increase, decrease, or not change. Changes in demand and supply in the opposite direction lead to reverse changes in price and quantity.

EXPANDED CHAPTER CHECKLIST

When you have completed this chapter, you will be able to:

1 **Distinguish between quantity demanded and demand and explain what determines demand.**
- Define quantity demanded and demand.
- State and explain the law of demand.
- Illustrate the law of demand using a demand schedule and a demand curve.
- Define market demand and derive the market demand curve from individual demand curves.
- List the influences on buying plans that change demand.
- Distinguish between a change in the quantity demanded and a change in demand.

2 **Distinguish between quantity supplied and supply and explain what determines supply.**
- Define quantity supplied and supply.
- State and explain the law of supply.
- Illustrate the law of supply using a supply schedule and a supply curve.
- Define market supply and derive the market supply curve from individual supply curves.
- List the influences on selling plans that change supply.
- Distinguish between a change in the quantity supplied and a change in supply.

3 **Explain how demand and supply determine price and quantity in a market and explain the effects of changes in demand and supply.**
- Find the equilibrium price and equilibrium quantity in a supply and demand diagram.
- Indicate the amount of a surplus or shortage if the price is not the equilibrium price.
- Illustrate the effects of a change in demand and a change in supply separately and simultaneously.

KEY TERMS

- Change in demand (page 84)
- Change in the quantity demanded (page 84)
- Change in the quantity supplied (page 91)
- Change in supply (page 91)
- Complement (page 85)
- Complement in production (page 92)
- Demand (page 81)
- Demand curve (page 82)
- Demand schedule (page 82)
- Equilibrium price (page 95)
- Equilibrium quantity (page 95)
- Inferior good (page 85)
- Law of demand (page 81)
- Law of market forces (page 96)
- Law of supply (page 88)
- Market demand (page 83)
- Market equilibrium (page 95)
- Market supply (page 90)
- Normal good (page 85)
- Quantity demanded (page 81)
- Quantity supplied (page 88)
- Shortage or excess demand (page 96)
- Substitute (page 84)
- Substitute in production (page 91)
- Supply (page 88)
- Supply curve (page 89)
- Supply schedule (page 89)
- Surplus or excess supply (page 96)

CHECKPOINT 4.1

■ **Distinguish between quantity demanded and demand and explain what determines demand.**

Practice Problem 4.1

In the market for scooters, several events occur one at a time. Explain the influence of each event on the quantity demanded of scooters and on the demand for scooters. Illustrate the effects of each event either by a movement along the demand curve or a shift in the demand curve for scooters and say which event (or events) illustrates the law of demand in action. These events are:

a. The price of a scooter falls.
b. The price of a bicycle falls.
c. Citing rising injury rates, cities and towns ban scooters from sidewalks.
d. Average income increases.
e. Rumour has it that the price of a scooter will rise next month.
f. The number of buyers increases.

Solution to Practice Problem 4.1

This problem studies the difference between a change in the quantity demanded and a change in demand.

Quick Review

- *Change in the quantity demanded* A change in the quantity of a good that people plan to buy that results from a change in the price of the good.
- *Change in demand* A change in the quantity that people plan to buy when any influence on buying plans other than the price of the good changes.

a. **The price of a scooter falls.**

A fall in the price of a scooter increases the quantity of scooters demanded, which is shown in the figure as a movement down along the demand curve. This event illustrates the law of demand in action.

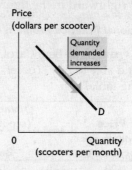

b. **The price of a bicycle falls.**

A fall in the price of a bicycle, which is a substitute for a scooter, decreases the demand for scooters. The demand curve for scooters shifts leftward in the figure from D_0 to D_1.

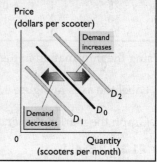

c. **Citing rising injury rates, cities and towns ban scooters from sidewalks.**

The ban on scooters changes preferences. The demand for scooters decreases and the demand curve for the scooters shifts leftward in the figure from D_0 to D_1.

d. **Average income increases.**

The demand for scooters increases when average income increases because a scooter is (likely) a normal good. The demand curve shifts rightward in the figure from D_0 to D_2.

e. **Rumour has it that the price of a scooter will rise next month.**

A rise in the expected future price of a scooter increases the demand for scooters now. The demand curve shifts rightward in the figure from D_0 to D_2.

f. **The number of buyers increases.**

When the number of buyers increase, the demand for scooters increases. The demand curve shifts rightward in the figure from D_0 to D_2.

Additional Practice Problem 4.1a

Each year Anna, Ben, Carol, and Dana are willing and able to buy scooters as shown in the following table.

Price (dollars per scooter)	Quantity demanded (scooters per year)			
	Anna	Ben	Carol	Dana
100	0	0	0	0
75	1	0	0	0
50	2	1	1	0
25	2	1	2	1

Using the information in the table:

a. Label the axes in Figure 4.1.

b. Graph the market demand curve.

■ **FIGURE 4.1**

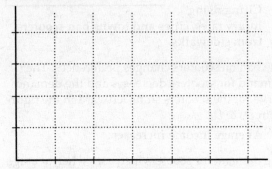

Solution to Additional Practice Problem 4.1a

a. **Label the axes in Figure 4.1.**

The axes are labelled in Figure 4.2

b. **Graph the market demand curve.**

The market demand curve is derived by adding the quantities demanded by Anna, Ben, Carol, and Dana at each price. The market demand curve is illustrated in Figure 4.2.

■ **FIGURE 4.2**
Price (dollars per scooter)

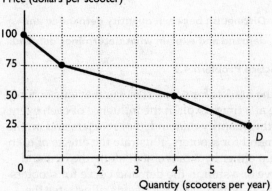

■ **Self Test 4.1**

Fill in the blanks

The ____ (demand schedule; law of demand) states that other things remaining the same, if the price of a good rises, the ____ (quantity demanded of; demand for) that good decreases. A ____ (demand; quantity) curve is a graph of the relationship between the quantity demanded of a good and the price when all other influences on buying plans remain the same. An increase in demand shifts the demand curve ____ (leftward; rightward). A rise in the price of a good ____ (does; does not) shift its demand curve.

True or false

1. The law of demand states that other things remaining the same, if the price of a good rises, the quantity demanded of that good increases.

2. If the quantity of ice cream demanded at each price increases and other influences on buying plans do not change, there is a movement along the demand curve for ice cream.

3. When Elizabeth's income increases, her demand for movies increases. For Elizabeth, movies are a normal good.

4. A rise in the price of a computer increases the demand for computers because a computer is a normal good.

5. If average income falls and all other influences on buying plans remain the same, the demand for computers will decrease and there will be a movement along the demand curve.

Multiple choice

1. The law of demand indicates that if Seneca College increases the price of tuition, all other things remaining the same _____ at Seneca College.
   a. the demand for classes will decrease
   b. the demand for classes will increase
   c. the quantity of classes demanded will increase
   d. the quantity of classes demanded will decrease

2. Other things remaining the same, the quantity of a good or service demanded will increase if the price of that good or service
   a. rises.
   b. falls.
   c. does not change.
   d. rises or falls.

3. If Phillip's demand for pop increases, everything else remaining the same
   a. market demand increases.
   b. market demand decreases.
   c. market demand does not change.
   d. there is a movement along the market demand curve.

4. One reason the demand for Dell laptop computers might increase is a
   a. decrease in the price of a Dell laptop computer.
   b. decrease in price of an Apple computer.
   c. change in preferences as laptops have become more portable.
   d. poor quality performance record for Dell laptop computers.

5. The number of buyers in the market for sport utility vehicles decreases sharply. As a result,
   a. the demand curve for sport utility vehicles shifts leftward.
   b. the demand curve for sport utility vehicles shifts rightward.
   c. there is neither a shift nor a movement along the demand curve for sport utility vehicles.
   d. there is a movement down along the demand curve for sport utility vehicles.

6. When moving along a demand curve, which of the following changes?
   a. the consumers' incomes
   b. the prices of other goods
   c. the number of buyers
   d. the price of the good

7. If the price of a CD falls,
   a. the demand for CDs will increase and the demand curve for CDs will shift rightward.
   b. the demand for CDs will be unaffected, so the demand curve for CDs will not shift.
   c. the quantity of CDs demanded will increase and there will be a movement along the demand curve for CDs.
   d. Both answers (b) and (c) are correct.

8. Pizza and tacos are substitutes. The price of a pizza rises. Which of the following correctly indicates what happens?
   a. The demand for pizzas decreases and the demand for tacos increases.
   b. The demand for both goods decreases.
   c. The quantity of tacos demanded increases and the quantity of pizza demanded decreases.
   d. The quantity of pizza demanded decreases and the demand for tacos increases.

Complete the graph

1. The demand schedule for cotton candy is given in the following table. In Figure 4.3, label the axes and draw the demand curve.

Price (dollars per bag of cotton candy)	Quantity (bags of cotton candy per month)
1	10,000
2	8,000
3	7,000
4	4,000

a. If the price of cotton candy is $2 a bag, what is the quantity of cotton candy demanded?

b. If the price of cotton candy is $3 a bag, what is the quantity of cotton candy demanded?

c. Does the demand curve slope upward or downward?

■ **FIGURE 4.3**

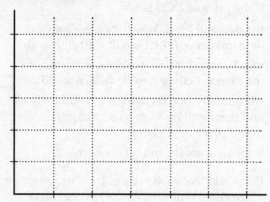

Short answer

1. Explain the difference between a change in the quantity demanded and a change in demand.

2. Explain the difference between a movement along a demand curve and a shift of a demand curve.

CHECKPOINT 4.2

■ **Distinguish between quantity supplied and supply and explain what determines supply.**

Practice Problem 4.2

In the market for timber beams, several events occur one at a time. Explain the influence of each event on the quantity supplied of timber beams and the supply of timber beams. Illustrate the effects of each event by either a movement along the supply curve or a shift in the supply curve of timber beams, and say which event (or events) illustrates the law of supply in action. The events are:

a. The wage rate of sawmill workers rises.

b. The price of sawdust rises.

c. The price of a timber beam rises.

d. The price of a timber beam is expected to rise next year.

e. Environmentalists convince Parliament to introduce a new law that reduces the amount of forest that can be cut for timber products.

f. A new technology lowers the cost of producing timber beams.

Solution to Practice Problem 4.2

This problem studies the difference between a change in the quantity supplied and a change in supply.

Quick Review

- *Change in the quantity supplied* A change in the quantity of a good that suppliers plan to sell that results from a change in the price of the good.

- *Change in supply* A change in the quantity that suppliers plan to sell when any influence on selling plans other than the price of the good changes.

a. The wage rate of sawmill workers rises.

Sawmill workers are a resource used to produce timber beams. A rise in their wage rate decreases the supply of timber beams. The supply curve in the figure shifts leftward from S_0 to S_1.

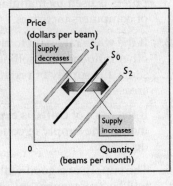

b. The price of sawdust rises.

Sawdust is produced when timber beams are produced, so sawdust and timber beams are complements in production. A rise in the price of a complement in production increases the supply of timber beams and the supply curve of timber beams in the figure shifts rightward from S_0 to S_2.

c. The price of a timber beam rises.

A rise in the price of a timber beam increases the quantity of timber beams supplied. There is a movement up along the supply curve in the figure. This event illustrates the law of supply in action.

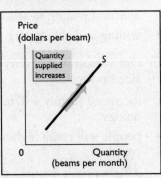

d. The price of a timber beam is expected to rise next year.

The higher expected price decreases the current supply of timber beams because producers plan to sell their timber beams next year when the price is higher. The supply curve in the figure shifts leftward from S_0 to S_1.

e. Environmentalists convince Parliament to introduce a new law that reduces the amount of forest that can be cut for timber products.

The new law decreases the supply of timber beams. The price of a tree, a resource for timber beams, rises. The supply curve of timber beams in the figure shifts leftward from S_0 to S_1.

f. A new technology lowers the cost of producing timber beams.

With the lower cost of production from the new technology, the supply of timber beams increases. The supply curve of timber beams in the figure shifts rightward from S_0 to S_2.

Additional Practice Problem 4.2a

Each month Eddy, Franco, George, and Helen are willing and able to sell plywood as shown in the following table.

Price (dollars per tonne of plywood)	Quantity supplied (tonnes of plywood per month)			
	Eddy	Franco	George	Helen
100	2	2	1	1
75	2	1	1	1
50	1	1	1	0
25	0	0	1	0

a. Label the axes in Figure 4.4.
b. Graph the market supply curve.

■ **FIGURE 4.4**

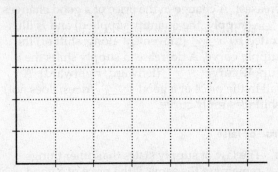

Solution to Additional Practice Problem 4.2a

a. **Label the axes in Figure 4.4.**

The axes are labelled in Figure 4.5.

a. **Graph the market supply curve.**

The market supply curve is derived by discovered by adding the quantities supplied by Eddy, Franco, George, and Helen at each price.

■ **FIGURE 4.5**

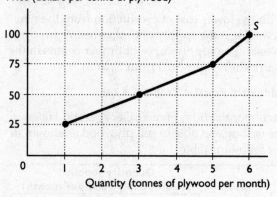

■ Self Test 4.2

Fill in the blanks

The ____ (quantity supplied; supply) of a good is the amount people are willing and able to sell during a specified period at a specified price. The law of supply states that other things remaining the same, if the price of a good rises, the quantity supplied ____ (decreases; increases). A change in the price of a good changes ____ (supply; the quantity supplied) and is illustrated by a ____ (movement along; shift of) the supply curve. A decrease in supply shifts the supply curve ____ (leftward; rightward). A fall in the price of a good ____ (does; does not) shift its supply curve.

True or false

1. The law of supply states that other things remaining the same, if the price of a good rises, the supply of the good increases.

2. When new technology for producing computers is used by manufacturers, the supply of computers increases.

3. If the wage rate paid to chefs rises and all other influences on selling plans remain the same, the supply of restaurant meals will increase.

4. If the price of coffee is expected to rise next month, the supply of coffee this month will decrease.

5. The supply of a good will increase and there will be a movement up along the supply curve of the good if the price of one of its substitutes in production falls.

Multiple choice

1. The quantity supplied is the amount that people are ____ during a specified period at a specified price.
   a. able to sell
   b. willing to sell
   c. able and willing to sell
   d. willing and able to buy

2. One reason supply curves have an upward slope is because
   a. increased supply will require increased technology.
   b. people will pay a higher price when less is supplied.
   c. a higher price brings a greater return than before, so people want to sell more of that good.
   d. None of the above because supply curves have a downward slope.

3. Which of the following indicates that the law of supply applies to makers of pop?
a. An increase in the price of a pop leads to an increase in the demand for pop.
b. An increase in the price of a pop leads to an increase in the supply of pop.
c. An increase in the price of a pop leads to an increase in the quantity of pop supplied.
d. A decrease in the price of a pop leads to an increase in the quantity of pop demanded.

4. The market supply curve is the
a. horizontal sum of the individual supply curves.
b. vertical sum of the individual supply curves.
c. horizontal sum of the individual supply curves minus the market demand.
d. vertical sum of the individual supply curves minus the market demand.

5. If the price of pepperoni and cheese, ingredients used in the production of pizza, rise what will happen in the market for pizza?
a. The supply of pizza will decrease.
b. The quantity of pizzas supplied will increase as sellers try to cover their costs.
c. Pizza will cease to be produced and sold.
d. The demand curve for pizza will shift leftward when the price of a pizza increases.

6. A rise in the price of a substitute in production for a good will lead to
a. an increase in the supply of that good.
b. a decrease in the supply of that good.
c. no change in the supply of that good.
d. a decrease in the quantity of that good supplied.

7. A technological advance in the production of jeans will bring about which of the following?
a. The quantity of jeans supplied will increase.
b. The supply of jeans will increase.
c. The demand for jeans increases because they are now more efficiently produced.
d. The impact on the supply of jeans is impossible to predict.

8. Suppose the price of leather used to produce shoes increases. As a result, there is ____ in the supply of shoes and the supply curve of shoes shifts ____.
a. an increase; rightward
b. an increase; leftward
c. a decrease; rightward
d. a decrease; leftward

Complete the graph

1. The supply schedule for cotton candy is given in the following table. In Figure 4.6, label the axes and draw the supply curve.

Price (dollars per bag of cotton candy)	Quantity (bags of cotton candy per month)
1	4,000
2	8,000
3	10,000
4	12,000

a. If the price of cotton candy is $2 a bag, what is the quantity supplied?
b. If the price of cotton candy is $3 a bag, what is the quantity supplied?
c. Does the supply curve slope upward or downward?

FIGURE 4.6

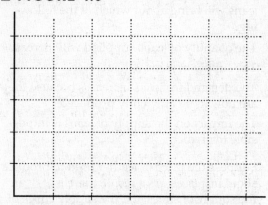

2. Figure 4.7 shows a supply curve of rubber bands. In Figure 4.7, illustrate the effect of a technological advance in the production of rubber bands.

FIGURE 4.7
Price (dollars per box of rubber bands)

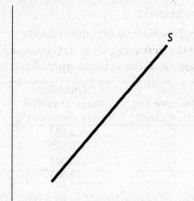

Quantity (boxes of rubber bands per year)

3. Figure 4.8 shows a supply curve for copper. The cost of the natural gas used to refine copper ore into copper rises. In Figure 4.8, show the effect of this event.

FIGURE 4.8
Price (dollars per tonne of copper)

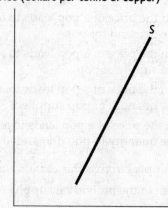

Quantity (tonnes of copper per year)

Short answer

1. What is the law of supply?
2. The following table gives the supply schedules for the three pizza producers in a small town.

Price (dollars per pizza)	Quantity supplied (pizzas per day)			Market supply
	Tom	Bob	Kate	
14	20	12	15	___
12	16	10	10	___
10	12	8	5	___
8	8	6	0	___

Calculate the market supply schedule in the last column.

3. What influence or influences cause a change in the quantity supplied?
4. What influence or influences cause a change in supply?

CHECKPOINT 4.3

■ Explain how demand and supply determine price and quantity in a market and explain the effects of changes in demand and supply.

Practice Problem 4.3

The table shows the demand and supply schedules for milk:

Price (dollars per carton)	Quantity demanded	Quantity supplied
	(cartons per day)	
1.00	200	110
1.25	175	130
1.50	150	150
1.75	125	170
2.00	100	190

a. What is the market equilibrium in the milk market?
b. Describe the situation in the milk market if the price were $1.75 a carton.
c. If the price is $1.75 a carton, explain how the market reaches equilibrium.
d. A drought decreases the quantity supplied by 45 cartons a day at each price. What is the new equilibrium and how does the market adjust to it?
e. Milk becomes more popular, and the quantity demanded increases by 5 cartons a day at each price. Better feeds increase the quantity of milk supplied by 50 cartons a day at each price. If there is no drought, what is the new equilibrium, and how does the market adjust to it?

Solution to Practice Problem 4.3

This Practice Problem studies market equilibrium and shows how changes in demand and supply change the equilibrium price and equilibrium quantity.

Quick Review

• *Market equilibrium* When the quantity demanded equals the quantity supplied—when buyers' and sellers' plans are consistent.

a. **What is the market equilibrium in the milk market?**

Find the row in which the quantity supplied and the quantity demanded are equal. The quantity is 150 cartons a day, which is the equilibrium quantity, and the equilibrium price is $1.50 a carton.

b. **Describe the situation in the milk market if the price were $1.75 a carton.**

When the price is higher than the equilibrium price, the quantity supplied exceeds the quantity demanded, so there is a surplus. At a price of $1.75 a carton, the surplus is 170 cartons minus 125 cartons, which is 45 cartons a day.

c. **If the price is $1.75 a carton, explain how the market reaches equilibrium.**

At $1.75 a carton, there is a surplus of milk. As suppliers lower the price, the quantity demanded increases, the quantity supplied decreases, and the surplus decreases. The price falls until the surplus disappears at a price of $1.50 a carton.

d. **A drought decreases the quantity supplied by 45 cartons a day at each price. What is the new equilibrium and how does the market adjust to it?**

Supply decreases by 45 cartons a day at each price. The table shows the new supply schedule and the original demand schedule.

Price (dollars per carton)	Quantity demanded	New quantity supplied
	(cartons per day)	
1.00	200	65
1.25	175	85
1.50	150	105
1.75	125	125
2.00	100	145

At the original equilibrium price of $1.50 a carton, there is a shortage of milk. The price rises, the quantity of milk demanded decreases, and the quantity supplied increases. The new equilibrium price is $1.75 a carton and the new equilibrium quantity is 125 cartons a day.

e. **Milk becomes more popular, and the quantity demanded increases by 5 cartons a day** at each price. **Better feeds increase the quantity of milk supplied by 50 cartons a day at each price. If there is no drought, what is the new equilibrium and how does the market adjust to it?**

The change in preferences increases demand by 5 cartons a day at each price and the advance in technology increases supply by 50 cartons a day at each price. The table shows the new quantity demanded and the new quantity supplied.

Price (dollars per carton)	New Quantity demanded	New Quantity supplied
	(cartons per day)	
1.00	205	160
1.25	180	180
1.50	155	200
1.75	130	220
2.00	105	240

A surplus exists at the initial equilibrium price. The price falls, the quantity of milk demanded increases, and the quantity of milk supplied decreases. The new equilibrium price is $1.25 a carton and the new equilibrium quantity is 180 cartons a day.

Additional Practice Problem 4.3a

In the market for hot dogs, the price of a hot dog bun falls and the number of hot dog producers increases. The effect of the fall in the price of a hot dog bun is less than the effect of the increase in the number of producers. Describe the new market equilibrium.

Solution to Additional Practice Problem 4.3a

The fall in the price of a complement, hot dog buns, increases the demand for hot dogs. The demand curve for hot dogs shifts rightward in the figure from D_0 to D_1. The increase in the number of producers increases the supply of hot dogs and the supply curve of hot dogs shifts

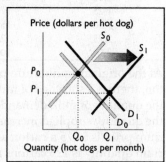

rightward in the figure from S_0 to S_1. Because the increase in supply exceeds the increase in demand, the price of a hot dog falls and the quantity increases, as shown in the figure.

■ Self Test 4.3

Fill in the blanks

The price at which the quantity demanded equals the quantity supplied is the ____ (demand; equilibrium) price. If price exceeds the equilibrium price, the price ____ (rises; falls). An increase in demand ____ (raises; lowers) the equilibrium price and ____ (increases; decreases) the equilibrium quantity. An increase in supply ____ (raises; lowers) the equilibrium price and ____ (increases; decreases) the equilibrium quantity. If both the demand and supply increase, the equilibrium ____ (price; quantity) increases but the equilibrium ____ (price; quantity) rises, falls, or remains the same.

True or false

1. If the price of asparagus is below the equilibrium price, there is a shortage of asparagus and the price of asparagus will rise until the shortage disappears.

2. When the demand for skateboards decreases and the supply of skateboards remains unchanged, the quantity supplied of skateboards decreases as the price rises.

3. Automakers expect the price of a SUV to fall next season. If the demand for SUVs does not change, the equilibrium price of a SUV today will fall and the equilibrium quantity today will increase.

4. As winter sets in, the demand for and supply of hamburger buns decrease. The price of a hamburger bun will definitely remain the same.

5. The number of buyers of grapefruit juice increases and at the same time severe frost decreases the supply of grapefruit. The price of grapefruit juice will rise.

Multiple choice

1. At the equilibrium price, the
a. quantity of the good demanded equals the quantity of the good supplied.
b. quantity of the good demanded is greater than the quantity of the good supplied.
c. quantity of the good demanded is less than the quantity of the good supplied.
d. demand for the good is equal to the supply of the good.

2. Which of the following is correct?
a. A surplus puts downward pressure on the price of a good.
b. A shortage puts upward pressure on the price of a good.
c. There is no surplus or shortage at equilibrium.
d. All of the above answers are correct.

3. The number of buyers of ceiling fans increases. This increase leads to an increase in the
a. quantity of ceiling fans demanded and a surplus of ceiling fans.
b. demand for ceiling fans and a rise in the price of a ceiling fan.
c. demand for ceiling fans and a surplus of ceiling fans.
d. supply of ceiling fans and no change in the price of a ceiling fan.

4. Which of the following is the best explanation for why the price of gasoline rises during the summer months?
a. Oil producers have lower costs of production in the summer.
b. More people walk or ride their bicycles to work in the summer.
c. Car travel increases in the summer as families go on their annual vacations.
d. Oil refineries increase production in the summer.

5. The price of lettuce used to produce tacos increases. The equilibrium price of a taco ____ and the equilibrium quantity ____.
a. rises; increases
b. rises; decreases
c. falls; increases
d. falls; decreases

6. Advances in technology associated with manufacturing computers have led to a _____ in the equilibrium price of a computer and ____ in the equilibrium quantity.
a. rise; an increase
b. rise; a decrease
c. fall; an increase
d. fall; a decrease

7. Candy makers accurately anticipate the increase in demand for candy for Halloween so that the supply of candy and demand for candy increase by the same amount. As a result, the price of candy ____ and the quantity of candy ____.
a. rises; does not change
b. falls; increases
c. does not change; increases
d. does not change; does not change

8. If the supply of gasoline decreases by a greater amount than the demand for gasoline increases, then the equilibrium price of gasoline _____ and the equilibrium quantity _____.

   a. rises; decreases
   b. rises; increases
   c. rises; does not change
   d. falls; does not change

Complete the graph

1. Figure 4.9 shows the demand and supply curves for cotton candy.

   a. Describe the market for cotton candy when the price of cotton candy is $1 a bag.
   b. Describe the market for cotton candy when the price of cotton candy is $3 a bag.
   c. What is the equilibrium price and equilibrium quantity of cotton candy?

■ **FIGURE 4.9**

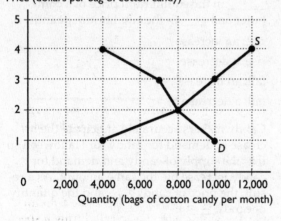

Short answer

1. Define shortage and surplus.

2. The table gives the demand and supply schedules for sweatshirts.

Price (dollars per sweatshirt)	Quantity demanded (sweatshirts per season)	Quantity supplied (sweatshirts per season)
35	13	32
30	15	25
25	19	19
20	27	12
15	37	8

What is the equilibrium quantity and the equilibrium price of sweatshirts?

3. People read that drinking orange juice helps prevent heart disease. What is the effect on the equilibrium price and the equilibrium quantity of orange juice?

4. The cost of memory chips used in computers falls. What is the effect on the equilibrium price and equilibrium quantity of computers?

5. New cars are a normal good. Suppose autoworkers receive a pay increase. What is the effect on the price and quantity of new cars?

SELF TEST ANSWERS

■ CHECKPOINT 4.1

Fill in the blanks

The law of demand states that other things remaining the same, if the price of a good rises, the quantity demanded of that good decreases. A demand curve is a graph of the relationship between the quantity demanded of a good and the price when all other influences on buying plans remain the same. An increase in demand shifts the demand curve rightward. A rise in the price of a good does not shift its demand curve.

True or false

1. False; page 81
2. False; page 84
3. True; page 85
4. False; page 85
5. False; page 86

Multiple choice

1. d; page 81
2. b; page 81
3. a; page 83
4. c; page 85
5. a; page 85
6. d; page 86
7. d; page 86
8. d; pages 85-86

Complete the graph

1. Figure 4.10 shows the demand curve.
   a. 8,000 bags a month
   b. 7,000 bags a month
   c. The demand curve slopes downward; pages 81-82

Short answer

1. A change in the quantity demanded is a change in the quantity of a good that people plan to buy that results from a change in the price of the good. A change in demand is a change in the quantity that people plan to buy when any influence on buying plans other than the price of the good changes; page 84.

2. A movement along a demand curve shows a change in the quantity demanded. A shift of a demand curve shows a change in demand; page 86.

■ FIGURE 4.10

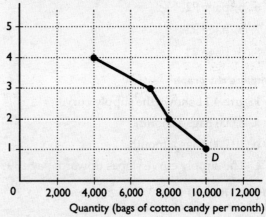

■ CHECKPOINT 4.2

Fill in the blanks

The quantity supplied of a good is the amount people are willing and able to sell during a specified period at a specified price. The law of supply states that other things remaining the same, if the price of a good rises, the quantity supplied increases. A change in the price of a good changes the quantity supplied and is illustrated by a movement along the supply curve. A decrease in supply shifts the supply curve leftward. A fall in the price of a good does not shift its supply curve.

True or false

1. False; page 88
2. True; page 92
3. False; page 92
4. True; page 92
5. False; page 93

Multiple choice

1. c; page 88
2. c; page 88
3. c; page 88
4. a; page 90
5. a; page 92
6. b; page 92
7. b; page 92
8. d; page 93

Complete the graph

1. Figure 4.11 shows the supply curve.
    a. 8,000 bags a month.
    b. 10,000 bags a month.
    c. The supply curve slopes upward; page 89

■ **FIGURE 4.11**
Price (dollars per bag of cotton candy)

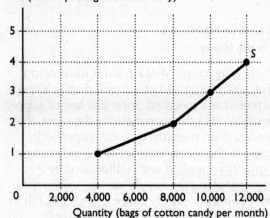

2. An advance in technology increases supply. Figure 4.12 shows the rightward shift of the supply curve from S_0 to S_1; pages 92-93.

■ **FIGURE 4.12**
Price (dollars per box of rubber bands)

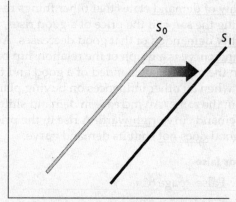

Quantity (boxes of rubber bands per year)

3. A rise in the price of a resource decreases supply. Figure 4.13 shows the leftward shift of the supply curve from S_0 to S_1; pages 92-93

■ **FIGURE 4.13**
Price (dollars per tonne of copper)

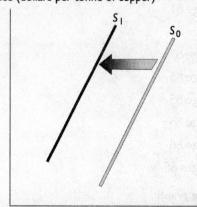

Quantity (tonnes of copper per year)

Short answer

1. Other things remaining the same, if the price of a good rises, the quantity supplied of that good increases; and if the price of a good falls, the quantity supplied of that good decreases ; page 88.

2. The market supply schedule is in the following table; page 90.

Price (dollars per pizza)	Market supply (pizzas per day)
14	47
12	36
10	25
8	14

3. Change in the price of the good; page 93.

4. Changes in: prices of related goods; prices of resources and other inputs; expectations; number of sellers; and productivity; page 91.

■ CHECKPOINT 4.3

Fill in the blanks

The price at which the quantity demanded equals the quantity supplied is the <u>equilibrium</u> price. If price exceeds the equilibrium price, the price <u>falls</u>. An increase in demand <u>raises</u> the equilibrium price and <u>increases</u> the equilibrium quantity. An increase in supply <u>lowers</u> the equilibrium price and <u>increases</u> the equilibrium quantity. If both the demand and supply increase, the equilibrium <u>quantity</u> increases but the equilibrium <u>price</u> rises, falls, or remains the same.

True or false

1. True; page 96
2. False; page 97
3. True; page 98
4. False; page 100
5. True; page 101

Multiple choice

1. a; page 95
2. d; page 96
3. b; page 97
4. c; page 97
5. b; page 98
6. c; page 98
7. c; page 100
8. a; page 101

Complete the graph

1. a. A shortage of 6,000 bags a month; page 96.
   b. A surplus of 3,000 bags a month; page 96.
   c. The equilibrium price is $2 a bag of cotton candy and the equilibrium quantity is 8,000 bags a month; page 95.

Short answer

1. A shortage is a situation in which the quantity demanded exceeds the quantity supplied. A surplus is a situation in which the quantity supplied exceeds the quantity demanded; page 96.

2. The equilibrium price is $25 a sweatshirt. The equilibrium quantity is 19 sweatshirts a season; page 95.

3. The change in preferences increases the demand for orange juice. The equilibrium price of orange juice rises and the equilibrium quantity increases; page 97.

4. The fall in the cost of the memory chips increases the supply of computers. The equilibrium price of a computer falls and the equilibrium quantity increases; page 98.

5. The pay increase received by autoworkers increases income and the demand for new cars increases. The autoworkers are a resource used to produce cars, so the increase in pay decreases the supply of new cars. When demand increases and supply decreases, the price of a new car rises, but the equilibrium quantity can increase, decrease, or remain the same; page 101.

Chapter 5
Elasticities of Demand and Supply

CHAPTER IN PERSPECTIVE

In Chapter 5 we study the price elasticity of demand, the price elasticity of supply, the cross elasticity of demand, and the income elasticity of demand.

■ **Define, explain the factors that influence, and calculate the price elasticity of demand.**

The price elasticity of demand is a measure of the extent to which the quantity demanded of a good changes when the price of the good changes and all other influences on buyers' plans remain the same. The price elasticity of demand equals the percentage change in the quantity demanded divided by the percentage change in price. Demand is elastic if the percentage change in the quantity demanded exceeds the percentage change in price. Demand is unit elastic if the percentage change in the quantity demanded equals the percentage change in price. Demand is inelastic if the percentage change in the quantity demanded is less than the percentage change in price. Elasticity is a *units-free* measure. Along a linear demand curve demand is unit elastic at the midpoint of the curve, demand is elastic at all points above the midpoint of the curve, and demand is inelastic at all points below the midpoint of the curve. The total revenue from the sale of a good equals the price of the good multiplied by the quantity sold. If price and total revenue change in opposite directions, demand is elastic. If a price change leaves total revenue unchanged, demand is unit elastic. If price and total revenue change in the same direction, demand is inelastic.

■ **Define, explain the factors that influence, and calculate the price elasticity of supply.**

The price elasticity of supply is a measure of the extent to which the quantity supplied of a good changes when the price of the good changes and all other influences on sellers' plans remain the same. The two main influences on the price elasticity of supply are production possibilities and storage possibilities. The price elasticity of supply equals the percentage change in the quantity supplied divided by the percentage change in the price. If the price elasticity of supply is greater than 1, supply is elastic. If the price elasticity of supply equals 1, supply is unit elastic. If the price elasticity of supply is less than 1, supply is inelastic.

■ **Define and explain the factors that influence the cross elasticity of demand and the income elasticity of demand.**

The cross elasticity of demand is a measure of the extent to which the demand for a good changes when the price of a substitute or complement changes, other things remaining the same. The cross elasticity of demand is positive for a substitute and negative for a complement. The income elasticity of demand is a measure of the extent to which the demand for a good changes when income changes, other things remaining the same. The income elasticity of demand is positive for a normal good and negative for an inferior good.

EXPANDED CHAPTER CHECKLIST

When you have completed this chapter, you will be able to:

1 Define, explain the factors that influence, and calculate the price elasticity of demand.

- Define price elasticity of demand.
- Use the midpoint method to calculate the percentage change in price and the percentage change in the quantity demanded.
- Define elastic demand, unit elastic demand, and inelastic demand.
- Use a graph to illustrate perfectly elastic demand and perfectly inelastic demand.
- List and explain the influences on the price elasticity of demand.
- Calculate price elasticity of demand.
- Discuss elasticity along a linear demand curve.
- Use the total revenue test to determine the price elasticity of demand.
- Discuss the relationship between farm prices and total revenue.
- Explain how we can use price elasticity of demand to design effective policies for dealing with addiction to drugs.

2 Define, explain the factors that influence, and calculate the price elasticity of supply.

- Define the price elasticity of supply.
- Define elastic supply, unit elastic supply, and inelastic supply.
- Use a graph to illustrate perfectly elastic supply and perfectly inelastic supply.
- List and explain the influences on the price elasticity of supply.
- Calculate the price elasticity of supply.

3 Define and explain the factors that influence the cross elasticity of demand and the income elasticity of demand.

- Define and calculate the cross elasticity of demand.
- Explain when the cross elasticity of demand is positive and when it is negative.
- Define and calculate the income elasticity of demand.
- Discuss the three ranges into which the income elasticity of demand falls.

KEY TERMS

- Cross elasticity of demand (page 125)
- Elastic demand (page 110)
- Elastic supply (page 120)
- Income elasticity of demand (page 126)
- Inelastic demand (page 110)
- Inelastic supply (page 120)
- Perfectly elastic demand (page 110)
- Perfectly elastic supply (page 120)
- Perfectly inelastic demand (page 110)
- Perfectly inelastic supply (page 120)
- Price elasticity of demand (page 108)
- Price elasticity of supply (page 120)
- Total revenue (page 116)
- Total revenue test (page 116)
- Unit elastic demand (page 110)
- Unit elastic supply (page 120)

CHECKPOINT 5.1

■ Define, explain the factors that influence, and calculate the price elasticity of demand.

Practice Problem 5.1

A 10 percent increase in the price of a good has led to a 2 percent decrease in the quantity demanded of that good.

a. How would you describe the demand for this good?
b. Are substitutes for this good easy to find or does it have poor substitutes?
c. Is this good more likely to be a necessity or a luxury? Why?
d. Is this good more likely to be narrowly or broadly defined? Why?
e. Calculate the price elasticity of demand for this good.
f. Has the total revenue from the sale of the good changed? Explain your answer.
g. The good might be which of the following goods: apple juice, bread, toothpaste, theatre tickets, clothing, blue jeans, Stanley Cup tickets? Why?

Solution to Practice Problem 5.1

The practice problem concentrates on the differences between elastic and inelastic demand.

Quick Review

- *Elastic demand* When the percentage change in the quantity demanded exceeds the percentage change in price.
- *Inelastic demand* When the percentage change in the quantity demanded is less than the percentage change in price.

a. **How would you describe the demand for this good?**

The demand for the good is inelastic because the percentage change in the quantity demanded is less than the percentage change in the price.

b. **Are substitutes for this good easy to find or does it have poor substitutes?**

The demand for a good is inelastic if a substitute for it is hard to find. Because demand is inelastic, this good probably has poor substitutes.

c. **Is this good more likely to be a necessity or a luxury? Why?**

This good is probably a necessity. An example of a necessity is food. A necessity has poor substitutes—you must eat—so the demand for a necessity is inelastic.

d. **Is this good more likely to be narrowly or broadly defined? Why?**

The good is probably broadly defined. The demand for a broadly defined good is inelastic. For example, the demand for a particular brand of coffee is elastic because another brand of coffee is a good substitute. But the demand for coffee is inelastic because tea is a poor substitute for it.

e. **Calculate the price elasticity of demand for this good.**

Price elasticity of demand equals the percentage change in the quantity demanded divided by the percentage change in the price, which is (2 percent) ÷ (10 percent) = 0.2.

f. **Has the total revenue from the sale of the good changed? Explain your answer.**

When demand for a good is inelastic, price and total revenue change in the same direction. So when the price increases, total revenue increases.

g. **The good might be which of the following goods: apple juice, bread, toothpaste, theatre tickets, clothing, blue jeans, Stanley Cup tickets? Why?**

The good might be bread because bread is a necessity. The good might be toothpaste because toothpaste has poor substitutes. Or the good might be clothing because clothing is broadly defined.

Additional Practice Problem 5.1a

The table gives the demand schedule for bags of cat food.

Price (dollars per bag of cat food)	Quantity demanded (bags of cat food per year)	Total revenue (dollars)
5	4	____
4	8	____
3	12	____
2	16	____
1	20	____

A graph of this demand schedule gives a linear demand curve.

a. Finish the table by calculating the total revenue for each row.
b. When is the demand elastic? inelastic? unit elastic?
c. Explain your answers to part (b).

Solution to Additional Practice Problem 5.1a

a. **Finish the table by calculating the total revenue for each row.**

The completed table is below.

Price (dollars per bag of cat food)	Quantity demanded (bags of cat food per year)	Total revenue (dollars)
5	4	20
4	8	32
3	12	36
2	16	32
1	20	20

Total revenue equals price times the quantity sold.

b. **When is the demand elastic? inelastic? unit elastic?**

The demand is elastic at prices greater than $3 a bag. The demand is inelastic at prices less than $3 a bag. The demand is unit elastic at a price of $3 a bag.

c. **Explain your answers to part (b).**

Demand is unit elastic at the midpoint of the demand curve. When demand is unit elastic, a price change leaves total revenue unchanged. The midpoint of the curve occurs when the price is $3 a bag, so demand is unit elastic at a price of $3 a bag.

Demand is elastic at all points above the midpoint of the demand curve. When demand is elastic, price and total revenue change in opposite directions. So when the price is greater than $3 a bag, demand is elastic. For example, when the price rises from $4 a bag to $5 a bag, total revenue decreases from $32 to $20.

Demand is inelastic at all points below the midpoint of the demand curve. When demand is inelastic, price and total revenue change in the same direction. So when the price is less than $3 a bag, demand is inelastic. For example, when the price rises from $1 a bag to $2 a bag, total revenue increases from $20 to $32.

■ Self Test 5.1

Fill in the blanks

To calculate the percentage change in price, the midpoint formula divides the change in price by the _____ (initial price; new price; average of the initial and the new price) and then multiplies by 100. If the percentage change in the quantity demanded exceeds the percentage change in the price, demand is _____ (elastic; inelastic). The demand for a product is more elastic if there are _____ (more; fewer) substitutes for it. The price elasticity of demand equals the percentage change in the _____ (price; quantity demanded) divided by the percentage change in the _____ (price; quantity demanded). Moving along a straight-line demand curve, the slope _____ (is constant; varies) and the elasticity _____ (is constant; varies). If demand is elastic, an increase in price _____ (increases; decreases) total revenue.

True or false

1. The price elasticity of demand equals the magnitude of the slope of the demand curve.
2. If the price increases by 10 percent and the quantity demanded decreases by 8 percent, the price elasticity of demand equals 1.25.
3. If as the price of a good increases, the quantity demanded of it remains the same, then demand for the good is perfectly inelastic.
4. Above the midpoint of a straight-line demand curve, demand is elastic.
5. When the price of a service increases by 5 percent the quantity demanded decreases by 5 percent. Total revenue remains unchanged.

Multiple choice

1. The price elasticity of demand is a measure of the extent to which the quantity demanded of a good changes when _____ changes and all other influences on buyers' plans remain the same.
   a. income changes
   b. the price of a related good
   c. the price of the good
   d. the demand

2. According to the midpoint method, what is the percentage change in the price of a movie when the price falls from $9 to $7?
   a. 33 percent
   b. −33 percent
   c. 25 percent
   d. −25 percent

3. Demand for a good is elastic if
   a. the percentage change in the quantity demanded exceeds the percentage change in price.
   b. a large percentage change in price brings about a small percentage change in quantity demanded.
   c. a small percentage change in price brings about a small percentage change in quantity demanded.
   d. the quantity demanded does not change when the price changes.

4. If when the price of natural gas increases the quantity demanded decreases only a little, the demand for natural gas is
   a. inelastic.
   b. elastic.
   c. unit elastic.
   d. perfectly elastic.

5. If substitutes for a good are readily available, the demand for that good will
   a. be small.
   b. be elastic.
   c. be inelastic.
   d. not change substantially if the price changes.

6. If the price of a product increases by 5 percent and the quantity demanded decreases by 5 percent, then the elasticity of demand is
   a. 0.
   b. 1.
   c. indeterminate.
   d. 5.

7. The price of a bag of pretzels rises from $2 to $3 and the quantity demanded decreases from 100 to 60. What is the price elasticity of demand?
   a. 1.0
   b. 1.25
   c. 40.0
   d. 20.0

8. When a firm raises the price of its product, what happens to total revenue?
   a. If demand is elastic, total revenue will decrease.
   b. If demand is unit elastic, total revenue will increase.
   c. If demand is inelastic, total revenue will decrease.
   d. If demand is elastic, total revenue will increase.

Complete the graph

1. In Figure 5.1, label the axes and draw a demand curve for a good that has a perfectly elastic demand.

■ FIGURE 5.1

2. In Figure 5.2, label the point on the demand curve at which demand is unit elastic.

■ FIGURE 5.2

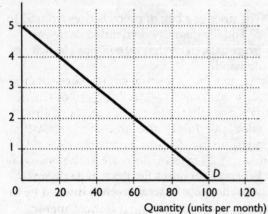

Short answer

1. Complete the table below by calculating the price elasticity of demand.

	Percentage change in price	Percentage change in quantity demanded	Price elasticity of demand
A	5	10	___
B	8	4	___
C	3	0	___
D	6	6	___
E	1	8	___

a. Which row has the most elastic demand?
b. Which row has the least elastic demand?

2. Suppose the price elasticity of demand for oil is 0.3. If the quantity of oil demanded decreases by 6 percent, what will be the effect on the price of oil?

3. What does it mean when the demand for a good is inelastic?

4. What is the relationship between how narrowly a good is defined and the number of substitutes it has?

5. What is the relationship between a rise in price, the elasticity of demand for the good, and the change in total revenue?

CHECKPOINT 5.2

■ **Define, explain the factors that influence, and calculate the price elasticity of supply.**

Practice Problem 5.2

You are told that a 10 percent increase in the price of a good has led to a 1 percent increase in the quantity supplied of the good after one month. Use this information to answer the following questions:

a. How would you describe the supply of this good?
b. What can you say about the production possibilities of this good?
c. Calculate the price elasticity of supply.
d. If after one year, the quantity supplied has increased by 25 percent, describe how the supply has changed over the year.
e. Calculate the elasticity of supply after one year.

Solution to Practice Problem 5.2

Practice Problem 5.2 is similar to Practice Problem 5.1. Note that to calculate both the price elasticity of supply and the price elasticity of demand we divide the percentage change in the quantity (supplied or demanded) by the percentage change in price.

Quick Review

- *Price elasticity of supply* A measure of the extent to which the quantity supplied of a good changes when the price of the good changes and all other influences on sellers' plans remain the same.

a. **How would you describe the supply of this good?**

The supply of this good is inelastic because the percentage change in the quantity supplied is less than the percentage change in the price.

b. **What can you say about the production possibilities of this good?**

The factors of production that are used to produce this good are likely to be quite unique because the percentage increase in the quantity supplied after one month is not large.

c. **Calculate the price elasticity of supply.**

The price elasticity of supply is the percentage change in the quantity supplied divided by the percentage change in price, which is (1 percent) ÷ (10 percent) = 0.1.

d. **If after one year, the quantity supplied has increased by 25 percent, describe how the supply has changed over the year.**

The supply of the good has become more elastic during the year. With the increase in price more producers have entered the market.

e. **Calculate the elasticity of supply after one year.**

The price elasticity of supply equals the percentage change in the quantity supplied divided by percentage change in price, which is (25 percent) ÷ (10 percent) = 2.5.

Additional Practice Problem 5.2a

Over one month the elasticity of supply of avocados is 0.1 and over 5 years the elasticity of supply of avocados is 2.0. If the price of avocados rises 10 percent, what is the increase in the quantity supplied in one month and in 5 years? Why is there a difference in the quantities?

Solution to Additional Practice Problem 5.2a

The increase in the quantity supplied equals the percentage change in the price times the elasticity of supply. In one month, the quantity supplied increases by (10 percent) × (0.1), which is 1 percent. In 5 years, the quantity supplied increases by (10 percent) × (2.0), which is 20 percent. The increase in the quantity supplied is much greater after 5 years because eventually, additional avocado trees can be planted, mature, and then be harvested. The supply of avocados becomes more elastic as time passes.

■ **Self Test 5.2**

Fill in the blanks

When a good has a vertical supply curve, then the supply of the good is perfectly ____ (elastic; inelastic). Goods that can be produced at an almost constant opportunity cost have an ____ (elastic; inelastic) supply. As time passes, the elasticity of supply ____ (increases; decreases). The price elasticity of supply equals the percentage change in the ____ (price; quantity supplied) divided by the percentage change in the ____ (price; quantity supplied).

True or false

1. If the percentage change in the quantity supplied is zero when the price changes, supply is perfectly elastic.

2. Goods that are produced at a constant opportunity cost have an elastic supply.

3. The supply of apples is perfectly elastic on the day of a price change.

4. The supply of a storable good is perfectly inelastic.

5. When the price of a pizza is $20, 10 pizzas are supplied and when the price rises to $30 a pizza, 14 pizzas are supplied. The price elasticity of supply of pizzas is 0.83.

Multiple choice

1. The price elasticity of supply is a measure of the extent to which the quantity supplied of a good changes when the _____ and all other influences on sellers' plans remain the same.
   a. cost of producing the product increases
   b. quantity of the good demanded increases
   c. supply increases
   d. price of the good changes

2. When the percentage change in the quantity supplied exceeds the percentage change in price, then the good has _____ supply.
   a. an elastic
   b. an inelastic
   c. a unit elastic
   d. a perfectly inelastic

3. The supply of lakefront property in Muskoka is
   a. elastic.
   b. unit elastic.
   c. negative.
   d. inelastic.

4. If a good has a rapidly increasing opportunity cost of producing additional units, we would expect that _____ that good is _____.
   a. demand for; elastic
   b. supply of; elastic
   c. demand for; inelastic
   d. supply of; inelastic

5. The greater the amount of time that passes after a price change, the
   a. less elastic supply becomes.
   b. more elastic supply becomes.
   c. more negative supply becomes.
   d. more positive supply becomes.

6. The price elasticity of supply equals the percentage change in the
   a. quantity demanded divided by the percentage change in the price of a substitute.
   b. quantity supplied divided by the percentage change in price.
   c. quantity demanded divided by the percentage change in price.
   d. quantity demanded divided by the percentage change in income.

7. If a firm supplies 200 units at a price of $50 and 100 units at a price of $40, what is the price elasticity of supply?
   a. 0.33
   b. 1.00
   c. 3.00
   d. 0

8. If the price of a good increases by 10 percent and the quantity supplied increases by 5 percent, then the elasticity of supply is
   a. greater than one and supply is elastic.
   b. negative and supply is inelastic.
   c. less than one and supply is elastic.
   d. less than one and supply is inelastic.

Complete the graph

1. In Figure 5.3, label the axes and then draw a supply curve for a good that has a perfectly inelastic supply.

■ **FIGURE 5.3**

Short answer

1. If the elasticity of supply of wheat is 0.3 and the price of wheat rises 10 percent, what is the increase in the quantity of wheat supplied? If the elasticity of supply of magazines is 1.3 and the price of a magazine rises 10 percent, what is the increase in the quantity of magazines supplied?

2. The table gives a supply schedule.

	Price (dollars)	Quantity supplied (units per week)
A	5	10
B	15	30
C	25	50
D	35	90

   Calculate the price elasticity of supply between points A and B; between points B and C; and between points C and D.

3. Describe the elasticity of supply of a good that can be stored.

4. Why does the elasticity of supply increase as time passes after a price change?

CHECKPOINT 5.3

■ **Define and explain the factors that influence the cross elasticity of demand and the income elasticity of demand.**

Practice Problem 5.3

1. If the quantity demanded of good A increases by 5 percent when the price of good B rises by 10 percent and other things remain the same:

   a. Are goods A and B complements or substitutes? Why?
   b. Describe how the demand for good A changes.
   c. Calculate the cross elasticity of demand of good A with respect to good B.

2. If, when income rises by 5 percent and other things remain the same, the quantity demanded of good C increases by 1 percent:

   a. Is good C a normal good or an inferior good? Why?
   b. Describe how the demand for good C changes when income increases.
   c. Calculate the income elasticity of demand for good C.

Solution to Practice Problem 5.3

This practice problem studies cross elasticity of demand and income elasticity of demand. Remember that when you calculate the cross elasticity of demand for a good that you must divide by the percentage change in the price of one of the good's substitutes or complements.

Quick Review

- *Cross elasticity of demand* A measure of the extent to which the demand for a good changes when the price of a substitute or complement changes, other things remaining the same.
- *Income elasticity of demand* A measure of the extent to which the demand for a good changes when income changes, other things remaining the same.

1a. Are goods A and B complements or substitutes? Why?

A rise in the price of a substitute brings an increase in the quantity demanded of the good. A rise in the price of good B increases the quantity of good A demanded, so A and B are substitutes.

1b. Describe how the demand for good A changes.

As the price of good B rises, the demand for good A increases and the demand curve for good A shifts rightward.

1c. Calculate the cross elasticity of demand of good A with respect to good B.

The cross elasticity of demand equals the percentage change in the quantity demanded of good A divided by the percentage change in the price of good B, which is (5 percent) ÷ (10 percent) = 0.50.

2a. Is good C a normal good or an inferior good? Why?

Good C is a normal good because when income increases the quantity demanded increases.

2b. Describe how the demand for good C changes when income increases.

As income increases, the demand for good C increases and its demand curve shifts rightward.

2c. Calculate the income elasticity of demand for good C.

The income elasticity of demand equals the percentage change in the quantity demanded divided by the percentage change in income, which is (1 percent) ÷ (5 percent) = 0.20.

Additional Practice Problem 5.3a

Pepsi and Coke are substitutes. Pepsi and Tropicana juice also are substitutes. Which pair of substitutes has the larger cross elasticity of demand?

Solution to Additional Practice Problem 5.3a

For many people, Pepsi and Coke are close substitutes. A slight rise in the price of a Coke increases the quantity of Pepsi demanded significantly. The cross elasticity is large. Pepsi and Tropicana juice are less close substitutes. An increase in the price of Tropicana orange increases the demand for Pepsi by a small amount and the cross elasticity is small.

■ Self Test 5.3

Fill in the blanks

The ____ (price; cross; income) elasticity of demand is a measure of the extent to which the demand for a good changes when the price of a substitute or complement changes, other things remaining the same. The cross elasticity of demand is ____ (positive; negative) for a complement. The income elasticity of demand equals the percentage change in ____ (quantity demanded; income) divided by the percentage change in ____ (the quantity demanded; income). The income elasticity of demand is ____ (positive; negative) for a normal good.

True or false

1. If the cross elasticity of demand is negative, the two goods are substitutes.
2. If the cross elasticity between hamburgers and hot dogs is positive, then hamburgers and hot dogs are substitutes.
3. An inferior good has a negative income elasticity of demand.
4. When the income elasticity of demand of a good is positive, the good is a normal good.
5. A normal good is a good that has a positive cross elasticity of demand

Multiple choice

1. The measure used to determine whether two goods are complements or substitutes is the
   a. price elasticity of supply.
   b. cross elasticity of demand.
   c. price elasticity of demand.
   d. income elasticity.

2. If beef and pork are substitutes, the cross elasticity of demand between the two goods
   a. is negative.
   b. is positive.
   c. cannot be determined.
   d. is elastic.

3. When the price of a pizza is $10, the quantity of pop demanded is 300 cans. When the price of pizza is $15, the quantity of pop demanded is 100 cans. The cross elasticity of demand equals
   a. −0.25.
   b. −0.40.
   c. −2.50.
   d. −25.00.

4. If two goods have a cross elasticity of –2, then when the price of one good increases, the demand curve of the other good
   a. shifts rightward.
   b. shifts leftward.
   c. remains unchanged.
   d. may shift rightward, leftward or remain unchanged.

5. Income elasticity of demand equals the percentage change in
   a. quantity demanded divided by the percentage change in the price of a substitute.
   b. quantity supplied divided by the percentage change in price.
   c. quantity demanded divided by the percentage change in price.
   d. quantity demanded divided by the percentage change in income.

6. When income increases from $20,000 to $30,000 the number of home delivered pizzas per year increases from 22 to 40. The income elasticity of demand for home delivered pizza equals
   a. 1.45.
   b. 0.69.
   c. 0.58.
   d. 0.40.

7. If a product is a normal good, then its income elasticity of demand is
   a. zero.
   b. positive.
   c. negative.
   d. indeterminate.

8. The income elasticity of demand for used cars is less than zero. A used car is
   a. an inferior good.
   b. a normal good.
   c. an inelastic good.
   d. a perfectly inelastic good.

Complete the graph

1. The income elasticity of demand for large screen televisions is positive. In Figure 5.4, show how the demand for large screen televisions changes when income increases.

■ **FIGURE 5.4**

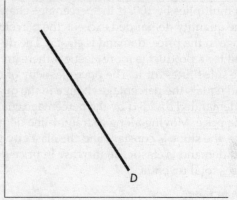

Short answer

1. The income elasticity of demand for inter-city bus trips is negative. What does this fact tell you about inter-city bus trips?

2. Complete the table below.

	Percentage change in income	Percentage change in quantity demanded	Income elasticity of demand
A	5	10	___
B	5	–10	___
C	5	2	___
D	6	6	___

Which row indicates an inferior good and which row indicates a good that is income elastic?

SELF TEST ANSWERS

■ CHECKPOINT 5.1

Fill in the blanks

To calculate the percentage change in price, the midpoint formula divides the change in price by the <u>average of the initial and the new price</u> and then multiplies by 100. If the percentage change in the quantity demanded exceeds the percentage change in the price, demand is <u>elastic</u>. The demand for a product is more elastic if there are <u>more</u> substitutes for it. The price elasticity of demand equals the percentage change in the <u>quantity demanded</u> divided by the percentage change in the <u>price</u>. Moving along a straight-line demand curve, the slope <u>is constant</u> and the elasticity <u>varies</u>. If demand is elastic, an increase in price <u>decreases</u> total revenue.

True or false

1. False; page 114
2. False; page 112
3. True; page 110
4. True; page 114
5. True; page 116

Multiple choice

1. c; page 108
2. d; page 108
3. a; page 110
4. a; page 110
5. b; page 110
6. b; page 112
7. b; page 112
8. a; page 116

Complete the graph

1. Figure 5.5 labels the axes and illustrates a demand curve for a good with perfectly elastic demand; page 111.

■ **FIGURE 5.5**

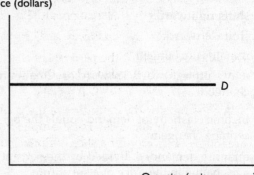

2. In Figure 5.6, demand is unit elastic at the midpoint of the curve; page 114.

■ **FIGURE 5.6**

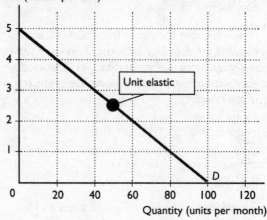

Short answer

1. The complete table is below; page 112.

	Percentage change in price	Percentage change in quantity demanded	Price elasticity of demand
A	5	10	2.0
B	8	4	0.5
C	3	0	0.0
D	6	6	1.0
E	1	8	8.0

a. The most elastic demand is in row E; page 112.
b. The least elastic demand is in row C (the demand is perfectly inelastic); page 112.
2. The price rises by 20 percent; page 112.
3. Demand is inelastic if the percentage change in the quantity demanded is less than the percentage change in price; page 110.
4. The more narrow the definition of the good, the more substitutes exist. For example, there are more substitutes for a slice of Pizza Hut pizza than for pizza in general; page 112.
5. When the price of a good rises, total revenue increases if demand is inelastic, total revenue does not change if demand is unit elastic, and total revenue decreases if demand is elastic; page 116.

■ CHECKPOINT 5.2

Fill in the blanks

When a good has a vertical supply curve, then the supply of the good is perfectly <u>inelastic</u>. Goods that can be produced at an almost constant opportunity cost have an <u>elastic</u> supply. As time passes, the elasticity of supply <u>increases</u>. The price elasticity of supply equals the percentage change in the <u>quantity supplied</u> divided by the percentage change in the <u>price</u>.

True or false

1. False; page 120
2. True; page 120
3. False; page 122
4. False; page 122
5. True; page 122

Multiple choice

1. d; page 120
2. a; page 120
3. d; page 120
4. d; page 120
5. b; page 122
6. b; page 122
7. c; page 122
8. d; page 122

Complete the graph

1. Figure 5.7 labels the axes and illustrates a supply curve for a good with a perfectly inelastic supply; page 121.

■ FIGURE 5.7

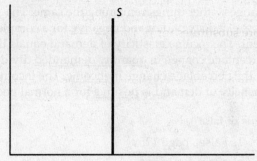

Short answer

1. If the price of wheat rises 10 percent, the increase in the quantity supplied equals (10 percent) × (0.3) = 3 percent. If the price of a magazine rises 10 percent, the increase in the quantity supplied equals (10 percent) × (1.3) = 13 percent; page 122.
2. The price elasticity of supply between points A and B is 1.00; between points B and C is 1.00; and between points C and D is 1.71; page 122.
3. The elasticity of supply of a good that can be stored depends on the decision to keep the good in storage or offer it for sale. A small price change can make a big difference to this decision, so the supply of a storable good is highly elastic; page 122.
4. As time passes after a price change, it becomes easier to change production plans and supply becomes more elastic. For example, many manufactured goods have an inelastic supply if production plans have had only a short period in which to change. But after all

the technologically possible ways of adjusting production have been exploited, supply is extremely elastic for most manufactured items; page 122.

■ CHECKPOINT 5.3

Fill in the blanks

The cross elasticity of demand is a measure of the extent to which the demand for a good changes when the price of a substitute or complement changes, other things remaining the same. The cross elasticity of demand negative for a complement. The income elasticity of demand equals the percentage change in quantity demanded divided by the percentage change in income. The income elasticity of demand is positive for a normal good.

True or false

1. False; page 125
2. True; page 125
3. True; page 126
4. True; page 126
5. False; page 126

Multiple choice

1. b; page 125
2. b; page 125
3. c; page 125
4. b; pages 125-126
5. d; page 126
6. a; page 126
7. b; page 126
8. a; page 126

Complete the graph

1. Because the income elasticity of demand is positive, large screen televisions are a normal good. In Figure 5.8 an increase in income shifts the demand curve rightward from D_0 to D_1; page 126.

■ FIGURE 5.8

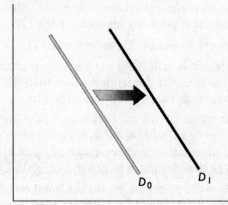

Short answer

1. The fact that the income elasticity of demand for inter-city bus trips is negative indicates that an inter-city bus trip is an inferior good. When people's incomes increase, they take fewer inter-city bus trips and instead fly, drive, or take the train; page 126.

2. The completed table is below. The good in Row B is an inferior good. The good in row A is income elastic; page 126.

	Percentage change in income	Percentage change in quantity demanded	Income elasticity of demand
A	5	10	2.0
B	5	−10	−2.0
C	5	2	0.4
D	6	6	1.0

Chapter 6

Efficiency and Fairness of Markets

CHAPTER IN PERSPECTIVE

In Chapter 6 we study the equilibrium quantities of goods, services, and factors of production to determine if markets are efficient. Chapter 6 also studies the main ideas about fairness and determines if competitive markets result in fair outcomes.

- **Distinguish between value and price and define consumer surplus.**

Value is what we get, and price is what we pay. In economics, the everyday idea of value is called *marginal benefit*, which is the maximum price that people are willing to pay for another unit of the good or service. The demand curve tells us this price. A demand curve is a marginal benefit curve. When people buy something for less than it is worth to them, they receive a consumer surplus. Consumer surplus is the marginal benefit from a good or service minus the price paid for it, summed over the quantity consumed.

- **Distinguish between cost and price and define producer surplus.**

Cost is what a seller must give up to produce a good, and price is what a seller receives when the good is sold. The cost of producing one more unit of a good or service is its *marginal cost*. It is just worth producing one more unit of a good or service if the price for which it can be sold equals marginal cost. The supply curve tells us this price. A supply curve is a marginal cost curve. When the price exceeds marginal cost, the firm obtains a producer surplus. Producer surplus is the price of a good minus the marginal cost of producing it, summed over the quantity produced.

- **Explain the conditions in which markets are efficient and inefficient.**

Markets are efficient when resources are used to produce the goods and services people value most highly. When marginal benefit equals marginal cost, the efficient quantity is produced. The sum of consumer surplus and producer surplus is maximized at a competitive equilibrium. According to Adam Smith, each participant in a competitive market is "led by an invisible hand to promote an end [the efficient use of resources] which was no part of his intention." Externalities, public goods, and monopoly are obstacles to achieving an efficient allocation of resources. Governments can create inefficiency when they implement price ceilings and price floors, and taxes, subsidies, and quotas.

- **Explain the main ideas about fairness and evaluate claims that competitive markets result in unfair outcomes.**

The symmetry principle is the requirement that people in similar situations be treated similarly. Two views of fairness are it's not fair if the *result* isn't fair and it's not fair if the *rules* aren't fair. Utilitarianism is a principle that states that we should strive to achieve "the greatest happiness for the greatest number." The utilitarian idea of complete equality ignores the cost of making income transfers, which leads to the big tradeoff—a tradeoff between efficiency and fairness.

EXPANDED CHAPTER CHECKLIST

When you have completed this chapter, you will be able to:

1 Distinguish between value and price and define consumer surplus.

- Discuss the difference between value and price.
- Explain why a demand curve is a marginal benefit curve.
- Define consumer surplus and illustrate it in a figure.

2 Distinguish between cost and price and define producer surplus.

- Discuss the difference between cost and price.
- Explain why a supply curve is a marginal cost curve.
- Define producer surplus and illustrate it in a figure.

3 Explain the conditions in which markets are efficient and inefficient.

- Explain why a competitive equilibrium is efficient.
- Discuss Adam Smith and the "invisible hand".
- List the obstacles to achieving an efficient allocation of resources.
- Define and illustrate deadweight loss.

4 Explain the main ideas about fairness and evaluate claims that competitive markets result in unfair outcomes.

- Define the symmetry principle.
- Discuss the two broad views of fairness.

- Define utilitarianism and discuss the one big problem with the utilitarian idea of complete equality.
- Discuss fairness in the face of a natural disaster.

KEY TERMS

- Big tradeoff (page 148)
- Consumer surplus (page 135)
- Deadweight loss (page 144)
- Producer surplus (page 138)
- Symmetry principle (page 147)
- Utilitarianism (page 148)

CHECKPOINT 6.1

■ Distinguish between value and price and define consumer surplus.

Practice Problem 6.1

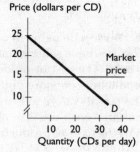

The figure shows the demand for CDs and the market price of a CD. Use the figure to answer the following questions:

a. What is the value of the 10th CD?
b. What is the willingness to pay for the 20th CD?
c. What is the consumer surplus on the 10th CD?
d. What are the quantity of CDs bought and the consumer surplus?
e. What is the amount paid for CDs in question (d)?
f. What is the total benefit from CDs in question (d)?
g. If the price of a CD rises to $20, what is the consumer surplus?

Solution to Practice Problem 6.1

This practice problem illustrates the relationship between the demand curve and the marginal benefit curve. A demand curve is a marginal benefit curve. Marginal benefit is the maximum price that people are willing to pay for another unit of a good or service. The demand curve tells us this price.

Quick Review

- *Value* In economics, the everyday idea of value is called *marginal benefit*, which we measure as the maximum price that people are willing to pay for another unit of a good or service.
- *Consumer surplus* The marginal benefit from a good or service minus the price paid for it, summed over the quantity consumed.

a. What is the value of the 10th CD?

The value of the 10th CD is the marginal benefit of the 10th CD. The value of the 10th CD is also equal to the maximum price that someone is willing to pay for it. In the figure, the demand curve shows that if 10 CDs are available, the maximum price willingly paid for the 10th CD is $20.

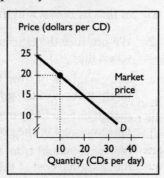

b. What is the willingness to pay for the 20th CD?

The willingness to pay for the 20th CD is equal to the maximum price that someone is willing to pay for the 20th CD. In the figure, the demand curve shows that if 20 CDs are available, the maximum price willingly paid for the 20th CD is $15.

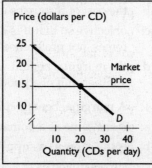

c. What is the consumer surplus on the 10th CD?

The consumer surplus on the 10th CD is the marginal benefit of 10th CD minus the price of a CD. In the figure, the marginal benefit of the 10th CD is $20 and the price is $15, so consumer surplus is $20 − $15, which is $5.

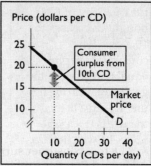

d. What are the quantity of CDs bought and the consumer surplus?

In the figure, the quantity of CDs bought is 20, which is the quantity where the market price line and the demand curve intersect.

The consumer surplus equals the area of the grey triangle in the figure. The area of the triangle is ½ × ($25 − $15) × 20, which is $100.

e. What is the amount paid for the CDs in question (d)?

The amount paid for the CDs equals the price multiplied by the quantity bought. The amount paid is $15 × 20, which is $300.

f. What is the total benefit from the CDs in question (d)?

The total benefit from the CDs is the amount paid for the CDs, which is $300, plus the consumer surplus, which is $100. The total benefit is $400.

g. If the price of a CD rises to $20, what is the consumer surplus?

When the price is $20, the quantity of CDs bought decreases to 10 a day. The consumer surplus equals the area of the grey triangle in the figure. The area of the triangle is ½ × ($25 − $20) × 10, which is $25.

Additional Practice Problem 6.1a

Estelle paid a lawyer $50 to write a letter to settle a rent dispute. What is Estelle's value of this service, her marginal benefit, and consumer surplus?

Solution to Additional Practice Problem 6.1a

The value that Estelle receives from the service provided by the lawyer is the same as her marginal benefit. And Estelle's marginal benefit is the maximum price that she is willing to pay to have the letter prepared. The consumer surplus from the service provided by the lawyer is equal to Estelle's marginal benefit minus the price she pays. If the price that Estelle pays for the letter is less than her marginal benefit, then Estelle receives a consumer surplus.

■ Self Test 6.1

Fill in the blanks

The benefit a person receives from consuming one more unit of a good is its ____ (marginal; opportunity) benefit. The opportunity cost of producing one more unit of a good is its ____ (marginal benefit; marginal cost). Allocative efficiency occurs at the quantity where marginal benefit is ____ (greater than; equal to; less than) marginal cost. The demand curve ____ (is; is not) a marginal benefit curve. The consumer surplus equals the marginal benefit of a good ____ (plus; multiplied by; minus) the price paid for it, summed over the quantity consumed.

True or false

1. The efficient quantity of lip gloss is the quantity at which the marginal benefit from a lip gloss equals the marginal cost of a lip gloss.
2. Value and price refer to the same thing.
3. A demand curve is a marginal benefit curve.
4. Consumer surplus is the marginal benefit from a good or service minus the price paid for it, summed over the quantity consumed.

Multiple choice

1. As the consumption of a good increases, the marginal benefit from consuming that good
   a. increases.
   b. decreases.
   c. stays the same.
   d. at first increases and then decreases.

2. We produce the efficient quantity of a good when the
   a. marginal benefit from the good exceeds the marginal cost of the good.
   b. marginal benefit from the good equals the marginal cost of the good.
   c. marginal benefit from the good is lower than the marginal cost of the good.
   d. the marginal cost of the good stops increasing.

3. Value is
   a. the price we pay for a good.
   b. the cost of resources used to produce a good.
   c. objective so that it is determined by market forces, not preferences.
   d. the marginal benefit we get from consuming another unit of a good or service.

4. A marginal benefit curve
   a. is the same as a demand curve.
   b. is the same as a supply curve.
   c. slopes upwards.
   d. is a vertical line.

5. The difference between the marginal benefit from a new pair of shoes and the price of the new pair of shoes is
   a. the consumer surplus from that pair of shoes.
   b. what we get.
   c. what we have to pay.
   d. the price when the marginal benefit is maximized.

6. Suppose the price of a scooter is $199 and Cora Lee is willing to pay $250. Cora Lee's
   a. consumer surplus from that scooter is $199.
   b. consumer surplus from that scooter is $51.
   c. total benefit from that scooter is $199.
   d. None of the above answers are correct.

Complete the graph

1. Figure 6.1 shows the marginal benefit curve and marginal cost curve for roller blades.

■ **FIGURE 6.1**

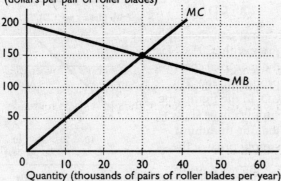

   a. What is the efficient quantity of roller blades?
   b. Is the market for roller blades efficient if more than 30,000 pairs of roller blades are produced a year?

2. Figure 6.2 shows the demand curve for bags of potato chips.

■ **FIGURE 6.2**

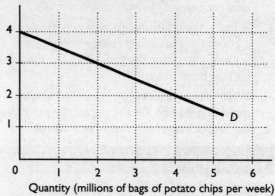

   a. What is the maximum price a consumer is willing to pay for the 2 millionth bag of chips?
   b. What is the marginal benefit from the 2 millionth bag of chips? What is the relationship between your answer to part (a) and your answer to this part?
   c. If the price of a bag of chips equals $2, in Figure 6.2 shade the area that equals the amount of the consumer surplus.
   d. If the price of a bag of chips equals $2, what is the amount of the consumer surplus?

Short answer

1. The table gives the demand schedule for MP3 players.

Price (dollars per MP3 player)	Quantity (millions of MP3 players per year)	Consumer surplus (dollars)
500	4	___
400	8	___
300	12	___
200	16	___
100	20	___

Suppose the price of an MP3 player is $200.

   a. Complete the table by calculating the consumer surplus. In the first row, calculate the consumer surplus for the 4 millionth MP3 player; in the second row, calculate the consumer surplus for the 8 millionth MP3 player; and so on.

b. As more MP3 players are purchased, what happens to the consumer surplus of the last unit purchased? Why?

2. What is the relationship between the value of a good, the maximum price a consumer is willing to pay for the good, and the marginal benefit from the good?

3. What is the relationship between the marginal benefit of a slice of pizza, the price paid for the slice, and its consumer surplus?

CHECKPOINT 6.2

■ **Distinguish between cost and price and define producer surplus.**

Practice Problem 6.2

The figure shows the supply of CDs and the market price of a CD. Use the figure to answer the following questions:

b. What is the marginal cost of the 10th CD?
b. What is the minimum supply price of the 20th CD?
c. What is the producer surplus on the 10th CD?
d. What are the quantity of CDs sold and the producer surplus?
e. What is the total revenue from the sales of CDs in question (d)?
f. What is the cost of producing the CDs sold in question (d)?
g. If the price of a CD falls to $10, what now is the producer surplus?

Solution to Practice Problem 6.2

This practice problem illustrates the relationship between the supply curve and the marginal cost curve. A supply curve is a marginal cost curve. It is just worth producing one more unit of a good or service if the price for which it can be sold equals marginal cost. The supply curve tells us this price.

Quick Review

- *Cost* Cost is what the seller must give up to produce a good.
- *Producer surplus* The price of a good minus the marginal cost of producing it, summed over the quantity produced.

a. **What is the marginal cost of the 10th CD?**

The marginal cost of the 10th CD is equal to the minimum supply price of the 10th CD. The supply curve tells us this price. In the figure, the supply curve shows that the marginal cost of the 10th CD is $10.

b. **What is the minimum supply price of the 20th CD?**

The minimum supply price of the 20th CD is the marginal cost of producing the 20th CD. In the figure, the supply curve shows that the minimum supply price of the 20th CD is $15.

b. **What is the producer surplus on the 10th CD?**

The producer surplus on the 10th CD is the price of a CD minus the marginal cost of producing it. In the figure the producer surplus is $15 − $10, which is $5.

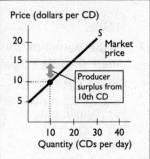

d. What are the quantity of CDs sold and the producer surplus?

At the market price of $15, 20 CDs are sold. The producer surplus equals the area of the grey triangle in the figure. The area of the triangle is ½ × 20 × ($15 − $5), which equals $100.

e. What is the total revenue from the sales of CDs in question (d)?

Total revenue equals price multiplied by quantity sold. Total revenue is $15 × 20 = $300.

f. What is the cost of producing the CDs sold in question (d)?

The total cost of producing 20 CDs equals the total revenue minus the producer surplus. The total cost is $300 − $100, which is $200.

g. If the price of a CD falls to $10, what now is the producer surplus?

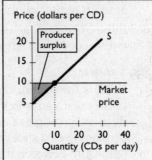

When the price falls to $10, the quantity of CDs sold decreases to 10 a day. The producer surplus equals the area of the grey triangle in the figure. The grey area equals ½ × 10 × ($10 − $5), which is $25.

Additional Practice Problem 6.2a

Why is the minimum price that a seller will produce a good equal to the good's marginal cost?

Solution to Additional Practice Problem 6.2a

A seller is willing to produce a good when the price he receives covers all the costs of producing the good. So the minimum price for which a seller is willing to produce a unit of a good is the amount that just equals the cost of producing that unit. The cost of producing a unit of a good is its marginal cost, so the minimum supply price equals the marginal cost.

■ Self Test 6.2

Fill in the blanks

____ (Price; Cost) is what a seller must give up to produce a good and ____ (price; cost) is what a seller receives when the good is sold. A ____ (demand; supply) curve is a marginal cost curve. A firm receives a producer surplus when price is ____ (greater; less) than marginal cost.

True or false

1. In economics, cost and price are the same.
2. The minimum price for which Bob will grow another kilogram of carrots is 50¢, so the marginal cost of an additional kilogram of carrots is 50¢.
3. A supply curve is a marginal benefit curve.
4. Producer surplus equals the marginal benefit of a good minus the cost of producing it.

Multiple choice

1. Cost is
   a. what the buyer pays to get the good.
   b. always equal to marginal benefit.
   c. what the seller must give up to produce the good.
   d. greater than market price.

2. If a firm is willing to supply the 1,000th unit of a good at a price of $23 or more, we know that $23 is the
   a. highest price the seller hopes to realize for this output.
   b. minimum price the seller must receive to produce this unit.
   c. average price of all the prices the seller could charge.
   d. price that sets the marginal benefit equal to the marginal cost.

3. A supply curve shows the _____ of producing one more unit of a good or service.
   a. producer surplus
   b. consumer surplus
   c. total benefit
   d. marginal cost

4. Producer surplus is
   a. equal to the marginal benefit from a good minus its price.
   b. equal to the price of a good minus the marginal cost of producing it, summed over the quantity produced.
   c. always equal to consumer surplus.
   d. Both answers (a) and (c) are correct.

5. You are willing to tutor your friend for $10 an hour. Your friend pays you $15 an hour. What is your producer surplus?
   a. $5 an hour
   b. $10 an hour
   c. $15 an hour
   d. $25 an hour

6. In a figure that shows a supply curve and a demand curve, producer surplus is the area
   a. below the demand curve and above the market price.
   b. below the supply curve and above the market price.
   c. above the demand curve and below the market price.
   d. above the supply curve and below the market price.

Complete the graph

1. Figure 6.3 shows the supply curve for bags of potato chips.

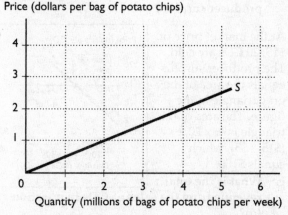

■ FIGURE 6.3
Price (dollars per bag of potato chips)

   a. What is the minimum price for which a supplier is willing to produce the 2 millionth bag of chips?
   b. What is the marginal cost of the 2 millionth bag of chips? What is the relationship between your answer to part (a) and your answer to this part?
   c. If the price of a bag of chips equals $2, in Figure 6.3 shade the area that equals the amount of the producer surplus.
   d. If the price of a bag of chips equals $2, calculate the producer surplus.

Short answer

1. What is the relationship between the minimum price a supplier must receive to produce a slice of pizza and the marginal cost of producing that slice of pizza? What is the relationship between the marginal cost curve and the supply curve?

2. What is producer surplus? As the price of a good or service rises and the supply curve does not shift, what happens to the amount of the producer surplus?

CHECKPOINT 6.3

■ Explain the conditions in which markets are efficient and inefficient.

Practice Problem 6.3

The figure shows the market for paper. Use the figure to answer the following questions:

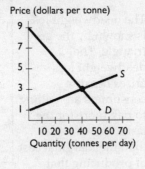

a. What are the equilibrium price and the equilibrium quantity of paper?
b. In market equilibrium, what is the consumer surplus?
c. In market equilibrium, what is the producer surplus?
d. Is the market for paper efficient? Why or why not?
e. If a news magazine lobby group persuaded the government to pass a law requiring paper producers to sell 50 tonnes of paper a day, would the market for paper be efficient? Why or why not?
f. In the situation described in part (e), shade the deadweight loss on the figure.
g. If an environmental lobby group persuaded the government to pass a law that allows producers of paper to sell only 20 tonnes of paper a day, would the market for paper be efficient? Why or why not?
h. In the situation described in part (g), shade the deadweight loss on the figure.

Solution to Practice Problem 6.3

The efficient use of resources occurs when marginal benefit equals marginal cost. When production in a market occurs at an inefficient level, a deadweight loss occurs.

Quick Review

- *Efficiency of competitive equilibrium* The condition that marginal benefit equals marginal cost delivers an efficient use of resources. It allocates resources to the activities that create the greatest possible value. So a competitive equilibrium is efficient.

- *Deadweight loss* The decrease in consumer surplus and producer surplus that results from an inefficient level of production.

a. What are the equilibrium price and the equilibrium quantity of paper?

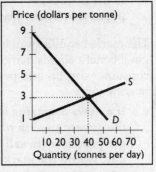

In the figure, the equilibrium price and the equilibrium quantity of paper occur at the intersection of the demand curve, D, and the supply curve, S. The equilibrium quantity is 40 tonnes a day and the equilibrium price is $3 a tonne.

b. In market equilibrium, what is the consumer surplus?

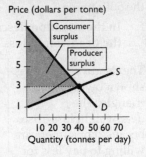

The consumer surplus equals the area of the dark triangle. Consumer surplus equals ½ × (40 tonnes) × ($9 − $3), which is $120.

c. In market equilibrium, what is the producer surplus?

The producer surplus equals the area of the light grey triangle. Producer surplus equals ½ × (40 tonnes) × ($3 − $1), which is $40.

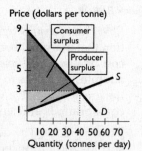

d. Is the market for paper efficient? Why or why not?

The market equilibrium is efficient because marginal benefit equals marginal cost and the sum of consumer surplus and producer surplus is maximized.

e. If a news magazine lobby group persuaded the government to pass a law requiring paper producers to sell 50 tonnes of paper a day, would the market be efficient? Why or why not?

When producers sell 50 tonnes of paper a day the market is inefficient because the marginal cost of the 50th tonne exceeds the marginal benefit of the 50th tonne.

f. In the situation described in part (e), shade the deadweight loss on the figure.

The deadweight loss is shown by the grey triangle. The deadweight loss arises because consumers are willing to pay less for the last tonne of paper than the marginal cost of producing that tonne.

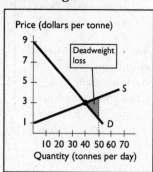

g. If an environmental lobby group persuaded the government to pass a law that allows producers of paper to sell only 20 tonnes of paper a day, would the market for paper be efficient? Why or why not?

When producers sell 20 tonnes of paper a day the market is inefficient because the marginal cost of the 20th tonne is less than the marginal benefit of the 20th tonne.

h. In the situation described in part (g), shade the deadweight loss on the figure.

The deadweight loss is shown by the grey triangle. The deadweight loss arises because consumers are willing to pay more for the last tonne of paper than the marginal cost of producing that tonne.

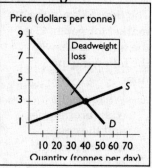

Additional Practice Problem 6.3a

Who gains from a deadweight loss?

Solution to Additional Practice Problem 6.3a

No one gains from a deadweight loss. Deadweight loss is the decrease in consumer surplus and producer surplus that results from an inefficient level of production. The deadweight loss is borne by the entire society. It is not a loss for the consumers and a gain for the producer. It is a social loss.

■ Self Test 6.3

Fill in the blanks

Equilibrium in a competitive market ____ (is; is not) efficient. Adam Smith believed that each participant in a competitive market is "led by _____" (an invisible hand; market forces). _____ (An externality; A public good) is a good or service that is consumed simultaneously by everyone, even if they don't pay for it. A price _____ (ceiling; floor) is a regulation that makes it illegal to charge a price higher than a specified level. Deadweight loss is the decrease in _____ (consumer surplus; consumer surplus and producer surplus; producer surplus) that results from an inefficient level of production.

True or false

1. In a competitive equilibrium, resource use is efficient.
2. When the efficient quantity of a good is produced, the consumer surplus is always zero.
3. According to Adam Smith, competitive markets require government action to ensure that resources are allocated efficiently.
4. Producing less than the efficient quantity of a good results in a deadweight loss but producing more than the efficient quantity does not result in a deadweight loss.

Multiple choice

1. When a market is efficient
   a. the sum of consumer surplus and producer surplus is maximized.
   b. the consumer surplus is as large as possible.
   c. the quantity produced is maximized.
   d. marginal cost is less than marginal benefit.

2. When a market is efficient
   a. producers earn the highest income possible.
   b. production costs equal total benefit.
   c. consumer surplus equals producer surplus.
   d. resources are used to produce the goods and services that people value most highly

3. The concept of "the invisible hand" suggests that markets
   a. do not produce the efficient quantity.
   b. are always fair.
   c. produce the efficient quantity.
   d. are unfair.

4. What can cause a market to produce an inefficient quantity of a good?
   a. a monopoly
   b. an external cost or an external benefit
   c. a public good
   d. All of the above.

5. When underproduction occurs,
   a. producers realize more surplus at the expense of consumers.
   b. marginal cost is greater than marginal benefit.
   c. consumer surplus grows to a harmful amount.
   d. there is a deadweight loss that is borne by the entire society.

6. When production moves from the efficient quantity to a point of overproduction
   a. consumer surplus definitely increases.
   b. the sum of producer surplus and consumer surplus increases.
   c. there is a deadweight loss.
   d. consumers lose and producers gain.

Complete the graph

1. In Figure 6.4, what is the equilibrium quantity of automobiles? What is the efficient quantity of automobiles? Show the consumer surplus and the producer surplus.

■ **FIGURE 6.4**
Price (thousands of dollars per automobile)

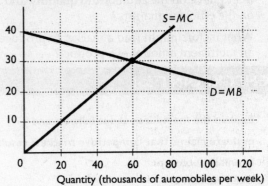

2. Figure 6.5 is identical to Figure 6.4. Now, suppose that 80,000 automobiles are produced. If there is a deadweight loss, shade it light grey. Next suppose that 40,000 automobiles are produced. If there is a deadweight loss, shade it dark grey.

■ **FIGURE 6.5**

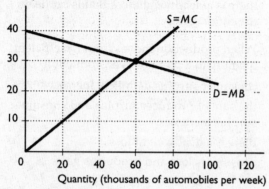

Price (thousands of dollars per automobile)

Short answer

1. What is the relationship between a competitive market, efficiency, and the invisible hand?
2. Suppose the demand for cotton clothing increases. What effect does the increase in demand have on the equilibrium quantity and on the efficient quantity?
3. What factors might lead a market to produce an inefficient amount of a product?

CHECKPOINT 6.4

■ **Explain the main ideas about fairness and evaluate claims that competitive markets result in unfair outcomes.**

Practice Problem 6.4

A winter storm cuts the power supply and isolates a small town in the mountains. The people rush to buy candles from the town store, which is the only source of supply of candles. The store owner decides to ration the candles to one per family but keep the price of a candle unchanged.

a. Who gets to consume the candles?
b. Who receives the consumer surplus on candles?
c. Who receives the producer surplus on candles?
d. Is the outcome efficient?
e. Is the outcome fair according to the utilitarian principle?
f. Is the process fair according to the symmetry principle?
g. If the town government declares a state of emergency and gives every family $100 to cope with the crisis, does this produce a more efficient and fairer outcome?

Solution to Practice Problem 6.4

This problem challenges you to use what you have learned about fairness and think carefully about what is fair and what is unfair.

Quick Review

- *Utilitarianism* A principle that states that we should strive to achieve "the greatest happiness for the greatest number."
- *Symmetry principle* The requirement that people in similar situations be treated similarly.

a. **Who gets to consume the candles?**

The answer that each family gets to consume one candle is incorrect because it ignores that candles can be resold. A buyer from the town store will sell his candle if the price exceeds his marginal benefit. The consumers of the candles are those who are willing to pay the most.

b. **Who receives the consumer surplus on candles?**

The consumer surplus is received by families that buy and consume the candles. A family that buys and then sells a candle, does not receive any consumer surplus because it does not consume the candle.

c. **Who receives the producer surplus on candles?**

The town store owner receives the same producer surplus as normal. The families who initially purchase the candles from the town store and then resell them to other families also receive some producer surplus.

d. **Is the outcome efficient?**

The outcome is efficient because the families that most highly value the candles are the families that buy and consume the candles.

e. **Is the outcome fair according to the utilitarian principle?**

The outcome is not fair according to the utilitarian principle. Utilitarians would have the candles shared equally, so that every family gets the same number of candles. But the outcome has the candles shared unequally because some families sell their candles.

f. **Is the process fair according to the symmetry principle?**

The process is fair according to the symmetry principle because all the exchanges are voluntary. Families that want to sell their candles are free to do so and families that want to buy candles are free to do so.

g. **If the town government declares a state of emergency and gives every family $100 to cope with the crisis, does this produce a more efficient and fairer outcome?**

When the government provides every family with $100, the demand for candles increases, and the equilibrium price of a candle rises. But the quantity of candles available does not change. To pay the $100, the town government must raise taxes, which might be fair or unfair.

Additional Practice Problem 6.4a

If Bill Gates gives $1,000 to a homeless person, would the transaction be fair? If Mr. Gates is taxed $1,000 by the government and the government gives the $1,000 to the same homeless person, would the transaction be fair?

Solution to Additional Practice Problem 6.4a

If Mr. Gates gives $1,000 to a homeless person, the exchange is considered fair according to the symmetry principle because the exchange is voluntary. The outcome is fair according to the utilitarian principle because there is more equality of income. If Mr. Gates is taxed by the government, the outcome is fair according to the utilitarian principle because there is more equality of income. But the transaction is not fair according to the symmetry principle because the exchange does not occur voluntarily.

■ Self Test 6.4

Fill in the blanks

Two views of fairness are that "it's not fair if the ____ (result; income distribution) isn't fair;" and "it's not fair if the ____ (rules; tradeoffs between efficiency and income) aren't fair." _____ (Symmetry; Utilitarianism) is a principle that states that we should strive to achieve "the greatest happiness for the greatest number". According to Robert Nozick, fair-rules ideas require _____ (government intervention; property rights and voluntary exchange).

True or false

1. The symmetry principle is the idea that all people should receive symmetric incomes.

2. The goal of utilitarianism is to achieve the greatest happiness for the greatest number of people.

3. The big tradeoff is the tradeoff between efficiency and happiness.

4. According to the "fair-rules" view of fairness, in times of natural disasters, it is fair to force people to make available necessary goods and services at lower than usual prices.

Multiple choice

1. The requirement that people in similar situations be treated similarly is the ____ principle.
   a. equity
   b. symmetry
   c. market
   d. fairness

2. The principle that states that we should strive to achieve "the greatest happiness for the greatest number" is
   a. equity.
   b. fairness.
   c. market equilibrium.
   d. utilitarianism.

3. Which of the following is an example in which "the big tradeoff" can occur?
   a. the government redistributes income from the rich to the poor
   b. Ford increases the price of a pickup truck
   c. a basketball player signs a $5 million contract
   d. a college lowers tuition

4. The "fair-rules" view of fairness is based on
   a. income transfers from the rich to the poor.
   b. property rights and voluntary exchange.
   c. utilitarianism.
   d. the big tradeoff.

5. An unequal distribution of income is considered fair according to Robert Nozick if
   a. marginal cost equals marginal benefit.
   b. the cost of administering a welfare system is minimized.
   c. property rights are enforced and voluntary exchange occurs.
   d. the economy is producing its maximum total output.

6. Suppose an ice storm strikes eastern Ontario. The price of firewood jumps from $15 a box to $28. If the government buys all the firewood at $28 a box and offers it to consumers for $15 a box, which of the following is true?
   a. There is enough firewood for everyone at $15 a box.
   b. There is a surplus of firewood at $15 a box.
   c. Some people who buy firewood from the government at $15 a box will resell the firewood to consumers who are willing to pay $28 a box, and earn a producer surplus.
   d. Because the government is buying and selling the firewood, the market is efficient.

Short answer

1. In Canada, richer people generally pay a larger fraction of their income as taxes than do poorer people. Is this arrangement fair? Answer from a fair-results view and from a fair-rules view.

2. Suppose that during their working lifetimes, Matt and Pat earned identical incomes as computer programmers. Matt spent all of his income and Pat saved a large portion of hers. Now that they are retired, Pat's income is higher than Matt's because of Pat's saving. Is it fair for Pat's income to be higher than Matt's? Answer from a fair-results view and from a fair-rules view.

3. What is the effect of the big tradeoff in transferring income from people with high incomes to people with low incomes?

4. Is it fair for the government to limit the prices sellers charge for bottled water after a flood destroys a town's water supply?

SELF TEST ANSWERS

■ CHECKPOINT 6.1

Fill in the blanks

The benefit a person receives from consuming one more unit of a good is its <u>marginal</u> benefit. The opportunity cost of producing one more unit of a good is its <u>marginal cost</u>. Allocative efficiency occurs at the quantity where marginal benefit is <u>equal to</u> marginal cost. The demand curve <u>is</u> a marginal benefit curve. The consumer surplus equals the marginal benefit of a good <u>minus</u> the price paid for it, summed over the quantity consumed.

True or false

1. True; page 133
2. False; page 134
3. True; page 134
4. True; page 135

Multiple choice

1. b; page 132
2. b; page 133
3. d; page 134
4. a; page 134
5. a; page 135
6. b; page 135

Complete the graph

1. a. The efficient quantity is 30,000 roller blades a year because at that quantity, marginal benefit equals marginal cost; page 133.

   b. If the quantity produced is more than 30,000 pairs of roller blades a year, the marginal cost of a pair of roller blades exceeds the marginal benefit from a pair of roller blades. The market is inefficient; page 133.

2. a. The maximum price is $3; page 134.

   b. The marginal benefit is $3. The marginal benefit is the maximum price a consumer is willing to pay for another bag of chips; page 134.

   c. Figure 6.6 shades the area of the consumer surplus; page 135.

■ FIGURE 6.6

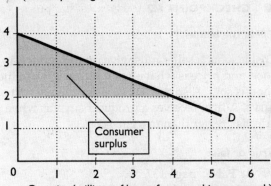

   d. The consumer surplus equals the area of the shaded triangle in Figure 6.6, which is ½ × ($4 − $2) × 4 million, which is $4 million; page 135.

Short answer

1. a. The table gives the consumer surpluses.

Price (dollars per MP3 player)	Quantity (millions of MP3 players per year)	Consumer surplus (dollars)
500	4	300
400	8	200
300	12	100
200	16	0
100	20	None

The consumer surplus is zero for the 20 millionth MP3 player because when the price of an MP3 player is $200, the 20 millionth MP3 player is not purchased. For the remaining quantities, the consumer surplus equals marginal benefit, which is the maximum price willing to be paid minus the price; page 135.

b. The consumer surplus decreases as more MP3 players are purchased because the value of an additional MP3 player decreases as more are purchased; page 135.

2. The value of a good is equal to the maximum price a buyer is willing to pay, which also equals the marginal benefit; page 134.

3. The marginal benefit of the slice of pizza equals the price paid plus the consumer surplus on that slice; page 135.

■ **CHECKPOINT 6.2**

Fill in the blanks

<u>Cost</u> is what a seller must give up to produce a good and <u>price</u> is what a seller receives when the good is sold. A <u>supply</u> curve is a marginal cost curve. A firm receives a producer surplus when price is <u>greater</u> than marginal cost.

True or false

1. False; page 137
2. True; page 137
3. False; page 137
4. False; page 138

Multiple choice

1. c; page 137
2. b; page 137
3. d; page 137
4. b; page 138
5. a; page 138
6. d; page 138

Complete the graph

1. a. The minimum price is $1; page 137.

   b. The marginal cost is $1. The marginal cost of the 2 millionth bag is the minimum price for which a supplier is willing to produce that bag of chips; page 137.

   c. Figure 6.7 shades the area of the producer surplus; page 138.

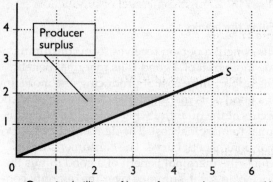

■ **FIGURE 6.7**
Price (dollars per bag of potato chips)

   d. The consumer surplus equals the area of the grey triangle in Figure 6.7. Producer surplus is ½ × $2 × 4 million, which equals $4 million; page 138.

Short answer

1. The minimum price for which a firm will produce a slice of pizza equals the marginal cost of producing that slice. It is just worth producing one more slice of pizza if the price for which it can be sold equals its marginal cost. The supply curve tells us this price. So the supply curve is the same as the marginal cost curve; page 137.

2. Producer surplus equals the price of a good minus the marginal cost of producing it, summed over the quantity produced. As the price of a good rises and the supply curve does not shift, the producer surplus increases; page 138.

■ **CHECKPOINT 6.3**

Fill in the blanks

Equilibrium in a competitive market <u>is</u> efficient. Adam Smith believed that each participant in a competitive market is "led by <u>an invisible hand</u>". <u>A public good</u> is a good or service that is consumed simultaneously by everyone, even if they don't pay for it. A price <u>ceiling</u> is a regulation that makes it illegal to charge a price higher than a specified level. Deadweight loss is the decrease in <u>consumer surplus and producer surplus</u> that results from an inefficient level of production.

True or false

1. True; page 140
2. False; pages 140-141
3. False; page 141
4. False; page 144

Multiple choice

1. a; page 141
2. d; page 141
3. c; page 141
4. d; page 143
5. d; page 144
6. c; page 144

Complete the graph

1. In Figure 6.8, the equilibrium quantity of automobiles is 60,000 a week. The efficient quantity of automobiles is also 60,000 a week because that is the quantity at which the marginal benefit equals the marginal cost. The consumer surplus and producer surplus are shown in the figure; pages 140.

■ **FIGURE 6.8**

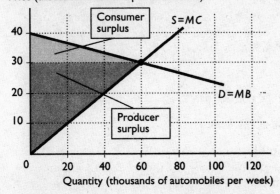

2. When 80,000 automobiles are produced, a deadweight loss occurs. For every automobile that is produced over 60,000, marginal cost exceeds marginal benefit. People are willing to pay less for the marginal car than it costs to produce. The deadweight loss is the area of the light grey triangle in Figure 6.9.

When 40,000 automobiles are produced, a deadweight loss occurs. For each of the 40,000 automobiles produced, marginal benefit exceeds marginal cost. Consumers are willing to pay more for the marginal automobile than it costs to produce. The amount of the deadweight loss is the area of dark grey triangle in Figure 6.9; page 144.

■ **FIGURE 6.9**

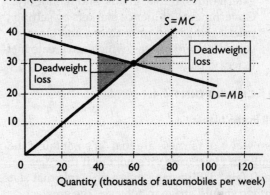

Short answer

1. Adam Smith believed that each participant in a competitive market is "led by an invisible hand to promote an end [the efficient use of resources] which was no part of his intention"; page 141.

2. If the demand for cotton clothing increases, the demand curve for cotton clothing shifts rightward and the equilibrium quantity increases. The demand curve is the marginal benefit curve, so the marginal benefit curve also shifts rightward. The efficient quantity also increases; pages 140-141.

3. The most significant obstacles to achieving an efficient allocation of resources involve externalities, public goods, and monopoly. Governments influence markets by setting price ceilings and price floors, and taxes, subsidies, and quotas, which can create inefficiency; page 143, 144.

■ CHECKPOINT 6.4

Fill in the blanks

Two views of fairness are that "it's not fair if the result isn't fair;" and "it's not fair if the rules aren't fair." Utilitarianism is a principle that states that we should strive to achieve "the greatest happiness for the greatest number". According to Robert Nozick, fair-rules ideas require property rights and voluntary exchange.

True or false

1. False; page 147
2. True; page 148
3. False; page 148
4. False; page 149

Multiple choice

1. b; page 147
2. d; page 148
3. a; page 148
4. b; page 149
5. c; page 149
6. c; page 150

Short answer

1. The tax arrangement is fair from a fair-results view. It leads to a greater equality of income. The tax arrangement is not fair from a fair-results view because the tax is not a voluntary exchange; pages 148-149

2. From a fair-results view, it is not fair for Pat's income to be substantially higher than Matt's. From a fair-rules view, it is fair because Pat and Matt had the same opportunities; pages 148-149.

3. Income is transferred from people with high incomes to people with low incomes by taxing incomes, which discourages work. It results in the quantity of labour being less than the efficient quantity. Similarly, taxing income from capital discourages saving, which results in the quantity of capital being less than the efficient quantity. The greater the amount of income redistribution through income taxes, the greater is the inefficiency and the smaller is the economic pie; page 148.

4. Limiting the price that can be charged is unfair because it compels the seller to help and such compulsion is unfair; page 150.

Chapter 7

Government Influences on Markets

CHAPTER IN PERSPECTIVE

In Chapter 7 we study how governments influence markets when they collect taxes. We also look at the inefficiency that is created when the government applies a rent ceiling in the housing market or a minimum wage in the labour market.

■ **Explain the effects of taxes on goods and labour and determine who pays the taxes.**

When goods or services are taxed, the burden of the tax might fall on the buyer, the seller, or both. The division of the burden of the tax between the buyer and the seller depends on the elasticities of demand and supply. For a given elasticity of supply, the buyer pays a larger share of the tax the more inelastic is the demand for the good. And, for a given elasticity of demand, the seller pays a larger share of the tax the more inelastic is the supply of the good. The buyer pays the entire tax when demand is perfectly inelastic or supply is perfectly elastic. The seller pays the entire tax when demand is perfectly elastic or supply is perfectly inelastic. The elasticities of demand and supply, not the government, determine who pays the income tax and who pays a payroll tax. The excess burden of a tax is the deadweight loss from a tax—the amount by which the burden of a tax exceeds the tax revenue received by the government.

■ **Explain how a rent ceiling creates a housing shortage, inefficiency, and unfairness.**

A price ceiling is the highest price at which it is legal to trade a particular good, service, or factor of production. A rent ceiling is an example of a price ceiling. A rent ceiling set above the equilibrium rent is ineffective. A housing shortage occurs when a rent ceiling is set below the equilibrium rent because the quantity of housing demanded exceeds the quantity of housing supplied. A black market is an illegal market that operates alongside a government-regulated market. When a rent ceiling creates a shortage of housing, search activity, which is the time spent looking for someone with whom to do business, increases. A rent ceiling creates a deadweight loss and decreases consumer surplus and producer surplus. Rent controls violate the fair-rules view of fairness because they block voluntary exchange.

■ **Explain how the minimum wage creates unemployment, inefficiency, and unfairness.**

A minimum wage law is a government regulation that makes hiring labour for less than a specified wage illegal. A minimum wage law is an example of a price floor. A minimum wage set below the equilibrium wage rate is ineffective. Unemployment occurs when the minimum wage is set above the equilibrium wage rate because the quantity of labour supplied exceeds the quantity of labour demanded. A minimum wage increases job search activity. Some firms and workers might agree to do business at an illegal wage rate below the minimum wage. The minimum wage creates a deadweight loss, delivers an unfair result, and imposes unfair rules.

EXPANDED CHAPTER CHECKLIST

When you have completed this chapter, you will be able to:

1 Explain the effects of taxes on goods and labour and determine who pays the taxes.

- Define tax incidence.
- Explain how the burden of a tax depends on the elasticities of demand and supply.
- Determine who bears the tax burden if demand is perfectly inelastic or supply is perfectly elastic.
- Determine who bears the tax burden if demand is perfectly elastic or supply is perfectly inelastic.
- Show how a payroll tax and the income tax can deliver the same outcome.
- Illustrate the deadweight loss from a tax.

2 Explain how a rent ceiling creates a housing shortage, inefficiency, and unfairness.

- Define rent ceiling and price ceiling.
- Explain why a rent ceiling that exceeds the equilibrium price is ineffective.
- Illustrate the effects of a rent ceiling set below the equilibrium rent.
- Define black market and search activity.
- Illustrate the deadweight loss created by a rent ceiling.
- Discuss the fairness of rent ceilings.

3 Explain how the minimum wage creates unemployment, inefficiency, and unfairness.

- Define minimum wage law and price floor.
- Explain why a minimum wage set below the equilibrium wage rate is ineffective.
- Illustrate the effects of a minimum wage set above the equilibrium wage rate and discuss how a minimum wage can lead to increased job search activity and illegal hiring.
- Illustrate the deadweight loss created by a minimum wage.
- Discuss the fairness of the minimum wage.

KEY TERMS

- Black market (page 167)
- Excess burden (page 164)
- Minimum wage law (page 174)
- Payroll tax (page 163)
- Price ceiling (page 166)
- Price floor (page 174)
- Rent ceiling (page 166)
- Search activity (page 168)
- Tax incidence (page 158)

CHECKPOINT 7.1

■ Explain the effects of taxes on goods and labour and determine who pays the taxes.

Practice Problems 7.1

1. The figure shows the market for golf balls. The government imposes a sales tax on golf balls at 60 cents a ball:

   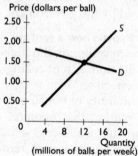

   a. What is the increase in the price that buyers pay for golf balls?
   b. What is the decrease in the price that sellers receive?
   c. What is the decrease in the quantity of golf balls?
   d. What is the tax revenue from golf ball sales?

e. Which is more inelastic: the demand for golf balls or the supply of golf balls? How can you tell?

f. What is the excess burden of the sales tax on golf balls?

2. The supply of labour in Newfoundland is elastic and the demand for labour is inelastic.

a. Does the employer or the worker pay more of the tax on labour income?

b. If a payroll tax replaces the income tax in part (a), does the employer or the worker pay more of the tax?

Solution to Practice Problems 7.1

To work these Practice Problems, remember that a tax is like an increase in the suppliers' cost. Supply decreases and the supply curve shifts leftward.

Quick Review

- *Tax incidence and elasticities of demand and supply* For a given elasticity of supply, the buyer pays a larger share of the tax the more inelastic is the demand for the good. For a given elasticity of demand, the seller pays a larger share of the tax the more inelastic is the supply of the good.
- *Payroll tax* A tax on employers based on the wages they pay their workers.

1a. What is the increase in the price that buyers pay for golf balls?

The figure shows the effect of the tax. The tax decreases supply. The new supply curve is S + tax. The length of the vertical arrow equals the amount of the tax, which is 60 cents a golf ball.

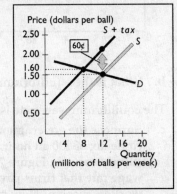

The price paid by buyers rises from $1.50 to $1.60.

b. What is the decrease in the price that sellers receive?

The seller receives $1.60 minus the 60 cents tax, which is $1.00 per ball. So the price that sellers receive falls from $1.50 to $1.00, a decrease of 50 cents.

c. What is the decrease in the quantity of golf balls?

The figure shows that the quantity decreases from 12 million golf balls a week to 8 million golf balls a week.

d. What is the tax revenue from golf ball sales?

The tax is 60 cents a ball and 8 million balls a week are sold. The tax revenue equals (60 cents) × (8 million balls), which is $4.8 million a week.

e. Which is more inelastic: the demand for golf balls or the supply of golf balls? How can you tell?

The price the seller receives falls from $1.50 to $1.00 so the seller pays 50 cents of the tax. The price the buyer pays rises from $1.50 to $1.60 so the buyer pays 10 cents of the tax. The seller pays more of the tax so the supply is more inelastic than the demand.

f. What is the excess burden of the sales tax on golf balls?

The excess burden is the deadweight loss of the tax, which equals the area of the grey triangle in the figure. The deadweight loss equals ½ × 4 million golf balls × 60 cents, which equals $1.2 million.

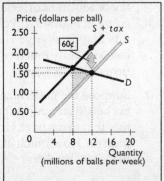

2. The supply of labour in Newfoundland is elastic and the demand for labour is inelastic.

a. Does the employer or the worker pay more of the tax on labour income?

The employer pays more of the income tax because the demand for labour is less elastic than the supply of labour.

b. If a payroll tax replaces the income tax in part (a), does the employer or the worker pay more of the tax?

Whether the tax is an income tax or a payroll tax, the tax incidence is the same.

Additional Practice Problem 7.1a

The table shows the supply schedule and the demand schedule for labour.

Wage rate (dollars per hour)	Quantity demanded	Quantity supplied
	(workers)	
50	28	46
40	34	43
30	40	40
20	46	37
10	52	34

a. Label the axes in Figure 7.1 and draw the labour demand curve and the labour supply curve.

b. What is the equilibrium wage rate?

c. Suppose the government imposes an income tax of $30 an hour. Show the new supply curve in Figure 7.1. What is the new wage rate that firms pay? How much do workers receive? How much of the tax is paid by firms? By workers?

d. Suppose the government imposes a payroll tax of $30 an hour. What is the new wage rate that firms pay? How much do workers receive? How much of the tax is paid by firms? By workers?

e. How do your answers to parts (c) and (d) compare?

■ FIGURE 7.1

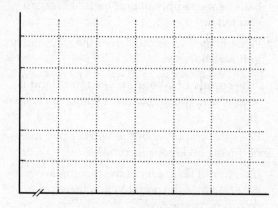

Solution to Additional Practice Problem 7.1a

a. Label the axes in Figure 7.1 and draw the labour demand curve and the labour supply curve.

The axes are labelled and curves are drawn in Figure 7.2.

■ FIGURE 7.2

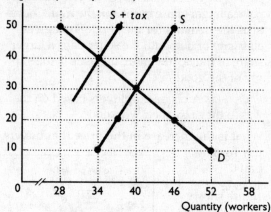

b. What is the equilibrium wage rate?

The equilibrium wage rate is $30 an hour.

c. Suppose the government imposes an income tax of $30 an hour. Show the new supply curve in Figure 7.1. What is the new wage rate that firms pay? How much do workers receive? How much of the tax is paid by firms? By workers?

The new supply curve is the curve S + *tax* in Figure 7.2. Firms pay $40 an hour and workers receive $10 an hour. Firms pay $10 of the tax and workers pay $20.

d. Suppose the government imposes a payroll tax of $30 an hour. What is the new wage rate that firms pay? How much do workers receive? How much of the tax is paid by firms? By workers?

Firms pay $40 an hour and workers receive $10 an hour. Firms pay $10 of the tax and workers pay $20.

e. How do your answers to parts (c) and (d) compare?

The payroll tax delivers the same outcome as the income tax. The answers to parts (c) and (d) are the same.

■ Self Test 7.1

Fill in the blanks

The tax ____ (elasticity; incidence) is the division of the burden of a tax between the buyer and the seller. For a given elasticity of supply, the buyer pays a larger share of the tax the more _____ (elastic; inelastic) is the demand for the good. If the supply is perfectly ____ (elastic; inelastic), the seller pays the entire tax. An income tax and a payroll tax both ____ (raise; lower) the wage rate that employees receive and ____ (increase; decrease) employment. Taxes ____ (create; do not create) a deadweight loss.

True or false

1. When the government imposes a tax on the sale of a good, the burden of the tax falls entirely on the buyer.
2. When the government taxes a good that has a perfectly elastic supply, the buyer pays the entire tax.
3. The introduction of an income tax decreases the equilibrium quantity of labour and lowers the wage rate paid by employers.
4. When the government introduces a payroll tax, the demand for labour decreases.
5. A tax on fast-food meals does not create a deadweight loss because the supply of fast-food meals does not change.

Multiple choice

1. Tax incidence refers to
   a. how government taxes are spent by the government.
   b. the incidences of tax revolts by tax payers.
   c. the amount of a tax minus its burden.
   d. the division of the burden of a tax between the buyer and the seller.

2. If neither the supply of nor demand for a good is perfectly elastic or perfectly inelastic, imposing a tax on the good results in a ____ in the price paid by buyers and ____ in the equilibrium quantity.
   a. rise; an increase
   b. rise; a decrease
   c. fall; an increase
   d. fall; a decrease

3. If neither the supply of nor demand for a good is perfectly elastic or perfectly inelastic, imposing a tax on the good results in a ____ in the price received by sellers and a ____ in the price paid by buyers.
   a. rise; rise
   b. rise; fall
   c. fall; rise
   d. fall; fall

4. To determine who will bear the greater share of a tax, we compare
   a. the number of buyers to the number of sellers.
   b. the elasticity of supply to the elasticity of demand.
   c. the size of the tax to the price of the good.
   d. government tax revenue to business revenue.

5. Suppose the demand for barley is perfectly elastic. The supply curve of barley is upward sloping. If a tax is imposed on barley,
   a. barley sellers pay the entire tax.
   b. barley buyers pay the entire tax.
   c. the government pays the entire tax.
   d. the tax is split evenly between barley buyers and sellers.

6. When an income tax is imposed, the level of employment ____ and when a payroll tax is imposed, the level of employment ____.
   a. increases; increases
   b. increases; decreases
   c. decreases; increases
   d. decreases; decreases

7. The deadweight loss from a tax is called the ____ the tax
   a. marginal benefit of
   b. marginal cost of
   c. excess burden of
   d. net gain from

8. A sales tax creates a deadweight loss because
   a. there is some paperwork opportunity cost of sellers paying the sales tax.
   b. demand and supply both decrease.
   c. less is produced and consumed.
   d. citizens value government goods less than private goods.

Complete the graph

1. The supply curve and the demand curve for pizza slices are shown in Figure 7.3. The price is in dollars per slice and the quantity is thousands of pizza slices per day. Label the axes.

■ FIGURE 7.3

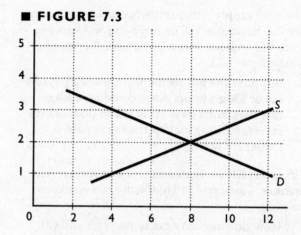

   a. What is the equilibrium price and quantity of pizza slices?
   b. Suppose the government imposes a sales tax of $2 a slice of pizza. In Figure 7.3, draw the new supply curve after the tax is imposed.
   c. After the tax is imposed, what is the price paid by buyers for a slice of pizza? What is the price received by sellers for a slice of pizza? What is the incidence of the tax?
   d. In Figure 7.3, darken the area of the deadweight loss from the tax.

2. Figure 7.4 shows a labour supply curve and a labour demand curve.

■ FIGURE 7.4

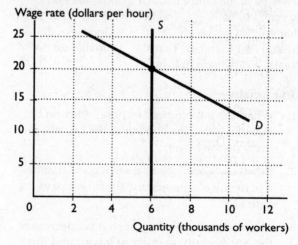

The government imposes a $5 an hour payroll tax on firms. In the figure, show the effect of this tax. What is the wage rate that workers receive before the tax and after the tax? How is the burden of the tax split?

Short answer

1. The table gives the monthly demand and supply schedules for golf balls at the College Hills Golf Shop.

Price (dollars per ball)	Quantity demanded	Before-tax quantity supplied	After-tax quantity supplied
	(golf balls per month)		
0.50	1,100	600	0
1.00	1,000	620	0
1.50	900	680	0
2.00	700	700	0
2.50	600	850	____
3.00	300	950	____
3.50	60	1,180	680

   With no tax, what is the equilibrium price and quantity?

   Suppose a $2 per ball tax is imposed.

   a. Complete the last column of the table.
   b. What is the equilibrium price and quantity after the tax is imposed?
   c. How much of the tax is paid by the buyer? How much is paid by the seller?
   d. How much tax revenue does the government collect?

2. The government decides to tax high blood-pressure medicine. The supply by drug companies is elastic; the demand by patients is inelastic. Will the drug companies bear the entire tax burden?

3. The government mandates that half of a payroll tax has to be paid by the employer and the other half has to be paid by the worker. Does this law mean that the burden of the payroll tax is shared equally by the employer and worker?

CHECKPOINT 7.2

■ **Explain how a rent ceiling creates a housing shortage, inefficiency, and unfairness.**

Practice Problem 7.2

The figure shows the rental market for apartments in a Winnipeg suburb:

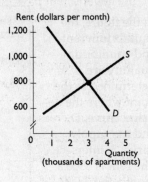

a. What is the rent in this suburb and how many apartments are rented?

b. If the city of Winnipeg imposes a rent ceiling of $900 a month, what is the rent in this suburb and how many apartments are rented?

c. If the city of Winnipeg imposes a rent ceiling of $600 a month, what is the rent in this suburb and how many apartments are rented?

d. With a strictly enforced $600 rent ceiling, is the housing market efficient? Explain why or why not.

e. If the city strictly enforces the rent ceiling, is the housing market fair? Explain why or why not.

f. If a black market develops, how high could the black market rent be? Explain your answer.

Solution to Practice Problem 7.2

To answer this Practice Problem, remember that a rent ceiling is effective only when it is set below the equilibrium price.

Quick Review

- *Rent ceiling* A government regulation that makes it illegal to charge more than a specified rent for housing.

- *Effective rent ceiling* When a rent ceiling is set below the equilibrium rent, the quantity of housing demanded is greater than the equilibrium quantity and the quantity of housing supplied is less than the equilibrium quantity. A housing shortage occurs.

a. **What is the rent in this suburb and how many apartments are rented?**

In the figure, the equilibrium rent and equilibrium quantity are determined at the point where the demand curve, D, and the supply curve, S, intersect. The rent is $800 a month and 3,000 apartments are rented.

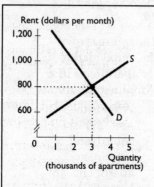

b. **If the city of Winnipeg imposes a rent ceiling of $900 a month, what is the rent in this suburb and how many apartments are rented?**

A rent ceiling of $900 a month is above the equilibrium rent. So the rent ceiling is ineffective. The rent remains at $800 a month and 3,000 apartments are rented.

c. **If the city of Winnipeg imposes a rent ceiling of $600 a month, what is the rent in this suburb and how many apartments are rented?**

The rent ceiling is below the equilibrium rent. In the figure, when the rent falls to $600 a month, the quantity of apartments supplied, which equals the quantity of apartments rented decreases to 1,000.

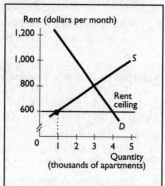

d. **With a strictly enforced $600 rent ceiling, is the housing market efficient? Explain why or why not.**

The housing market is inefficient and a deadweight loss arises. In the figure the deadweight loss is shown by the grey triangle. The market is inefficient because the marginal benefit of the last apartment rented, the 1,000th apartment, exceeds the marginal cost of that apartment.

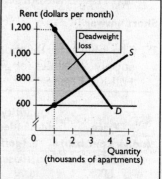

e. **If the city strictly enforces the rent ceiling, is the housing market fair? Explain why or why not.**

The housing market is unfair by the fair-rules view because the rent ceiling prevents voluntary exchange. It is unfair by the fair-results view because poorer people do not necessarily get the apartments.

f. **If a black market develops, how high could the black market rent be? Explain your answer.**

The black market rent could be as high as $1,200 a month. This rent equals the willingness of someone to pay for the 1,000th apartment.

Additional Practice Problem 7.2a

The table gives the supply and demand schedules for rounds of golf.

Price (dollars per round of golf)	Quantity demanded	Quantity supplied
	(rounds per week)	
50	2,000	2,800
40	2,300	2,700
30	2,600	2,600
20	2,900	2,500
10	3,200	2,400

a. What is the equilibrium price and equilibrium quantity of rounds of golf?

b. Suppose the city government imposes a price ceiling of $40 a round of golf. What will be the price and quantity of rounds of golf? Is there a shortage?

c. Suppose the city government imposes a price ceiling of $20 a round of golf. What will be the price and quantity of rounds of golf? Is there a shortage?

Solution to Additional Practice Problem 7.2a

a. **What is the equilibrium price and equilibrium quantity of rounds of golf?**

The equilibrium price is $30 a round of golf and the equilibrium quantity is 2,600 rounds a week.

b. **Suppose the city government imposes a price ceiling of $40 a round of golf. What will be the price and quantity of rounds of golf? Is there a shortage?**

The price ceiling is above the equilibrium price, so the price remains at $30 a round and the quantity remains at 2,600 rounds a week. There is no shortage.

c. **Suppose the city government imposes a price ceiling of $20 a round of golf. What will be the price and quantity of rounds of golf? Is there a shortage?**

The price ceiling is below the equilibrium price. The price falls to $20 a round. The quantity played equals the quantity supplied at $20, which is 2,500 rounds a week. There is a shortage of 400 rounds a week.

■ Self Test 7.2

Fill in the blanks

A price ceiling is the _____ (highest; lowest) price at which it is legal to trade a particular good, service, or factor of production. A rent ceiling is effective if it is set ____ (above; below) the equilibrium rent. A rent ceiling can create a housing ____ (shortage; surplus), which leads to _____ (decreased; increased) search activity. Rent ceilings ____ (are; are not) efficient. The ____ (less; more) inelastic the demand for housing or the supply of housing, the smaller the deadweight loss created by a rent ceiling. Rent ceilings ____ (are; are not) fair. There is _____ (little; plenty of) political support for rent ceilings.

True or false

1. A rent ceiling always lowers the rent paid.
2. When a rent ceiling is higher than the equilibrium rent, a black market emerges.
3. The opportunity cost of a dorm room is equal to its rent plus the value of the search time spent finding the dorm room.
4. Rent ceilings are efficient because they lower the cost of housing to low-income families.
5. The total loss from a rent ceiling exceeds the deadweight loss.

Multiple choice

1. A price ceiling is a government regulation that makes it illegal to charge a price
a. below the equilibrium price.
b. above the equilibrium price.
c. for a good or service.
d. above some specified level.

2. When a price ceiling is set below the equilibrium price the quantity supplied ____ the quantity demanded and a ____ exists.
a. is less than; surplus
b. is less than; shortage
c. is greater than; surplus
d. is greater than; shortage

3. In a housing market with a rent ceiling set below the equilibrium rent,
a. some people seeking an apartment to rent will not be able to find one.
b. the total cost of renting an apartment will decrease for all those seeking housing.
c. some landlords will not be able to find renters to fill available apartments.
d. None of the above answers are correct.

4. A rent ceiling on housing creates a problem of allocating the available housing units because
a. the demand for housing decreases and the demand curve shifts leftward.
b. the supply of housing increases and the supply curve shifts rightward.
c. a shortage of apartments occurs.
d. a surplus of apartments occurs.

5. Rent ceilings
a. increase search activity.
b. result in surpluses.
c. are efficient.
d. benefit producers.

6. Suppose that the government imposes a price ceiling on gasoline that is below the equilibrium price. The black market for gasoline is ___ market in which the price ___ the ceiling price.
a. a legal; exceeds
b. an illegal; exceeds
c. a legal; is less than
d. an illegal; is less than

7. A rent ceiling creates a deadweight loss
a. if it is set below the equilibrium rent.
b. if it is set equal to the equilibrium rent.
c. if it set above the equilibrium rent.
d. never, because if it did create a deadweight loss, the government would not impose it.

8. Rent ceilings
a. eliminate the problem of scarcity.
b. allocate resources efficiently.
c. ensure that housing goes to the poorer people.
d. benefit renters living in rent-controlled apartments.

Complete the graph

1. The table gives the demand and supply schedules for housing in a small town. In Figure 7.5, label the axes and graph the demand and supply curves. What is the equilibrium rent and quantity of housing?

Rent (dollars per month)	Quantity demanded	Quantity supplied
	(housing units per month)	
900	200	350
800	300	300
700	400	250
600	500	200
500	600	150

■ **FIGURE 7.5**

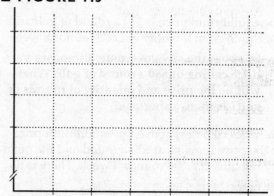

Suppose the government imposes a $600 a month rent ceiling.

a. With the rent ceiling, what is the quantity of housing demanded and the quantity of housing supplied?
b. Does the rent ceiling result in a shortage or a surplus of housing? Indicate the shortage or surplus on Figure 7.5.

Short answer

1. What is a price ceiling?

2. The table gives the demand and supply schedules for milk.

Price (dollars per carton)	Quantity demanded	Quantity supplied
	(cartons per day)	
1.00	200	110
1.25	175	130
1.50	150	150
1.75	125	170
2.00	100	190

a. What is the market equilibrium in the milk market?
b. Suppose the government imposes a price ceiling of $1.25 per carton. What is the price of a carton of milk and what quantity is purchased? Is there a shortage or surplus of milk?
c. Suppose the government imposes a price ceiling of $1.75 per carton. What is the price of a carton of milk and what quantity is purchased? Is there a shortage or surplus of milk?
3. Are rent ceilings efficient?
4. Are rent ceilings fair?

CHECKPOINT 7.3

■ **Explain how the minimum wage creates unemployment, inefficiency, and unfairness.**

Practice Problem 7.3

The figure shows the market for tomato pickers in southern Ontario.

a. What is the equilibrium wage rate of tomato pickers and what is the equilibrium quantity of tomato pickers employed?
b. Is the market for tomato pickers efficient?
c. If Ontario introduces a minimum wage for tomato pickers of $4 an hour, how many tomato pickers are employed and how many are unemployed?
d. If Ontario introduces a minimum wage for tomato pickers of $8 an hour, how many tomato pickers are employed and how many are unemployed?
e. Is the minimum wage of $8 an hour efficient? Is it fair?
f. Who gains and who loses from the minimum wage of $8 an hour?

Solution to Practice Problem 7.3

To answer this practice problem, remember that a minimum wage is effective only when it is set above the equilibrium wage rate.

Quick Review

- *Minimum wage law* A government regulation that makes hiring labour for less than a specified wage illegal.
- *Effective minimum wage law* When the minimum wage is set above the equilibrium wage rate, the quantity of labour demanded is less than the equilibrium quantity and the quantity of labour supplied is greater than the equilibrium quantity. Unemployment occurs.

a. **What is the equilibrium wage rate of tomato pickers and what is the equilibrium quantity of tomato pickers employed?**

The equilibrium wage rate is $6.00 an hour and the equilibrium quantity of pickers is 4,000 at the intersection of the labour demand curve, *D*, and labour supply curve, *S*.

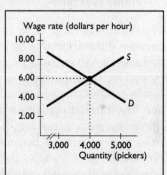

b. **Is the market for tomato pickers efficient?**

The market is efficient. At the equilibrium, the marginal benefit to the tomato growers equals the marginal cost borne by the pickers.

c. **If Ontario introduces a minimum wage for tomato pickers of $4 an hour, how many tomato pickers are employed and how many are unemployed?**

A minimum wage of $4 an hour is less than the equilibrium wage rate. The minimum wage is ineffective. 4,000 pickers are employed and none are unemployed.

d. **If Ontario introduces a minimum wage for tomato pickers of $8 an hour, how many tomato pickers are employed and how many are unemployed?**

The minimum wage of $8 an hour is above the equilibrium wage rate. In the figure, 3,000 tomato pickers are employed (the quantity of labour demanded when the wage rate is $8 an hour) and 5,000

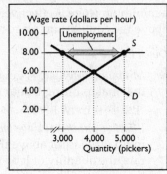

people would like to work as tomato pickers (the quantity of labour supplied when the wage rate is $8 an hour). The number of people unemployed is 5,000 − 3,000, which is 2,000.

e. **Is the minimum wage of $8 an hour efficient? Is it fair?**

The minimum wage of $8 an hour is not efficient because the marginal benefit to growers (on the demand curve) exceeds the marginal cost borne by pickers (on the supply curve). A deadweight loss is created. An additional loss arises as unemployed tomato pickers search for jobs. The minimum wage is not fair. It violates the fair-rules view of fairness because it prevents voluntary exchange. It violates the fair-results view of fairness because some workers lose their jobs and are made poorer.

f. **Who gains and who loses from the minimum wage of $8 an hour?**

Tomato pickers who find jobs at the higher wage rate gain because they earn $8 an hour rather than $6. Unemployed tomato pickers lose and all tomato growers lose.

Additional Practice Problem 7.3a

The table gives the supply and demand schedules for sugar.

Price (cents	Quantity demanded	Quantity supplied
	(kilograms of sugar per year)	
10	300	225
15	275	275
20	250	325
25	225	375
30	200	425

a. What is the equilibrium price and quantity of sugar?
b. If the government imposes a price floor of 25¢ a kilogram, what is the quantity demanded and the quantity supplied? Is there a shortage or surplus and if so, how much?
c. Who gains from a price floor of 25¢ a kilogram? Who loses?

Solution to Additional Practice Problem 7.3a

a. **What is the equilibrium price and quantity of sugar?**

The equilibrium price is 15¢ a kilogram and the equilibrium quantity is 275 kilograms a year.

b. **If the government imposes a price floor of 25¢ a kilogram, what is the quantity demanded and the quantity supplied? Is there a shortage or surplus and if so, how much?**

The quantity demanded at 25¢ a kilogram is 225 kilograms and the quantity supplied is 375 kilograms. There is a surplus of 150 kilograms.

c. **Who gains from a price floor of 25¢ a kilogram? Who loses?**

Gainers from the price floor are sugar growers who sell their sugar at 25¢ a kilogram rather than 15¢ a kilogram. Losers include sugar producers who cannot sell their sugar and all buyers of sugar.

■ Self Test 7.3

Fill in the blanks

A minimum wage is a price _____ (ceiling; floor). A price floor is the _____ (highest; lowest) price at which it is legal to trade a particular good, service, or factor of production. A minimum wage set above the equilibrium wage rate is _____ (effective; not effective). A minimum wage _____ (creates; does not create) unemployment and _____ (decreases; increases) job search activity. An efficient allocation of labour occurs when the marginal _____ (benefit; cost) to firms _____ (equals; is greater than) the marginal _____ (benefit; cost) borne by workers. Labour unions ____ (do not support; support) the minimum wage.

True or false

1. Firms hire labour, so they determine how much labour to supply in a market.
2. A minimum wage is effective when it is set above the equilibrium wage rate.
3. A minimum wage law can lead to increased job search activity and illegal hiring.
4. A minimum wage is fair because low-income workers receive an increase in take-home pay.
5. A minimum wage set above the equilibrium wage rate is efficient.

Multiple choice

1. A price floor
   a. sets the maximum price it is legal to charge.
   b. is the lowest price at which it is legal to trade a particular good, service, or factor of production.
   c. is an illegal price to charge.
   d. is the equilibrium price when the stock market crashes.

2. An efficient minimum wage is set
   a. above the equilibrium wage rate.
   b. below the equilibrium wage rate.
   c. equal to the equilibrium wage rate.
   d. below $5.

3. A minimum wage set above the equilibrium wage rate
   a. increases the quantity of labour supplied.
   b. decreases the quantity of labour supplied.
   c. has no effect on the quantity of labour supplied.
   d. shifts the labour supply curve rightward.

4. Suppose the current equilibrium wage rate for lifeguards in Halifax is $7.85 an hour. If the government introduces a minimum wage of $8.50 an hour, there is
   a. a surplus of lifeguards in Halifax.
   b. a shortage of lifeguards in Halifax.
   c. no changes in the lifeguard market.
   d. a change in the quantity of lifeguards supplied but no change in the quantity of lifeguards demanded.

5. An increase in the minimum wage ____ employment and ____ unemployment.
   a. increases; increases
   b. increases; decreases
   c. decreases; increases
   d. decreases; decreases

6. If a minimum wage is introduced that is above the equilibrium wage rate,
   a. the quantity of labour demanded increases.
   b. job search activity increases.
   c. the supply of labour increases and the supply of labour curve shifts rightward.
   d. unemployment decreases because more workers accept jobs at the higher minimum wage.

7. Does the minimum wage create inefficiency when it is set above the equilibrium wage rate?
   a. Yes.
   b. No.
   c. Only if the supply of labour is inelastic.
   d. Only if the demand for labour is elastic.

8. When the minimum wage rises, the _____ union labour _____.
   a. demand for; increases
   b. demand for; decreases
   c. supply of; increases
   d. supply of; decreases

Complete the graph

1. The table gives the demand and supply schedules for labour in a small town.

Wage rate (dollars per hour)	Quantity demanded	Quantity supplied
	(workers per day)	
4	3,500	2,750
5	3,000	3,000
6	2,500	3,250
7	2,000	3,500
8	1,500	3,750

   In Figure 7.6, label the axes. Draw the labour demand curve and the labour supply curve. Indicate the equilibrium wage rate and employment.

■ **FIGURE 7.6**

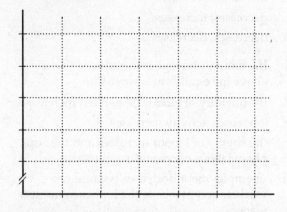

a. Suppose the government imposes a $4 an hour minimum wage. What is the effect on the wage rate and levels of employment and unemployment?

b. Suppose the government raises the minimum wage from $4 an hour to $7 an hour. What is the effect on the wage rate and levels of employment and unemployment? Indicate any unemployment in the figure.

Short answer

1. What is the effect of a minimum wage set below the equilibrium wage rate?
2. How does a minimum wage affect the time needed to find a job?
3. Do all low-wage workers benefit from a minimum wage?

SELF TEST ANSWERS

■ CHECKPOINT 7.1

Fill in the blanks

The tax <u>incidence</u> is the division of the burden of a tax between the buyer and the seller. For a given elasticity of supply, the buyer pays a larger share of the tax the more <u>inelastic</u> is the demand for the good. If the supply is perfectly <u>inelastic</u>, the seller pays the entire tax. An income tax and a payroll tax both <u>lower</u> the wage rate that employees receive and <u>decrease</u> employment. Taxes <u>create</u> a deadweight loss.

True or false

1. False; page 158
2. True; page 160
3. False; page 162
4. True; page 163
5. False; page 164

Multiple choice

1. d; page 158
2. b; page 159
3. c; page 159
4. b; page 159
5. a; page 160
6. d; pages 162-163
7. c; page 164
8. c; page 164

Complete the graph

1. The axes are labelled in Figure 7.7.
   a. The price is $2 a slice and the quantity is 8,000 slices a day; pages 158-159.
   b. Figure 7.7 shows the supply curve after the tax is imposed, S + tax; pages 158-159.
   c. Buyers pay $3 a slice; sellers receive $1 a slice. The tax is split equally; pages 158-159.
   d. The deadweight loss is the grey triangle in Figure 7.7; page 164.

■ FIGURE 7.7

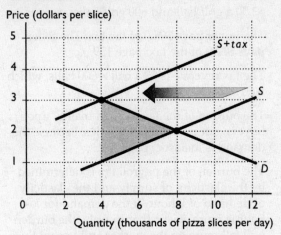

2. Figure 7.8 shows the effect of the tax. The wage rate before the tax is $20 an hour and the wage rate after the tax is $15 an hour. The workers pay all the tax; page 163.

■ FIGURE 7.8

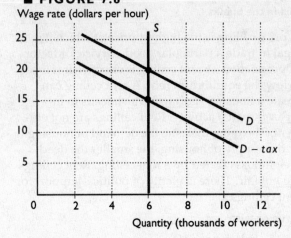

Short answer

1. The equilibrium price is $2.00 a golf ball and the equilibrium quantity is 700 golf balls.
   a. The supply schedule is completed in the table; page 158.

Price (dollars per golf ball)	After-tax quantity supplied (golf balls per month)
2.50	600
3.00	620

b. $2.50 a golf ball and 600 golf balls; page 159.

c. The buyer pays $0.50 of the tax. The seller pays $1.50 of the tax; page 159.

d. The tax revenue is $2 a ball × 600 balls, which is $1,200; page 159.

2. The burden of the tax will fall mainly upon buyers, not the drug companies, because the demand is inelastic; page 159.

3. The burden of the payroll tax is determined by the elasticity of supply and the elasticity of demand of labour. If the demand for labour is more elastic than supply, the burden will fall more on the worker and less on the employer. The government can legislate how the tax will be collected, but cannot legislate the division of the tax's burden; page 162.

■ CHECKPOINT 7.2

Fill in the blanks

A price ceiling is the <u>highest</u> price at which it is legal to trade a particular good, service, or factor of production. A rent ceiling is effective if it is set <u>below</u> the equilibrium rent. A rent ceiling can create a housing <u>shortage</u>, which leads to <u>increased</u> search activity. Rent ceilings <u>are not</u> efficient. The <u>more</u> inelastic the demand of housing or the supply of housing, the smaller the deadweight loss created by a rent ceiling. Rent ceilings <u>are not</u> fair. There is <u>plenty of</u> political support for rent ceilings.

True or false

1. False; page 166
2. False; page 167
3. True; page 168
4. False; page 170
5. True; page 170

Multiple choice

1. d; page 166
2. b; pages 166-167
3. a; page 167
4. c; page 167
5. a; page 168
6. b; pages 167-168
7. a; page 170
8. d; page 171

Complete the graph

1. Figure 7.9 shows the demand and supply curves. The equilibrium rent is $800 a month and the quantity is 300 units a month.

■ FIGURE 7.9

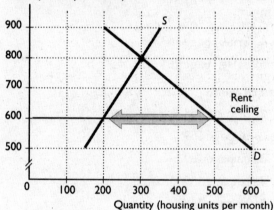

a. The quantity of housing demanded is 500 units a month; the quantity supplied is 200 units a month; page 167.

b. The shortage of 300 units a month is indicated by the arrow; page 167.

Short answer

1. A price ceiling is the highest price at which it is legal to trade a particular good, service, or factor of production. A rent ceiling is an example of a price ceiling; page 166.

2a. The equilibrium price is $1.50 a carton and the equilibrium quantity is 150 cartons a day.

b. The price is $1.25 a carton and 130 cartons a day are purchased. There is a shortage of 45 cartons a day; page 167.

c. The price ceiling is ineffective. The price is $1.50 a carton, 150 cartons a day are purchased, and there is neither a shortage nor a surplus; page 166.

3. Rent ceilings are not efficient; page 170.

4. Rent ceilings are not fair. They violate the fair-results view and the fair-rules view of fairness; page 171.

■ **CHECKPOINT 7.3**

Fill in the blanks

A minimum wage is a price <u>floor</u>. A price floor is the <u>lowest</u> price at which it is legal to trade a particular good, service, or factor of production. A minimum wage set above the equilibrium wage rate is <u>effective</u>. A minimum wage <u>creates</u> unemployment and <u>increases</u> job search activity. An efficient allocation of labour occurs when the marginal <u>benefit</u> to firms <u>equals</u> the marginal <u>cost</u> borne by workers. Labour unions <u>support</u> the minimum wage.

True or false

1. False; page 173
2. True; page 174
3. True; page 175
4. False; page 177
5. False; page 176

Multiple choice

1. b; page 174
2. a; page 174
3. a; page 174
4. a; page 174
5. c; pages 174-175
6. b; page 175
7. a; page 176

8. a; page 177

Complete the graph

1. Figure 7.10 shows the demand curve and the supply curve. The equilibrium wage rate is $5.00 an hour and equilibrium employment is 3,000 workers a day.

■ **FIGURE 7.10**

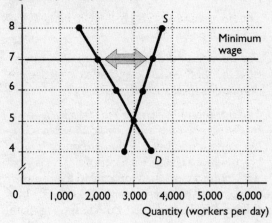

a. The $4 minimum wage is below the equilibrium wage and has no effect; page 174.

b. The $7 minimum wage raises the wage rate to $7. Employment decreases to 2,000 workers. The number of people who would like to work is 3,500. Unemployment equals 3,500 − 2,000, which is 1,500 workers. The amount of unemployment is shown by the arrow in Figure 7.10; page 174.

Short answer

1. A minimum wage set below the equilibrium wage rate has no effect on the wage rate or amount of employment; page 174.

2. By decreasing the quantity of labour demanded and creating unemployment, a minimum wage increases the time spent searching for a job; page 175.

3. A minimum wage harms low-wage workers who lose their jobs or cannot find jobs because of the minimum wage; page 177.

Chapter 8

Externalities

CHAPTER IN PERSPECTIVE

An externality in an unregulated market leads to inefficiency and creates a deadweight loss. Chapter 8 explains the role of the government in markets where an externality is present and how government intervention can result in an efficient level of production.

■ **Explain why negative externalities lead to inefficient overproduction and how property rights, pollution charges, or taxes can achieve a more efficient outcome.**

Marginal private cost is the cost of producing an additional unit of a good or service that is borne by the producer of that good or service. Marginal external cost is the cost of producing an additional unit of a good or service that falls on people other than the producer. And marginal social cost, which is the marginal cost incurred by the entire society is the sum of marginal private cost and marginal external cost. Producers take account only of marginal private cost and overproduce when there is a marginal external cost. Sometimes it is possible to reduce the inefficiency arising from an externality by establishing a property right where one does not currently exist. The Coase theorem is the proposition that if property rights exist, only a small number of parties are involved, and transactions costs are low, then private transactions are efficient and the outcome is not affected by who is assigned the property right. When property rights cannot be assigned, the three main methods that governments can use to cope with externalities are emission charges, marketable permits, and taxes.

■ **Explain why positive externalities lead to inefficient underproduction and how public provision, subsidies, vouchers, and patents can achieve a more efficient outcome.**

Marginal private benefit is the benefit from an additional unit of a good or service that the consumer of that good or service receives. Marginal external benefit is the benefit from an additional unit of a good or service that people other than the consumer of the good or service enjoy. And marginal social benefit, which is the marginal benefit enjoyed by society, is the sum of marginal private benefit and marginal external benefit. External benefits from education arise because better-educated people tend to be better citizens, commit fewer crimes, and support social activities. External benefits from research arise because once someone has worked out a basic idea others can copy. When people make decisions about how much schooling to undertake, they undervalue its external benefits and place most emphasis on its private benefits. The result is that if education were provided by private schools that charged full-cost tuition, we would produce too few college graduates. Four devices that governments can use to achieve a more efficient allocation of resources in the presence of external benefits are public provision, private subsidies, vouchers, and patents and copyrights.

EXPANDED CHAPTER CHECKLIST

When you have completed this chapter, you will be able to:

1 Explain why negative externalities lead to inefficient overproduction and how property rights, pollution charges, or taxes can achieve a more efficient outcome.

- Give an example of a negative externality and an example of a positive externality.
- Define marginal private cost, marginal external cost, and marginal social cost.
- Draw a figure that shows the relationship between marginal private cost, marginal external cost, and marginal social cost.
- Draw a figure that shows the inefficiency with an external cost.
- Explain the Coase theorem.
- Describe how emission charges, marketable permits, and taxes can lead to efficiency in a market with an external cost.

2 Explain why positive externalities lead to inefficient underproduction and how public provision, subsidies, vouchers, and patents can achieve a more efficient outcome.

- Define marginal private benefit, marginal external benefit, and marginal social benefit.
- Draw a figure that shows the relationship between marginal private benefit, marginal external benefit, and marginal social benefit.
- Draw a figure that shows the inefficiency with an external benefit.
- Describe how public provision, private subsidies, vouchers, and patents and copyrights can lead to efficiency in a market with an external benefit.

KEY TERMS

- Coase theorem (page 188)
- Copyright (page 199)
- Externality (page 182)
- Intellectual property rights (page 199)
- Marginal external benefit (page 194)
- Marginal external cost (page 184)
- Marginal private benefit (page 194)
- Marginal private cost (page 184)
- Marginal social benefit (page 194)
- Marginal social cost (page 184)
- Negative externality (page 182)
- Patent (page 199)
- Positive externality (page 182)
- Property rights (page 187)
- Public provision (page 196)
- Subsidy (page 197)
- Transactions costs (page 188)
- Voucher (page 198)

CHECKPOINT 8.1

■ Explain why negative externalities lead to inefficient overproduction and how property rights, pollution charges, or taxes can achieve a more efficient outcome.

Practice Problem 8.1

The figure illustrates the unregulated market for pesticide. When the factories produce pesticide, they also create waste, which they dump into a lake on the outskirts of the town. The marginal external cost

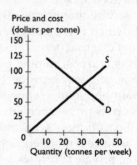

of the dumped waste is equal to the marginal private cost of producing the pesticide, so the marginal social cost of producing the pesticide is double the marginal private cost.

a. What is the quantity of pesticide produced if no one owns the lake?
b. What is the efficient quantity of pesticide?
c. If the residents of the town own the lake, what is the quantity of pesticide produced and how much do the pesticide factories pay to residents of the town?
d. If the pesticide factories own the lake, how much pesticide is produced and how much does the town pay the factories to produce the efficient quantity of pesticide?
e. Suppose that no one owns the lake but the government levies a pollution tax. What is the tax per tonne of pesticide that will achieve the efficient outcome?

Solution to Practice Problem 8.1

This Practice Problem studies the negative production externality of pollution. Part (c) and part (d) use the Coase theorem. According to the Coase theorem, the outcome is efficient if the residents own the lake or if the pesticide factories own the lake.

Quick Review

- *Marginal private cost* The cost of producing an additional unit of a good or service that is borne by the producer of that good or service.
- *Marginal external cost* The cost of producing an additional unit of a good or service that falls on people other than the producer.
- *Marginal social cost* The marginal cost incurred by the entire society—by the producer and by everyone else on whom the cost falls. It is the sum of marginal private cost and marginal external cost.

a. **What is the quantity of pesticide produced if no one owns the lake?**

If no one owns the lake, the market supply curve is the marginal private cost curve. In the figure the quantity of pesticide produced is the quantity where the demand curve, $D = MB$, intersects the marginal private cost curve, $S = MC$. The quantity of pesticide produced is 30 tonnes a week.

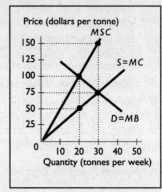

b. **What is the efficient quantity of pesticide?**

At the efficient quantity, the marginal benefit to the factories equals the marginal social cost. The marginal social cost is the sum of the marginal private cost and the marginal external cost. In the figure, the efficient quantity is the quantity where the demand curve, $D = MB$, intersects the marginal social cost curve, MSC. The efficient quantity is 20 tonnes a week.

c. **If the residents of the town own the lake, what is the quantity of pesticide produced and how much do the pesticide factories pay to residents of the town?**

The quantity of pesticide produced is the efficient quantity, which is 20 tonnes a week. The factories pay the townspeople the marginal external cost. In the figure, the marginal external cost is the distance between the marginal private cost curve, $S = MC$, and the marginal social cost curve, MSC. The marginal external cost is $50 a tonne.

d. **If the pesticide factories own the lake, how much pesticide is produced and how much does the town pay the factories to produce the efficient quantity of pesticide?**

The quantity of pesticide produced is the efficient quantity, which is 20 tonnes a week. The town pays the factories nothing because the factories own the lake and the *MSC* curve becomes the factories' private *MC* curve.

e. **Suppose that no one owns the lake but the government levies a pollution tax. What is the tax per tonne of pesticide that will achieve the efficient outcome?**

At the efficient quantity of 20 tonnes a week, the marginal external cost is $50 a tonne. A tax of $50 a tonne will set firms' marginal private cost equal to marginal social cost and result in the efficient quantity being produced.

Additional Practice Problem 8.1a

Two factories each emit 10 tonnes of the pollutant sulfur dioxide a week. The cost to eliminate a tonne of sulfur dioxide to Factory A is $4 and the cost to Factory B is $2. The government wants to eliminate 10 tonnes of sulfur dioxide a week.

a. If the government requires that Firm A decrease emissions by 10 tonnes a week, what is the cost of eliminating the pollution?

b. If the government requires that Firm B decrease emissions by 10 tonnes a week, what is the cost of eliminating the pollution?

c. If the government gives each firm 5 marketable permits, each good for 1 tonne of pollution a week, what will occur?

Solution to Additional Practice Problem 8.1a

a. **If the government requires that Firm A decrease emissions by 10 tonnes a week, what is the cost of eliminating the pollution?**

The cost is $4 a tonne multiplied by 10 tonnes, which is $40 a week.

b. **If the government requires that Firm B decrease emissions by 10 tonnes a week, what is the cost of eliminating the pollution?**

The cost is $2 a tonne multiplied by 10 tonnes, which is $20 a week.

c. **If the government gives each firm 5 marketable permits, each good for 1 tonne of pollution, what will occur?**

Firm A will buy permits from Firm B for any price less than $4 a permit; Firm B will sell permits to Firm A for any price greater than $2 a permit. The companies settle on a price and Firm A buys 5 permits from Firm B. Firm B decreases its pollution and incurs a cost of $20 a week.

■ Self Test 8.1

Fill in the blanks

Marginal private cost equals marginal social cost ____ (minus; plus) marginal external cost. A pollution externality creates an _____ (efficient; inefficient) equilibrium. According to the Coase theorem, if property rights exist, only a small number of parties are involved, and transactions costs are low, then private transactions are efficient and the outcome _____ (is; is not) affected by who is assigned the property right. By setting the tax rate equal to the marginal _____ (external; private; social) cost, firms behave in the same way as they would if they bore the cost of the externality directly.

True or false

1. All externalities are negative.

2. Smoking on a plane creates a negative externality.

3. Marginal social cost equals marginal private cost minus marginal external cost.

4. Copper mining creates land pollution. If the copper mining industry is unregulated, then the quantity of copper mined is less than the efficient quantity.

5. The Coase theorem concludes that if property rights to a polluted river are assigned to the polluter, the quantity of pollution will increase.

6. Emission charges allow the government to set the price for a unit of pollution.

7. By issuing marketable permits, the government sets the price for each unit of pollution produced.

8. If the government imposes a pollution tax on lead mining equal to its marginal external cost, the quantity of lead mined will be the efficient quantity.

Multiple choice

1. An externality is
   a. something that is external to the economy.
   b. a sales tax on a good.
   c. an effect of a transaction felt by someone other than the consumer or producer.
   d. anything produced in other countries

2. The cost of producing one more unit of a good or service that is borne by the producer of that good or service
   a. is the marginal social cost.
   b. equals marginal cost minus marginal benefit.
   c. is the marginal private cost.
   d. is the external cost.

3. The cost of producing an additional unit of a good or service that falls on people other than the producer is
   a. the marginal cost.
   b. represented by the demand curve.
   c. represented by the supply curve.
   d. the marginal external cost.

4. Pollution is an example of a
   a. negative production externality.
   b. negative consumption externality.
   c. positive production externality.
   d. positive consumption externality.

5. An example of an external cost is
   a. second-hand smoke.
   b. sulfur emitting from a smoke stack.
   c. garbage on the roadside.
   d. All of the above answers are correct.

6. The marginal cost of production that is borne by the entire society is the _____ cost.
   a. marginal private
   b. marginal social
   c. marginal external
   d. total external

7. If the marginal private cost of producing one kilowatt of power is five cents and the marginal social cost of each kilowatt is nine cents, then the marginal external cost is
   a. five cents a kilowatt.
   b. nine cents a kilowatt.
   c. four cents a kilowatt.
   d. zero cents a kilowatt.

8. When the production of a good has a marginal external cost, which of the following will occur in an unregulated market?
   a. Overproduction relative to the efficient level will occur.
   b. The market price will be less the marginal social cost of the equilibrium quantity.
   c. A deadweight loss will occur.
   d. All of the above will occur.

9. The Coase theorem is the proposition that if property rights exist, a small number of parties are involved, and transactions costs are low, then private transactions are
   a. inefficient.
   b. efficient.
   c. inequitable.
   d. illegal.

10. A marketable permit
    a. allows firms to maximize pollution.
    b. allows firms to buy and sell the right to pollute at government-controlled prices.
    c. eliminates pollution by setting the price of permits above the marginal cost of polluting.
    d. allows firms to buy and sell the right to pollute.

11. To work out the emission charge that achieves efficiency, the regulator must determine the _____ cost of pollution at different levels of output.

   a. marginal external
   b. marginal social
   c. total
   d. private

12. If a polluting producer is forced to pay an emission charge or a tax on its output, which of the following occurs?

   a. The quantity supplied along the firm's supply curve will increase.
   b. The firm's demand curve will shift leftward.
   c. The firm's supply curve will shift rightward.
   d. The firm's supply curve will shift leftward.

Complete the graph

1. The table shows the marginal private cost, marginal social cost, and marginal benefit schedules for generating electricity, an activity that creates pollution.

Quantity (megawatts per day)	Marginal private cost	Marginal social cost	Marginal benefit
	(dollars per megawatt)		
1	5	10	50
2	10	20	40
3	15	30	30
4	20	40	20

   a. In Figure 8.1, label the axes and then plot the marginal private cost curve, the marginal social cost curve and marginal benefit curve.
   b. How much electricity will an unregulated market produce? What is the marginal external cost at this amount of production?
   c. What is the efficient amount of electricity? Illustrate the deadweight loss resulting from the market equilibrium.
   d. At the efficient quantity of electricity, what is the marginal external cost? If the government imposes a tax on producing electricity to produce the efficient quantity, what should be the amount of tax?

■ FIGURE 8.1

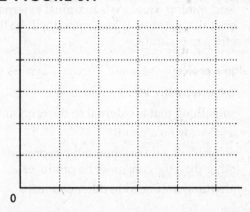

Short answer

1. If the marginal social cost curve lies above the marginal private cost curve, how do you calculate the marginal external cost?

2. The table shows the costs of producing pesticide. Complete the table.

Quantity (tonnes per day)	Marginal private cost	Marginal external cost	Marginal social cost
	(dollars per tonne)		
1	100	—	130
2	120	40	
3	—	60	210
4	190	—	280
5	240	120	—

3. According to the Coase theorem, when are private transactions efficient?

4. What is a marketable permit? What is the advantage of a marketable permit over an emission charge?

5. The production of fertilizer creates water pollution. How do emission charges and taxes result in the efficient quantity of pollution? What information must the government posses to use emission charges or taxes effectively?

CHECKPOINT 8.2

■ Explain why positive externalities lead to inefficient underproduction and how public provision, subsidies, vouchers, and patents can achieve a more efficient outcome.

Practice Problem 8.2

The figure shows the marginal private benefit from college education. The marginal cost of a college education is a constant $6,000 per year. The marginal external benefit from a college education is $4,000 per student per year.

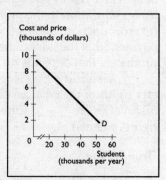

a. If colleges are private and government has no involvement in college education, how many people will undertake a college education and what will be the tuition?
b. What is the efficient number of students?
c. If the government decides to provide public colleges, what tuition will these colleges charge to achieve the efficient number of students? How much will taxpayers have to pay?
d. If the government decides to subsidize private colleges, what subsidy will achieve the efficient number of college students?
e. If the government offers vouchers to those who enrol at a college and no subsidy, what is the value of the voucher that will achieve the efficient number of students?

Solution to Practice Problem 8.2

Practice Problem 8.2 studies the important issue of external benefits and education. Because education has external benefits, an unregulated market will result in less than the efficient provision of education.

Quick Review

- *Marginal private benefit* The benefit from an additional unit of a good or service that the consumer of that good or service receives.
- *Marginal external benefit* The benefit from an additional unit of a good or service that people other than the consumer of the good or service enjoy.
- *Marginal social benefit* The marginal benefit enjoyed by society—by the consumers of a good or service and by everyone else who benefits from it. It is the sum of marginal private benefit and marginal external benefit.

a. If colleges are private and government has no involvement in college education, how many people will undertake a college education and what will be the tuition?

If the government has no involvement, the tuition and number of students is determined at the intersection of the supply curve, which is the marginal private cost curve and the demand curve, which is the marginal private benefit curve.

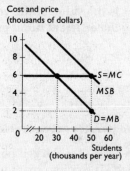

In the figure, tuition equals $6,000 a year and enrolment is 30,000 students a year at the intersection of the $D = MB$ curve and the $S = MC$ curve.

b. What is the efficient number of students?

The efficient number of students is determined at the quantity where marginal cost equals marginal social benefit, which is 50,000 students a year. This quantity is shown in the figure where the $S = MC$ curve and MSB curve intersect.

c. If the government decides to provide public colleges, what tuition will these colleges charge to achieve the efficient number of students? How much will taxpayers have to pay?

The efficient quantity of students is 50,000. The demand curve in the figure, $D = MB$, shows that to have 50,000 students enrol, the tuition must be $2,000 a student. The MC curve shows that the marginal cost for each student is $6,000, so taxpayers must pay $4,000 a student.

d. **If the government decides to subsidize private colleges, what subsidy will achieve the efficient number of college students?**

To have the efficient quantity of 50,000 students attend college the demand curve shows that tuition must be $2,000. The marginal cost of each student is $6,000, so private colleges must be paid a subsidy of $6,000 − $2,000, which is $4,000 a student. The subsidy is equal to the marginal external benefit.

e. **If the government offers vouchers to those who enrol at a college and no subsidy, what is the value of the voucher that will achieve the efficient number of students?**

The enrolment is the efficient quantity of 50,000 students when tuition is $2,000. The private college tuition is $6,000, so the value of the voucher must be $6,000 − $2,000, which is $4,000.

Additional Practice Problem 8.2a

A vaccine for chicken pox was recently developed. The government will make the vaccine available if the marginal benefit of vaccination exceeds the marginal cost. The producer of the vaccine reports that the marginal cost of a dose of vaccine is $80. The marginal benefit to the child being vaccinated is estimated to be $30 and an additional marginal benefit to the child's parents is estimated at $60. Based on these data, should the vaccine be made available?

Solution to Additional Practice Problem 8.2a

To determine if the government should make the vaccine available, we need to compare the marginal cost with the marginal social benefit. The marginal social benefit equals the marginal private benefit to the child of $30 plus the marginal external benefit to the parent of $60, which is $90. The marginal social benefit is greater than the marginal cost, and so the vaccine should be made available.

■ Self Test 8.2

Fill in the blanks

Marginal _____ (external; social) benefit is the benefit enjoyed by society. If the government leaves education to the private market _____ (overproduction; underproduction) occurs. A payment that the government makes to private producers that depends on the level of output is _____ (a subsidy; public provision). The property rights of the creators of knowledge and other discoveries are _____ (intellectual property rights; patents).

True or false

1. The marginal private benefit from a good or service must exceed the marginal external benefit.
2. The expanded job opportunities from a college degree is a marginal private benefit enjoyed by college graduates.
3. A flu vaccination has an external benefit, so the marginal private benefit curve for flu vaccinations lies above the marginal social benefit curve for flu vaccinations.
4. An unregulated market underproduces products with external benefits, such as education.
5. A public community college is an example of public provision of a good that has an external benefit.
6. To overcome the inefficiency in the market for a good with an external benefit, the government can either tax or subsidize the good.
7. Vouchers can help overcome the inefficiency created by a good with an external cost but not the inefficiency created by a good with an external benefit.
8. A patent protects intellectual property rights by giving the patent holder a monopoly.

Multiple choice

1. The benefit the consumer of a good or service receives is the
   a. social benefit.
   b. external benefit.
   c. private benefit.
   d. public benefit.

2. An external benefit is a benefit from a good or service that someone other than the _____ receives.
   a. seller of the good or service
   b. government
   c. foreign sector
   d. consumer

3. When Ronald takes another economics class, other people in society benefit. The benefit to these other people is the marginal ____ benefit of the class.
   a. social
   b. private
   c. external
   d. opportunity

4. Marginal social benefit equals
   a. marginal external benefit.
   b. marginal private benefit.
   c. marginal private benefit minus marginal external benefit.
   d. marginal private benefit plus marginal external benefit.

5. If an external benefit is present, then the
   a. marginal private benefit curve lies above the marginal private cost curve.
   b. marginal social benefit curve lies above the marginal private benefit curve.
   c. marginal social cost curve lies above the marginal private benefit curve.
   d. marginal social benefit is equal to the marginal social cost.

6. In an unregulated market with an external benefit, the
   a. quantity produced is greater than the efficient quantity.
   b. price charged is too high for efficiency.
   c. quantity produced is less than the efficient quantity.
   d. producer is causing pollution but not paying for it.

7. If all education in Canada were provided by private, tuition-charging institutions,
   a. students would consume too much education.
   b. there would be too little education consumed.
   c. the economically efficient level of education would be provided.
   d. the government would provide students with vouchers.

8. Which of the following is a method used by government to cope with the situation in which production of a good creates an external benefit?
   a. removing property rights
   b. paying subsidies
   c. issuing marketable permits
   d. running a lottery

9. If the government provides a subsidy to colleges, then we _____ the marginal _____ of education to find the colleges' supply curve.
   a. subtract the subsidy from; cost
   b. subtract the subsidy from; benefit
   c. add the subsidy to; cost
   d. add the subsidy to; benefit

10. A public university is a service that is an example of
   a. patent protection.
   b. vouchers.
   c. private subsidies.
   d. public provision.

11. A voucher is a token that _____ provides to _____.
   a. firms; households
   b. households; firms
   c. the government; households and firms
   d. the government; households

12. Which government device is associated with intellectual property rights?
   a. public provision
   b. private subsidies
   c. vouchers
   d. patents and copyrights

Complete the graph

1. Figure 8.2 illustrates the market for honey.

   ■ FIGURE 8.2

   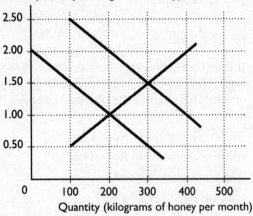

   a. Label the curves in the figure.
   b. Based on Figure 8.2, does the production of honey create an external cost? An external benefit?
   c. What is the efficient quantity of honey? What is the quantity of honey that will be produced in an unregulated market?
   d. Shade the area that equals the deadweight loss in an unregulated market.

Short answer

1. When is the efficient quantity produced in a market with an external benefit?

2. Most elementary schools require that children be vaccinated before allowing the child to attend school. Can this policy be justified using economic analysis?

3. Is a private subsidy or a tax the correct government policy for a product that has an external benefit?

4. What is a voucher? How do vouchers work? Why is a voucher a proper policy to deal with the inefficiency created by a good or service that has an external benefit?

SELF TEST ANSWERS

■ CHECKPOINT 8.1

Fill in the blanks

Marginal private cost equals marginal social cost <u>minus</u> marginal external cost. A pollution externality creates an <u>inefficient</u> equilibrium. According to the Coase theorem, if property rights exist, only a small number of parties are involved, and transactions costs are low, then private transactions are efficient and the outcome <u>is not</u> affected by who is assigned the property right. By setting the tax rate equal to the marginal <u>external</u> cost, firms behave in the same way as they would if they bore the cost of the externality directly.

True or false

1. False; page 182
2. True; page 183
3. False; page 184
4. False; page 186
5. False; page 188
6. True; page 189
7. False; page 189
8. True; page 190

Multiple choice

1. c; page 182
2. c; page 184
3. d; page 184
4. a; page 182
5. d; page 184
6. b; page 184
7. c; page 184
8. d; page 186
9. b; page 188
10. d; page 189
11. a; page 189
12. d; page 190

Complete the graph

1. a. Figure 8.3 shows the *MSC*, *MC*, and *MB* curves; page 186.

■ **FIGURE 8.3**

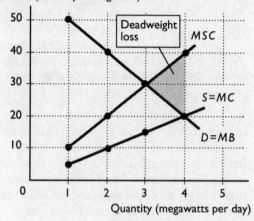

b. An unregulated market will produce 4 megawatts of electricity a day. The marginal external cost at this production level is $20 a megawatt; page 186.

c. The efficient amount of electricity is 3 megawatts a day. The deadweight loss is illustrated in the figure; page 186.

d. At the efficient quantity of electricity, the marginal external cost is $15 a megawatt. The tax is $15 a megawatt. With the tax, 3 megawatts of electricity are produced and the price is $30 a megawatt; page 189.

Short answer

1. The marginal external cost is the distance between the marginal social cost curve and the marginal private cost curve at each quantity of output; page 185.

2. The completed table is below; page 184.

Quantity (tonnes per day)	Marginal private cost	Marginal external cost	Marginal social cost
		(dollars per tonne)	
1	100	30	130
2	120	40	160
3	150	60	210
4	190	90	280
5	240	120	360

3. The Coase theory is the proposition that if property rights exist, only a small number of parties are involved, and transactions costs are low, then private transactions are efficient; page 188.

4. A marketable permit is a permit issued by the government that allows each firm to emit a certain amount of pollution. Firms that have a low marginal cost of reducing pollution sell their permits, and firms that have a high marginal cost of reducing pollution buy permits. To work out the emission charge that achieves efficiency, the government must determine the marginal external cost of pollution at different levels of output and levy a charge on polluters that equals that cost. With marketable permits, the government does not need this information; page 189.

5. Emission charges and taxes are designed to charge polluting firms the cost of their pollution. By forcing the firm to pay this cost, a firm's marginal private cost becomes equal to the marginal social cost. To use emission charges or taxes to overcome the problem of pollution, the government must know the marginal external cost at different levels of output; pages 189-190.

■ **CHECKPOINT 8.2**

Fill in the blanks

Marginal social benefit is the benefit enjoyed by society. If the government leaves education to the private market underproduction occurs. A payment that the government makes to private producers that depends on the level of output is a subsidy. The property rights of the creators of knowledge and other discoveries are intellectual property rights.

True or false

1. False; page 194
2. True; page 194
3. False; page 194
4. True; page 195
5. True; page 196
6. False; page 196
7. False; page 198
8. True; page 199

Multiple choice

1. c; page 194
2. d; page 194
3. c; page 194
4. d; page 194
5. b; page 194
6. c; page 195
7. b; page 195
8. b; page 196
9. a; page 197
10. d; page 196
11. d; page 198
12. d; page 199

Complete the graph

1. a. Figure 8.4 labels the curves; page 195.

■ FIGURE 8.4

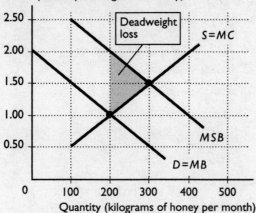

b. The production of honey has an external benefit but no external cost; page 194.

c. The efficient quantity of honey is 300 kilograms a month at the intersection of the *MSB* curve and the *S = MC* curve. In an unregulated market, the quantity produced is 200 kilograms a month at the intersection of the *D = MB* curve and the *S = MC* curve; page 195.

d. Figure 8.4 shades the deadweight loss; page 195.

Short answer

1. The efficient quantity is produced when marginal social benefit equals marginal cost; page 195.

2. Vaccination protects not only the child who is vaccinated, but also makes it less likely for the classmates to catch the disease. So a vaccination has an external benefit. Although the marginal cost of a vaccination may be greater than the marginal private benefit of a vaccination, the marginal social benefit equals the marginal cost and the market is efficient; page 194.

3. The correct government action to deal with a product that has an external benefit is a private subsidy, not a tax; page 197.

4. A voucher is a token that the government gives to households, which they can use to buy specified goods or services. Vouchers increase the demand for the good or service and shift the marginal private benefit curve rightward, closer to the marginal social benefit curve. Vouchers reduce the inefficiency created by a good or service with an external benefit; page 198.

Chapter 9

Public Goods and the Tax System

CHAPTER IN PERSPECTIVE

Chapter 9 studies the services that the government provides and the taxes that pay for these services.

■ **Distinguish between public goods and private goods, explain the free-rider problem, and explain how the quantity of public goods is determined.**

A public good is a good or service that can be consumed simultaneously by everyone and from which no one can be excluded. A private good is a good or service that can be consumed by only one person at a time and only by those people who have bought it or own it. A good is rival if consumption by one person decreases the quantity of the good that is available for others and nonrival if consumption by one person does not decrease the quantity of the good available for someone else. A good is excludable if it is technologically possible to prevent a person from enjoying its benefits and nonexcludable if it is technologically impossible, or extremely costly, to prevent someone from benefiting from it. A pure public good is a good that is both nonrival and nonexcludable. A pure public good is a good that is both rival and excludable. Public goods create a free-rider problem. The economy's marginal benefit curve of a public good is the vertical sum of the individual marginal benefit curves. The efficient quantity of a public good is the quantity where marginal benefit equals marginal cost. The tendency for political parties to propose identical policies to appeal to the maximum number of voters is an example of the principle of minimum differentiation. Rational ignorance is the decision not to acquire information because the marginal cost of doing so exceeds the expected marginal benefit. Rational ignorance, combined with the bureaucratic desire to maximize budgets, can lead to inefficient overprovision of public goods.

■ **Explain the effects of income taxes and review the main ideas about the fairness of the tax system.**

The marginal tax rate is the percentage of an additional dollar of income that is paid in tax; the average tax rate is the percentage of income that is paid in tax. A progressive tax is an increase in the average tax rate as income increases. A proportional tax is a constant average tax rate at all income levels. A tax on labour income decreases employment and creates a deadweight loss. Both the employer and the worker pay part of the tax. A tax on capital income decreases the quantity of capital and creates a deadweight loss. The supply of capital is highly elastic. If the supply of capital is perfectly elastic, then firms pay the entire tax. A tax on land or other unique resource does not decrease the quantity and creates no deadweight loss because the supply is perfectly inelastic. The entire burden of the tax falls on the landowners. The benefits principle is the proposition that people should pay taxes equal to the benefits they receive from public services. This arrangement is fair because those who benefit most pay the most. The ability-to-pay principle is the proposition that people should pay taxes according to how easily they can bear the burden. The ability-to-pay principle compares people along vertical and horizontal dimensions.

EXPANDED CHAPTER CHECKLIST

When you have completed this chapter, you will be able to:

1 **Distinguish between public goods and private goods, explain the free-rider problem, and explain how the quantity of public goods is determined.**

- Define public good and private good and discuss the two dimensions along which public and private goods are distinguished.
- Explain the free-rider problem.
- Describe how the marginal benefit for a public good is calculated.
- Explain why the economy's marginal benefit curve for a public good is different from the market demand curve for a private good.
- Show on a figure the efficient quantity of a public good.
- Define the principle of minimum differentiation and explain how it applies to the proposals of political parties.
- Define rational ignorance.
- Explain why government is large and grows.

2 **Explain the effects of income taxes and review the main ideas about the fairness of the tax system.**

- Define taxable income, marginal tax rate, and average tax rate.
- Compare progressive, regressive, and proportional taxes.
- Describe how the effect of a tax depends upon the elasticity of supply.
- Illustrate the effects of a tax on labour income, capital, and land income.
- Describe the difference in tax incidence when labour income, capital income, and land income are taxed. Discuss the size of the deadweight loss in each case.
- Explain why we have a progressive income tax.
- Discuss the two conflicting principles of fairness of taxes.

KEY TERMS

- Ability-to-pay principle (page 222)
- Average tax rate (page 215)
- Benefits principle (page 222)
- Excludable (page 204)
- Free rider (page 205)
- Horizontal equity (page 222)
- Marginal tax rate (page 215)
- Nonexcludable (page 204)
- Nonrival (page 204)
- Principle of minimum differentiation (page 210)
- Private good (page 204)
- Progressive tax (page 215)
- Proportional tax (page 216)
- Public good (page 204)
- Rational ignorance (page 211)
- Regressive tax (page 216)
- Rival (page 204)
- Taxable income (page 215)
- Vertical equity (page 223)

CHECKPOINT 9.1

■ **Distinguish between public goods and private goods, explain the free-rider problem, and explain how the quantity of public goods is determined.**

Practice Problems 9.1

1. Classify the following goods as public goods or private goods. With each good, is there a

free-rider problem? If not, how is it avoided? The goods are:

a. Weed control treatment for lawns
b. Fire protection
c. Car licences
d. The Trans-Canada Highway

2. The table provides information about a mosquito control program.

Quantity (square kilometres per day)	Marginal cost (dollars per day)	Marginal benefit (dollars per day)
0	0	0
1	1,000	5,000
2	2,000	4,000
3	3,000	3,000
4	4,000	2,000
5	5,000	1,000

a. What quantity of spraying would a private mosquito control program provide?
b. What is the efficient quantity of spraying?
c. In a single-issue election on the quantity of spraying, what quantity would the political outcome deliver?

Solution to Practice Problems 9.1

The first Practice Problem gives practice recognizing public and private goods and the two dimensions along which they are distinguished. The second Practice Problem studies the free-rider problem and the efficient amount of a public good.

Quick Review

- *Pure public good* A pure public good is one for which consumption is nonrival and from which it is impossible to exclude a consumer.
- *Pure private good* A pure private good is one for which consumption is rival and from which consumers can be excluded.
- *Free rider* A person who enjoys the benefits of a good or service without paying for it.

1. **Classify the following goods as public goods or private goods. With each good, is there a free-rider problem? If not, how is it avoided? The goods are:**

a. **Weed control treatment for lawns**

Weed control treatment is a private good because it is consumed by those people who buy it.

b. **Fire protection**

Fire protection is a public good. Private provision would create a free-rider problem. Public provision paid for by property taxes prevents the free-rider problem.

c. **Car licences**

A car licence is a private good. People who want to drive a car buy car licences.

d. **The Trans-Canada Highway**

The Trans-Canada Highway is nonrival, nonexcludable, and a public good. The free-rider problem is avoided because taxes pay the cost of the highway.

2. **The table provides information about a mosquito control program.**

a. **What quantity of spraying would a private mosquito control program provide?**

A private mosquito control program would provide no spraying. Because no one can be excluded from enjoying the benefits of the program, no one has an incentive to pay for it. A free-rider problem would prevail.

b. **What is the efficient quantity of spraying?**

The efficient quantity is to spray three square kilometres a day because that is the quantity at which the marginal benefit equals the marginal cost.

c. **In a single-issue election on the quantity of spraying, what quantity would the political outcome deliver?**

Each political party proposes three square kilometres of spraying to maximize votes. In this single-issue election, the quantity of spraying is the efficient quantity.

Additional Practice Problem 9.1a

It's a balmy, pleasant Sunday afternoon on a fall day in Toronto, where the Blue Jays are playing in the World Series. A variety of goods and services are being consumed. Classify each of the goods and services as rival, nonrival, excludable, and nonexcludable. State if any are pure public or pure private goods.

a. hot dogs eaten while watching the game
b. a pleasant, sunny afternoon
c. watching the World Series
d. listening to the national anthem

Solution to Additional Practice Problem 9.1a

a. **hot dogs eaten while watching the game**

A hot dog is rival and excludable and a pure private good.

b. **a pleasant, sunny afternoon**

The pleasant afternoon is nonrival and nonexcludable and a pure public good.

c. **watching the World Series**

Watching the World Series is excludable. Whether it is rival depends on whether the game is a sell out. If it is a sell out, then watching the game is rival; in the event that it is not sold out and so seats remain available, it is nonrival.

d. **listening to the national anthem**

Listening to the national anthem is nonrival and nonexcludable and a pure public good.

■ Self Test 9.1

Fill in the blanks

A good that is both nonrival and nonexcludable is a pure ____ (private; public) good and a good that is both rival and excludable is a pure ____ (private; public) good. A person who enjoys the benefit of a good or service without paying for it is a ____ (free rider; loafer). The marginal benefit curve for a public good is the ____ (horizontal; vertical) sum of the individual marginal benefit curves. The efficient quantity of a public good is the quantity at which the marginal benefit ____ (equals; equals or is greater than) the marginal cost. ____ (Rational ignorance; The principle of minimum differentiation) is the decision to not acquire information because the marginal cost of doing so exceeds the expected marginal benefit. Bureaucrats try to _____ (maximize; minimize) their budgets.

True or false

1. A donut from Tim Hortons is a public good.
2. A pure private good is nonrival and nonexcludable.
3. Beth is a free rider when she is protected by the city's police force but does not pay anything for the protection.
4. The marginal benefit curve for a public good slopes downward.
5. A private firm would produce too much of a public good.
6. The efficient quantity of a public good is the quantity at which marginal benefit equals marginal cost.
7. The principle of minimum differentiation is the tendency for voters to have similar preferences for public goods.
8. Rational ignorance can lead to the provision of more than the efficient amount of a public good.

Multiple choice

1. A public good
a. can be consumed simultaneously by everyone.
b. can only be consumed by one person at a time.
c. is any good provided by a company owned by a member of the public.
d. is any good provided by government.

2. Which of the following is the best example of a public good?
a. tickets to a concert
b. a Volvo S80
c. a city park
d. a college education

3. If I order a pizza and invite my neighbours to eat it, then the pizza
a. is a public good because many people ate it.
b. creates a free-rider problem.
c. is a private good.
d. in this particular situation, becomes a mixed good.

4. The fact that Heidi's enjoyment of a sunset on Vancouver Island does not preclude David from enjoying the same sunset is an example of
a. a good that is nonrival.
b. a good that is excludable.
c. a private good.
d. the rival nature of consumption.

5. A pure public good is
a. rival and excludable.
b. nonrival and nonexcludable.
c. rival and nonexcludable.
d. nonrival and excludable.

6. When someone enjoys the benefits of a good or service but does not pay for it, that person
a. is a free-range consumer.
b. is a free rider.
c. receives no marginal benefit from the good.
d. is consuming an excludable good.

7. The marginal benefit of a public good is the
a. sum of the marginal benefits of all individuals at each quantity.
b. marginal benefit of the individual person who places the lowest value on the good, multiplied by the number of people in the economy.
c. marginal benefit of the individual person who places the highest value on the good, multiplied by the number of people in the economy.
d. benefit of the last person's consumption.

8. Dredging a lake is a public good. If the marginal cost of dredging a lake is constant at $1,000 and 1,000 boaters benefit from the dredging, then it is efficient to dredge the lake
a. only if at least 1 of the 1,000 boaters has a marginal benefit that is equal to or larger than $1,000.
b. if each of the 1,000 boaters has a marginal benefit of $1.
c. if the boaters each agree to pay $1,000.
d. if the government raises the $1,000 by taxation.

9. The efficient quantity of a public good is
a. the quantity produced by private firms.
b. the quantity at which the marginal benefit equals the marginal cost.
c. impossible to determine because each person's marginal benefit is different.
d. the quantity at which the marginal benefit equals or is greater than the marginal cost.

10. The efficient quantity of a public good can't be produced by private firms because
a. only government has the necessary resources.
b. it is impossible to determine the efficient amount.
c. consumers have an incentive to free ride and not pay for their share of the good.
d. private firms aren't large enough.

11. _____ is the decision not to acquire information because the marginal cost of doing so exceeds the expected marginal benefit

a. Rational ignorance
b. The principle of minimum differentiation
c. A free rider
d. Consumer ignorance

12. Government bureaucracies over-provide public goods and grow larger because of their goal of ____ combined with ____ of the voters.

a. budget maximization; rational ignorance
b. budget minimization; irrational intelligence
c. budget maximization; irrational exuberance
d. budget maximization; rational exuberance

Complete the graph

1. Three shipping firms serve the west coast of a nation. The table has the firms' marginal benefit schedules for lighthouses. Lighthouses are a public good and the marginal cost of constructing a lighthouse is constant at $120,000.

Quantity (lighthouses)	Firm A's marginal benefit	Firm B's marginal benefit	Firm C's marginal benefit
	(thousands of dollars per lighthouse)		
1	50	50	50
2	45	45	45
3	40	40	40
4	35	35	35

a. Complete the table below.

Quantity (lighthouses)	Economy's marginal benefit (thousands of dollars per lighthouse)
1	
2	
3	
4	

Then graph the economy's marginal benefit and marginal cost curves in Figure 9.1.

■ FIGURE 9.1

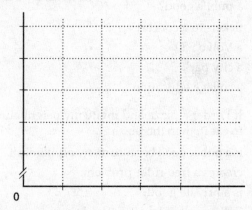

b. What is the efficient number of lighthouses to build?

c. If all three firms agree to split the cost of building lighthouses equally, how much would each firm pay per lighthouse and how many lighthouses will be built?

d. Suppose that one firm decides to free ride and not pay for the construction of any lighthouses. How much would each of the two other firms pay per lighthouse and how many lighthouses will be built?

e. In the situation described in part (d), how might government action overcome the problem?

Short answer

1. What is a pure public good, a pure private good, and a mixed good?

2. What is a free rider? Why is free riding not a problem for private goods?

3. A condominium complex has 10 residents. Each resident has a $10 marginal benefit from 1 unit of a private good and a $10 marginal benefit from 1 unit of a public good. What is one combination of marginal benefit and quantity on the economy's marginal benefit curve for the private good and what is one combination on the economy's marginal benefit curve for the public good? Explain the difference.

4. How does free riding affect the private provision of a public good? How does rational ignorance affect the public provision of a public good?

CHECKPOINT 9.2

■ **Explain the effects of income taxes and review the main ideas about the fairness of the tax system.**

Practice Problems 9.2

1. Suppose that a province has the following taxes: a 5.5 percent corporate income tax, a 6 percent sales tax, a 13.3 percent excise tax on gasoline, a 33.9 cents a pack excise tax on cigarettes, a 13 cents a litre excise tax on beer, a 60 cents a litre excise tax on wine, and property taxes that vary across the counties and range from 1.4 percent to 2.0 percent of property values.

   Classify the province's taxes as progressive, proportional, and regressive.

2. In Hong Kong, the marginal tax rates on salaries range from 2 percent to 20 percent with a maximum average tax of 15 percent, which is reached on incomes of about $91,000 in Canadian dollars. Compare the tax rates in Hong Kong with Canada's federal tax rate. In which country is the personal income tax (tax on salaries) more progressive? Why?

Solution to Practice Problems 9.2

This Practice Problem helps you to recognize whether a tax is progressive or regressive or proportional.

Quick Review

- *Progressive tax* An increase in the average tax rate as income increases.
- *Proportional tax* A constant average tax rate at all income levels.
- *Regressive tax* A decrease in the average tax rate as income increases.

1. **Classify the province's taxes as progressive, proportional, and regressive.**

Proportional: The corporate income tax does not vary with income; it is a proportional tax.

Regressive: The 6 percent sales tax, and the excise taxes on gasoline, cigarettes, beer, and wine are regressive because these items consume a larger fraction of low income earners' spending and a smaller fraction of high income earners' spending.

Progressive: Property taxes are progressive if the counties with the higher tax rates are those with the higher property values.

2. **In Hong Kong, the marginal tax rates on salaries range from 2 percent to 20 percent with a maximum average tax of 15 percent, which is reached on incomes of about $91,000 in Canadian dollars. Compare the tax rates in Hong Kong with Canada's federal tax rate. In which country is the personal income tax (tax on salaries) more progressive? Why?**

The personal income tax in Canada is more progressive because the average tax rate in Canada rises from 0 to about 26 percent. In Hong Kong the average tax rate rises from 2 percent to 15 percent.

Additional Practice Problem 9.2a

"The only fair taxes are user fees, such as toll roads. The gas tax is fair because the funds raised go for road maintenance. All government-provided services need to be funded through user fees. To pay for parks, we need to charge entrance fees. The cost of garbage collection must be based on how much garbage the household creates. Any tax except a user fee is unfair and must be abolished!" Comment on the fairness principle being discussed.

Solution to Additional Practice Problem 9.2a

The speaker is advocating the benefits principle of taxation, which is the proposition that people should pay taxes equal to the benefits they receive from public services. Although user fees have merit, it is not possible to fund all government programs through user fees. For public goods such as law and order, everyone consumes the same amount. It is impossible to determine how much any particular person benefits and not possible to determine the proper fee. Some programs are designed to redistribute income to poorer people. It would be not make sense to tax welfare recipients an amount equal to the benefits they received.

■ Self Test 9.2

Fill in the blanks

The largest source of tax revenue in Canada in 2000 was ____ (personal income taxes; sales taxes; property taxes). The percentage of an additional dollar that is paid in tax is ____ (a progressive tax; a marginal tax; an average tax) rate. A tax is regressive if the average tax rate ____ (increases; decreases) as income increases. An income tax on low-wage workers ____ (creates; does not create) a deadweight loss and an income tax on high-wage workers ____ (creates; does not create) a deadweight loss. If the supply of capital is perfectly elastic, a tax on capital is paid entirely by the ____ (firms; suppliers of capital) and the tax ____ (creates; does not create) a deadweight loss. If the supply of land is _____ (inelastic; perfectly inelastic), a tax on land is paid entirely by the landowners and the tax ____ (creates; does not create) a deadweight loss. The _____ (ability-to-pay; benefits) principle is fair because those who benefit most pay the most.

True or false

1. Provincial sales taxes and the GST are the largest sources of government tax revenue.

2. When Hugh earns an additional dollar, he pays 30 cents in additional tax. Hugh's marginal tax rate is 30 percent.

3. If the average tax rate increases as income increases, the tax is a progressive tax.

4. Sam has $40,000 of taxable income and pays $4,000 income tax. Bert has $50,000 of taxable income and pays $4,500 income tax. Sam and Bert live in a country with a progressive income tax.

5. An income tax on labour creates a deadweight loss.

6. If the supply of capital is perfectly elastic, a tax on capital income decreases the demand for capital and decreases the interest rate.

7. If the revenue from gasoline taxes is used to pay for road repairs, the tax reflects the ability-to-pay principle of a fair tax system.

8. The Canadian income tax system, which uses progressive income taxes, can be considered fair based on the principle of vertical equity.

Multiple choice

1. The single largest source of tax revenue for the government is
a. corporate income taxes.
b. personal income taxes.
c. property taxes.
d. sales taxes.

2. The percentage of an additional dollar of income that is paid in tax is the
a. sales tax.
b. excise tax.
c. marginal tax rate.
d. personal income tax.

3. If the average tax rate increases as income increases, then the tax is
a. regressive.
b. progressive.
c. proportional.
d. a fair tax.

4. The sales tax in Ontario is 8 percent. This sales tax is
a. fair because everyone pays the same tax.
b. proportional.
c. regressive.
d. progressive.

5. If we tax labour, the tax
a. increases the quantity employed because the labour demand curve shifts rightward.
b. decreases the quantity employed because the labour supply curve shifts leftward.
c. increases the quantity employed because the labour supply curve shifts rightward.
d. decreases the quantity employed because the labour demand curve shifts rightward.

6. The incidence of an income tax on labour income is generally that the tax is
a. paid by workers.
b. paid by employers.
c. shared between workers and employers.
d. funded by the deadweight loss.

7. When governments tax capital, the equilibrium quantity of capital
a. increases because of the international mobility of capital.
b. does not change because the supply of capital is perfectly elastic.
c. decreases.
d. does not change because the supply of capital is perfectly inelastic.

8. A tax on land in Victoria would be borne entirely by landowners because the
a. demand for land is perfectly inelastic.
b. supply of land is perfectly inelastic.
c. supply of land is perfectly elastic.
d. demand for land is perfectly elastic.

9. We have a progressive income tax system because
a. the wealthy taxpayers have more influence than the poor over the system.
b. the median voter is a wealthy taxpayer.
c. more people are low-income voters and the median voter is in this group.
d. the average voter has less income than the median voter.

10. Which of the following taxes best illustrates the benefits principle of taxation?
a. property tax
b. income tax
c. corporate income tax
d. gasoline tax

11. The proposition that people should pay taxes according to how easily they can bear the burden is the _____ principle.
a. regressive tax
b. benefits
c. ability-to-pay
d. fairness

12. Vertical equity implies that
a. tax rates should be equal for all taxpayers.
b. people with higher income should pay more in taxes.
c. people with higher incomes should pay a lower average tax rate.
d. All of the above are implied vertical equity.

Complete the graph

1. Figure 9.2 shows the labour market.

   ■ FIGURE 9.2
   Wage rate (dollars per hour)

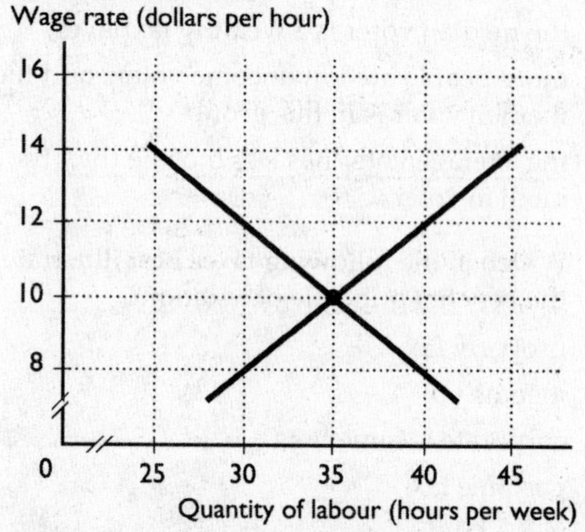

   a. Label the curves. What is the equilibrium wage rate and quantity of labour?
   b. Suppose the government imposes an income tax of $4 an hour on labour income. Illustrate the effect of this tax in the figure.
   c. After the tax is imposed, what is the wage rate paid by firms and what is the amount received by households?
   d. If a deadweight loss is created, shade its area. If a deadweight loss is not created, explain why not.

2. Figure 9.3 shows the market for land.
   a. What is the equilibrium rent and quantity of land?
   b. Suppose the government imposes a tax on land income of $10 a hectare. What is the new equilibrium rent paid by renters and what is the amount of rent kept by landowners? What is the equilibrium quantity of land?
   c. If a deadweight loss is created, shade its area. If a deadweight loss is not created, explain why not.

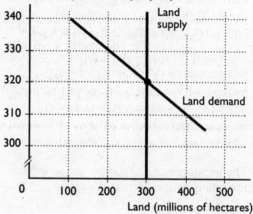

■ FIGURE 9.3
Rent (dollars per hectare per year)

Short answer

1. In Canada in 2000, what single tax generates the largest percentage of total tax revenue? What tax generates the second largest percentage?
2. Why is the supply of capital highly elastic? Who pays the tax on capital if the supply of capital is perfectly elastic?
3. What role does the median voter play in why we have a progressive income tax?

Chapter 9 · Public Goods and the Tax System   149

SELF TEST ANSWERS

■ CHECKPOINT 9.1

Fill in the blanks

A good that is both nonrival and nonexcludable is a pure <u>public</u> good and a good that is both rival and excludable is a pure <u>private</u> good. A person who enjoys the benefit of a good or service without paying for it is a <u>free rider</u>. The marginal benefit curve for a public good is the <u>vertical</u> sum of the individual marginal benefit curves. The efficient quantity of a public good is the quantity at which the marginal benefit <u>equals</u> the marginal cost. <u>Rational ignorance</u> is the decision to not acquire information because the marginal cost of doing so exceeds the expected marginal benefit. Bureaucrats try to <u>maximize</u> their budgets.

True or false

1. False; page 204
2. False; page 204
3. True; page 205
4. True; page 206
5. False; page 208
6. True; page 208
7. False; page 210
8. True; page 211

Multiple choice

1. a; page 204
2. c; page 204
3. c; page 204
4. a; page 204
5. b; page 204
6. b; page 205
7. a; page 206
8. b; page 208
9. b; page 208
10. c; page 208
11. a; page 211
12. a; pages 210-211

Complete the graph

1. a. The complete table and the completed Figure 9.4 are below; page 206.

Quantity (lighthouses)	Economy's marginal benefit (thousands of dollars per lighthouse)
1	150
2	135
3	120
4	105

■ **FIGURE 9.4**

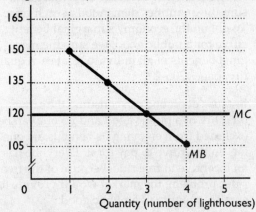

b. The efficient number of lighthouses to build is 3; page 208.

c. Each firm pays $40,000 per lighthouse and 3 lighthouses are built; page 208.

d. If one firm free rides, the other firms would need to pay $60,000 a lighthouse. No lighthouses would be built because $60,000 exceeds each firm's marginal benefit from any lighthouse; page 209.

e. The government could tax each firm $40,000 a lighthouse and use the tax revenue to build three lighthouses; page 209.

Short answer

1. A pure public good is a good that is both nonrival and nonexcludable. A pure private good is a good that is both rival and excludable. A mixed good is either nonexcludable and rival or excludable and nonrival; page 204.

2. A free rider is a person who enjoys the benefits of a good or service without paying for it. Free riding is not a problem for private goods because private goods are excludable; page 205.

3. For the private good, one combination on the economy's marginal benefit curve is: $10 marginal benefit and 10 units. For the public good, one combination is: $100 marginal benefit and 1 unit. To obtain the economy's marginal benefit curve for a private good, we sum the quantities demanded at each price. To obtain the economy's marginal benefit curve for a public good, we sum the marginal benefits of all individuals at each quantity; pages 206–207.

4. Because everyone can consume the same quantity of a public good and no one can be excluded from enjoying its benefits, no one has an incentive to pay for it. Everyone has an incentive to free ride. Because of the free-rider problem, the market would provide too small a quantity of a public good.

    Bureaucrats who maximize their budgets and voters who work in the industry exert a larger influence on public policy than voters who are rationally ignorant. This leads to overprovision; pages 205 and 212.

■ **CHECKPOINT 9.2**

Fill in the blanks

The largest source of tax revenue in Canada in 2000 was <u>personal income taxes</u>. The percentage of an additional dollar that is paid in tax is <u>a marginal tax</u> rate. A tax is regressive if the average tax rate <u>decreases</u> as income increases. An income tax on low-wage workers <u>creates</u> a deadweight loss and an income tax on high-wage workers <u>creates</u> a deadweight loss. If the supply of capital is perfectly elastic, a tax on capital is paid entirely by the <u>firms</u> and the tax <u>creates</u> a deadweight loss. If the supply of land is <u>perfectly inelastic</u>, a tax on land is paid entirely by the landowners and the tax <u>does not create</u> a deadweight loss. The <u>benefits</u> principle is fair because those who benefit most pay the most.

True or false

1. False; page 214
2. True; page 215
3. True; page 215
4. False; page 216
5. True; page 217
6. False; page 218
7. False; page 222
8. True; page 223

Multiple choice

1. b; page 214
2. c; page 215
3. b; page 215
4. c; pages 215-216
5. b; page 217
6. c; page 217
7. c; pages 218-219
8. b; page 220
9. c; page 221
10. d; page 222
11. c; page 222
12. b; page 223

Complete the graph

1. a. The curves are labelled LD and LS_0 in Figure 9.5. The equilibrium wage rate is $10

an hour and the equilibrium quantity of labour is 35 hours a week; page 217.

■ **FIGURE 9.5**
Wage rate (dollars per hour)

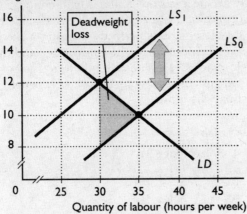

■ **FIGURE 9.6**
Rent (dollars per hectare per year)

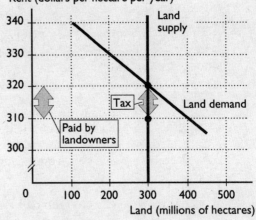

b. The income tax decreases the supply of labour. The labour supply curve shifts leftward from LS_0 to LS_1. The vertical distance between LS_0 and LS_1 is equal to the $4 tax; page 217.

c. Firms pay a wage rate of $12 an hour; workers receive a wage rate of $8 an hour; page 217.

d. The deadweight loss is the grey triangle in Figure 9.5; page 217.

2. a. In Figure 9.6, the equilibrium rent is $320 a hectare per year and the equilibrium quantity of land is 300 million hectares; page 220.

b. In the figure, the supply of land is perfectly inelastic. So after the tax, renters pay $320 a hectare and landowners keep $310 a hectare. The equilibrium quantity of land is 300 million hectares; page 220.

c. There is no deadweight loss created because the equilibrium quantity does not change; page 220.

Short answer

1. The tax that generates the largest percentage of total tax revenue is the personal income tax, which accounts for 38 percent of total tax revenue. Second is provincial sales taxes and the GST, which generate 25 percent of total tax revenue; page 214.

2. Because capital is internationally mobile, its supply is highly (perhaps perfectly) elastic. If the supply of capital is perfectly elastic, firms pay the entire tax on capital income and the quantity of capital decreases; page 218.

3. Suppose that government programs benefit everyone equally and are paid for by a proportional income tax. There is redistribution from high-income voters to low-income voters. But this situation is not the best one possible for the median voter.

Now suppose that the marginal tax rate is lowered for low-income voters and increased for high-income voters—a progressive tax. Low-income voters are now better off, and high-income voters are worse off. Low-income voters will support this change and high-income voters will oppose it. There are many more low-income voters than high-income voters, so the low-income voters will win. And the median voter is a low-income voter; page 221.

Chapter 10

Consumer Choice and Demand

CHAPTER IN PERSPECTIVE

Chapter 10 presents a model of consumer choice based on marginal utility and the fundamental idea that people make rational choices. We use marginal utility theory to derive a demand curve and explain the paradox of value.

■ **Calculate and graph a budget line that shows the limits to a person's consumption possibilities.**

A budget line describes the limits to a consumer's consumption possibilities. A consumer can afford any combination on the budget line and inside it, but she cannot afford any combination outside the budget line. When the price of a good changes, the slope of the budget line changes. The relative price is the price of one good in terms of another good—an opportunity cost. It equals the price of one good divided by the price of another good. The slope of the budget line is the relative price. An increase in the budget shifts the budget line rightward, and a decrease in the budget shifts the budget line leftward.

■ **Explain marginal utility theory and use it to derive a consumer's demand curve.**

Utility is the benefit or satisfaction that a person gets from the consumption of a good or service. Total utility is the total benefit that a person gets from the consumption of a good or service; marginal utility is the change in total utility that results from a one-unit increase in the quantity of a good consumed. As the quantity of a good consumed increases, its total utility increases but its marginal utility decreases. A consumer maximizes total utility when he allocates his entire available budget and makes the marginal utility per dollar spent the same for all goods. The marginal utility per dollar spent is the increase in total utility that comes from the last dollar spent on a good. If the price of a good falls, the marginal utility per dollar spent on that good rises at the current consumption level and the consumer buys more of that good. So when the price of a good falls, there is an increase in the quantity demanded and a movement down along the demand curve.

■ **Use marginal utility theory to explain the paradox of value: Why water is vital but cheap while diamonds are relatively useless but expensive.**

The paradox of value is that water, which is essential to life, is cheap, while diamonds, which are relatively useless, are expensive. We solve this puzzle by distinguishing between total utility and marginal utility. The total utility from water is enormous. But we use so much water that its marginal utility is a small value. We buy few diamonds, so diamonds have a large marginal utility. Diamonds have a high price and a high marginal utility. Water has a low price and a low marginal utility. When the high marginal utility of diamonds is divided by the high price of a diamond, the result is a number that equals the low marginal utility of water divided by the low price of water. Water is cheap but provides a large consumer surplus, while diamonds are expensive but provide a small consumer surplus.

EXPANDED CHAPTER CHECKLIST

When you have completed this chapter, you will be able to:

1 **Calculate and graph a budget line that shows the limits to a person's consumption possibilities.**

- Define and draw a budget line.
- Describe how the slope of the budget line changes when price changes.
- Discus the relationship between the slope of the budget line, opportunity cost, and relative price of a good or service.
- Show the effect of an increase or decrease in the consumer's budget on the budget line.

2 **Explain marginal utility theory and use it to derive a consumer's demand curve.**

- Define utility and total utility.
- Define and calculate marginal utility.
- Explain the principle of diminishing marginal utility.
- Use the utility-maximizing rule to choose the point on the budget line that maximizes total utility.
- Derive a demand curve using marginal utility theory.
- Describe the relationship between the price elasticity of demand and marginal utility.

3 **Use marginal utility theory to explain the paradox of value: Why water is vital but cheap while diamonds are relatively useless but expensive.**

- Explain how marginal utility theory resolves the paradox of value.
- Discuss the difference between the price and consumer surplus of water and diamonds.

KEY TERMS

- Budget line (page 230)
- Diminishing marginal utility (page 237)
- Marginal utility (page 237)
- Marginal utility per dollar spent (page 241)
- Relative price (page 233)
- Total utility (page 236)
- Utility (page 236)
- Utility-maximizing rule (page 240)

CHECKPOINT 10.1

■ Calculate and graph a budget line that shows the limits to a person's consumption possibilities.

Practice Problem 10.1

Jerry's burger and magazine budget is $12 a week. The price of a burger is $2, and the price of a magazine is $4.

a. List the combinations of burgers and magazines that Jerry can afford.
b. Draw a graph of Jerry's budget line with the quantity of burgers plotted on the x-axis.
c. What is the relative price of a magazine? Explain your answer.
d. Describe how the budget line in (b) changes if the following events occur one at a time other things remain the same:
   - The price of a magazine falls.
   - The price of a burger rises.
   - Jerry's budget for burgers and magazines increases.

Solution to Practice Problem 10.1

This Practice Problem studies the budget line. Remember that when the price of a good changes, the slope of the budget line changes and when the consumer's budget changes, there is a shift of the budget line.

Quick Review

- *Budget line* A line that describes the limits to consumption choices and that depends on a consumer's budget and the prices of goods and services.

a. **List the combinations of burgers and magazines that Jerry can afford.**

The combinations of burgers and magazines that Jerry can afford are listed in the table. To construct this table, select the combinations of burgers and magazines that spend all of Jerry's $12 budget.

Burgers	Magazines
0	3
2	2
4	1
6	0

b. **Draw a graph of Jerry's budget line with the quantity of burgers plotted on the *x*-axis.**

The figure shows Jerry's budget line. The maximum number of burgers Jerry can buy is 6, where the budget line intersects the *x*-axis and the maximum number of magazines Jerry can buy is 3, where the budget line intersects the *y*-axis.

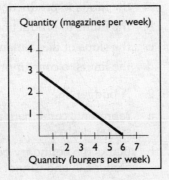

c. **What is the relative price of a magazine? Explain your answer.**

The relative price of a magazine equals the price of a magazine divided by the price of a burger, which is $4 per magazine ÷ $2 per burger = 2 burgers per magazine. The relative price of a magazine is the opportunity cost of a magazine, which is the number of burgers that Jerry must forgo to get 1 magazine.

d. **Describe how the budget line in (b) changes if the following events occur one at a time other things remain the same:**

- **The price of a magazine falls.**

When the price of a magazine falls, and Jerry spends all his budget on magazines, he can buy more magazines. But if Jerry spends all his budget on burgers, he can still buy only 6 burgers a week. The figure shows that Jerry's budget line rotates outward and becomes more steep. Jerry's consumption possibilities have expanded.

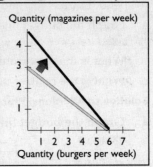

- **The price of a burger rises.**

When the price of a burger rises, and Jerry spends all his budget on burgers, he can buy fewer burgers. But if Jerry spends all his budget on magazines, he can still buy 3 magazines a week. The figure shows that Jerry's budget line rotates inward and becomes more steep. Jerry's consumption possibilities have decreased.

- **Jerry's budget for burgers and magazines increases.**

When Jerry's budget for burgers and magazines increases, his consumption possibilities expand. In the figure, Jerry's budget line shifts outward.

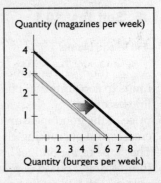

Additional Practice Problem 10.1a

Mark is dining at the Olive Garden. He has $30 to spend. Pizza is $15 and a salad is $5.

a. Graph the budget line with pizza on the x-axis.
b. What is the opportunity cost of a pizza?
c. What is the relative price of a pizza?

Solution to Additional Practice Problem 10.1a

a. **Graph the budget line with pizza on the x-axis.**

The figure shows Mark's budget line. The maximum number of pizzas he can buy is 2 and the maximum number of salads he can buy is 6.

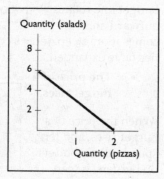

b. **What is the opportunity cost of a pizza?**

The slope of the budget line is the opportunity cost of a pizza. The slope is (6 salads) ÷ (2 pizzas), which equals 3 salads per pizza.

c. **What is the relative price of a pizza?**

The opportunity cost of a pizza is also its relative price. The relative price of a pizza is 3 salads per pizza.

■ Self Test 10.1

Fill in the blanks

A ____ (budget; consumption) line shows the limits to consumption possibilities. The budget line becomes ____ (less; more) steep when the price of the good measured along the x-axis increases and everything else remains the same. The slope of the budget line is equal to the ____ (opportunity; relative) price. When income increases, the budget line shifts ____ (inward; outward).

True or false

1. Dian's budget line shows the limits to what Dian can consume.
2. A fall in the price of the good measured along the x-axis, all other things remaining the same, rotates the budget line inward.
3. The slope of the budget line measures the opportunity cost of one more unit of the good plotted on the x-axis.
4. The price of one good plus the price of another good equals the relative price.
5. When Stan's budget increases, his budget line shifts outward.

Multiple choice

1. A budget line describes
   a. the limits to production possibilities.
   b. the limits to production opportunities.
   c. the slope of the demand curve.
   d. the limits to consumption possibilities.

2. A budget line
   a. represents combinations of goods a consumer desires.
   b. marks the boundary between what a consumer can and cannot afford.
   c. has a positive slope.
   d. is the same as the production possibilities frontier.

3. Linda has $10 a month to spend on ice cream cones and chocolate bars. If the price of an ice cream cone is $2 and the price of a chocolate bar is $1, which of the following is a point on Linda's budget line?
   a. 4 cones and 0 chocolate bars
   b. 1 cone and 8 chocolate bars
   c. 3 cones and 1 chocolate bar
   d. 5 cones and 10 chocolate bars

4. If a budget line rotates inward and becomes steeper, then the
   a. consumer's budget decreased.
   b. consumer's budget increased.
   c. price of one of the goods decreased.
   d. price of one of the goods increased.

5. A steeper budget line means a
   a. higher opportunity cost of the good measured on the *x*-axis.
   b. lower opportunity cost of the good measured on the *x*-axis.
   c. larger income.
   d. smaller income.

6. A relative price is the
   a. price of a substitute.
   b. price of a related good.
   c. price of one good divided by the price of another.
   d. absolute price of a good.

7. When a consumer's budget increases, the budget line
   a. rotates outward and its slope changes.
   b. rotates inward and its slope changes.
   c. shifts outward and its slope does not change.
   d. shifts inward and its slope does not change.

8. Rob buys fishing lures and steaks. If his budget increases, the maximum number of fishing lures he can purchase ____ and the maximum number of steaks he can purchase ____.
   a. increases; increases
   b. increases; decreases
   c. decreases; increases
   d. decreases; decreases

Complete the graph

1. Jack buys only magazines, which have a price of $3 each, and hamburgers, which have a price of $4 each. Jack's income is $12.
   a. In Figure 10.1, draw Jack's budget line.

   ■ **FIGURE 10.1**

   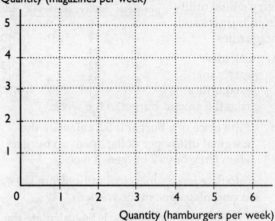

   b. What does the slope of the budget line equal? What is the interpretation of this slope?
   c. Can Jack buy 2 magazines and 1 hamburger? Can he buy 2 magazines and 3 hamburgers?
   d. Suppose the price of a hamburger falls to $2. In Figure 10.1, draw Jack's new budget line.
   e. What does the slope of the new budget line equal? How does the slope compare to your answer to part (b)?
   f. Can Jack now buy 2 magazines and 1 hamburger? Can he now buy 2 magazines and 3 hamburgers?

Short answer

1. How is a budget line similar to a production possibilities frontier? How is it dissimilar?
2. What does the slope of a budget line equal?
3. What is the relationship between the relative price of a good and its opportunity cost?
4. If a consumer's budget increases, what happens to the budget line? Does its slope change?

CHECKPOINT 10.2

■ **Explain marginal utility theory and use it to derive a consumer's demand curve.**

Practice Problem 10.2

The table shows Jerry's total utility from burgers and magazines.

Burgers		Magazines	
Quantity per week	Total utility	Quantity per week	Total utility
0	0	0	0
1	14	1	100
2	24	2	120
3	32	3	134
4	38	4	144

a. Calculate Jerry's marginal utility from the second burger in the week.
b. If the price of a burger is $2, calculate the marginal utility per dollar spent on burgers when Jerry buys 2 burgers a week.
c. Calculate Jerry's marginal utility from the second magazine in the week.
d. If the price of a magazine is $4, calculate the marginal utility per dollar spent on magazines when Jerry buys 2 magazines.
e. When the price of a burger is $2, the price of a magazine is $4, and Jerry has $12 a week to spend, Jerry buys 2 burgers and 2 magazines. Does he maximize his total utility? Explain your answer.

Solution to Practice Problem 10.2

The goal of a consumer is to allocate the available budget in a way that maximizes total utility. Total utility is maximized when the sum of the utilities obtained from all goods is as large as possible. This outcome occurs when a person follows the utility-maximizing rule: 1. Allocate the entire available budget and 2. Make the marginal utility per dollar spent the same for all goods.

Quick Review

- *Marginal utility* The change in total utility that results from a one-unit increase in the quantity of a good consumed.
- *Marginal utility per dollar spent* The increase in total utility that comes from the last dollar spent on a good.

a. **Calculate Jerry's marginal utility from the second burger in the week.**

The marginal utility from the second burger equals the total utility from 2 burgers, which is 24 minus the total utility from 1 burger, which is 14. So the marginal utility from the second burger is 24 − 14 = 10 units of utility.

b. **If the price of a burger is $2, calculate the marginal utility per dollar spent on burgers when Jerry buys 2 burgers a week.**

The marginal utility per dollar spent on 2 burgers a week equals the marginal utility of the second burger divided by the price, which is 10 ÷ $2 = 5.

c. **Calculate Jerry's marginal utility from the second magazine in the week.**

The marginal utility from the second magazine equals the total utility from 2 magazines, which is 120 minus the total utility from 1 magazine, which is 100. So the marginal utility from the second magazine is 120 − 100 = 20 units of utility.

d. **If the price of a magazine is $4, calculate the marginal utility per dollar spent on magazines when Jerry buys 2 magazines.**

The marginal utility per dollar spent on 2 magazines a week equals the marginal utility of the second magazine divided by the price, which is 20 ÷ $4 = 5.

e. **When the price of a burger is $2, the price of a magazine is $4, and Jerry has $12 a week to spend, Jerry buys 2 burgers and 2 magazines. Does he maximize his total utility? Explain your answer.**

Jerry maximizes his total utility when he allocates his entire available budget and the marginal utility per dollar spent on burgers equals the marginal utility per dollar spent on magazines. When the price of a burger is $2 and Jerry buys 2 burgers, he spends $4 and when the price of a magazine is $4 and Jerry buys 2 magazines, he spends $8. So Jerry is allocating his entire available budget. Jerry's marginal utility per dollar spent on burgers is 5 from part (b) and his marginal utility per dollar spent on magazines is also 5 from part (d). So Jerry is maximizing his total utility.

Additional Practice Problem 10.2a

If Jenny is allocating her entire available budget on movies and popcorn, explain the rule she must follow to maximize her total utility.

Solution to Additional Practice Problem 10.2a

If the marginal utility per dollar spent on movies exceeds the marginal utility per dollar spent on popcorn, then Jenny sees more movies and buys less popcorn; if the marginal utility per dollar spent on popcorn exceeds the marginal utility per dollar spent on movies, Jenny buys more popcorn and sees fewer movies. More generally, if the marginal gain from an action exceeds the marginal loss, take the action.

■ Self Test 10.2

Fill in the blanks

The total benefit a person gets from the consumption of a good or service is ____ (marginal; total) utility. The change in total utility that results from a one-unit increase in the quantity of a good consumed is ____ (marginal; elastic) utility. As the quantity of a good consumed increases, total utility ____ (increases; decreases) and marginal utility ____ (increases; decreases). The marginal utility per dollar spent equals the marginal utility of a good ____ (multiplied; divided) by the price of the good. When total utility is maximized, the marginal utility per dollar spent ____ (equals 1; is equal) for all goods. Diminishing marginal utility theory implies that other things remaining the same, the _____ (higher; lower) the price of a good, the smaller is the quantity demanded of that good. If, as the quantity consumed of a good increases, marginal utility decreases quickly, the demand for the good is____ (elastic; inelastic).

True or false

1. As Katie consumes more sushi, her total utility from sushi increases.
2. As Katie consumes more sushi, her marginal utility from sushi increases.
3. Kim maximizes her utility whenever she allocates her entire available budget.
4. Tommy is allocating his entire available budget. If Tommy's marginal utility per dollar spent on tacos is 8 and the marginal utility per dollar spent on burritos is 10, then Tommy is not maximizing his total utility.
5. Diminishing marginal utility theory implies that other things remaining the same, the higher the price of a good, the greater is the quantity demanded of that good.

Multiple choice

1. In economics, utility
   a. is always increasing.
   b. equals opportunity cost.
   c. is an index of how much a person wants something.
   d. is measured in the same units as relative price.

2. Marginal utility is the
   a. change in total utility that results from a one-unit increase in the quantity of a good consumed.
   b. total benefit from the consumption of a good or service.
   c. quantity of a good a consumer prefers.
   d. average utility per unit consumed.

3. As I drink additional cups of tea at breakfast, my
   a. marginal utility from tea decreases.
   b. total utility from tea increases.
   c. total utility from tea decreases.
   d. Both answers (a) and (b) are correct.

4. Marginal utility per dollar spent is calculated by _____ utility of a good by the price of the good.
   a. multiplying marginal
   b. dividing marginal
   c. multiplying total
   d. dividing total

5. When a household maximizes its total utility, then its entire available budget is allocated in such a way that the
   a. marginal utility of all goods is equal.
   b. marginal utility per dollar spent is equal for all goods.
   c. marginal utility is as large as possible for all goods.
   d. marginal utility will start decreasing if it consumes fewer goods.

6. Suppose that Jennifer likes pizza and hotdogs. If her marginal utility per dollar spent on pizza is 6 and on hotdogs is 5, Jennifer
   a. is maximizing her total utility.
   b. could increase her total utility by buying more hotdogs and less pizza.
   c. could increase her total utility by buying more pizza and fewer hotdogs.
   d. is maximizing her marginal utility.

7. You can use marginal utility theory to find the demand curve by changing
   a. the price of one good.
   b. income.
   c. the utility schedule.
   d. the prices of both goods.

8. If, as the quantity consumed of a good increases, marginal utility decreases slowly, the demand for that good is
   a. elastic or unit elastic.
   b. elastic.
   c. unit elastic.
   d. inelastic.

Complete the graph

1. Bertha consumes only pop and pizza. The table gives Bertha's total utility from pop and pizza.

   a. Complete the table.

Pizza			Pop		
Quantity (slices per day)	Total utility	Marginal utility	Quantity (cans per day)	Total utility	Marginal utility
0	0		0	0	
1	45	___	1	25	___
2	85	___	2	45	___
3	120	___	3	60	___
4	150	___	4	70	___
5	175	___	5	75	___
6	195	___	6	76	___

   b. The price of a can of pop is $1 and the price of a slice of pizza is $2. If Bertha's budget is $6, how many cans of pop and slices of pizza does she consume?

   c. If the price of a slice of pizza rises to $3, while the price of a can of pop and Bertha's budget do not change, how many cans of pop and slices of pizza does she consume?

   d. What are two points on Bertha's demand curve for pizza? Label the axes and then draw her demand curve in Figure 10.2.

   ■ FIGURE 10.2

   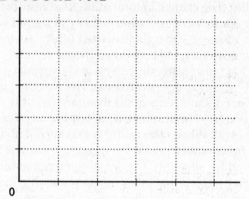

Short answer

1. Carlos drinks Aquafina bottled water. The table gives his total utility from this water. Calculate his marginal utility.

Quantity (bottles of Aquafina per day)	Total utility	Marginal utility
0	0	___
1	25	___
2	45	___
3	60	___
4	70	___
5	75	___
6	76	___

2. Lisa eats tacos and hamburgers. The quantities and marginal utilities from each are in the table below. Lisa's budget is $8.

Tacos		Hamburgers	
Quantity per week	Marginal utility	Quantity per week	Marginal utility
0	0	0	0
1	50	1	80
2	40	2	40
3	30	3	20
4	20	4	10
5	10	5	5

 a. If the price of taco is $1 and the price of a hamburger is $2, what quantity of tacos and hamburgers will Lisa purchase?

 b. If the price of a taco rises to $2 while neither Lisa's budget nor the price of a hamburger change, what quantity of tacos and hamburgers will Lisa purchase?

 c. How does Lisa respond to a change in the price of a taco?

3. What does it mean to "allocate the entire available budget?" How does saving fit into the picture?

4. What is the relationship between a good's marginal utility and its elasticity of demand?

5. What is marginal analysis? Why is making the marginal utility per dollar spent necessary for a consumer to maximize his or her utility?

CHECKPOINT 10.3

■ Use marginal utility theory to explain the paradox of value: Why water is vital but cheap while diamonds are relatively useless but expensive.

Practice Problem 10.3

Tony rents 500 videos a year at $3 each and buys 10,000 litres of tap water a year, for which he pays $50. Tony is maximizing total utility. If Tony's marginal utility from water is 0.5 unit per litre, what is his marginal utility from a video rental? Which good is the more valuable to Tony: water or videos? Why?

Solution to Practice Problem 10.3

To answer this Practice Problem, remember that when Tony is maximizing his utility that the marginal utility per dollar spent for tap water and videos is equal. And when we are discussing the value of videos and tap water, we are thinking about total utility and consumer surplus.

Quick Review

- *The paradox of value* Why is water, which is essential to life, cheap, but diamonds, which are relative useless, expensive?

Tony rents 500 videos a year at $3 each and buys 10,000 litres of tap water a year, for which he pays $50. Tony is maximizing total utility. If Tony's marginal utility from water is 0.5 unit per litre, what is his marginal utility from a video rental? Which good is the more valuable to Tony: water or videos? Why?

Tony is maximizing utility, so the marginal utility per dollar spent on tap water equals the marginal utility per dollar spent on videos. Tony buys 10,000 litres of tap water a year, for which he pays $50. So Tony pays $50 ÷ 10,000 litres, which is $0.005 a litre. Tony's marginal utility per dollar spent for water is 0.5 ÷ $0.005, which is 100.

The price of a video is $3, and the marginal utility of a video divided by the price of a video equals 100. So the marginal utility of a video equals 100 × $3, which is 300 units.

Water most likely generates more total utility for Tony and has a greater consumer surplus. Water is more valuable to Tony.

Additional Practice Problem 10.3a

In Practice Problem 10.3, why does Tony receive a lower marginal utility from his consumption of water?

Solution to Additional Practice Problem 10.3a

Tony rents 500 videos a year and buys 10,000 litres of tap water a year. As the quantity of a good consumed increases, the marginal utility tends to decrease. Because Tony is consuming much more water than videos, his total utility from water is greater than his total utility from videos, but his marginal utility from water is much less than his marginal utility from videos.

■ Self Test 10.3

Fill in the blanks

Marginal benefit is the maximum price a consumer is willing to pay for an extra unit of a good or service when ____ (marginal; total) utility is maximized. The paradox of value is resolved by noting that diamonds have a high price, a ____ (high; low) total utility, and a ____ (high; low) marginal utility. Water provides ____ (more; less) consumer surplus than diamonds.

True or false

1. Katie's demand curve for sushi shows the quantity of sushi she demands at each price when her total utility is maximized.

2. Marginal benefit is the maximum price a consumer is willing to pay for an extra unit of a good or service when total utility is maximized.

3. The paradox of value is that water, which is essential to life, is plentiful while diamonds, which are not essential to life, are much less plentiful.

4. The paradox of value is solved by noting that the total utility from water is small while the marginal utility from water is large.

5. The consumer surplus from water is greater than the consumer surplus from diamonds.

Multiple choice

1. At all points on a demand curve, the
   a. consumer's budget has been allocated to maximize total utility.
   b. quantity describes the quantity demanded at each price when total utility is maximized.
   c. price represents the marginal benefit the consumer gets from an extra unit of a good.
   d. All of the above answers are correct.

2. As more of a good is consumed, the marginal utility of an additional unit ____, so consumers are willing to pay ____ for an additional unit.
   a. decreases; less
   b. increases; less
   c. decreases; more
   d. increases; more

3. The paradox of value refers to the
   a. utility-maximizing rule.
   b. fact that water is vital but cheap while diamonds are relatively useless but expensive.
   c. fact that consumers have different preferences and utility schedules.
   d. law of demand.

4. One reason why water is cheap is because the
   a. marginal utility of water is enormous.
   b. marginal utility of water is small.
   c. marginal utility of water is negative.
   d. total utility of water is small.

5. In the paradox of value between expensive diamonds and inexpensive water, we see that
a. the consumer surpluses are very high for both goods.
b. diamonds have a low consumer surplus while water has a high consumer surplus.
c. diamonds have a high consumer surplus while water has a low consumer surplus.
d. the consumer surpluses are very low for both goods.

Complete the graph

1. Figure 10.3 shows the market for water. Indicate the equilibrium price and then shade in the area of the consumer surplus.

■ FIGURE 10.3
Price (dollars per thousand litres)

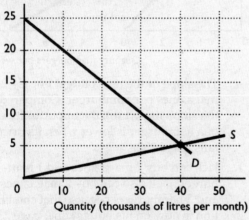

2. Figure 10.4 shows the market for rubies. Indicate the equilibrium price and then shade in the area of the consumer surplus.

■ FIGURE 10.4
Price (thousands of dollars per carat)

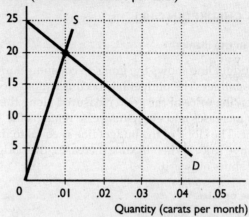

3. Based on Figures 10.3 and 10.4, is there more consumer surplus for water or rubies? Which is larger: the marginal utility of a litre of water or a carat of rubies?

Short answer

1. Bobby consumes potato chips and Gatorade and is maximizing his total utility. His marginal utility from the last bag of chips he eats is 40 and his marginal utility from the last bottle of Gatorade he drinks is 60. The price of a bag of chips is $2. What is the price of a bottle of Gatorade?

2. Does the price Bianca is willing to pay for another purse depend on her total utility from purses or her marginal utility? Explain your answer.

3. What is the paradox of value and what is its solution?

SELF TEST ANSWERS

■ CHECKPOINT 10.1

Fill in the blanks

A <u>budget</u> line shows the limits to consumption possibilities. The budget line becomes <u>more</u> steep when the price of the good measured along the *x*-axis increases and everything else remains the same. The slope of the budget line is equal to the <u>relative</u> price. When income increases, the budget line shifts <u>outward</u>.

True or false

1. True; page 230
2. False; page 231
3. True; page 232
4. False; page 233
5. True; page 234

Multiple choice

1. d; page 230
2. b; page 230
3. b; page 230
4. d; page 232
5. a; page 232
6. c; page 233
7. c; page 234
8. a; page 234

Complete the graph

1. a. The budget line in Figure 10.5, which is labelled Hamburgers $4 is Jack's budget line; page 230.
   b. The slope of the budget line equals (–4 magazines ÷ 3 hamburgers), which is –4/3 magazines per hamburger. The slope tells us that the opportunity cost of a hamburger is 4/3 magazines and the relative price of a hamburger is 4/3 magazines; page 233.
   c. Jack can buy 2 magazines and 1 hamburger. Jack cannot buy 2 magazines and 3 hamburgers because that combination is outside his budget line; page 231.
   d. The new budget line is in Figure 10.5, labelled Hamburgers $2; page 230.

■ **FIGURE 10.5**

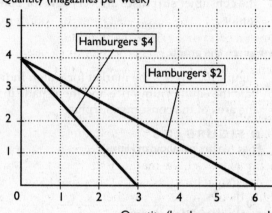

   e. The slope of the new budget line is –2/3 magazines per hamburger. Compared to the slope in part (b), the opportunity cost of a hamburger is lower when its price falls; page 232.
   f. Jack can buy 2 magazines and 1 hamburger. Jack also can buy 2 magazines and 3 hamburgers because that combination is now on his budget line; page 231.

Short answer

1. A budget line is similar to a production possibilities frontier. Both curves show a limit to what is feasible. The *PPF* is a technological limit that does not depend on prices. But the budget line does depend on prices. Consumption possibilities change when prices or the available budget change; page 231.

2. The slope of the budget line equals the opportunity cost and the relative price of the good measured along the *x*-axis; page 232.

3. The relative price is the price of one good in terms of another good. The relative price is an opportunity cost. It equals the price of one good divided by the price of another good; page 233.

4. The budget line shifts outward. Its slope does not change; page 234.

■ CHECKPOINT 10.2

Fill in the blanks

The total benefit a person gets from the consumption of a good or service is <u>total</u> utility. The change in total utility that results from a one-unit increase in the quantity of a good consumed is <u>marginal</u> utility. As the quantity of a good consumed increases, total utility <u>increases</u> and marginal utility <u>decreases</u>. The marginal utility per dollar spent equals the marginal utility of a good <u>divided</u> by the price of the good. When total utility is maximized, the marginal utility per dollar spent <u>is equal</u> for all goods. Diminishing marginal utility theory implies that other things remaining the same, the <u>higher</u> the price of a good, the smaller is the quantity demanded of that good. If, as the quantity consumed of a good increases, marginal utility decreases quickly, the demand for the good is <u>inelastic</u>.

True or false

1. True; page 236
2. False; page 237
3. False; page 240
4. True; page 240
5. False; pages 242-243

Multiple choice

1. c; page 236
2. a; page 237
3. d; page 237
4. b; page 241
5. b; page 240
6. c; page 242
7. a; page 242
8. b; page 244

Complete the graph

1. a. The completed table is below; page 237.

Pizza			Pop		
Quantity (slices per day)	Total utility	Marginal utility	Quantity (cans per day)	Total utility	Marginal utility
0	0	<u>0</u>	0	0	<u>0</u>
1	45	<u>45</u>	1	25	<u>25</u>
2	85	<u>40</u>	2	45	<u>20</u>
3	120	<u>35</u>	3	60	<u>15</u>
4	150	<u>30</u>	4	70	<u>10</u>
5	175	<u>25</u>	5	75	<u>5</u>
6	195	<u>20</u>	6	76	<u>1</u>

b. Bertha consumes 2 cans of pop and 2 slices of pizza. This combination allocates all her budget and the marginal utility per dollar spent for pop and pizza both equal 20; page 240.

c. Bertha now consumes 3 cans of pop and 1 slice of pizza. This combination allocates all of her budget and the marginal utility per dollar spent for pop and pizza both equal 15; page 240.

d. One point on her demand curve is $2 and 2 slices of pizza; another point is $3 and 1 slice of pizza. Figure 10.6 shows Bertha's demand curve; page 243.

■ FIGURE 10.6

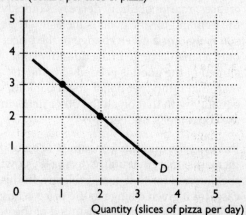

Short answer

1. The completed table is below; page 237.

Quantity (bottles of Aquafina per day)	Total utility	Marginal utility
0	0	
1	25	25
2	45	20
3	60	15
4	70	10
5	75	5
6	76	1

2a. Lisa will buy 4 tacos and 2 hamburgers because this combination allocates her entire budget and sets the marginal utility per dollar spent on tacos equal to the marginal utility per dollar spent on hamburgers; page 240.

b. Lisa will buy 2 tacos and 2 hamburgers. This combination allocates her entire budget and sets the marginal utility per dollar spent on tacos equal to the marginal utility per dollar spent on hamburgers; page 240.

c. When the price of a taco rises, the quantity of tacos demanded decreases; page 242.

3. To "allocate the entire available budget" means that we use the entire available budget. Using the entire budget doesn't mean not saving anything. The available budget is the amount available after choosing how much to save; page 240.

4. If, as the quantity consumed of a good increases, marginal utility decreases quickly, the demand for the good is inelastic. The reason is that for a given change in the price, only a small change in the quantity consumed of the good is needed to bring its marginal utility per dollar spent bank to equality with that on all the other items in the consumer's budget.

But if, as the quantity consumed of a good increases, marginal utility decreases slowly, the demand for that good is elastic. In this case, for a given change in the price, a large change in the quantity consumed of the good is needed to bring its marginal utility per dollar spent back to equality with that on all the other items in the consumer's budget; page 244.

5. Marginal analysis compares the marginal gain from having more of one good with the marginal loss from having less of another good. The "equalize the marginal utility per dollar spent" rule is the result of marginal analysis. Suppose the marginal utility per dollar spent on a blouse exceeds that of a dollar spent on a purse. Marginal analysis indicates that the consumer increases her total utility by spending a dollar less on purses and spending a dollar more on blouses because the gain in utility from the dollar spent on blouses exceeds the loss in utility from the dollar reduction on purses; page 244.

■ **CHECKPOINT 10.3**

Fill in the blanks

Marginal benefit is the maximum price a consumer is willing to pay for an extra unit of a good or service when total utility is maximized. The paradox of value is resolved by noting that diamonds have a high price, a low total utility, and a high marginal utility. Water provides more consumer surplus than diamonds.

True or false

1. True; page 246
2. True; page 246
3. False; page 246
4. False; page 246
5. True; page 246

Multiple choice

1. d; page 246
2. a; page 246
3. b; page 246
4. b; page 246
5. b; page 247

Complete the graph

1. The equilibrium price is $5 per thousand litres of water. The consumer surplus is the grey area in Figure 10.7; page 247.

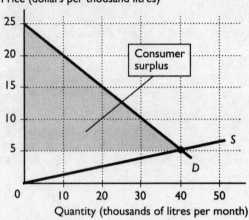

■ FIGURE 10.7

2. The equilibrium price is $20,000 a carat. Figure 10.8 shows the consumer surplus; page 247.

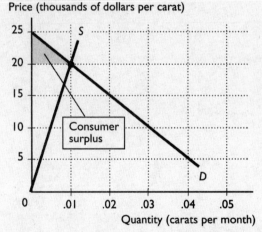

■ FIGURE 10.8

3. There is more consumer surplus for water than rubies. Because the price of a carat of rubies is much greater than the price of a litre of water, it must be the case that the marginal utility of a carat of rubies is much greater than the marginal utility of a litre of water; page 246.

Short answer

1. Bobby maximizes his total utility by consuming the combination of chips and Gatorade such that the marginal utility per dollar spent on chips equals the marginal utility per dollar spend on Gatorade. The marginal utility from the last bag of chips is 40 and the price of a bag of chips is $2, so the marginal utility per dollar spent is 40 ÷ $2 = 20. Because the marginal utility of the Gatorade is 60, the price is $3 to make the marginal utility per dollar spent equal to 20; page 246.

2. The price Bianca is willing to pay for another purse depends on marginal utility. Bianca maximizes her total utility by making her marginal utility per dollar spent equal for all goods. If her marginal utility from an additional purse is high, she is willing to pay a high price for the next purse; page 246.

3. The paradox of value is that water, which is essential for life, is cheap while diamonds are relatively useless but expensive. The solution to the paradox is that people consume a lot of water, so the marginal utility of an additional litre of water is very low. People consume only a few diamonds, so the marginal utility of an additional diamond is quite high. A household maximizes its total utility when the marginal utility per dollar spent is equal for all goods. So water has a low marginal utility and a low price and diamonds have a high marginal utility and a high price; page 246.

Chapter 10

Appendix: Indifference Curves

APPENDIX IN PERSPECTIVE

The appendix uses indifference curves and budget lines to derive a demand curve.

■ Indifference curves

An indifference curve is a line that shows combinations of goods among which a consumer is indifferent. All combinations above the indifference curve are preferred to those on the indifference curve and all combinations on the indifference curve are preferred to those below the indifference curve. The marginal rate of substitution, *MRS*, is the rate at which a person will give up good y (the good measured on the y-axis) to get more of good x (the good measured on the x-axis) and at the same time remain on the same indifference curve. The magnitude of the slope of the indifference curve equals the marginal rate of substitution. The marginal rate of substitution diminishes as the consumer moves along an indifference curve, increasing consumption of the good measured on the x-axis and decreasing consumption of the good measured on the y-axis. The consumer is at his best affordable point when he is on his budget line, is on his highest attainable indifference curve, and has a marginal rate of substitution equal to the relative price of the two goods. We can use the indifference curve model to generate a demand curve.

EXPANDED APPENDIX CHECKLIST

1 An indifference curve.
- Define and draw an indifference curve.
- State which consumption combinations are more preferred and which are less preferred to those on an indifference curve.

2 Marginal rate of substitution.
- Define the marginal rate of substitution and explain how the marginal rate of substitution is measured.
- Discuss the key assumption of consumer theory.

3 Consumer equilibrium.
- Describe the best affordable point.
- Discuss when the marginal rate of substitution of equals relative price.

4 Deriving the demand curve.
- Derive a demand curve using indifference curves and budget lines.

KEY TERMS

- Diminishing marginal rate of substitution (page 252)
- Indifference curve (page 251)
- Marginal rate of substitution (page 252)

CHECKPOINT A10.1

■ **Indifference curves**

Additional Practice Problems A10.1a

1. Figure A10.1 shows one of Maria's indifference curves between ice cream cones and milkshakes.

■ **FIGURE A10.1**

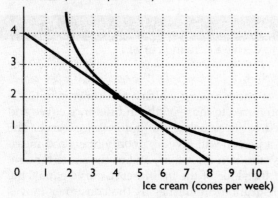

Lightly shade combinations of cones and milkshakes that are more preferred to those on the indifference curve. More heavily shade combinations that are less preferred to those on the indifference curve.

2. In Figure A10.1, what is Maria's marginal rate of substitution when she is consuming 4 ice cream cones and 2 milkshakes?

3. In Figure A10.2, what is Maria's best affordable point?

■ **FIGURE A10.2**

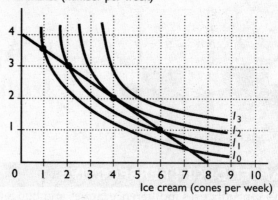

Solution to Additional Practice Problems 1

1. Figure A10.1 shows one of Maria's indifference curves between ice cream cones and milkshakes. Lightly shade combinations of cones and milkshakes that are more preferred to those on the indifference curve. More heavily shade combinations that are less preferred to those on the indifference curve.

Figure A10.3 shows that all combinations above the indifference curve are more preferred to those on it and all combinations below the indifference curve are less preferred to those on it.

■ **FIGURE A10.3**

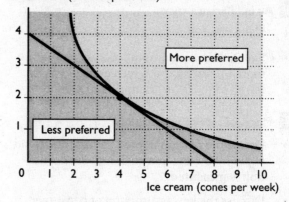

2. In Figure A10.1, what is Maria's marginal rate of substitution when she is consuming 4 ice cream cones and 2 milkshakes?

Maria's marginal rate of substitution equals the magnitude of the slope of the indifference curve. Use the straight line that touches the combination of 4 ice cream cones and 2 milkshakes and touches the indifference curve at only that point. The magnitude of the slope of this line is 1/2 of a milkshake per ice cream cone, so Maria's marginal rate of substitution is 1/2 of a milkshake per ice cream cone.

3. **In Figure A10.2, what is Maria's best affordable point?**

Figure A10.4 shows Maria's best affordable point. This point is on Maria's budget line and also on the highest attainable indifference curve, I_2.

■ **FIGURE A10.4**
Milkshakes (number per week)

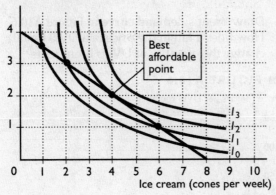

■ **Self Test 1**

Fill in the blanks

An ____ (equilibrium; indifference) curve is a curve that shows combinations of goods among which a consumer is indifferent. A consumer prefers being on a ____ (lower; higher) indifference curve. The magnitude of the slope of an indifference curve equals the ____ (marginal rate of substitution; rate of consumer equilibrium). The best affordable point occurs at the point on the highest attainable indifference curve where the magnitude of the slope of the budget line ____ (equals; is greater than; is less than) the marginal rate of substitution.

True or false

1. Tara is indifferent among combinations of goods that are on her indifference curve.

2. A consumer is indifferent among combinations on different indifference curves.

3. The marginal rate of substitution is the rate at which a person will give up the good measured on the y-axis to get more of the good measured on the x-axis and at the same time remain indifferent.

4. When Sara is on her budget line, she is always at her best affordable point.

5. Along a demand curve that is derived using indifference curves, the quantity of the good demanded increases when the price rises.

Multiple choice

1. An indifference curve is a line that shows combinations of goods among which a consumer
   a. prefers one over the other.
   b. places no value on any of the items.
   c. can afford to buy all the combinations.
   d. is indifferent.

2. What is the difference between a budget line and an indifference curve?
   a. One is measured in dollars while the other is measured in units of goods.
   b. One shows what is possible while the other shows what is preferred.
   c. One shows a positive relationship and the other shows a negative relationship.
   d. There is no difference.

3. In a preference map, combinations on higher indifference curves ____ on a lower indifference curve.
   a. always cost more than any combination
   b. are preferred to combinations on
   c. always cost less than any combination
   d. are less preferred than combinations

4. The marginal rate of substitution is
  a. the consumer surplus.
  b. the same as the consumer's budget line.
  c. equal to the magnitude of the slope of the indifference curve.
  d. equal to the magnitude of the slope of the consumer surplus curve.

5. At her best affordable point, Erin
  a. is on her budget line.
  b. is on the highest attainable indifference curve.
  c. has a marginal rate of substitution equal to the relative price of the goods.
  d. All of the above answers are correct.

6. When Ralph is at his best affordable point, the marginal rate of substitution is
  a. greater than the relative price.
  b. equal to the relative price.
  c. less than the relative price.
  d. maximized.

7. To derive a demand curve using indifference curves, you must change the
  a. consumer's preferences.
  b. consumer's budget.
  c. price of one good, holding the price of the other good and budget constant.
  d. price of both goods simultaneously.

Complete the graph

1. Figure A10.5 shows two of Brent's indifference curves.

  a. Brent's budget is $40 a month and the price of a movie and renting a DVD are $10 each. Draw Brent's budget line in Figure A10.5. How many DVDs does Brent rent a month?

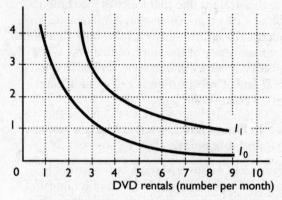

■ FIGURE A10.5
Movies (number per month)

  b. Draw Brent's new budget line in Figure A10.5 if the price of a DVD rental falls to $5 and everything else remains the same. How many DVDs does Brent now rent per month?

  c. Draw Brent's demand curve in Figure A10.6. How does a fall in the price of a DVD rental change the quantity of DVDs Brent rents?

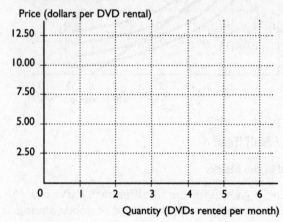

■ FIGURE A10.6
Price (dollars per DVD rental)

Short answer

1. Alberto's marginal rate of substitution between shirts and pants is 2 shirts per pair of pants. As Alberto obtains more pants, what happens to his marginal rate of substitution?

2. What is the difference between an indifference curve and a demand curve?

SELF TEST ANSWERS

CHECKPOINT 1

Fill in the blanks

An <u>indifference</u> curve is a curve that shows combinations of goods among which a consumer is indifferent. A consumer prefers being on a <u>higher</u> indifference curve. The magnitude of the slope of an indifference curve equals the <u>marginal rate of substitution</u>. The best affordable point occurs at the point on the highest attainable indifference curve where the magnitude of the slope of the budget line <u>equals</u> the marginal rate of substitution.

True or false

1. True; page 251
2. False; page 252
3. True; page 252
4. False; page 253
5. False; pages 254-255

Multiple choice

1. d; page 251
2. b; page 251
3. b; pages 251-252
4. c; page 252
5. d; page 253
6. b; page 253
7. c; page 255

Complete the graph

1a. Figure A10.7 shows the budget line. Brent rents 2 DVDs a month; page 254.

b. Figure A10.7 shows the new budget line. Brent now rents 4 DVDs a month; page 254.

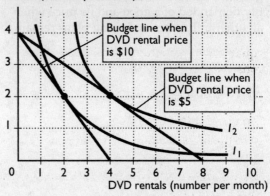

■ FIGURE A10.7

c. One point on Brent's demand curve is from part (a). When the price of a DVD rental is $10, the quantity of DVDs Brent rents is 2 a month. The other point is from part (b). When the price of a DVD rental is $5, Brent rents 4 DVDs a month. Figure A10.8 plots these two points and draws Brent's demand curve. A fall in the price of a DVD rental increases the quantity of DVDs Brent rents; page 255.

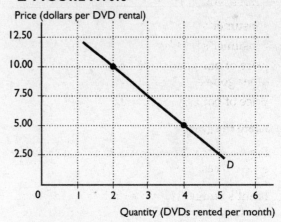

■ FIGURE A10.8

Short answer

1. The marginal rate of 2 shirts per pair of pants means that Alberto is willing to give up 2 shirts in order to get another pair of pants. As Alberto obtains more pants, his marginal rate of substitution decreases; page 252.

2. An indifference curve is a line that shows combinations of goods among which a consumer is indifferent. A demand curve is a graph of the relationship between the quantity demanded of a good and its price when all other influences on buying plans remain the same. We can use a preference map, which is a series of indifference curves to derive a demand curve; pages 251 and 255.

Chapter 11

Production and Cost

CHAPTER IN PERSPECTIVE

Chapter 11 studies the firm's costs and how these costs vary as the firm varies its output.

- **Explain how economists measure a firm's cost of production and profit.**

The firm's goal is to maximize profit. The highest-valued alternative forgone is the opportunity cost of a firm's production. A cost paid in money is an explicit cost. A firm incurs an implicit cost when it uses a factor of production but does not make a direct money payment for its use. The return to entrepreneurship is normal profit, which is part of a firm's opportunity cost because it is the cost of not running another firm. A firm's economic profit equals total revenue minus total cost, which is the sum of explicit costs and implicit costs and is the opportunity cost of production.

- **Explain the relationship between a firm's output and labour employed in the short run.**

The short run is the time frame in which the quantities of some resources are fixed; the long run is the time frame in which the quantities of all resources can be varied. Total product is the total output produced in a given period. Marginal product is the change in total product that results from a one-unit increase in the quantity of labour employed. As firms hire labour, initially increasing marginal returns occur but eventually decreasing marginal returns set in. Average product is total product divided by the quantity of an input. When marginal product exceeds average product, the average product curve slopes upward and average product increases as more labour is employed. And when marginal product is less than average product, the average product curve slopes downward and average product decreases as more labour is employed.

- **Explain the relationship between a firm's output and costs in the short run.**

Total cost is the sum of total fixed cost and total variable cost. Marginal cost is the change in total cost that results from a one-unit increase in output. Average total cost is the sum of average fixed cost and average variable cost. The U-shape of the average total cost curve arises from the influence of two opposing forces: spreading total fixed cost over a larger output and decreasing marginal returns. The marginal cost curve intersects the average variable cost and average total cost curves at their minimum points. The average cost curve and the marginal cost curve shift when technology changes or when the price of a factor of production changes.

- **Derive and explain a firm's long-run average cost curve.**

In the long run, all costs are variable. When a firm changes its plant size, it may experience economies of scale, diseconomies of scale, or constant returns to scale. The long-run average cost curve is a curve that shows the lowest average cost at which it is possible to produce each output when the firm has had sufficient time to change both its plant size and labor employed. The long-run average cost curve slopes downward with economies of scale and upward with diseconomies of scale.

EXPANDED CHAPTER CHECKLIST

When you have completed this chapter, you will be able to:

1 **Explain how economists measure a firm's cost of production and profit.**

- Explain the firm's goal.
- Compare the economic view and the accounting view of cost and profit.
- Define and give examples of explicit cost and implicit cost.
- Define normal profit and explain why it is part of a firm's opportunity cost.
- Define economic profit.

2 **Explain the relationship between a firm's output and labour employed in the short run.**

- Define short run and long run.
- Define total product and draw a total product curve.
- Define and calculate marginal product.
- Explain why increasing marginal returns and decreasing marginal returns occur.
- Define and calculate average product.
- Use a graph to explain the relationship between marginal product and average product.

3 **Explain the relationship between a firm's output and costs in the short run.**

- Define total cost, total fixed cost, and total variable cost, and illustrate the total cost curves.
- Define and calculate marginal cost.
- Define average total cost, average variable cost, and average fixed cost, and illustrate the average cost curves and the marginal cost curve.
- Explain why the average total cost curve is U-shaped.

4 **Derive and explain a firm's long-run average cost curve.**

- Define economies of scale, diseconomies of scale, and constant returns to scale.
- Explain how the long-run average cost curve is constructed and use it to illustrate economies and diseconomies of scale.

KEY TERMS

- Average fixed cost (page 271)
- Average product (page 266)
- Average total cost (page 271)
- Average variable cost (page 271)
- Constant returns to scale (page 278)
- Decreasing marginal returns (page 264)
- Diseconomies of scale (page 278)
- Economic depreciation (page 259)
- Economic profit (page 259)
- Economies of scale (page 277)
- Explicit cost (page 259)
- Implicit cost (page 259)
- Increasing marginal returns (page 264)
- Law of decreasing returns (page 266)
- Long run (page 262)
- Long-run average cost curve (page 278)
- Marginal cost (page 270)
- Marginal product (page 264)
- Normal profit (page 259)
- Short run (page 262)
- Total cost (page 269)
- Total fixed cost (page 269)
- Total product (page 263)
- Total variable cost (page 269)

CHECKPOINT 11.1

■ **Explain how economists measure a firm's cost of production and profit.**

Practice Problem 11.1

Lee was a store manager who earned $35,000 in 2000. But Lee was young and restless and decided to try a new career. He loves water sports, and in 2001 he opened a surfboard manufacturing business. At the end of the first year of operation, he submitted the following information to his accountant:

(i) He stopped renting out his cottage for $3,500 a year and used it as his factory.

(ii) He spent $50,000 on materials, phone, utilities, and the like.

(iii) He leased machines for $10,000 a year.

(iv) He paid $15,000 in wages.

(v) He used $10,000 from his savings account at the bank, which pays 5 percent a year interest.

(vi) He borrowed $40,000 at 10 percent a year from the bank.

(vii) He sold $160,000 worth of surfboards.

(viii) Normal profit is $25,000 a year.

a. Calculate Lee's explicit costs.
b. Calculate Lee's implicit costs.
c. What does the accountant calculate for Lee's profit?
d. Calculate Lee's economic profit.

Solution to Practice Problem 11.1

This Practice Problem studies the difference between an explicit cost and an implicit cost and the difference between the economic view and the accounting view of cost and profit.

Quick Review

- *Explicit cost* A cost paid in money.
- *Implicit cost* An opportunity cost incurred by a firm when it uses a factor of production for which it does not make a direct money payment.

- *Normal profit* The return to entrepreneurship. Normal profit is part of a firm's opportunity cost because it is the cost of not running another firm.

- *Economic profit* A firm's total revenue minus total cost.

a. **Calculate Lee's explicit costs.**

An explicit cost is a cost paid in money. Lee's explicit costs are $50,000 for materials, phone, utilities, and the like; $10,000 to lease machines; $15,000 for wages; and 10 percent of $40,000, which is $4,000 for interest payments. Lee's explicit costs are $79,000.

b. **Calculate Lee's implicit costs.**

Lee incurs an implicit cost when he uses a factor of production but does not make a direct money payment for its use. Lee's implicit costs are: $35,000 for wages forgone; $3,500 that could have been earned as rent for the cottage; forgone bank interest, equal to 5 percent of $10,000, which is $500; and normal profit of $25,000. Lee's implicit costs are $64,000.

c. **What does the accountant calculate for Lee's profit?**

An accountant calculates profit as total revenue minus explicit costs. Lee's total revenue is $160,000 and his explicit costs are $79,000, so the accountant calculates Lee's profit as $160,000 − $79,000, which is $81,000.

d. **Calculate Lee's economic profit.**

Economic profit is total revenue minus total cost. Total cost is the sum of explicit costs and implicit costs. So Lee's total cost is $79,000 + $64,000, which is $143,000. Lee's economic profit equals $160,000 − $143,000, which is $17,000.

Additional Practice Problem 11.1a

Gary manufactures toy gliders made of balsa wood. Each week, Gary pays $200 in wages, buys balsa wood for $400, pays $50 to lease saws and sanders, and pays $150 in rent for the workspace.

To fund his operations, Gary withdrew $162,500 from his savings account at the bank, which paid interest of $250 a week. The normal profit for a glider company is $250 a week. Gary sells $1,500 worth of gliders a week.

a. How much are the weekly explicit costs?
b. How much are the weekly implicit costs?
c. What does an accountant compute for the weekly profit?
d. What does an economist compute for the weekly economic profit?

Solution to Additional Practice Problem 11.1a

a. How much are the weekly explicit costs?

The explicit costs are the money Gary spends on wages, the balsa wood, the leased saws and sanders, and rent. The weekly explicit costs are $200 + $400 + $50 + $150, which equals $800.

b. How much are the weekly implicit costs?

The implicit costs are the forgone interest and the normal profit. The weekly implicit costs are $250 + $250, which equals $500.

c. What does an accountant compute for the weekly profit?

Accountants calculate profit as total revenue minus explicit costs, which is $1,500 − $800 = $700.

d. What does an economists compute for the weekly economic profit?

Economic profit is total revenue minus total cost. Total cost is the sum of explicit costs and implicit costs. So Gary's total cost is $800 + $500, which is $1,300. Gary's economic profit equals $1,500 − $1,300, which is $200.

■ Self Test 11.1

Fill in the blanks

The firm's goal is to maximize ____ (growth; market share; profit). A cost paid in money is an ____ (explicit; implicit) cost; a cost incurred when a firm uses a factor of production for which it does not make a direct money payment is an ____ (explicit; implicit) cost. The return to entrepreneurship is ____ (normal; economic) profit and ____ (is; is not) part of the firm's opportunity cost. A firm's total revenue minus total cost is ____ (normal; economic) profit.

True or false

1. The firm's goal is to maximize profit.
2. An accountant measures profit as total revenue minus opportunity cost.
3. All of a firm's costs must be paid in money.
4. If a firm earns an economic profit, the return to the entrepreneur exceeds normal profit.

Multiple choice

1. The goal of a firm is to
   a. maximize profit.
   b. maximize sales.
   c. maximize total revenue.
   d. minimize costs.

2. For a business, opportunity cost measures
   a. only the cost of labour and materials.
   b. only the implicit costs of the business.
   c. the amount the firm must pay the owners of the factors of production it employs to attract them from their best alternative use.
   d. only the explicit costs the firm must pay.

3. The cost paid in money to attract a resource from its best alternative use is
   a. normal profit.
   b. an implicit cost.
   c. an explicit cost.
   d. an alternative-use cost.

4. Which of the following is an example of an implicit cost?
   a. wages paid to employees
   b. interest paid to a bank on a building loan
   c. the value of capital an owner donates to the business
   d. dollars paid to a supplier for materials used in production

5. The opportunity cost of a firm using capital that it owns is
a. economic depreciation.
b. depreciation.
c. economic loss.
d. normal loss.

6. The difference between a firm's total revenue and its total cost is ____ profit.
a. explicit
b. normal
c. economic
d. accounting

Short answer

1. What is likely to happen to a firm that does not maximize profit?
2. Bobby quits his job as a dentist to open a model train store. Bobby made $80,000 a year as a dentist. The first year his train store is open, Bobby pays a helper $26,000. He also pays $24,000 in rent, $10,000 in utilities, and buys $200,000 of model trains. Bobby had a good year because he sold all of his model trains for $300,000. Bobby's normal profit is $30,000.
   a. What would an accountant calculate as Bobby's profit?
   b. What is Bobby's total opportunity cost? What is his economic profit?
3. Why are wages a cost to a business? Why is a normal profit a cost to a business?

CHECKPOINT 11.2

■ **Explain the relationship between a firm's output and labour employed in the short run.**

Practice Problem 11.2

Tom leases a farmer's field and grows strawberries. Tom hires students to pick and pack the strawberries. The table sets out Tom's total product schedule.

Labour (students per day)	Total product (boxes per day)
0	0
1	100
2	220
3	300
4	360
5	400
6	420
7	430

a. Calculate the marginal product of the third student.
b. Calculate the average product of three students.
c. Over what numbers of students does marginal product increase?
d. When marginal product increases, compare average product and marginal product.

Solution to Practice Problem 11.2

This Practice Problem emphasizes the relationship between marginal product and average product. For employment levels at which marginal product exceeds average product, the average product curve slopes upward and average product increases as more labour is employed. For employment levels at which marginal product is less than average product, the average product curve slopes downward and average product decreases as more labour is employed.

Quick Review

- *Marginal product* The change in total product that results from a one-unit increase in the quantity of labour employed. Marginal product equals the change in total product divided by the change in the quantity of labour.

a. **Calculate the marginal product of the third student.**

The marginal product of the third student is the change in total product that results from hiring the third student. The marginal product of the third students equals the total product of 3 students, which is 300 boxes of strawberries a day minus the total product of 2 students, which is 220 boxes a day. So the marginal product of the third student is 300 boxes a day − 220 boxes a day, which is 80 boxes of strawberries a day.

b. **Calculate the average product of three students.**

Average product is calculated as total product divided by the quantity of labour. When Tom hires 3 students, total product is 300 boxes of strawberries a day. So the average product of three students is (300 boxes a day) ÷ (3 students), which is 100 boxes a day per student.

c. **Over what numbers of students does marginal product increase?**

The marginal product of the first student is 100 boxes of strawberries a day. The marginal product of the second student is 120 boxes of strawberries a day. And the marginal product of the third student is 80 boxes of strawberries a day. Marginal product increases when Tom hires the first and second students.

d. **When marginal product increases, compare average product and marginal product.**

When Tom hires 1 student, marginal product is 100 boxes of strawberries a day and average product is also 100 boxes of strawberries a day. When Tom hires 2 students, marginal product is 120 boxes of strawberries a day and average product is 110 boxes of strawberries a day. When marginal product increases, average product also increases, and marginal product is greater than average product.

Additional Practice Problem 11.2a

The first five members of the men's basketball squad are each 185 centimetres tall. A sixth player, whose height is 215 centimetres, is added. Has the average height increased or decreased with the addition of this player? A seventh player, whose height is 155 centimetres, is added. What happens to the team's average height? An eighth player, whose height is 185 centimetres, is added. What is the effect on the average height? What is the general rule about how the marginal player's height changes the average height of the team?

Solution to Additional Practice Problem 11.2a

The player who is 215 centimetres tall is above the average height, so adding him to the team increases the average height. The player who is 155 centimetres tall is below the average height, so adding him decreases the average height. When the player who is 185 centimetres tall is added, the team's average height equals 185 centimetres, so his addition has no effect on the average height. The general rule is that when a marginal value lies above the average, the average rises. When the marginal value is below the average, the average falls. And when the marginal value equals the average, the average does not change.

■ **Self Test 11.2**

Fill in the blanks

The time frame in which the quantities of some resources are fixed is the ____ (long; market; short) run and the time frame in which the quantities of all resources can be changed is the _____ (long; market; short) run. Marginal product equals ____ (total product; the change in total product) divided by the ____ (quantity of labour; change in the quantity of labour). Average product equals ____ (total product; the change in total product) divided by the ____ (quantity of labour; change in quantity of labour). The law of decreasing returns states that as a firm uses more of a ____ (fixed; variable) input, with a given quantity of ____ (fixed; variable) inputs, the marginal product of the ____ (fixed; variable) input eventually decreases. If marginal product exceeds average product, the average product curve slopes ____ (downward; upward).

True or false

1. In the short run, the firm's fixed inputs cannot be changed.

2. Points on and below the total product curve are efficient.

3. Most production processes initially have decreasing marginal returns followed eventually by increasing marginal returns.
4. When the marginal product of labour exceeds the average product of labour, the average product curve is downward sloping.

Multiple choice

1. The short run is a time period during which
a. some of the firm's resources are fixed.
b. all of the firm's resources are fixed.
c. all of the firm's resources are variable.
d. the firm cannot increase its output.

2. In the short run, firms increase output by
a. increasing the size of their plant.
b. decreasing the size of their plant.
c. increasing the amount of labour used.
d. decreasing the amount of labour used.

3. If we compare the short run to the long run, we find that the
a. short run for a firm can be longer than the long run for the same firm.
b. short run is the same for all firms.
c. long run is the time frame in which the quantities of all resources can be changed.
d. long run is the time frame in which all resources are fixed.

4. Marginal product is
a. the total product produced by a certain amount of labour.
b. the change in total product that results from a one-unit increase in the quantity of labour employed.
c. total product divided by the quantity of labour.
d. the amount of labour needed to produce an increase in production.

5. Increasing marginal returns occur when the
a. average product of an additional worker is less than the average product of the previous worker.
b. marginal product of an additional worker exceeds the marginal product of the previous worker.
c. marginal product of labour is less than the average product of labour.
d. total output of the firm is at its maximum.

6. If 25 workers can pick 100 flats of strawberries an hour, then average product is
a. 100 flats an hour.
b. 125 flats an hour.
c. 75 flats an hour.
d. 4 flats an hour.

Complete the graph

1. The table gives the total product schedule at Al's Turkey Town Farm.

Quantity of labour (workers)	Total product (turkeys per day)	Average product (turkeys per worker)	Marginal product (turkeys per worker)
0	0	xx	
			100
1	100	100	
			___
2	300	___	
			___
3	450	___	
			30
4	___	___	
			___
5	___	100	

a. Complete this table. (The marginal product is entered midway between rows to emphasize that it is the result of changing inputs, that is, moving from one row to the next.)
b. In Figure 11.1 label the axes and plot the marginal product (*MP*) curve and average product (*AP*) curve. (Plot the *MP* curve midway between the quantities of labour.) Where do the two curves intersect?

■ FIGURE 11.1

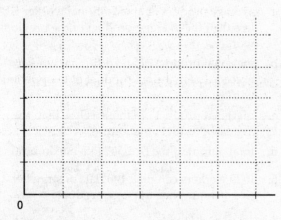

Short answer

1. What is the difference between the short run and the long run?
2. A pizzeria opens in your town. As the owner adds workers, what happens to their marginal product? Why?
3. What is the law of decreasing returns?
4. If the marginal product of a new worker exceeds the average product, what happens to the average product?

CHECKPOINT 11.3

■ **Explain the relationship between a firm's output and costs in the short run.**

Practice Problem 11.3

Tom leases a farmer's field for $120 a day and grows strawberries. Tom pays students $100 a day to pick and pack the strawberries. Tom leases capital at $80 a day. The table gives the daily output.

Labour (students per day)	Output (boxes per day)
0	0
1	100
2	220
3	300
4	360
5	400
6	420
7	430

a. Construct the total cost schedule.
b. Construct the average total cost schedule.
c. Construct the marginal cost schedule.
d. At what output is Tom's average total cost a minimum?

Solution to Practice Problem 11.3

This Practice Problem gives you practice in calculating different types of costs. Total cost is the sum of total fixed cost and total variable cost; average total cost equals total cost divided by the quantity produced; and marginal cost is the change in total cost that results from a one-unit increase in output.

Quick Review

- *Total cost* The cost of all the factors of production used by a firm.
- *Marginal cost* The change in total cost that results from a one-unit increase in output.
- *Average total cost* Total cost per unit of output, which equals average fixed cost plus average variable cost.

a. Construct the total cost schedule.

Labour	Output	TC	MC	ATC
0	0	200		
			1.00	
1	100	300		3.00
			0.83	
2	220	400		1.82
			1.25	
3	300	500		1.67
			1.67	
4	360	600		1.67
			2.50	
5	400	700		1.75
			5.00	
6	420	800		1.91
			10.00	
7	430	900		2.09

Total cost is the sum of total fixed cost and total variable cost. Tom's total fixed cost is the sum of his lease payments for the field, $120, and for the capital, $80, which equals $200 a day. His total variable cost is the wages of the students, $100 a day per student. For example, if Tom hires 2 students a day, his fixed cost is $200, his variable cost is $200, and his total cost is $400. The *TC* column in the table above shows the total cost schedule.

b. **Construct the average total cost schedule.**

Average total cost is total cost divided by output. For example, when Tom hires 2 students a day, they pick and pack 220 boxes of strawberries. Tom's total cost is $400. Average total cost is $400 ÷ 220 boxes, which is $1.82 a box. The *ATC* column in the table shows the average total cost schedule.

c. **Construct the marginal cost schedule.**

The marginal cost is the change in total cost that results from picking and packing an additional box of strawberries a day. The total cost of picking and packing 220 boxes a day is $400 and the total cost of picking and packing 300 boxes a day is $500. The increase in the number of boxes is 80, and the increase in total cost is $100. Marginal cost equals $100 ÷ 80 boxes, which is $1.25 a box. The *MC* column in the table above shows the marginal cost schedule.

d. **At what output is Tom's average total cost a minimum?**

Average total cost is a minimum at the output where average total cost equals marginal cost. The output is 330 boxes of strawberries.

Additional Practice Problem 11.3a

Pearl owns a company that produces pools. Pearl has total fixed cost of $2,000 a month and pays each of her workers $2,500 a month. The table below shows the number of pools Pearl's company can produce in a month.

Labour	Output	TC	MC	TC	MC
0	0	___		___	
			___		___
1	1	___		___	
			___		___
2	5	___		___	
			___		___
3	9	___		___	
			___		___
4	12	___		___	
			___		___
5	14	___		___	
			___		___
6	15	___		___	

a. Complete the left side of the table.

b. **Suppose that the wage Pearl pays her workers increases to $3,000 a month. Complete the right side of the table.**

c. **What was the effect of the wage hike on Pearl's marginal cost?**

Solution to Additional Practice Problem 11.3a

a. **Complete the left side of the table.**

Labour	Output	TC	MC	TC	MC
0	0	2,000		2,000	
			2,500		3,000
1	1	4,500		5,000	
			625		750
2	5	7,000		8,000	
			625		750
3	9	9,500		11,000	
			833		1,000
4	12	12,000		14,000	
			1,250		1,500
5	14	14,500		17,000	
			2,500		3,000
6	15	17,000		20,000	

The completed table is above. Total cost equals the sum of total fixed cost plus total variable cost. For example, when Pearl hires 6 workers, the total cost is ($2,000) + (6 × $2,500), which is $17,000.

The marginal cost equals the change in the total cost divided by the change in output. For example, when output increases from 14 to 15 pools, marginal cost is ($17,000 − $14,500) ÷ (15 − 14), which is $2,500.

b. **Suppose that the wage Pearl pays her workers increases to $3,000 a month. Complete the right side of the table.**

The completed table is above.

c. **What was the effect of the wage hike on Pearl's marginal cost?**

The increase in the wage rate increased Pearl's marginal cost at every level of output.

Self Test 11.3

Fill in the blanks

Total cost equals total fixed cost ____ (plus; minus; times) total variable cost. ____ (Marginal; Average) cost is the change in total cost that results from a one-unit increase in output. Average total cost equals average fixed cost ____ (plus; minus; times) average variable cost. The average total cost curve is ____ (S-shaped; U-shaped). When the firm hires the quantity of labour so that the marginal product is at its maximum, marginal cost is at its ____ (maximum; minimum).

True or false

1. In the short run, total fixed cost does not change when the firm changes its output.
2. Marginal cost is always less than average total cost.
3. The average total cost curve is U-shaped because of the influence of increasing and decreasing marginal returns.
4. An increase in the wage rate shifts the marginal cost curve upward.

Multiple choice

1. Total cost is equal to the sum of total
   a. revenue and total cost.
   b. variable cost and total product.
   c. variable cost and total fixed cost.
   d. fixed cost and total product.

2. Total fixed cost is the cost of
   a. labour.
   b. production.
   c. a firm's fixed factors of production.
   d. implicit factors of production.

3. Jay set up his hot dog stand near the business district. His total variable cost includes the
   a. annual insurance for the hot dog stand.
   b. cost of buying the hot dog stand.
   c. cost of the hot dogs and condiments.
   d. interest he pays on the funds he borrowed to pay for advertising.

4. Marginal cost is equal to
   a. the total cost of a firm's production.
   b. the difference between total cost and fixed cost.
   c. a cost that is not related to the quantity produced.
   d. the change in total cost that results from a one-unit increase in output.

5. Average total cost equals
   a. marginal cost divided by output.
   b. average fixed cost plus average variable cost.
   c. total fixed cost plus total variable cost.
   d. marginal cost plus opportunity cost.

6. One of the major reasons for the U-shaped average total cost curve is the fact that
   a. there are increasing returns from labour regardless of the number of workers employed.
   b. there eventually are decreasing returns from labour as more workers are employed.
   c. the price falls as output increases.
   d. the average fixed cost increases as more output is produced.

Complete the graph

1. Sue hires workers to produce subs at Sue's Sub Shop. Sue pays her workers $10 an hour and has fixed costs of $30 an hour. The table on the next page shows Sue's total product schedule.

Labour	Output	TC	ATC	MC
0	0	___	xx	
				___
1	10	___	___	
				___
2	25	___	___	
				___
3	35	___	___	
				___
4	40	___	___	
				___
5	43	___	___	
				___
6	45	___	___	

a. Complete the table.
b. Plot Sue's *ATC* curve and *MC* curve in Figure 11.2. (Plot the marginal cost midway between the quantities.)

■ **FIGURE 11.2**

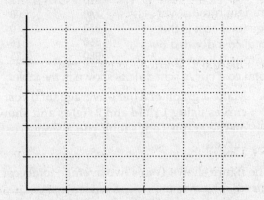

c. Sue's rent increases and her fixed cost rises to $75 an hour. Complete the following table.

Labour	Output	TC	ATC	MC
0	0	___	xx	
				___
1	10	___	___	
				___
2	25	___	___	
				___
3	35	___	___	
				___
4	40	___	___	
				___
5	43	___	___	
				___
6	45	___	___	

d. Plot Sue's new *ATC* curve and *MC* curve in Figure 11.2. (Plot the marginal cost midway between the quantities.)

e. How does the increase in total fixed cost change Sue's average total cost curve? Her marginal cost curve?

2. Label the cost curves in Figure 11.3.

■ **FIGURE 11.3**

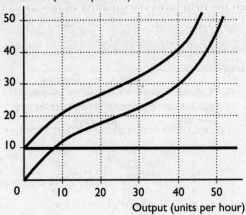

Short answer

1. What is the difference between marginal cost and average total cost?
2. Why is the average total cost curve U-shaped?
3. Where does the marginal cost curve intersect the average variable cost curve?
4. What two factors shift the cost curves?

CHECKPOINT 11.4

■ Derive and explain a firm's long-run average cost curve.

Practice Problem 11.4

Tom grows strawberries. He leases a farmer's field for $120 a day and capital for $80 a day. He hires students at $100 a day. Suppose that Tom now leases 2 fields for $240 a day and twice as much capital for $160 a day. Tom discovers that his output is the numbers in the third column of the table. The numbers in the second column are his output with 1 field and the original amount of capital.

Labour (students per day)	Output with 1 field (boxes of strawberries per day)	Output with 2 fields
0	0	0
1	100	220
2	220	460
3	300	620
4	360	740
5	400	820
6	420	860
7	430	880

a. Find Tom's average total cost curve schedule when he operates with two fields.

b. Make a graph of Tom's average total cost curves using 1 field and 2 fields and show on the graph Tom's long-run average cost curve.

c. Over what output range will Tom operate with 1 field and over what output range will he operate with 2 fields?

d. What happens to Tom's average total cost curve if he farms 2 fields and doubles his capital?

e. Does Tom experience economies or diseconomies of scale?

Solution to Practice Problem 11.4

This Practice Problem studies the construction of the long-run average cost curve and gives practice in identifying when economies and diseconomies of scale are present.

Quick Review

• *Long-run average cost curve* A curve that shows the lowest average cost at which it is possible to produce each output when the firm has had sufficient time to change both its plant size and labour employed.

a. Find Tom's average total cost curve schedule when he operates with two fields.

Total cost is the fixed cost of $400 a day plus the variable cost of $100 a day for each student hired. Average total cost is the total cost divided by output. The average total cost curve schedule is shown in the table.

Output (boxes per day)	Average total cost (dollars per box)
0	xx
220	2.27
460	1.30
620	1.13
740	1.08
820	1.10
860	1.16
880	1.25

b. Make a graph of Tom's average total cost curves using 1 field and 2 fields and show on the graph Tom's long-run average cost curve.

The figure shows Tom's two average total cost curves. The average total cost curve with 1 field is labelled ATC_1 and uses the average total costs from Practice Problem 11.3. The average total cost curve with 2 fields is labelled ATC_2. Tom's long-run average cost curve is the lower segments of these two ATC curves, highlighted in the figure.

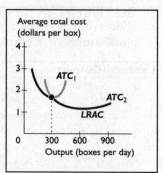

c. Over what output range will Tom operate with 1 field and over what output range will he operate with 2 fields?

Tom will operate with 1 field if he produces up to 300 boxes of strawberries a day because for this range of output, his average total cost is less with 1 field. For more than 300 boxes a day, Tom will operate with 2 fields.

d. **What happens to Tom's average total cost curve if he farms 2 fields and doubles his capital?**

Tom's average total cost increases at lower levels of output (up to 300 boxes a day) and decreases at higher levels of output (greater than 300 boxes a day).

e. **Does Tom experience economies or diseconomies of scale?**

Tom experiences economies of scale because as he increases his plant, the average total cost of picking and packing strawberries decreases.

Additional Practice Problem 11.4a

Describe economies of scale and diseconomies of scale along a long-run average cost curve.

Solution to Additional Practice Problem 11.4a

When economies of scale are present, the *LRAC* curve slopes downward. When the *LRAC* curve is horizontal, constant returns to scale are present. And when the *LRAC* curve slopes upward, diseconomies of scale are present.

■ **Self Test 11.4**

Fill in the blanks

In the long run, a firm ____ (can; cannot) vary its quantity of labour and ____ (can; cannot) vary its quantity of capital. Economies of scale occur if when a firm increases its plant size and labour employed by the same percentage, the firm's average total cost ____ (increases; decreases). When the firm has ____ (economies; diseconomies) of scale, its long-run average cost curve slopes upward.

True or false

1. All costs are fixed in the long run.
2. When a firm increases its plant size and labour, greater specialization of capital and labour can lead to economies of scale.
3. Constant returns to scale occur if when the firm increases its plant size and labour employed by the same percentage, output increases by the same percentage.
4. The long-run average cost curve is derived from the marginal cost curves for different possible plant sizes.

Multiple choice

1. Economies of scale is a condition in which
a. marginal cost decreases as production increases.
b. total cost increases as production is increased by increasing all inputs by the same percentage.
c. marginal product increases as labour increases and capital decreases.
d. when a firm increases its plant size and labour employed by the same percentage, its output increases by a larger percentage and its average total cost decreases.

2. The main source of economies of scale is
a. better management.
b. constant returns to plant.
c. specialization.
d. long-run cost curves eventually sloping downward.

3. Diseconomies of scale can occur as a result of which of the following?

a. increasing marginal returns as the firm increases its size
b. lower total fixed cost as the firm increases its size
c. management difficulties as the firm increases its size
d. greater specialization of labour and capital as the firm increases its size

4. Constant returns to scale occur when an increase in plant size

a. increases total cost.
b. does not change total cost.
c. increases average total cost.
d. does not change average total cost.

5. A firm's long-run average cost curve shows the ____ average cost at which it is possible to produce each output when the firm has had ____ time to change both its labour force and its plant.

a. highest; sufficient
b. lowest; sufficient
c. lowest; insufficient
d. highest insufficient

6. Economies of scale and diseconomies of scale explain

a. cost behaviour in the short run.
b. profit maximization in the long run.
c. the U-shape of the long-run average cost curve.
d. the U-shape of the short-run cost curves.

Complete the graph

1. In Figure 11.4, darken the firm's long-run average cost curve.

■ **FIGURE 11.4**

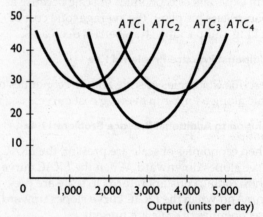

Short answer

1. Describe how a long-run average cost curve is constructed.

2. What are economies of scale? What leads to economies of scale?

SELF TEST ANSWERS

■ CHECKPOINT 11.1

Fill in the blanks

The firm's goal is to maximize <u>profit</u>. A cost paid in money is an <u>explicit</u> cost; a cost incurred when a firm uses a factor of production for which it does not make a direct money payment is an <u>implicit</u> cost. The return to entrepreneurship is <u>normal</u> profit and <u>is</u> part of the firm's opportunity cost. A firm's total revenue minus total cost is <u>economic</u> profit.

True or false

1. True; page 258
2. False; page 258
3. False; page 259
4. True; page 259

Multiple choice

1. a; page 258
2. c; pages 258-259
3. c; page 259
4. c; page 259
5. a; page 259
6. c; page 259

Short answer

1. A firm that does not seek to maximize profit is either eliminated or bought by firms that do seek that goal; page 258.

2a. An accountant calculates profit as total revenue minus explicit costs. Bobby's explicit costs are $26,000 + $24,000 + $10,000 + $200,000, which equals $260,000. The accountant calculates profit as $300,000 − $260,000, which is $40,000; page 258.

b. Bobby's opportunity cost is the sum of his explicit costs and his implicit costs. Bobby's explicit costs are $260,000. His implicit costs are the sum of his income forgone as a dentist, $80,000 and normal profit, 30,000. So Bobby's implicit costs are $110,000. Total opportunity cost is $260,000 + $110,000, which is $370,000. Bobby's economic profit is $300,000 − $370,000, which is −$70,000. Bobby incurs an economic loss; page 259.

3. Wages are a cost because they are paid to hire a factor of production, labour. A normal profit is a cost because it is paid to obtain the use of another factor of production, entrepreneurship; page 259.

■ CHECKPOINT 11.2

Fill in the blanks

The time frame in which the quantities of some resources are fixed is the <u>short</u> run and the time frame in which the quantities of all resources can be changed is the <u>long</u> run. Marginal product equals <u>the change in total product</u> divided by the <u>change in the quantity of labour</u>. Average product equals <u>total product</u> divided by the <u>quantity of labour</u>. The law of decreasing returns states that as a firm uses more of a <u>variable</u> input, with a given quantity of <u>fixed</u> inputs, the marginal product of the <u>variable</u> input eventually decreases. If marginal product exceeds average product, the average product curve slopes <u>upward</u>.

True or false

1. True; page 262
2. False; page 264
3. False; page 264
4. False; page 266

Multiple choice

1. a; page 262
2. c; page 262
3. c; page 262
4. b; page 264
5. b; page 264
6. d; page 266

Complete the graph

1. a. The completed table is below; pages 263, 264, 266.

Quantity of labour (workers)	Total product (turkeys per day)	Average product (turkeys per worker)	Marginal product (turkeys per worker)
0	0	xx	
			100
1	100	100	
			200
2	300	150	
			150
3	450	150	
			30
4	480	120	
			20
5	500	100	

b. Figure 11.5 plots the MP curve and the AP curve. The curves intersect where the AP curve is at its maximum; page 266.

■ FIGURE 11.5

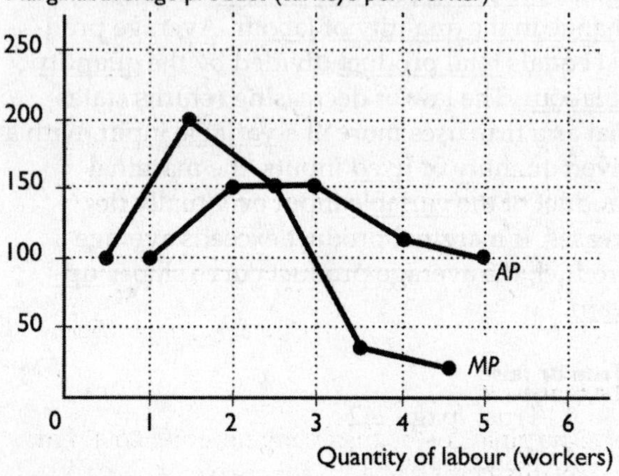

Marginal/average product (turkeys per worker)

[Graph showing MP curve peaking at 200 between workers 1-2, and AP curve peaking at 150 around workers 2-3. X-axis: Quantity of labour (workers) 0 to 6. Y-axis: 0 to 250.]

Short answer

1. The short run is the time frame in which the quantities of some resources are fixed. The long run is the time frame in which the quantities of *all* resources can be changed; page 262.

2. As the pizzeria initially adds workers, the marginal product of each additional worker exceeds the marginal product of the previous worker. The marginal product increases because the workers can specialize—some workers can make the pizzas and others can deliver them. As more workers are added, eventually the marginal product of each additional worker is less than the marginal product of the previous worker. The marginal product decreases because more workers are using the same equipment, so there is less productive work for each new worker; page 264.

3. The law of decreasing returns states that as a firm uses more of a variable input, with a given quantity of fixed inputs, the marginal product of the variable input eventually decreases; page 266.

4. If the marginal product of a worker exceeds the average product, then hiring the worker will increase the average product; page 267.

■ CHECKPOINT 11.3

Fill in the blanks

Total cost equals total fixed cost <u>plus</u> total variable cost. <u>Marginal</u> cost is the change in total cost that results from a one-unit increase in output. Average total cost equals average fixed cost <u>plus</u> average variable cost. The average total cost curve is <u>U-shaped</u>. When the firm hires the quantity of labour so that the marginal product is at its maximum, marginal cost is at its <u>minimum</u>.

True or false

1. True; page 269
2. False; page 272
3. False; page 273
4. True; page 275

Multiple choice

1. c; page 269
2. c; page 269
3. c; page 269
4. d; page 270
5. b; page 271
6. b; page 273

Complete the graph

1. a. The completed table is below; page 271.

Labour	Output	TC	ATC	MC
0	0	30	xx	
				1.00
1	10	40	4.00	
				0.67
2	25	50	2.00	
				1.00
3	35	60	1.71	
				2.00
4	40	70	1.75	
				3.33
5	43	80	1.86	
				5.00
6	45	90	2.00	

b. Figure 11.6 plots the curves as ATC_0 and MC; page 272

■ **FIGURE 11.6**
Average and marginal cost (dollars per sub)

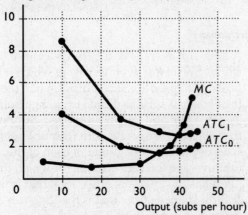

c. The completed table is in the next column; page 272.

d. Figure 11.6 plots the curves as ATC_1 and MC; page 272.

Labour	Output	TC	ATC	MC
0	0	75	xx	
				1.00
1	10	85	8.50	
				0.67
2	25	95	3.80	
				1.00
3	35	105	3.00	
				2.00
4	40	115	2.88	
				3.33
5	43	125	2.91	
				5.00
6	45	135	3.00	

e. The average cost curve shifts upward; the marginal cost curve does not change; page 274.

2. The labelled figure, Figure 11.7, is below; page 270.

■ **FIGURE 11.7**
Total cost (dollars per unit)

Short answer

1. Marginal cost is the change in total cost that results from a one-unit increase in output. Average total cost is total cost per unit of output, which equals average fixed cost plus average variable cost; pages 270-271.

2. When output increases, the firm spreads its total fixed costs over a larger output and its average fixed cost decreases—its average fixed cost curve slopes downward.

   Decreasing marginal returns means that as output increases, ever larger amounts of labour are needed to produce an additional unit of output. So average variable cost eventually increases, and the *AVC* curve eventually slopes upward.

Initially as output increases, both average fixed cost and average variable cost decrease, so average total cost decreases and the *ATC* cure slopes downward. But as output increases further and decreasing marginal returns set in, average variable cost begins to increase. Eventually, average variable cost increases more quickly than average fixed cost decreases, so average total cost increases and the *ATC* curve slopes upward; page 273.

3. The marginal cost curve intersects the average variable cost at the point where the average variable cost is at its minimum; page 272.

4. Cost curves shift if there is a change in technology or a change in the price of a factor of production; page 274.

■ CHECKPOINT 11.4

Fill in the blanks

In the long run, a firm <u>can</u> vary its quantity of labour and <u>can</u> vary its quantity of capital. Economies of scale occur if when a firm increases its plant size and labour employed by the same percentage, the firm's average total cost <u>decreases</u>. When the firm has <u>diseconomies</u> of scale, its long-run average cost curve slopes upward.

True or false

1. False; page 277
2. True; page 277
3. True; page 278
4. False; page 278

Multiple choice

1. d; page 277
2. c; page 277
3. c; page 278
4. d; page 278
5. b page 278
6. c; page 278

Complete the graph

1. Figure 11.8 darkens the firm's long-run average cost curve; page 279.

■ **FIGURE 11.8**

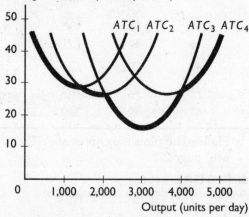

Short answer

1. A long-run average cost curve is a curve that shows the lowest average cost at which it is possible to produce each output when the firm has had sufficient time to change both its plant size and labour employed. Suppose that Alfred can operate with four different sizes of plant. The segment of each of the four average total cost curves for which that plant has the lowest average total cost is the scallop-shaped curve that is the long-run average cost curve; page 278.

2. Economies of scale is a condition in which, when a firm increases its plant size and labour employed by the same percentage, its output increase by a larger percentage and its average total cost decreases. The main source of economies of scale is greater specialization of both labour and capital; page 277.

Chapter 12
Perfect Competition

CHAPTER IN PERSPECTIVE

Chapter 12 studies perfect competition, the market that arises when demand for a product is large relative to the output of a single producer.

■ **Explain a perfectly competitive firm's profit-maximizing choices and derive its supply curve.**

Perfect competition exists when: many firms sell an identical product to many buyers; there are no restrictions on entry into (or exit from) the market; established firms have no advantage over new firms; and sellers and buyers are well informed about prices. A firm in perfect competition is a price taker—it cannot influence the price of its product. The market demand curve is downward sloping. A perfectly competitive firm faces a perfectly elastic demand. Marginal revenue is the change in total revenue that results from a one-unit increase in the quantity sold. In perfect competition, marginal revenue equals price. A firm maximizes its profit at the output level at which total revenue exceeds total cost by the largest amount. Another way to find the profit-maximizing output is to use marginal analysis. A firm maximizes its profit at the output level at which marginal revenue equals marginal cost. The shutdown point is the output and price at which price equals minimum average variable cost. A firm's supply curve is the upward-sloping part of its marginal cost curve above minimum average variable cost.

■ **Explain how output, price, and profit are determined in the short run.**

The market supply curve in the short run shows the quantity supplied at each price by a fixed number of firms. Market demand and market supply determine the price and quantity bought and sold. Each firm takes the price as given and produces its profit-maximizing output. A perfectly competitive firm earns an economic profit when price exceeds average total cost and incurs an economic loss when price is less than average total cost.

■ **Explain how output, price, and profit are determined in the long run.**

Economic profit is an incentive for new firms to enter a market, but as they do so, the price falls and the economic profit of each existing firm decreases. Economic loss is an incentive for firms to exit a market, but as they do so, the price rises and the economic loss of each remaining firm decreases. In the long run, a firm earns a normal profit and there is no entry or exit. External economies are factors beyond the control of an individual firm that lower its costs as the *market* output increases. External diseconomies are factors beyond the control of a firm that raise the firm's costs as *market* output increases. In a market undergoing technological change, firms that adopt the new technology make an economic profit. So new-technology firms have an incentive to enter. Firms that stick with the old technology incur economic losses. They either exit the market or switch to the new technology. Competition eliminates economic profit in the long run.

EXPANDED CHAPTER CHECKLIST

When you have completed this chapter, you will be able to:

1 **Explain a perfectly competitive firm's profit-maximizing choices and derive its supply curve.**

- Describe the four market types.
- Explain why a firm in perfect competition is a price taker.
- Describe the market demand curve and a firm's demand curve in perfect competition.
- Define marginal revenue.
- Discuss how a perfectly competitive firm determines its profit-maximizing output.
- Explain when a firm makes a decision to temporarily shutdown and locate the shutdown point on a graph.
- Derive and draw a firm's short-run supply curve.

2 **Explain how output, price, and profit are determined in the short run.**

- Derive the market supply curve in the short run.
- Illustrate a perfectly competitive firm that is earning an economic profit and calculate the amount of the economic profit.
- Illustrate a perfectly competitive firm that is incurring an economic loss and calculate the amount of the economic loss.

3 **Explain how output, price, and profit are determined in the long run.**

- Illustrate the case of a perfectly competitive firm in long-run equilibrium, when it earns only a normal profit.
- Explain how economic profit attracts entry, and discuss the effect entry has on the market supply, the price, and the existing firms' economic profit.
- Explain how economic loss creates exit, and discuss the effect exit has on the market supply, the price, and the surviving firms' economic loss.
- Define external economies and external diseconomies, give an example of the cause of each, and recognize them on a graph.
- Define and graph the long-run market supply curve.
- Describe the forces at work in markets with technological change.

KEY TERMS

- External diseconomies (page 302)
- External economies (page 302)
- Long-run market supply curve (page 303)
- Marginal revenue (page 287)
- Monopolistic competition (page 286)
- Monopoly (page 286)
- Oligopoly (page 286)
- Perfect competition (page 286)
- Price taker (page 287)
- Shutdown point (page 291)

CHECKPOINT 12.1

■ **Explain a perfectly competitive firm's profit-maximizing choices and derive its supply curve.**

Practice Problems 12.1

1. Sarah's Salmon Farm produces 1,000 fish a week. The marginal cost is $30 a fish, average variable cost is $20 a fish, and the market price is $25 a fish. Is Sarah maximizing profit? Explain why or why not. If Sarah is not maximizing profit, to do so will she increase or decrease the number of fish she produces in a week?

2. Trout farming is a perfectly competitive industry, and all trout farms have the same cost curves. The market price is $25 a fish.

To maximize profit, each farm produces 200 fish a week. Average total cost is $20 a fish and average variable cost is $15 a fish. Minimum average variable cost is $12 a fish.

a. If the price falls to $20 a fish, will trout farms continue to produce 200 fish a week? Explain why or why not.

b. If the price falls to $12 a fish, what will the trout farmer do?

c. What is one point on the trout farm's supply curve?

Solution to Practice Problems 12.1

To answer these Practice Problems remember that a perfectly competitive firm maximizes profit when it produces the output such that marginal revenue equals marginal cost. Also remember that a firm shuts down when price is less than minimum average variable cost.

Quick Review

- *A firm's short-run supply curve* A perfectly competitive firm's short-run supply curve has two separate parts: At prices that exceed minimum average variable cost, the supply curve is the same as the marginal cost curve above the shutdown point. And at prices below minimum average variable cost, the supply curve runs along the vertical axis.

- *Shutdown point* The output and price at which price equals minimum average variable cost.

1. Sarah's Salmon Farm produces 1,000 fish a week. The marginal cost is $30 a fish, average variable cost is $20 a fish, and the market price is $25 a fish. Is Sarah maximizing profit? Explain why or why not. If Sarah is not maximizing profit, to do so will she increase or decrease the number of fish she produces in a week?

The profit-maximizing output occurs when marginal revenue equals marginal cost. And for a firm in perfect competition, marginal revenue equals price. When Sarah produces 1,000 fish a week, marginal cost is $30 a fish and marginal revenue, which equals price is $25 a fish. To maximize profit, Sarah must decrease the quantity of fish until she reaches the output at which marginal cost is $25 a fish.

2. Trout farming is a perfectly competitive industry, and all trout farms have the same cost curves. The market price is $25 a fish. To maximize profit, each farm produces 200 fish a week. Average total cost is $20 a fish and average variable cost is $15 a fish. Minimum average variable cost is $12 a fish.

a. If the price falls to $20 a fish, will trout farms continue to produce 200 fish a week? Explain why or why not.

Trout farms will produce fewer than 200 fish per week. In the figure, the initial marginal revenue curve is MR_0. Trout farms produce 200 fish because that is the quantity that sets marginal revenue equal to marginal cost. When the price falls to $20 a fish, the marginal revenue curve shifts downward to MR_1. At the lower marginal revenue, trout farms cut their production to less than 200 fish a week, at the quantity MC and MR_1 intersect.

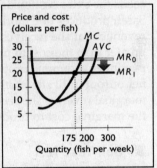

b. If the price falls to $12 a fish, what will the trout farmer do?

At $12 a fish, trout farmers cut production to the output where marginal cost equals $12. But $12 is minimum average variable cost, so trout farmers are at the shutdown point. Farms are indifferent between producing the profit-maximizing output and producing nothing. Regardless of their decision, they incur an economic loss equal to total fixed cost.

c. What is one point on the trout farm's supply curve?

At prices less than $12 a fish, the quantity supplied is zero fish. At $12 a fish, the quantity supplied might be zero or it may be the quantity determined by the intersection of the marginal cost curve and the marginal revenue curve at the price of $12. And at a price of $25 a fish, the quantity supplied is 200 fish.

Additional Practice Problem 12.1a

Suppose that Sarah, of Sarah's Salmon Farm in Practice Problem 12.1 cuts her production to a point where marginal revenue is greater than marginal cost. Explain why she is not maximizing profit.

Solution to Additional Practice Problem 12.1a

If marginal revenue exceeds marginal cost, then the extra revenue from selling one more fish exceeds the extra cost incurred to produce it. So if Sarah produces one more fish, then the marginal revenue that she receives from selling that fish is greater than the cost to produce that fish. To maximize economic profit, Sarah should increase her output until she reaches the point where the marginal revenue she receives from a fish equals the marginal cost to produce it.

■ Self Test 12.1

Fill in the blanks

The conditions that define perfect competition arise when the market demand for the product is _____ (large; small) relative to the output of a single producer. A perfectly competitive firm faces an _____ (elastic; inelastic) demand. The change in total revenue that results from a one-unit increase in the quantity sold is marginal_____ (cost; price; revenue). When a perfectly competitive firm maximizes profit, marginal revenue equals _____ (average variable; marginal) cost. When a firm shuts down, it incurs a loss equal to its total _____ (variable; fixed) cost. A firm will shut down if price is less than _____ (marginal; average total; minimum average variable) cost. A perfectly competitive firm's supply curve is its marginal _____ (cost; revenue) curve above minimum average _____ (total; variable) cost.

True or false

1. A perfectly competitive market has many firms.
2. A firm in perfect competition is a price taker.
3. To maximize profit, a perfectly competitive firm makes the vertical difference between its marginal revenue curve and marginal cost curve as large as possible.
4. Stan's U-Pick blueberry farm, a perfectly competitive firm, will shut down if its total revenue is less than its total cost.
5. A perfectly competitive firm's short-run supply curve is its average total cost curve above minimum average variable cost.

Multiple choice

1. The four market types are
a. perfect competition, imperfect competition, monopoly, and oligopoly.
b. oligopoly, monopsony, monopoly, and imperfect competition.
c. perfect competition, monopoly, monopolistic competition, and oligopoly.
d. oligopoly, oligopolistic competition, monopoly, and perfect competition.

2. Perfect competition exists when
a. many firms sell an identical product to many buyers.
b. there are no restrictions on entry into (or exit from) the market, and established firms have no advantage over new firms.
c. sellers and buyers are well informed about prices.
d. All of the above.

3. A perfectly competitive firm is a price taker because
a. many other firms produce the same product.
b. only one firm produces the product.
c. many firms produce a slightly differentiated product.
d. a few firms compete.

4. The demand curve faced by a perfectly competitive firm is
   a. horizontal.
   b. vertical.
   c. downward sloping.
   d. upward sloping.

5. The marginal revenue curve faced by a wheat producer in Saskatchewan is
   a. downward sloping.
   b. the same as his demand curve.
   c. upward sloping.
   d. U-shaped.

6. A perfectly competitive firm maximizes its profit by producing at the point where
   a. total revenue equals total cost.
   b. marginal revenue equals marginal cost.
   c. total revenue equals marginal revenue.
   d. total cost is at its minimum.

7. If the market price is lower than a perfectly competitive firm's average total cost, the firm will
   a. immediately shut down.
   b. continue to produce if the price exceeds average fixed cost.
   c. continue to produce if the price exceeds minimum average variable cost.
   d. shut down if the price exceeds average fixed cost.

8. One part of a perfectly competitive firm's supply curve is its
   a. marginal cost curve below the shutdown point.
   b. entire marginal cost curve.
   c. marginal cost curve above the shutdown point.
   d. average variable cost curve above the shutdown point.

Complete the graph

1. Figure 12.1 shows a perfectly competitive fish firm's cost curves.

   ■ FIGURE 12.1

   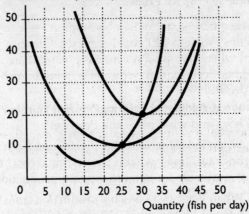

   a. Label the curves.
   b. If the market price is $40 a fish, what is the firm's equilibrium output and price?
   c. If the market price is $20 a fish, what is the firm's equilibrium output and price?
   d. What is the firm's shutdown price?
   e. Darken the firm's supply curve.

Short answer

1. What are the conditions that define perfect competition?

2. What is a "price taker?" Why are perfectly competitive firms price takers?

3. What is the difference between a perfectly competitive firm's demand curve and the market demand curve?

4. Willy, a perfectly competitive wheat farmer, can sell 999 baskets of wheat for $3 each or 1,000 baskets for $3 each. What is Willy's marginal revenue and total revenue if he sells 1,000 baskets of wheat?

5. Peter owns Peter's Porkers, a small hog farm. The table on the following page gives Peter's total cost schedule. Peter is in a perfectly

competitive market and can sell each hog for $200.

Quantity (hogs)	Total cost (dollars)	Total revenue (dollars)	Economic profit (dollars)
0	300	—	—
1	350	—	—
2	425	—	—
3	575	—	—
4	825	—	—
5	1,200	—	—

a. Complete the table.
b. What is Peter's profit-maximizing number of hogs and what price will Peter set?
c. When Peter increases his production from 2 hogs to 3 hogs, what is the marginal cost? Is it profitable for Peter to increase production?
d. When Peter increases his production from 3 hogs to 4 hogs, what is the marginal cost? Is it profitable for Peter to increase production?
e. What is the marginal cost of the third hog?
6. When will a firm temporarily shut down?

CHECKPOINT 12.2

■ Explain how output, price, and profit are determined in the short run.

Practice Problem 12.2

Tulip growing is a perfectly competitive industry, and all tulip growers have the same cost curves. The market price of tulips is $25 a bunch, and each grower maximizes profit by producing 2,000 bunches a week. The average total cost of producing tulips is $20 a bunch, and the average variable cost is $15 a bunch. Minimum average variable cost is $12 a bunch.

a. What is the economic profit that each grower is making in the short run?
b. What is the price at the grower's shutdown point?
c. What is each grower's profit at the shutdown point?

Solution to Practice Problem 12.2

In the short run, a firm can make an economic profit or incur an economic loss. This Practice Problem gives you practice in calculating economic profit.

Quick Review

• *Economic profit* A firm earns an economic profit when price exceeds average total cost.
• *Economic loss* A firm incurs an economic loss when price is less than average total cost.

Tulip growing is a perfectly competitive industry, and all tulip growers have the same cost curves. The market price of tulips is $25 a bunch, and each grower maximizes profit by producing 2,000 bunches a week. The average total cost of producing tulips is $20 a bunch, and the average variable cost is $15 a bunch. Minimum average variable cost is $12 a bunch.

a. **What is the economic profit that each grower is making in the short run?**

The economic profit on each bunch of tulips is the price minus average total cost, which is $25 – $20 = $5. Each grower produces 2,000 bunches a week, so each grower's total economic profit is (2,000 bunches) × ($5), which is $10,000 a week.

b. **What is the price at the grower's shutdown point?**

The shutdown point is at a price equal to the minimum average variable cost. The shutdown point is at a price of $12 a bunch.

c. **What is each grower's profit at the shutdown point?**

At the shutdown point, the grower incurs an economic loss equal to total fixed cost. $ATC = AVC + AFC$. So $AFC = ATC - AVC$. When 2,000 bunches are grown, $ATC = \$20$ a bunch and $AVC = \$15$ a bunch, so $AFC = \$20$ a bunch – $15 a bunch, which is $5 a bunch. Total fixed cost equals quantity times average fixed cost, which is (2,000 bunches a week) × ($5) = $10,000 a week. So the economic loss at the shutdown point is $10,000 a week.

Additional Practice Problem 12.2a

Quantity (roses per week)	Average total cost (dollars per rose)	Marginal cost
100	2.00	1.50
200	1.50	1.50
300	1.67	2.50
400	2.00	5.00

1. Growing roses is a perfectly competitive industry. There are 100 rose growers and all have the same cost curves. The table above gives the costs of one of the growers, Rosita's Roses. Minimum average variable cost is $150 a rose. The table to the right has the market demand schedule for roses.

Price (dollars per rose)	Quantity demanded (roses per week)
1.00	50,000
1.50	45,000
2.00	40,000
2.50	30,000
3.00	20,000

   a. Plot the market supply curve and the market demand curve in the figure to the right.

   b. What is the equilibrium price of a rose?

   c. How many roses does Rosita produce? What is her economic profit or loss?

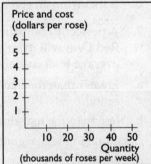

Solution to Additional Practice Problem 12.2a

a. **Plot the market supply curve and the market demand curve in the figure.**

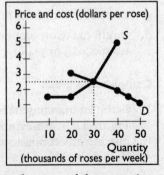

The market demand curve and the market supply curve are plotted in the figure. The quantity supplied in the market at any price is the sum of the quantities supplied by each firm at that price. Because each firm is identical, the market quantity supplied is 100 times the quantity supplied by any one firm. The firm's supply curve is its marginal cost curve above the minimum average variable cost. For example, when the price is $2.50 a rose, Rosita's marginal cost schedule shows she will supply 300 roses a week. So the quantity supplied in the market equals 100 × (300 roses a week), which is 30,000 roses a week.

b. **What is the equilibrium price of a rose?**

The figure shows that the equilibrium price of a rose is $2.50.

c. **How many roses does Rosita produce? What is her economic profit or loss?**

Rosita produces 300 roses a week and makes an economic profit. Her economic profit per rose equals the price of a rose minus the average total cost, which is $2.50 − $1.67 = $0.83. Rosita produces 300 roses a week, so total economic profit is (300 roses a week) × ($0.83) = $249 a week.

■ Self Test 12.2

Fill in the blanks

In a perfectly competitive industry, the quantity supplied in the market at any price is ____ (determined by the market demand curve; equal to the sum of the quantities supplied by all firms at that price). A firm earns an economic profit when price exceeds ____ (marginal revenue; average total cost). A firm ____ (can; cannot) incur an economic loss in the short run.

True or false

1. The market supply curve in the short run shows the quantity supplied at each price by a fixed number of firms.

2. Market supply in a perfectly competitive market is perfectly elastic at all prices.

3. A perfectly competitive firm earns an economic profit if price equals average total cost.

4. In a perfectly competitive industry, a firm's economic profit is equal to price minus marginal revenue multiplied by quantity.

5. A perfectly competitive firm incurs an economic loss if price is less than the marginal cost.

Multiple choice

1. If the market supply curve and the market demand curve intersect at 600,000 units and there are 10,000 identical firms in the market, then each firm is producing
   a. 600,000 units.
   b. 60,000,000,000 units.
   c. 60,000 units.
   d. 60 units.

2. A perfectly competitive firm earns an economic profit in the short run if price is
   a. equal to marginal cost.
   b. equal to average total cost.
   c. greater than average total cost.
   d. greater than marginal cost.

3. For a perfectly competitive firm earning an economic profit, which of the following is correct?
   a. price equals marginal revenue
   b. marginal revenue equals marginal cost
   c. price is greater than average total cost
   d. All of the above are correct.

4. The market for apples in British Columbia is perfectly competitive. An apple producer earning a normal profit could earn an economic profit if the _____ cost of selling apples _____.
   a. average total; does not change
   b. average total; increases
   c. average total; decreases
   d. marginal; does not change

5. Juan's Software Service Company is in a perfectly competitive industry. Juan's makes 1,000 services calls a month. Juan has total fixed cost of $25,000 a month, the average variable cost for 1,000 service calls is $45, and marginal revenue is $75. What is his economic profit?
   a. $5,000 a month
   b. $25,000 a month
   c. $45,000 a month
   d. It is impossible to determine with the information given.

6. If a perfectly competitive firm finds that price is less than its average total cost, then the firm
   a. will raise its price to increase its economic profit.
   b. will lower its price to increase its economic profit.
   c. is earning an economic profit.
   d. is incurring an economic loss.

7. A perfectly competitive video-rental firm in Red Deer will incur an economic loss if the average total cost of each video rental is
   a. greater than the marginal revenue of each rental.
   b. less than the marginal revenue of each rental.
   c. equal to the marginal revenue of each rental.
   d. equal to zero.

8. In the short run, a perfectly competitive firm
   a. must make an economic profit.
   b. must suffer an economic loss.
   c. must earn a normal profit.
   d. might make an economic profit, incur an economic loss, or make a normal profit.

Complete the graph

1. Is the lawn maintenance firm illustrated in Figure 12.2 earning an economic profit or incurring an economic loss? Shade the area that shows the economic profit or economic

loss. What is the amount of economic profit or economic loss?

■ **FIGURE 12.2**
Price and cost (dollars per lawn)

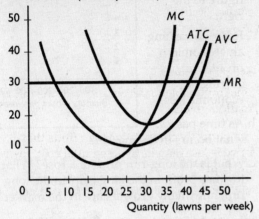

Short answer

1. In a perfectly competitive market, how is the market supply calculated?
2. If price is less than average total cost, is the firm earning an economic profit or incurring an economic loss?

CHECKPOINT 12.3

■ **Explain how output, price, and profit are determined in the long run.**

Practice Problem 12.3

Tulip growing is a perfectly competitive industry, and all tulip growers have the same cost curves. The market price of tulips is $15 a bunch, and each grower maximizes profit by producing 1,500 bunches a week. The average total cost of producing tulips is $21 a bunch. Minimum average variable cost is $12 a bunch, and the minimum average total cost is $18 a bunch. Tulip growing is a constant cost industry.

a. What is a tulip grower's economic profit in the short run?
b. How does the number of tulip growers change in the long run?
c. What is the price in the long run?
d. What is the economic profit in the long run?

Solution to Practice Problem 12.3

A perfectly competitive firm earns a normal profit in the long run. A firm will not incur an economic loss in the long run because it will shut down. And a perfectly competitive firm cannot earn an economic profit in the long run because the presence of an economic profit attracts entry, which drives down the price and eliminates economic profit. Competitive firms cannot prevent entry into their market and so they cannot protect an economic profit.

Quick Review

- *Entry* Economic profit is an incentive for new firms to enter a market, but as they do so, the price falls and the economic profit of each existing firm decreases.
- *Exit* Economic loss is an incentive for firms to exit a market, but as they do so, the price rises and the economic loss of each remaining firm decreases.

Tulip growing is a perfectly competitive industry, and all tulip growers have the same cost curves. The market price of tulips is $15 a bunch, and each grower maximizes profit by producing 1,500 bunches a week. The average total cost of producing tulips is $21 a bunch. Minimum average variable cost is $12 a bunch, and the minimum average total cost is $18 a bunch. Tulip growing is a constant cost industry.

a. What is a tulip grower's economic profit in the short run?

The tulip growers are incurring an economic loss because price is less than average total cost. The price is $15 a bunch and average total cost is $21 a bunch, so the economic loss is $21 − $15, which is $6 a bunch. Each tulip grower producers 1,500 bunches a week, so the economic loss is 1,500 bunches × $6, which is $9,000 a week. Notice that the tulip growers continue to produce because price is greater than minimum average variable cost.

b. **How does the number of tulip growers change in the long run?**

Because firms are incurring an economic loss, some firms exit the market and the number of tulip growers decreases.

c. **What is the price in the long run?**

As tulip growers exit the market, the market supply decreases, and the price rises. The price rises as long as growers are exiting, and growers exit as long as they incur an economic loss. The growers stop exiting when they earn a normal profit, which occurs when price equals minimum average total cost. So in the long run, the price rises to $18 a bunch.

d. **What is the economic profit in the long run?**

In a perfectly competitive market, the economic profit in the long run is zero. In the long run, the tulip growers will make normal profit.

Additional Practice Problem 12.3a

Growing roses is a perfectly competitive industry. Initially there are 100 rose growers and all have the same cost curves.

Quantity (roses per week)	Average total cost (dollars per rose)	Marginal cost (dollars per rose)
100	2.00	1.50
200	1.50	1.50
300	1.67	2.50
400	2.00	5.00

The above table gives the costs of one of the growers, Rosita's Roses. The table to the right gives the market demand schedule for roses. The equilibrium price for a rose is $2.50.

Price (dollars per rose)	Quantity demanded (roses per week)
1.00	50,000
1.50	45,000
2.00	40,000
2.50	30,000
3.00	20,000

a. Plot Rosita's marginal cost curve and marginal revenue curve in the figure to the right. Is Rosita earning an economic profit or incurring an economic loss?

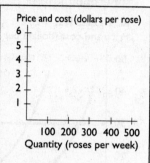

b. As time passes, what occurs in the market?

c. What is the long-run price of a rose? What is Rosita's profit in the long run? In the long run, how many growers are in the market?

Solution to Additional Practice Problem 12.3a

a. **Plot Rosita's marginal cost curve and marginal revenue curve in the figure. Is Rosita earning an economic profit or incurring an economic loss?**

The figure shows Rosita's marginal cost curve and marginal revenue curve. She is producing 300 roses a week and earning an economic profit because the price of a rose exceeds the average total cost.

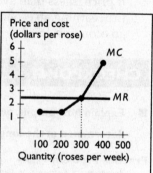

b. **As time passes, what occurs in the market?**

Because rose growers are earning an economic profit, more rose growers enter the market. The supply of roses increases. The equilibrium price of a rose falls and the market equilibrium quantity increases.

c. **What is the long-run price of a rose? What is Rosita's profit in the long run? In the long run how many growers are in the market?**

The long-run price of a rose will be $1.50, which is the minimum average total cost and rose growers earn a normal profit. When the price of a rose is $1.50, the quantity demanded is 45,000 roses a week. At a price of $1.50, each grower produces 200 roses a week. So there will be 225 growers, each producing 200 roses a week.

■ Self Test 12.3

Fill in the blanks

In the long run, a perfectly competitive firm ____ (can; cannot) earn an economic profit. In the long run, a perfectly competitive firm ____ (does not produce; produces) the quantity at minimum average total cost. Entry into an industry shifts the market ____ (demand; supply) curve ____ (rightward; leftward). Firms exit an industry when they are ____ (making a normal profit; incurring an economic loss). In a market with external diseconomies, the long-run supply curve is ____ (upward; downward) sloping. A technological change results in perfectly competitive firms ____ (temporarily; permanently) earning an economic profit.

True or false

1. When price equals average total cost, the firm earns a normal profit.
2. Entry into a perfectly competitive market lowers the price.
3. In the long run, a firm incurring an economic loss exits a perfectly competitive market.
4. External economies are factors that lower a firm's costs as its output increases.
5. New technology shifts a firm's cost curves upward.

Multiple choice

1. In the long run, new firms enter a perfectly competitive market when
   a. normal profits are greater than zero.
   b. economic profits are equal to zero.
   c. normal profits are equal to zero.
   d. economic profits are greater than zero.

2. In a perfectly competitive market, if firms are earning an economic profit, the economic profit
   a. attracts entry by more firms, which lowers the market price.
   b. can be earned both in the short run and the long run.
   c. is less than the normal profit.
   d. leads to a decrease in demand.

3. When firms leave a perfectly competitive market, the market
   a. supply curve shifts leftward.
   b. supply curve does not change.
   c. demand curve shifts rightward.
   d. supply curve shifts rightward.

4. In the long run, as firms exit a perfectly competitive industry, the economic losses of the surviving firms
   a. increase.
   b. decrease until they equal zero.
   c. decrease until economic profits are earned.
   d. do not change.

5. Factors outside the control of a firm that raise the firm's costs as market output increases are
   a. internal economies.
   b. external diseconomies.
   c. external economies.
   d. internal diseconomies.

6. In the long run, a firm in a perfectly competitive market will
   a. earn zero economic profit, that is, it will earn a normal profit.
   b. earn zero normal profit but it will earn an economic profit.
   c. remove all competitors and become a monopolistically competitive firm.
   d. incur an economic normal loss.

7. In a market with no external economies or diseconomies, the long-run market supply curve is
   a. perfectly elastic.
   b. perfectly inelastic.
   c. positively sloped.
   d. negatively sloped.

8. Technological change brings a ____ to firms that adopt the new technology.
   a. permanent economic profit
   b. temporary economic profit
   c. permanent economic loss
   d. temporary economic loss

Complete the graph

1. Through the point in Figure 12.3, draw one long-run market supply curve for an industry with external economies and another for an industry with external diseconomies.

2. Figure 12.4 shows cost curves for two firms in the maple syrup industry undergoing technological change. Firm 1 uses the old technology and has average total cost curve ATC_1 and marginal cost curve MC_1. Firm 2 uses the new technology and has average total cost curve ATC_2 and marginal cost curve MC_2. Initially the price of the product is $6 a can.

   a. At the price of $6 a can, do firm 1 and firm 2 earn an economic profit, normal profit, or incur an economic loss?

   b. As more firms adopt the new technology, what happens to market supply and price? Do firms 1 and 2 earn an economic profit, normal profit, or incur an economic loss?

   c. In the long run, what will be the new price? Will the firms an economic profit, a normal profit, or incur an economic loss?

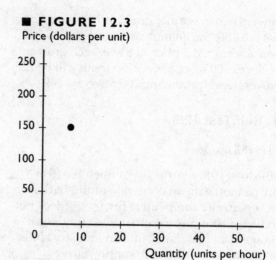

■ FIGURE 12.3
Price (dollars per unit)

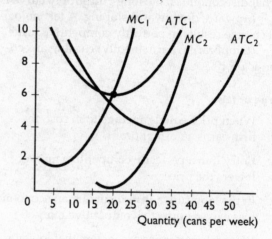

■ FIGURE 12.4
Price and cost (dollars per can)

Short answer

1. Why are perfectly competitive firms unable to earn an economic profit in the long run? Why won't they incur an economic loss in the long run?

2. What are external economies and external diseconomies? What relationship do they have to the long-run market supply curve?

SELF TEST ANSWERS

■ CHECKPOINT 12.1

Fill in the blanks

The conditions that define perfect competition arise when the market demand for the product is <u>large</u> relative to the output of a single producer. A perfectly competitive firm faces an <u>elastic</u> demand. The change in total revenue that results from a one-unit increase in the quantity sold is marginal <u>revenue</u>. When a perfectly competitive firm maximizes profit, marginal revenue equals <u>marginal</u> cost. When a firm shuts down, it incurs a loss equal to its total <u>fixed</u> cost. A firm will shut down if price is less than <u>minimum average variable</u> cost. A perfectly competitive firm's supply curve is its marginal <u>cost</u> curve above minimum average <u>variable</u> cost.

True or false

1. True; page 286
2. True; page 287
3. False; page 288
4. False; page 291
5. False; page 291

Multiple choice

1. c; page 286
2. d; page 286
3. a; page 287
4. a; pages 287-288
5. b; pages 287-288
6. b; page 290
7. c; page 291
8. c; page 291

Complete the graph

1a. Figure 12.5 labels the curves; page 292.
 b. Output is 35 units and the price is $40 a fish; page 290.
 c. Output is 30 units and the price is $20 a fish; page 290.
 d. The shutdown price is $10 a fish; page 291.
 e. The firm's supply curve is darkened in Figure 12.5; page 292.

■ FIGURE 12.5

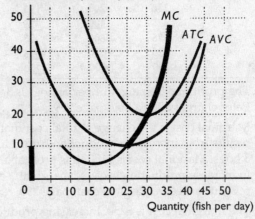

Price and cost (dollars per fish)

Short answer

1. Perfect competition exists when: many firms sell an identical product to many buyers; there are no restrictions on entry into (or exit from) the market; established firms have no advantage over new firms; and sellers and buyers are well informed about prices; page 286.

2. A price taker is a firm that cannot influence the price of the good or service it produces. Perfectly competitive firms are price takers because there are many competing firms, each selling an identical product. Any individual firm is such a small part of the market that its actions cannot affect the price; page 287.

3. A perfectly competitive firm's demand is perfectly elastic because all sellers produce goods that are perfect substitutes. So the firm's demand curve is horizontal. The market demand curve is downward sloping; pages 287-288.

4. Willy's marginal revenue equals the price of a basket of wheat, which is $3. His total revenue equals price multiplied by quantity, which is $3,000; page 288.

5a. The completed table is below; page 288.

Quantity (hogs)	Total cost (dollars)	Total revenue (dollars)	Economic profit (dollars)
0	300	0	−300
1	350	200	−150
2	425	400	−25
3	575	600	25
4	825	800	−25
5	1,200	1,000	−200

b. The profit maximizing number of hogs is 3. Peter charges $200 a hog; page 289.

c. Marginal cost is the change in total cost that results from increasing production from 2 to 3 hogs. Marginal cost is $150. It is profitable to increase production because marginal revenue exceeds marginal cost; page 290.

d. The marginal cost is $250. Increasing production is not profitable because marginal cost exceeds marginal revenue; page 290.

e. The marginal cost of the third hog is $200, which is the average of the marginal cost of increasing production from 2 to 3 hogs and increasing production from 3 to 4 hogs. Because marginal cost of the third hog equals marginal revenue, 3 hogs is the profit-maximizing output; page 290.

6. If a firm shuts down, it incurs an economic loss equal to total fixed cost. If the firm produces some output, it incurs an economic loss equal to total fixed cost plus total variable cost minus total revenue. If total revenue exceeds total variable cost, the firm's economic loss is less than total fixed cost. So it pays the firm to produce. But if total revenue is less than total variable cost, the firm's economic loss exceeds total fixed cost. So the firm shuts down temporarily; page 291.

■ CHECKPOINT 12.2

Fill in the blanks

In a perfectly competitive industry, the quantity supplied in the market at any price is <u>equal to the sum of the quantities supplied by all firms at that price</u>. A firm earns an economic profit when price exceeds <u>average total cost</u>. A firm <u>can</u> incur an economic loss in the short run.

True or false

1. True; page 294
2. False; page 294
3. False; page 295
4. False; page 295
5. False; page 296

Multiple choice

1. d; page 294
2. c; page 295
3. d; page 295
4. c; page 295
5. a; page 295
6. d; page 296
7. a; page 296
8. d; pages 295-296

Complete the graph

1. The firm is earning an economic profit. Figure 12.6 illustrates the economic profit.

■ **FIGURE 12.6**
Price and cost (dollars per lawn)

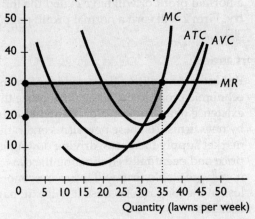

Economic profit per lawn equals the price minus average total cost, which is $30 − $20 = $10 per lawn. The quantity is 35 lawns, so economic profit is ($10 a lawn) × (35 lawns a week), which is $350 a week; page 295.

Short answer

1. The market supply in the short run is the quantity supplied at each price by a fixed number of firms. The quantity supplied at a given price is the sum of the quantities supplied by all firms at that price. For example, if there are 100 firms in the geranium market and each produces 50 geraniums when the price is $3, then the quantity supplied in the market at $3 is 5,000 geraniums; page 294.

2. The firm is incurring an economic loss. If price is less than average total cost, the firm is incurring an economic loss on each unit produced and has an overall economic loss; page 296.

■ **CHECKPOINT 12.3**
Fill in the blanks

In the long run, a perfectly competitive firm <u>cannot</u> earn an economic profit. In the long run, a perfectly competitive firm <u>produces</u> the quantity at minimum average total cost. Entry into an industry shifts the market <u>supply</u> curve <u>rightward</u>. Firms exit an industry when they are <u>incurring an economic loss</u>. In a market with external diseconomies, the long-run supply curve is <u>upward</u> sloping. A technological change results in perfectly competitive firms <u>temporarily</u> earning an economic profit.

True or false

1. True; page 298
2. True; page 299
3. True; page 301
4. False; page 302
5. False; page 304

Multiple choice

1. d; page 299
2. a; page 299
3. a; page 300
4. b; page 301
5. b; page 302
6. a; page 298
7. a; page 303
8. b; page 304

Complete the graph

1. Figure 12.7 shows the two long-run market supply curves. LS_1 slopes downward, reflecting the presence of external economies. LS_2 slopes upward, reflecting the presence of external diseconomies; page 303.

■ FIGURE 12.7
Price (dollars per unit)

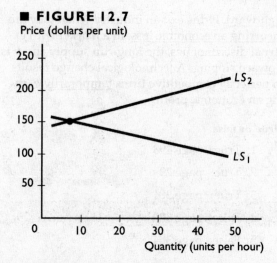

2a. At the price of $6 a can, the marginal revenue curve is MR_0 in Figure 12.8. Firm 1 produces 20 cans a week and earns a normal profit because the $6 price equals average total cost. Firm 2 produces 35 cans a week and earns an economic profit because the $6 price exceeds average total cost; pages 298, 304.

■ FIGURE 12.8
Price and cost (dollars per can)

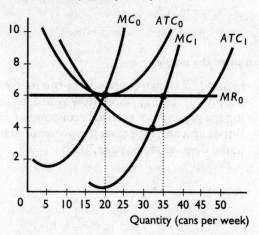

b. Market supply increases and the price falls. Firm 1 now incurs an economic loss and firm 2 earns a smaller economic profit; page 304.

c. In the long run, the new price will be $4 a can because that is the minimum of the new average total cost. Firm 1 will either have adopted the new technology and be earning a normal profit or will have exited the industry. Firm 2 will earn a normal profit; page 304.

Short answer

1. Perfectly competitive firms cannot earn an economic profit in the long run because the existence of an economic profit invites entry by new firms. As these new firms enter, the market supply increases, driving down the price and eventually eliminating the economic profit. No firm will incur an economic loss in the long run because it will exit; pages 300, 301.

2. External economies are factors beyond the control of an individual firm that lower its costs as the *market* output increases. External diseconomies are factors outside the control of a firm that raise the firm's costs as *market* output increases. An industry with external economies has a downward-sloping long-run market supply curve and an industry with external diseconomies has an upward-sloping long-run market supply curve; pages 302-303.

Chapter 13

Monopoly

CHAPTER IN PERSPECTIVE

Chapter 13 studies how a monopoly chooses its price and quantity and discusses whether a monopoly is efficient or fair.

■ **Explain how monopoly arises and distinguish between single-price monopoly and price-discriminating monopoly.**

A monopoly is a market with a single supplier of a good or service that has no close substitutes and in which natural or legal barriers to entry prevent competition. A monopolist faces a tradeoff between price and the quantity sold. A single-price monopoly is a monopoly that must sell each unit of its output for the same price to all its customers. A price-discriminating monopoly is a monopoly that is able to sell different units of a good or service for different prices.

■ **Explain how a single-price monopoly determines its output and price.**

The demand curve for a monopoly is the downward-sloping market demand curve. For a single-price monopoly, marginal revenue is less than price, so the marginal revenue curve lies below the demand curve. A monopoly maximizes profit by producing the quantity at which marginal revenue equals marginal cost and finds the highest price at which it can sell this output on the demand curve. A monopoly never profitably produces an output in the inelastic range of its demand curve.

■ **Compare the performance of single-price monopoly with that of perfect competition.**

Compared to a perfect competition, a single-price monopoly produces a smaller output and charges a higher price. A monopoly is inefficient because it creates a deadweight loss. A monopoly redistributes consumer surplus so that the producer gains and the consumers lose. Rent seeking is the act of obtaining special treatment by the government to create economic profit or to divert consumer surplus or producer surplus away from others. Rent seeking restricts competition and often creates a monopoly.

■ **Explain how price discrimination increases profit.**

To be able to price discriminate a firm must be able to identify and separate different types of buyers and sell a product that cannot be resold. Price discrimination converts consumer surplus into economic profit. Perfect price discrimination charges every consumer the maximum price the consumer is willing to pay. Perfect price discrimination eliminates consumer surplus but is efficient.

■ **Explain how monopoly regulation influences output, price, economic profit, and efficiency.**

Monopolies exist and have a potential advantage over a competitive alternative because of economies of scale and incentives to innovate. A marginal cost pricing rule sets price equal to marginal cost and the monopoly produces the efficient quantity. An average cost pricing rule, which sets price equal to average cost, covers a firm's costs and provides a normal profit but is inefficient.

EXPANDED CHAPTER CHECKLIST

When you have completed this chapter, you will be able to:

1 Explain how monopoly arises and distinguish between single-price monopoly and price-discriminating monopoly.

- Define monopoly and state the two conditions under which monopoly arises.
- Define barrier to entry, natural monopoly and legal monopoly.
- Describe how a price-discriminating monopoly differs from single-price monopoly.

2 Explain how a single-price monopoly determines its output and price.

- Calculate marginal revenue and explain why marginal revenue is less than price for a single-price monopoly.
- Explain the relationship between marginal revenue and elasticity.
- Use a total revenue curve and a total cost curve to find the profit-maximizing level of output for a single-price monopoly.
- Describe a single-price monopoly's output and price decision.

3 Compare the performance of single-price monopoly with that of perfect competition.

- Compare the output and price of perfect competition and single-price monopoly.
- Discuss the efficiency and fairness of monopoly.
- Define rent seeking and discuss its effects.

4 Explain how price discrimination increases profit.

- State the two conditions necessary for price discrimination.
- Explain why a firm practices price discrimination.

- Define perfect price discrimination and explain how a perfectly price-discriminating monopoly chooses its level of output.
- Discuss the relationship between price discrimination and efficiency.

5 Explain how monopoly regulation influences output, price, economic profit, and efficiency.

- List two potential advantages of monopoly over perfect competition.
- Define and illustrate a marginal cost pricing rule and an average cost pricing rule.

KEY TERMS

- Average cost pricing rule (page 331)
- Barrier to entry (page 310)
- Legal monopoly (page 311)
- Marginal cost pricing rule (page 331)
- Natural monopoly (page 310)
- Perfect price discrimination (page 326)
- Price-discriminating monopoly (page 312)
- Rent seeking (page 321)
- Single-price monopoly (page 312)

CHECKPOINT 13.1

■ Explain how monopoly arises and distinguish between single-price monopoly and price-discriminating monopoly.

Practice Problems 13.1

1. Monopoly arises in which of the following situations?
   a. Coca-Cola cuts its price below that of Pepsi-Cola in an attempt to increase its market share.
   b. A single firm, protected by a barrier to entry, produces a personal service that has no close substitutes.
   c. A barrier to entry exists, but some close substitutes for the good exist.

d. A firm offers discounts to students and seniors.

e. A firm can sell any quantity it chooses at the going price.

f. The government issues Souvenir Canada, Inc. an exclusive licence to produce souvenirs of Parliament Hill and the National Capital Region.

g. A firm experiences economies of scale even when it produces the quantity that meets the entire market demand.

2. Which of the cases in Problem 1 are natural monopolies and which are legal monopolies? Which can price discriminate, which cannot, and why?

Solution to Practice Problems 13.1

To answer this Practice Problem remember that a monopoly arises when there are no close substitutes and barriers to entry exist.

Quick Review

- *Barrier to entry* A natural or legal constraint that protects a firm from competitors.

1. Monopoly arises in which of the following situations?

a. Coca-Cola cuts its price below that of Pepsi-Cola in an attempt to increase its market share.

A monopoly is a market with a single firm. More than one firm exists so there is no monopoly.

b. A single firm, protected by a barrier to entry, produces a personal service that has no close substitutes.

A monopoly is a market with a single supplier of a good or service that has no close substitutes and in which natural or legal barriers to entry prevent competition. Part (b) describes a monopoly.

c. A barrier to entry exists, but some close substitutes for the good exist.

A monopoly does not arise because close substitutes for the good exist.

d. A firm offers discounts to students and seniors.

Firms other than a monopoly can price discriminate, so price discrimination by itself is not proof of a monopoly.

e. A firm can sell any quantity it chooses at the going price.

When a firm can sell any quantity it chooses at the going price, demand for the good that the firm produces is perfectly elastic. This situation occurs when the firm is in perfect competition.

f. The government issues Souvenir Canada, Inc. an exclusive licence to produce souvenirs of Parliament Hill and the National Capital Region.

When the government grants a licence, it is creating a legal monopoly.

g. A firm experiences economies of scale even when it produces the quantity that meets the entire market demand.

When a firm experiences economies of scale when it produces the quantity that meets the entire market demand, it produces that quantity at a lower price than two or more firms could. This firm is a natural monopoly.

2. Which of the cases in Problem 1 are natural monopolies and which are legal monopolies? Which can price discriminate, which cannot, and why?

A natural monopoly is a monopoly that arises because one firm can meet the entire market demand at a lower price than two or more firms could. Part (g) describes a natural monopoly. Part (b) could be a natural monopoly, but the type of barrier to entry is not specified.

A legal monopoly is a market in which competition and entry are restricted by the concentration of ownership of a natural resource or by the granting of a public franchise, government licence, patent, or copyright. Part (f) describes a legal monopoly. Part (b) could be a legal monopoly, but the type of barrier to entry is not specified.

Monopoly (b) can price discriminate because a personal service cannot be resold. Monopoly (f) cannot price discriminate because souvenirs can be resold. There is not enough information given about the type of good in monopoly (g) to determine if monopoly (g) can price discriminate.

Additional Practice Problem 13.1a

Describe the monopoly in the Canadian postal delivery market.

Solution to Additional Practice Problem 13.1a

There are legal barriers to entry in the market for the delivery of first class mail. Canada Post has the legal monopoly to deliver first class mail. But this monopoly is being weakened by substitutes such as the fax machine and courier services.

■ Self Test 13.1

Fill in the blanks

One of the requirements for monopoly is that there _____ (are; are no) close substitutes for the good. A _____ (legal; natural) monopoly exists when one firm can meet the entire market demand at a lower price than two or more firms could. A monopoly that is able to sell different units of a good or service for different prices is a _____ (legal-price; natural-price; price-discriminating) monopoly.

True or false

1. A legal barrier creates a natural monopoly.
2. A firm experiences economies of scale along a downward-sloping long-run average cost curve.
3. A monopoly always charges all customers the same price.

Multiple choice

1. A monopoly market has
   a. a few firms.
   b. a single firm.
   c. a few firms, but two dominate the market.
   d. only two firms in it.

2. There are two types of barriers to entry:
   a. legal and illegal.
   b. natural and legal.
   c. natural and illegal.
   d. natural and unnatural.

3. A natural monopoly is one that arises from
   a. patent law.
   b. copyright law.
   c. a firm buying up a natural resource.
   d. economies of scale.

4. A legal barrier is created when a firm
   a. has economies of scales.
   b. is granted a public franchise, government licence, patent, or copyright.
   c. produces a unique product or service.
   d. produces a standardized product or service.

5. A pizza producer who sets the price of a second pizza far below the first is an example of
   a. monopoly.
   b. a barrier to entry.
   c. behaviour that is not profit maximizing.
   d. price discrimination.

Short answer

1. What conditions define monopoly?
2. What are the two types of barriers to entry?
3. What are the two pricing strategies a monopoly can use?

CHECKPOINT 13.2

■ **Explain how a single-price monopoly determines its output and price.**

Practice Problem 13.2

Minnie's Mineral Springs is a single-price monopoly. The first two columns of the table show the demand schedule for Minnie's spring water, and the middle and third columns show the firm's total cost schedule.

Price (dollars per bottle)	Quantity (bottles per hour)	Total cost (dollars per hour)
10	0	1.0
9	1	1.5
8	2	2.5
7	3	5.5
6	4	10.5
5	5	17.5

a. Calculate Minnie's total revenue schedule and marginal revenue schedule.
b. Sketch Minnie's demand curve and marginal revenue curve.
c. Calculate Minnie's profit-maximizing output, price, and economic profit.
d. If the owner of the water source that Minnie uses increases the fee that Minnie pays by $15.50 an hour, what are Minnie's new profit-maximizing output, price, and economic profit?
e. If instead of increasing the fee that Minnie pays by $15.50 an hour, the owner of the water source increases the fee that Minnie pays by $4.00 a bottle, what are Minnie's new profit-maximizing output, price, and economic profit?

Solution to Practice Problem 13.2

To answer this Practice Problem, remember that a monopoly maximizes profit by producing the output at which marginal revenue equals marginal cost and charges the maximum price that consumers are willing to pay for that output.

Quick Review

- *Marginal revenue* The change in total revenue that results from a one-unit increase in the quantity sold.

a. **Calculate Minnie's total revenue schedule and marginal revenue schedule.**

Total revenue equals price times quantity and is reported in the middle column of the table. Marginal revenue is equal to the change in total revenue when Minnie increases her output by 1 bottle an hour and is reported in the third column in the table.

b. **Sketch Minnie's demand curve and marginal revenue curve.**

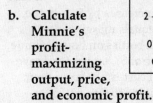

Quantity (bottles per hour)	Total revenue (dollars per hour)	Marginal revenue (dollars per bottle)
0	0	
1	9	9
2	16	7
3	21	5
4	24	3
5	25	1

The demand curve and marginal revenue curve are in the figure to the right. The marginal revenue curve lies below the demand curve.

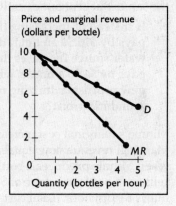

b. **Calculate Minnie's profit-maximizing output, price, and economic profit.**

The figure plots the marginal revenue curve, the marginal cost curve, and the demand curve. To find Minnie's marginal cost, find the change in total cost when output increases by 1 bottle. For example, when Minnie increases production from 2 bottles to 3 bottles an hour, total cost increases from $2.50 an hour to $5.50 an hour. So the marginal cost of increasing production from 2 to 3 bottles an hour is $3.00. The profit-maximizing output is 3 bottles an hour, where marginal revenue equals marginal cost. Minnie can sell 3 bottles an hour at $7 a bottle, so her total revenue is

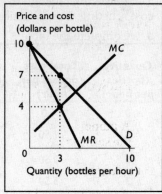

$21. And her total cost of producing 3 bottles an hour is $5.50. Minnie's economic profit is $21.00 − $5.50, which is $15.50 an hour.

d. **If the owner of the water source that Minnie uses increases the fee that Minnie pays by $15.50 an hour, what are Minnie's new profit-maximizing output, price, and economic profit?**

When the fee increases, Minnie's fixed cost increases, but her marginal cost does not change. The profit-maximizing output and price remain the same. But economic profit falls to zero.

e. **If instead of increasing the fee that Minnie pays by $15.50 an hour, the owner of the water source increases the fee that Minnie pays by $4.00 a bottle, what are Minnie's new profit-maximizing output, price, and economic profit?**

Minnie's marginal cost increases by $4 a bottle. Marginal revenue now equals marginal cost when Minnie produces 2 bottles an hour. Minnie sells each bottle at a price of $8, so her total revenue is $16 an hour. Total cost is $10.50 an hour. Minnie's economic profit is $16.00 − $10.50, which is $5.50 an hour.

Additional Practice Problem 13.2a

The following table gives part of Minnie's total cost schedule from Practice Problem 13.2.

a. Complete the table.

Quantity (bottles per hour)	Total cost (dollars per hour)	Average total cost (dollars per bottle)	Marginal cost (dollars per bottle)
0	1.0		
1	1.50	___	___
2	2.50	___	___
3	5.50	___	___
4	10.50	___	___

b. Using information in the table and in Practice Problem 13.2, plot Minnie's demand curve, marginal revenue curve, average total cost curve, and marginal cost curve. Indicate the equilibrium quantity and price, and show Minnie's economic profit.

Solution to Additional Practice Problem 13.2a

a. **Complete the table.**

The completed table below.

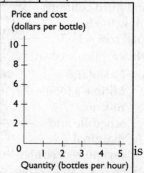

Quantity (bottles per hour)	Total cost (dollars per hour)	Average total cost (dollars per bottle)	Marginal cost (dollars per bottle)
0	1.00		
			0.50
1	1.50	1.50	
			1.00
2	2.50	1.25	
			3.00
3	5.50	1.83	
			5.00
4	10.50	2.63	

b. **Using information in the table and in Practice Problem 13.2, plot Minnie's demand curve, marginal revenue curve, average total cost curve, and marginal cost curve. Indicate the equilibrium quantity and price, and show Minnie's economic profit.**

The completed figure is to the right. The equilibrium quantity is the quantity where the MR and MC curves intersect, which is 3 bottles an hour. The price is $7 a bottle from the demand curve. The economic profit is equal to the area of the grey rectangle.

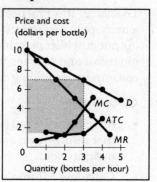

Self Test 13.2

Fill in the blanks

For each level of output, marginal revenue for a single-price monopoly is ____ (greater than; equal to; less than) price. When demand is inelastic, marginal revenue is ____ (positive; negative). A single-price monopoly maximizes profit by producing the quantity at which marginal revenue ____ (is greater than; equals; is less than) marginal cost and then finds the highest price it can sell that output by using the ____ (demand; marginal revenue; average total cost) curve.

True or false

1. For a single-price monopoly, marginal revenue exceeds price.
2. A monopoly can profitably produce an output in the inelastic range of its demand curve.
3. A single-price monopoly maximizes profit by producing the quantity that makes marginal revenue equal to marginal cost.

Multiple choice

1. For a single-price monopoly, price is ____ marginal revenue.
   a. greater than
   b. less than
   c. equal to
   d. unrelated to

2. A single-price monopoly can sell 1 unit for $9.00 or 2 units for $8.50 a unit. The marginal revenue from selling the second unit is
   a. $17.50.
   b. $17.00.
   c. $8.50.
   d. $8.00.

3. When demand is elastic, marginal revenue is
   a. positive.
   b. negative.
   c. zero.
   d. increasing as output increases.

4. A single-price monopoly produces where
   a. the difference between marginal revenue and marginal cost is as large as possible.
   b. marginal revenue equals marginal cost.
   c. average total cost is at its minimum.
   d. the marginal cost curve intersects the demand curve.

5. A monopolist charges a price that
   a. is determined by the intersection of the marginal revenue and marginal cost curves.
   b. minimizes marginal cost.
   c. is determined by its demand curve.
   d. is independent of the amount produced.

Complete the graph

1. The table gives the demand schedule for the monopoly seller of hamburgers in small town.

Quantity (hamburgers per hour)	Price (dollars per hamburger)	Marginal revenue (dollars per hamburger)
1	8.00	
2	7.00	____
3	6.00	____
4	5.00	____
5	4.00	____

   Complete the table by calculating the marginal revenue and then draw the demand curve and marginal revenue curve in Figure 13.1.

2. Figure 13.2 shows a monopoly. Label the curves. Identify the quantity produced by labelling it Q and the price charged by labelling it P. Is the monopoly earning an

economic profit or incurring an economic loss? Shade the area that shows the economic profit or economic loss.

■ FIGURE 13.1
Price and marginal revenue (dollars per hamburger)

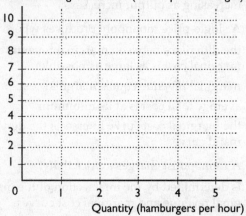

■ FIGURE 13.2
Price and cost (dollars per unit)

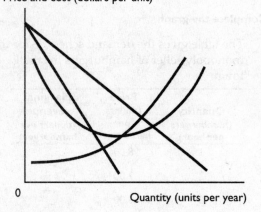

Short answer

1. What is the relationship between the elasticity of demand and marginal revenue?
2. Both perfectly competitive and monopoly firms maximize their profit by producing where $MR = MC$. Why do both use the same rule?
3. Why can a monopoly earn an economic profit in the long run?

CHECKPOINT 13.3

■ **Compare the performance of single-price monopoly with that of perfect competition.**

Practice Problem 13.3

Township is a small isolated community served by one newspaper that can meet the market demand at a lower cost than two or more newspapers could. There is no local radio or TV station and no Internet access. The *Township Gazette* is the only source of news. The figure shows the marginal cost of printing the *Township Gazette* and the demand for it. The *Township Gazette* is a profit-maximizing, single-price monopoly.

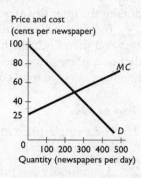

a. How many copies of the *Township Gazette* are printed each day?
b. What is the price of the *Township Gazette*?
c. What is the efficient number of copies of the *Township Gazette*?
d. What is the price at which the efficient number of copies could be sold?
e. Is the number of copies printed the efficient quantity? Explain why or why not.
f. On a graph, show the consumer surplus that is redistributed from consumers to the *Township Gazette*.
g. On a graph, show the deadweight loss that arises from the monopoly of the *Township Gazette*.

Solution to Practice Problem 13.3

Single-price monopolies create a deadweight loss. The key to this Practice Problem is to remember that a monopoly produces where $MR = MC$ but efficiency requires production where $MB = MC$.

Quick Review

- *Monopoly and competition compared* Compared to perfect competition, a single-price monopoly produces a smaller output and charges a higher price.
- *Monopoly and efficiency* A single-price monopoly creates a deadweight loss.

a. **How many copies of the *Township Gazette* are printed each day?**

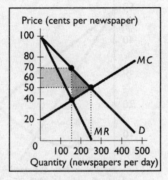

The marginal revenue curve extends from the intersection of the demand curve and the y-axis to the x-axis, halfway between the origin and the point where the demand curve intersects the x-axis. To maximize profit, the firm produces 150 papers a day, the quantity at which marginal revenue equals marginal cost.

b. **What is the price of the *Township Gazette*?**

Using the demand curve, the price that corresponds to the quantity of 150 newspapers a day is 70¢ a newspaper.

c. **What is the efficient number of copies of the *Township Gazette*?**

The efficient quantity is the quantity where marginal benefit equals marginal cost. The demand curve is the marginal benefit curve, so the efficient quantity is 250 newspapers a day.

d. **What is the price at which the efficient number of copies could be sold?**

From the demand curve, 250 newspapers a day will be bought at 50¢ each.

e. **Is the number of copies printed the efficient quantity? Explain why or why not.**

The *Township Gazette* is not printing the efficient quantity. The marginal benefit of the 150th newspaper is greater than the marginal cost.

f. **On a graph, show the consumer surplus that is redistributed from consumers to the *Township Gazette*.**

The redistributed consumer surplus is the light rectangle in the figure.

g. **On a graph, show the deadweight loss that arises from the monopoly of the *Township Gazette*.**

The dark triangular area is the deadweight loss from the monopoly.

Additional Practice Problem 13.3a

Throughout the future suppose that the *Township Gazette's* economic profit is $2 million. If the *Township Gazette* is put up for sale and bidding is a competitive process, what do you expect will be the price for which the newspaper is sold?

Solution to Additional Practice Problem 13.3a

Bidders will be willing to pay up to $2 million for the *Township Gazette* because if they can buy it for any price less than $2 million, they will receive an economic profit. Because the bidding is competitive, the price of the *Township Gazette* will be bid up to $2 million, and the winning bidder will earn a normal profit. This result demonstrates a rent-seeking equilibrium in which rent seeking costs exhaust economic profit.

■ **Self Test 13.3**

Fill in the blanks

Compared to perfect competition, a single-price monopoly produces a ____ (larger; smaller) output and charges a ____ (higher; lower) price. A single-price monopoly ____ (creates; does not create) a deadweight loss. The act of obtaining special treatment by the government to create an economic profit is called ____ (government-surplus; rent seeking). Rent seeking ____ (decreases; increases) the amount of deadweight loss.

True or false

1. A monopoly charges a higher price than a perfectly competitive industry would charge.

2. A monopoly redistributes consumer surplus so that the consumers gain and the producer loses.

3. The buyer of a monopoly always makes an economic profit.

Multiple choice

1. If a perfectly competitive industry is taken over by a single firm that operates as a single-price monopoly, the price will ____ and the quantity will ____.
   a. fall; decrease
   b. fall; increase
   c. rise; decrease
   d. rise; increase

2. Comparing single-price monopoly to perfect competition, we see that ____ consumer surplus.
   a. monopoly increases the amount of
   b. monopoly has the same amount of
   c. perfect competition has no
   d. monopoly decreases the amount of

3. Is a single-price monopoly efficient?
   a. Yes, because it creates a deadweight loss.
   b. No, because it creates a deadweight loss.
   c. Yes, because producer surplus decreases.
   d. Yes, because consumers surplus decreases.

4. Monopolies are
   a. always fair but not efficient.
   b. efficient but might or might not be fair.
   c. inefficient and might or might not be fair.
   d. both fair and efficient.

5. In equilibrium, rent seeking eliminates the
   a. deadweight loss.
   b. economic profit.
   c. consumer surplus.
   d. demand for the product.

Complete the graph

1. Figure 13.3 shows the ostrich farming market after one farmer buys all of the farms and operates as a single-price monopoly. Label the curves and show the deadweight loss. What is the competitive price and quantity? What is the monopoly price and quantity?

■ **FIGURE 13.3**
Price and cost (dollars per ostrich)

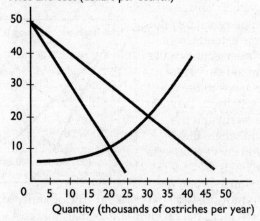

Quantity (thousands of ostriches per year)

Short answer

1. How does the quantity produced and the price set by a single-price monopoly compare to those in a perfectly competitive market?

2. What happens to consumer surplus with a single-price monopoly?

3. What is rent seeking? How does rent seeking affect society?

CHECKPOINT 13.4

■ **Explain how price discrimination increases profit.**

Practice Problem 13.4

Village, a small isolated town, has one veterinarian. For treating pets, the doctor charges a rich person twice as much as a poor person.

a. Does the veterinarian practise price discrimination?

b. Does the veterinarian's pricing system redistribute consumer surplus? If so, explain how.
c. Is the veterinarian using resources efficiently? Explain your answer.
d. If the veterinarian decided to charge everyone the maximum price that he or she would be willing to pay, what would be the consumer surplus?
e. In part (d), is the market for veterinarian service in Village efficient?

Solution to Practice Problem 13.4

To answer this Practice Problem, remember that the key idea behind price discrimination is to convert consumer surplus into economic profit.

Quick Review

- *Price discrimination* Charging different prices for a single good or service because the willingness to pay varies across buyers.

a. **Does the veterinarian practise price discrimination?**

Charging different prices to rich and poor people for the same service is price discrimination.

b. **Does the veterinarian's pricing system redistribute consumer surplus? If so, explain how.**

The veterinarian is setting the price closer to the maximum each consumer is willing to pay. Each consumer receives less consumer surplus, which is converted into economic profit.

c. **Is the veterinarian using resources efficiently? Explain your answer.**

The veterinarian is not using resources efficiently. Price discrimination creates a deadweight loss unless the monopolist can practice perfect price discrimination.

d. **If the veterinarian decided to charge everyone the maximum price that he or she would be willing to pay, what would be the consumer surplus?**

The veterinarian is now practicing perfect price discrimination. All of the consumer surplus would be converted into economic profit and consumer surplus would be zero.

e. **In part (d), is the market for veterinarian service in Village efficient?**

The demand curve becomes the marginal revenue curve in perfect price discrimination. The demand curve is also the marginal benefit curve. The veterinarian provides services until marginal revenue equals marginal cost, which is the same thing as when marginal benefit equals marginal cost and resource use is efficient.

Additional Practice Problem 13.4a

Why is the price to attend a movie less on a weekday evening than on a weekend evening?

Solution to Additional Practice Problem 13.4a

The movie cinema is practising price discrimination between two groups of buyers. Each group has a different average willingness to pay. By having two different prices, the movie cinema maximizes profit by converting consumer surplus into economic profit.

■ Self Test 13.4

Fill in the blanks

It is ____ (sometimes; never) possible for a monopoly to charge different customers different prices. The key idea behind price discrimination is to convert ____ (consumer surplus; producer surplus) into economic profit. Price discrimination results in consumers with a higher willingness to pay paying a ____ (higher; lower) price than consumers with a lower willingness to pay. Perfect price discrimination results in _____ (maximum; zero) consumer surplus.

True or false

1. Price discrimination lowers a firm's profit.
2. Price discrimination converts producer surplus into consumer surplus.
3. With perfect price discrimination, the demand curve is the marginal revenue curve.

Multiple choice

1. A firm that price discriminates
   a. divides buyers into different groups according to their willingness to pay.
   b. sells a good that cannot be resold.
   c. identifies into which group a buyer falls.
   d. All of the above answers are correct.

2. Which of the following is NOT price discrimination?
   a. different prices based on different production costs
   b. charging business flyers a higher airfare than tourists
   c. charging consumers who buy a larger quantity a lower price
   d. pricing on the basis of some easily distinguishing characteristic of buyers

3. When a monopolist price discriminates, it
   a. increases the amount of consumer surplus.
   b. decreases the monopolist's economic profit.
   c. converts consumer surplus into economic profit.
   d. converts economic profit into consumer surplus.

4. If a monopolist is able to perfectly price discriminate, consumer surplus is
   a. equal to zero.
   b. maximized.
   c. unchanged from what it is with a single-price monopoly.
   d. unchanged from what it is in a perfectly competitive industry.

5. With perfect price discrimination, the quantity of output produced by the monopolist is _____ the quantity produced by a perfectly competitive industry.
   a. greater than
   b. less than
   c. equal to
   d. almost always greater than

Complete the graph

1a. In Figure 13.4, show the economic profit earned by a dry cleaner that owns a single-price monopoly.

b. Calculate the economic profit earned by a perfect price discriminating monopoly and show the economic profit in the figure.

■ FIGURE 13.4

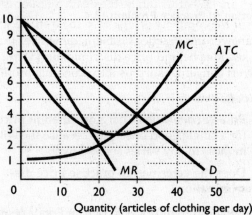

Short answer

1. Explain the effect of price discrimination on consumer surplus and economic profit.

2. When does a price discriminating monopoly produce the efficient quantity of output?

CHECKPOINT 13.5

■ **Explain how monopoly regulation influences output, price, economic profit, and efficiency.**

Practice Problem 13.5

The local water company is a natural monopoly. The figure shows the demand for water and the water company's cost of providing water.

a. If the company is an unregulated profit-maximizing firm:

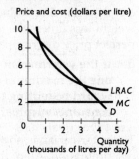

i. What is the price of water?
ii. What quantity of water would be supplied?
iii. What would be the deadweight loss?

b. If the company is regulated to make normal profit:
   i. What is the price of water?
   ii. What quantity of water would be supplied?
   iii. What would be the deadweight loss?

c. If the company is regulated to be efficient:
   i. What is the price of water?
   ii. What quantity of water would be supplied?
   iii. What would be the deadweight loss?

Solution to Practice Problem 13.5

This Practice Problem studies the implications of monopoly regulation.

Quick Review

- *Marginal cost pricing rule* A price rule for a natural monopoly that sets price equal to marginal cost.
- *Average cost pricing rule* A price rule for a natural monopoly that sets the price equal to average cost and enables the firm to cover its costs and earn a normal profit.

a. If the company is an unregulated profit-maximizing firm:
   i. What is the price of water?
   ii. What quantity of water would be supplied?
   iii. What would be the deadweight loss?

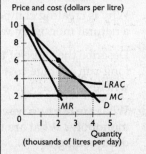

The firm produces where marginal revenue equals marginal cost. In the figure, the price of water is $6 a litre, the quantity of water supplied is 2,000 litres a day, and the deadweight loss is $4,000 a day, which is the area of the grey triangle.

b. If the company is regulated to make a normal profit:
   i. **What is the price of water?**
   ii. **What quantity of water would be supplied?**
   iii. **What would be the deadweight loss?**

The company is regulated using an average cost pricing rule. In the figure, the price is $4 a litre and the quantity supplied is 3,000 litres a day, at the intersection of the long-run average cost curve and the demand curve. The deadweight loss is the area of the grey triangle, which is $1,000 a day.

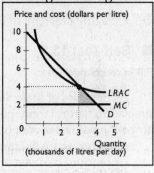

c. If the company is regulated to be efficient:
   i. What is the price of water?
   ii. What quantity of water would be supplied?
   iii. What would be the deadweight loss?

The company is regulated using a marginal cost pricing rule. In the figure, the price is $2 a litre and the quantity supplied is 4,000 litres a day at the intersection of the marginal cost curve and the demand curve. Deadweight loss is zero.

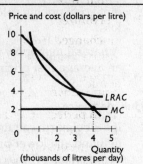

Additional Practice Problem 13.5a

If you are the owner of the natural monopoly would you want to be regulated or unregulated? If regulated, would you prefer an average cost pricing rule or a marginal cost pricing rule?

Solution to Additional Practice Problem 13.5a

You would prefer not to be regulated. If you are not regulated, price is greater than average cost and you earn an economic profit. And, if you are regulated, you would prefer the average cost pricing rule. With this rule you earn a normal profit. If a marginal cost pricing rule is imposed, you incur an economic loss.

■ Self Test 13.5

Fill in the blanks

____ (Economies of scale; Incentives to innovate) can lead to natural monopoly. Efficiency is attained if a natural monopoly is regulated using ____ (a marginal; an average) cost pricing rule. ____ (A marginal; An average) cost pricing rule allows a natural monopoly to earn a normal profit.

True or false

1. Large firms with monopoly power innovate more than smaller competitive firms which lack monopoly power.
2. A natural monopoly regulated using a marginal cost pricing rule incurs an economic loss.
3. A natural monopoly that is regulated using an average cost pricing rule incurs an economic loss.

Multiple choice

1. If a single firm can meet the entire market demand at a lower price than a larger number of smaller firms can, the single firm is
a. price discriminating.
b. a natural monopoly.
c. a legal monopoly.
d. efficient when profit maximizing.

2. What are the potential advantages of monopoly over competition for the economy?
a. There are none.
b. Monopolists earn more profit.
c. Monopolies have a higher rate of productivity growth.
d. Economies of scale and incentives to innovate are potential advantages.

3. When the government regulates a natural monopoly, the government
a. determines the price the monopoly charges.
b. insures that there is enough competition.
c. always uses the marginal cost pricing rule.
d. All of the above answers are correct.

4. With a marginal cost pricing rule, a natural monopoly produces an ____ amount of output and ____.
a. efficient; earns an economic profit
b. efficient; incurs an economic loss
c. inefficient; earns an economic profit
d. inefficient; incurs an economic loss

5. With an average cost pricing rule, a natural monopoly produces an ____ amount of output and ____.
a. efficient; earns an economic profit
b. efficient; incurs an economic loss
c. inefficient; earns a normal profit
d. inefficient; earns an economic profit

Short answer

1. Why is creating competition in a market with a natural monopoly wasteful?
2. Describe the slope of the natural monopoly's long-run average cost curve at the point where it intersects the demand curve.
3. What are the two ways to regulate a natural monopoly? What are their advantages and disadvantages?

SELF TEST ANSWERS

■ CHECKPOINT 13.1

Fill in the blanks

One of the requirements for monopoly is that there <u>are no</u> close substitutes for the good. A <u>natural</u> monopoly exists when one firm can meet the entire market demand at a lower price than two or more firms could. A monopoly that is able to sell different units of a good or service for different prices is a <u>price-discriminating</u> monopoly.

True or false

1. False; page 310
2. True; page 310
3. False; page 312

Multiple choice

1. b; page 310
2. b; page 310
3. d; page 310
4. b; page 311
5. d; page 312

Short answer

1. Monopoly occurs when there is a market with a single firm selling a good or service that has no close substitutes and in which the firm is protected by either a natural or a legal barrier to entry; page 310.

2. Barriers to entry are anything that protects a firm from the entry of new competitors. Barriers to entry are either natural barriers (the result of economies of scale) or legal barriers (the result of government actions); pages 310-311.

3. A monopoly can sell each unit of its output for the same price to all its customers or it can price discriminate by selling different units of its good or service at different prices; page 312.

■ CHECKPOINT 13.2

Fill in the blanks

For each level of output, marginal revenue for a single-price monopoly is <u>less than</u> price. When demand is inelastic, marginal revenue is <u>negative</u>. A single-price monopoly maximizes profit by producing the quantity at which marginal revenue <u>equals</u> marginal cost and then finds the highest price it can sell that output by using the <u>demand</u> curve.

True or false

1. False; page 314
2. False; pages 315-316
3. True; page 316

Multiple choice

1. a; page 314
2. d; page 314
3. a; page 315
4. b; page 316
5. c; page 316

Complete the graph

1. The completed table is below.

Quantity (hamburgers per hour)	Price (dollars per hamburger)	Marginal revenue (dollars per hamburger)
1	8.00	
		<u>6.00</u>
2	7.00	
		<u>4.00</u>
3	6.00	
		<u>2.00</u>
4	5.00	
		<u>0.00</u>
5	4.00	

Figure 13.5 plots the demand curve and marginal revenue curve; page 314.

■ FIGURE 13.5
Price and marginal revenue (dollars per hamburger)

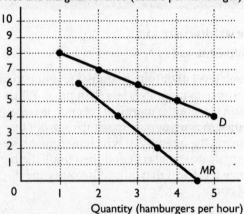

2. The curves, quantity, price, and economic profit are labelled and illustrated in Figure 13.6; page 317.

■ FIGURE 13.6
Price and cost (dollars per unit)

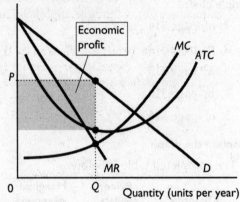

Short answer

1. If demand is elastic, marginal revenue is positive; if demand is unit elastic, marginal revenue is zero; and if demand is inelastic, marginal revenue is negative; page 315.

2. Both competitive and monopoly firms maximize profit by producing where $MR = MC$ because for *any* firm, a unit of output is produced if $MR > MC$ and is not produced if $MR < MC$. As long as $MR > MC$, *any* firm continues to produce additional output until it reaches the point at which $MR = MC$; page 316.

3. A monopoly can earn an economic profit in the long run because it is protected by a barrier to entry. Other firms might want to enter the market to earn an economic profit, but they cannot do so; page 317.

■ CHECKPOINT 13.3
Fill in the blanks

Compared to perfect competition, a single-price monopoly produces a smaller output and charges a higher price. A single-price monopoly creates a deadweight loss. The act of obtaining special treatment by the government to create an economic profit is called rent seeking. Rent seeking increases the amount of deadweight loss.

True or false

1. True; page 319
2. False; page 321
3. False; page 321

Multiple choice

1. c; page 319
2. d; page 320
3. b; page 320
4. c; page 321
5. b; page 322

Complete the graph

1. Figure 13.7 shows that the perfectly competitive price is $20 an ostrich and the quantity is 30,000 ostriches a year. The monopoly price is $30 an ostrich and the quantity is 20,000 ostriches a year. The deadweight loss is the area of the grey triangle; page 320.

■ FIGURE 13.7
Price and cost (dollars per ostrich)

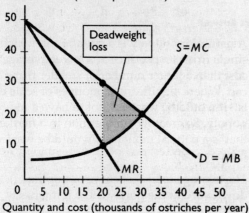

Quantity and cost (thousands of ostriches per year)

Short answer

1. The price set by a monopoly firm exceeds the price in a competitive market and the quantity produced by a monopoly is less than the quantity produced in a competitive market; page 319.

2. Consumer surplus decreases with a single-price monopoly. Consumer surplus decreases because the monopoly produces less output and charges a higher price; page 320.

3. Rent seeking is the act of obtaining special treatment by the government to create economic profit or to divert consumer surplus or producer surplus away from others. Rent seeking harms society because in a competitive rent-seeking equilibrium, the amount of the deadweight loss increases; page 322.

■ CHECKPOINT 13.4
Fill in the blanks

It is <u>sometimes</u> possible for a monopoly to charge different customers different prices. The key idea behind price discrimination is to convert <u>consumer surplus</u> into economic profit. Price discrimination results in consumers with a higher willingness to pay paying a <u>higher</u> price than consumers with a lower willingness to pay. Perfect price discrimination results in <u>zero</u> consumer surplus.

True or false

1. False; page 324
2. False; page 324
3. True; page 327

Multiple choice

1. d; page 324
2. a; page 324
3. c; page 324
4. a; pages 326-327
5. c; page 328

Complete the graph

1. a. The economic profit is the light grey rectangle in Figure 13.8. The economic profit equals the area of the rectangle, which is $60 a day; page 325.

   b. The economic profit is increased by the addition of the two dark grey areas. The economic profit is now the sum of the initial economic profit plus the additional economic profit, which is a total of $120 a day; page 327.

■ FIGURE 13.8
Price and cost (dollars per article of clothing)

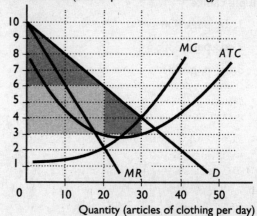

Quantity (articles of clothing per day)

Short answer

1. Price discrimination decreases consumer surplus and increases economic profit. Price discrimination allows the firm to charge a price closer to the maximum the consumer is willing to pay, which is the marginal benefit of the good. Consumer surplus is converted into economic profit; page 324.

2. With perfect price discrimination, the monopoly increases output to the point at which price equals marginal cost. This output is identical to that of perfect competition. Deadweight loss with perfect price discrimination is zero. So perfect price discrimination produces the efficient quantity; page 328.

■ CHECKPOINT 13.5
Fill in the blanks

<u>Economies of scale</u> can lead to natural monopoly. Efficiency is attained if a natural monopoly is regulated using <u>a marginal</u> cost pricing rule. <u>An average</u> cost pricing rule allows a natural monopoly to earn a normal profit.

True or false

1. False; page 330
2. True; page 331
3. False; page 331

Multiple choice

1. b; page 330
2. d; page 330
3. a; page 331
4. b; page 331
5. c; page 331

Short answer

1. A natural monopoly is a situation in which a single firm can produce at a lower average cost than a larger number of smaller firms can. Where significant economies of scale exist, it would be wasteful not to have a monopoly. So creating competition in a market that is a natural monopoly would be wasteful; page 330.

2. The average total cost curve is sloping downward at the point where it intersects the demand curve; page 331.

3. A natural monopoly can be regulated using a marginal cost pricing rule or an average cost pricing rule. The marginal cost pricing rule is a price rule for a natural monopoly that sets price equal to marginal cost. The advantage of this rule is that the firm produces the efficient quantity. The disadvantage is that the firm incurs an economic loss. An average cost pricing rule is a price rule for a natural monopoly that sets the price equal to average cost and enables the firm to cover its costs and earn an normal profit. The advantage of this rule is that the firm earns a normal profit. The disadvantage is that the firm produces less than the efficient quantity of output and a deadweight loss is created; pages 330, 331.

Chapter 14

Monopolistic Competition and Oligopoly

CHAPTER IN PERSPECTIVE

Chapter 14 studies the two market structures that lie between the extremes of perfect competition and monopoly: monopolistic competition and oligopoly.

■ **Explain how price and quantity are determined in monopolistic competition.**

Monopolistic competition is a market structure in which a large number of firms compete; each firm produces a differentiated product; firms compete on product quality, price, and marketing; and firms are free to enter and exit. The four-firm concentration ratio and the Herfindahl-Hirschman Index are indexes that measure the extent to which a market is dominated by a small number of firms. A firm in monopolistic competition maximizes profit by producing the output at which marginal revenue equals marginal cost. The price is determined by the demand curve. Entry and exit result in zero economic profit and excess capacity in long-run equilibrium. In monopolistic competition price exceeds marginal cost — a sign of inefficiency — but the inefficiency arises from product differentiation — a gain for consumers.

■ **Explain why selling costs are high in monopolistic competition.**

To maintain economic profit, firms in monopolistic competition innovate and develop new products, and incur huge costs to ensure that buyers appreciate the differences between their own products and those of their competitors. Selling costs such as advertising increase a firm's total cost, but they might lower average total cost if they increase the quantity sold by a large enough amount.

■ **Explain the dilemma faced by firms in oligopoly.**

An oligopoly is a market structure in which a small number of firms compete and natural or legal barriers prevent the entry of new firms. Firms in oligopoly would make the same economic profit as a monopoly if they could act together to restrict output to the monopoly level. Each firm can make a larger economic profit by increasing production, but this action decreases the economic profit of the other firms.

■ **Use game theory to explain how price and quantity are determined in oligopoly.**

Game theory is the tool economists use to analyze strategic behaviour. Games have rules, strategies, and payoffs. The prisoners' dilemma is a game between two prisoners that shows why it is hard to co-operate, even when it would be beneficial to both players to do so. The equilibrium of a game occurs when each player takes the best possible action given the action of the other player. This equilibrium concept is called Nash equilibrium. The equilibrium of the prisoners' dilemma game is not the best outcome. An oligopoly game is like the prisoners' dilemma. In a repeated game, a punishment strategy can produce a monopoly output, price, and economic profit.

EXPANDED CHAPTER CHECKLIST

When you have completed this chapter, you will be able to:

1 **Explain how price and quantity are determined in monopolistic competition.**

- Describe monopolistic competition.
- Define product differentiation.
- Calculate the four-firm concentration ratio and the Herfindahl-Hirschman Index.
- Illustrate the firm's profit-maximizing decision in monopolistic competition in the short run and in the long run.
- Discuss efficiency of monopolistic competition.
- Illustrate the excess capacity of firms in monopolistic competition.

2 **Explain why selling costs are high in monopolistic competition.**

- Explain why firms in monopolistic competition are continuously developing new products.
- Discuss the efficiency of product innovation.
- Illustrate how an increase in sales brought about by advertising can lower average total cost.

3 **Explain the dilemma faced by firms in oligopoly.**

- Define oligopoly and explain how one firm's actions can decrease the profits of other firms.
- Define cartel and explain why collusion usually breaks down.

4 **Use game theory to explain how price and quantity are determined in oligopoly.**

- Define game theory and discuss the three features of games.
- Describe the prisoners' dilemma.
- Define Nash equilibrium and be able to recognize the Nash equilibrium in a payoff matrix.
- Explain why a repeated game might lead to the monopoly outcome.

KEY TERMS

- Capacity output (page 341)
- Cartel (page 348)
- Duopoly (page 348)
- Four-firm concentration ratio (page 338)
- Game theory (page 353)
- Herfindahl-Hirschman Index (page 338)
- Nash equilibrium (page 354)
- Payoff matrix (page 354)
- Prisoners' dilemma (page 353)
- Product differentiation (page 336)
- Strategies (page 354)

CHECKPOINT 14.1

■ **Explain how price and quantity are determined in monopolistic competition.**

Practice Problem 14.1

Natti is a dot.com entrepreneur who has established a Web site at which people can design and buy a pair of cool sunglasses. Natti pays $4,000 a month for her Web server and Internet connection. The glasses that her customers design are made to order by another firm, and Natti pays this firm $50 a pair. Natti has no other costs. The table shows the demand schedule for Natti's sunglasses.

Price (dollars per pair)	Quantity demanded (pairs per month)
250	0
200	50
150	100
100	150
50	200
0	250

a. Calculate Natti's profit-maximizing output, price, and economic profit.

b. Do you expect other firms to enter the Web sunglasses business and compete with Natti?

c. What happens to the demand for Natti's sunglasses in the long run?

d. What happens to Natti's economic profit in the long run?

Solution to Practice Problem 14.1

Firms in monopolistic competition are similar to firms in perfect competition because both industries have no barriers to entry. When answering this Practice Problem remember that when possible, firms enter a market if they expect to earn an economic profit.

Quick Review

- *The firm's profit-maximizing decision* A firm in monopolistic competition produces the quantity at which marginal revenue equals marginal cost. The price is determined by the demand curve.

a. **Calculate Natti's profit-maximizing output, price, and economic profit.**

Natti will produce the quantity where marginal cost equals marginal revenue. The marginal cost is $50. The table shows Natti's marginal revenue.

Price (dollars per pair)	Quantity demanded (pairs per month)	Total revenue (dollars per month)	Marginal revenue (dollars per pair)
250	0	0	
			200
200	50	10,000	
			100
150	100	15,000	
			0
100	150	15,000	
			−100
50	200	10,000	
			−200
0	250	0	

When 100 pairs of sunglasses are produced, marginal revenue is $50 a pair (which is the average of $100 and $0). To maximize profit, Natti produces 100 pairs of sunglasses and sets a price of $150 a pair. Economic profit equals total revenue minus total cost. Natti's total revenue is 100 pairs × $150 a pair, which is $15,000. Total cost is the fixed cost of $4,000 plus variable cost of 100 pairs × $50 a pair, which is $5,000. So total cost is $9,000. Natti's economic profit is $15,000 − $9,000, which is $6,000 a month.

b. **Do you expect other firms to enter the Web sunglasses business and compete with Natti?**

Natti is earning an economic profit, so other firms will enter because they have an incentive to do so.

c. **What happens to the demand for Natti's sunglasses in the long run?**

As other firms enter, the demand for Natti's sunglasses will decrease. Natti's demand curve will shift leftward.

d. **What happens to Natti's economic profit in the long run?**

As the demand for Natti's sunglasses decreases her economic profit decreases. In the long run, Natti earns zero economic profit.

Additional Practice Problem 14.1a

The table gives some hypothetical data on sales in the fast-food hamburger market.

Firm	Sales (millions of dollars)	Market share (percent)
McDonald's	1,200	
Burger King	600	
Wendy's	600	
Harvey's	300	
A&W	100	
Other 20 smaller firms	800	

Complete the table and then calculate the four-firm concentration ratio. Based on the hypothetical concentration ratio, in what market structure would you classify the fast-food hamburger market?

Solution to Additional Practice Problem 14.1a

To calculate the market shares, first calculate the total sales within the market, which is $3,600 million. A firm's market share equals 100 times its sales divided by the total sales. The market shares are in the table below.

Firm	Sales (millions of dollars)	Market share (percent)
McDonald's	1,200	33.3
Burger King	600	16.7
Wendy's	600	16.7
Harvey's	300	8.3
A&W	100	2.8
Other 20 smaller firms	800	22.2

The four-firm concentration ratio is the percentage of the value of sales accounted for by the four largest firms in the industry, which is 33.3 percent + 16.7 percent + 16.7 percent + 8.3 percent = 75.0 percent. The fast-food hamburger market is an oligopoly.

■ Self Test 14.1

Fill in the blanks

In monopolistic competition there are a ____ (large; small) number of firms producing ____ (identical; differentiated) products. The square of the percentage market share of each firm summed over the 50 largest firms is the ____ (50-firm concentration ratio; Herfindahl-Hirschman Index). A firm in monopolistic competition produces the quantity where marginal revenue ____ (is greater than; equals; is less than) marginal cost. In the long run, a firm in monopolistic competition ____ (can; cannot) earn an economic profit. A firm in monopolistic competition ____ (does not have; has) excess capacity in the long run.

True or false

1. A firm in monopolistic competition faces a downward-sloping demand curve.
2. The larger the four-firm concentration ratio, the more competitive the industry.
3. A firm in monopolistic competition can make an economic profit in the short run.
4. In a broader view of efficiency, monopolistic competition brings gains for consumers.

Multiple choice

1. In monopolistic competition there
   a. are a large number of firms.
   b. are several large firms.
   c. is one large firm.
   d. might be many, several, or one firm.

2. Product differentiation means
   a. making a product that has perfect substitutes.
   b. making a product that is entirely unique.
   c. the inability to set your own price.
   d. making a product that is slightly different from products of competing firms.

3. If the four-firm concentration ratio for the market for pizza is 28 percent, then this industry is best characterized as
   a. a monopoly.
   b. monopolistic competition.
   c. an oligopoly.
   d. perfect competition.

4. A monopolistically competitive firm maximizes profit by equating
   a. price and marginal revenue.
   b. price and marginal cost.
   c. demand and marginal cost.
   d. marginal revenue and marginal cost.

5. In the long run, a firm in monopolistic competition
   a. earns a normal profit.
   b. produces at minimum average total cost.
   c. has deficient capacity.
   d. None of the above answers is correct.

6. At a firm's capacity output
   a. marginal cost is at a minimum.
   b. average total cost is at a minimum.
   c. profit is maximized.
   d. marginal revenue is at a maximum.

Complete the graph

1. Figure 14.1 shows the demand curve and marginal revenue curve for Seaside Pizza, a firm in monopolistic competition. Draw the average total cost curve and marginal cost curve so that Seaside's output is 40 pizzas a day and its economic profit is $160. Is this a short-run or long-run equilibrium?

■ **FIGURE 14.1**
Price and cost (dollars per pizza)

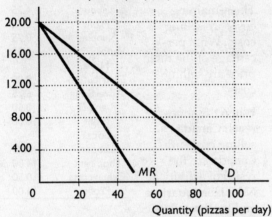

2. Figure 14.2 shows the demand curve and marginal revenue curve for Surf Pizza, a firm in monopolistic competition. Draw the average total cost curve and marginal cost curve so that Surf's output is 20 pizzas a day and its economic profit is $0. Does your figure illustrate a short-run or long-run equilibrium?

Short answer

1. What conditions define monopolistic competition?
2. Industry A has 1 firm with a market share of 57 percent and 43 other firms, each with a market share of 1 percent. Industry B has 4 firms, each with a market share of 15 percent, and 40 other firms, each with a market share of 1 percent.
   a. Calculate the four-firm concentration ratio for the two industries.
   b. Calculate the Herfindahl-Hirschman Index for the two industries.
3. Why do firms in monopolistic competition earn zero economic profit in the long run?
4. Is monopolistic competition efficient?

■ **FIGURE 14.2**
Price and cost (dollars per pizza)

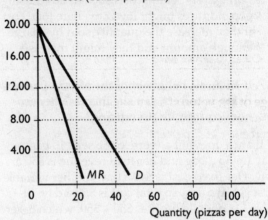

CHECKPOINT 14.2

■ Explain why selling costs are high in monopolistic competition.

Practice Problem 14.2

Bianca bakes delicious cookies. Her total fixed cost is $40 a day, and her average variable cost is $1 a bag. Few people know about Bianca's Cookies, and she is maximizing her profit by selling 10 bags a day for $5 a bag. Bianca thinks that if she spends $50 a day on advertising, she can increase her market and sell 25 bags a day for $5 a bag.

a. If Bianca's belief about the effect of advertising is correct, can she increase her economic profit by advertising?
b. If she advertised, would her average total cost increase or decrease at the quantity produced?
c. If Bianca's belief about the effect of advertising is correct, would she continue to sell her cookies for $5 a bag, or would she raise or lower her price?

Solution to Practice Problem 14.2

The Practice Problem helps you to understand why firms in monopolistic competition advertise.

Quick Review

- *Selling costs* Selling costs such as advertising expenditures might lower average total cost if they increase the quantity sold by a large enough amount and they might increase demand.

a. If Bianca's belief about the effect of advertising is correct, can she increase her economic profit by advertising?

If Bianca does not advertise she sells 10 bags a day for $5 a bag and her total revenue is $50 a day. Her fixed cost is $40 a day and her variable cost is $10 a day, so total cost is $50 a day. Bianca's economic profit is $50 − $50, which is zero.

If Bianca advertises, she sells 25 bags a day for $5 a bag and her total revenue is $125 a day. Her fixed cost if $90 a day, the sum of her original fixed cost and advertising cost, and her variable cost is $25 a day. Total cost is $115 a day. Bianca's economic profit is $125 − $115, which is $10 a day. So Bianca can increase her economic profit by advertising.

b. If she advertised, would her average total cost increase or decrease at the quantity produced?

Average total cost is total cost divided by quantity. Before advertising, average total cost is $50 ÷ 10 bags, which is $5 a bag. After advertising, ATC is $115 ÷ 25 bags, which is $4.60 a bag. Advertising decreases her average total cost.

c. If Bianca's belief about the effect of advertising is correct, would she continue to sell her cookies for $5 a bag, or would she raise or lower her price?

The price at which Bianca sells her cookies depends on how her demand curve shifts. And when the demand curve shifts, the marginal revenue curve also shifts. Bianca produces the quantity where marginal revenue equals marginal cost and the price is taken from the demand curve. We do not have sufficient information to determine if she would raise or lower her price.

Additional Practice Problem 14.2a

The table gives the cost of producing a pair of Nike running shoes.

a. The cost of producing and shipping a pair of Nikes to Canada is $32. The remaining costs are selling costs. What percentage of the retail price are selling costs?

b. When the shoes reach Canada, selling costs in Canada are the result of activity at Nike Headquarters and local retailers. What proportion of the $110 price are attributable to Nike and what proportion to local retailers?

Cost	Expenditure (dollars)
Asia	
Material	14.25
Capital	4.75
Labour	4.25
Profit	2.75
Shipping	0.75
Import duty	5.25
Nike	
Distribution	8.00
Advertising	6.25
R and D	0.50
Profit	10.00
Local	
Labour	14.75
Shop rent	14.00
Other costs	10.50
Profit	14.00

Solution to Additional Practice Problem 14.2a

a. What percentage of the retail price are selling costs?

Selling costs account for ($78 ÷ $110) × 100, which is 70.9 percent of the price.

b. What proportion of the $110 price are attributable to Nike and what proportion to local retailers?

Nike accounts for ($24.75 ÷ $110) × 100, which is 22.5 percent of the price and local retailers account for ($53.25 ÷ $110) × 100, which is 48.4 percent of the price.

Self Test 14.2

Fill in the blanks

Firms in monopolistic competition ____ (are; are not) continuously developing new products. In monopolistic competition, product improvement ____ (does; does not) equal its efficient level. Advertising costs ____ (are; are not) large in monopolistic competition. Advertising costs are a ____ (fixed; variable) cost and shift the average total cost curve ____ (downward; upward). Monopolistic competition ____ (definitely is; might be; definitely is not) efficient.

True or false

1. Firms in monopolistic competition innovate without regard to cost.
2. Firms in monopolistic competition often undertake extensive advertising.
3. Because advertising increases demand for a firm's product, increasing the amount of advertising shifts the firm's cost curves downward.
4. Whether monopolistic competition is inefficient depends on the value people place on product variety.

Multiple choice

1. To enjoy economic profits, firms in monopolistic competition must continuously
   a. shut down.
   b. exit the industry.
   c. innovate and develop new products.
   d. declare bankruptcy.

2. A firm in monopolistic competition that introduces a new and differentiated product will temporarily have a ____ demand for its product and be able to charge a ____ price.
   a. less elastic, lower
   b. less elastic, higher
   c. more elastic, lower
   d. more elastic, higher

3. The decision to innovate
   a. depends on the marketing department's needs.
   b. depends on whether the firm wants to benefit its customers.
   c. is based on the marginal cost and the marginal revenue of innovation.
   d. None of the above answers is correct.

4. Advertising costs and other selling costs are
   a. efficient.
   b. fixed costs.
   c. variable costs.
   d. marginal costs.

5. For a firm in monopolistic competition, selling costs
   a. increase costs and reduce profits.
   b. increase demand and increase profits.
   c. can change the quantity produced and lower the average total cost.
   d. can lower total cost.

6. The efficiency of monopolistic competition
   a. is as clear-cut as the efficiency of perfect competition.
   b. depends on whether the gain from extra product variety offsets the selling costs and the extra cost arising from excess capacity.
   c. comes from its excess capacity.
   d. is eliminated in the long run.

Short answer

1. Why do firms in monopolistic competition engage in innovation and product development?
2. How might advertising lower average total cost?
3. Is advertising and product differentiation efficient?

CHECKPOINT 14.3

■ Explain the dilemma faced by firms in oligopoly.

Practice Problem 14.3

Isolated Island has two natural gas wells, one owned by Tom and the other owned by Jerry. Each well has a valve that controls the rate of flow of gas, and the marginal cost of producing gas is zero. The table gives the demand schedule for gas on this island. What will the price of gas be on Isolated Island if Tom and Jerry:

Price (dollars per unit)	Quantity demanded (units per day)
12	0
11	1
10	2
9	3
8	4
7	5
6	6
5	7
4	8
3	9
2	10
1	11
0	12

a. Form a cartel and maximize their joint profit?
b. Are forced to sell at the perfectly competitive price?
c. Compete as duopolists?

Solution to Practice Problem 14.3

This Practice Problem compares the price and output of monopoly, duopoly, and perfect competition.

Quick Review

- *Duopoly* A market in which there are only two firms.
- *Cartel* A group of firms acting together to limit output, raise price, and increase economic profit.

a. **What is the price if Tom and Jerry form a cartel and maximize their joint profit?**

Tom and Jerry will charge the monopoly price and produce the monopoly quantity. A monopoly produces at the quantity at which marginal revenue equals marginal cost. Marginal cost is zero. Marginal revenue is zero when total revenue is at its maximum. Total revenue is at a maximum when 6 units a day are produced. And from the demand schedule, the highest price at which 6 units a day can be sold is $6 a unit.

b. **What is the price if Tom and Jerry are forced to sell at the perfectly competitive price?**

In perfect competition, marginal revenue equals price. Firms produce at the point where marginal revenue equals marginal cost. Marginal cost equals zero, so price is also zero.

c. **What is the price if Tom and Jerry compete as duopolists?**

When Tom and Jerry compete as duopolists, they will increase production beyond the monopoly output and the price will fall. But they will not increase production to the point where the price falls to zero.

Additional Practice Problem 14.3a

Suppose Tom and Jerry from Practice Problem 14.3 agree to operate as a monopoly. Tom and Jerry agree that each will produce 3 units. There are no fixed costs.

a. What is Tom's profit? Jerry's profit? The combined profit?
b. Suppose Tom decides to cheat on the agreement by producing 4 units. Jerry sticks to the agreement. If 7 units are produced, what is the price? What is Tom's profit? Jerry's profit? The combined profit?
c. Why would Tom consider cheating on the agreement he made with Jerry?

Solution to Additional Practice Problem 14.3a

a. **What is Tom's profit? Jerry's profit? The combined profit?**

Profit is equal to total revenue. Combined profit is equal to $36 dollars a day, Tom's profit is $18 a day, and Jerry's profit is also $18 a day.

b. **Suppose Tom decides to cheat on the agreement by producing 4 units. Jerry sticks to the agreement. If 7 units are produced, what is the price? What is Tom's profit? Jerry's profit? The combined profit?**

If 7 units are produced, the price is $5 a unit. Tom's profit on his 4 units is $20 and Jerry's profit on his 3 units is $15. Combined profit is $35.

c. **Why would Tom consider cheating on the agreement he made with Jerry?**

Tom considers cheating because cheating increases *his* profit. Tom realizes that when he alone cheats, his profit will be more, $20 versus $18. Jerry's profit falls more than Tom's rises but Tom is concerned only about his own profit.

■ **Self Test 14.3**

Fill in the blanks

In an oligopoly a ____ (large; small) number of firms compete. A ____ (cartel; duopoly) is a group of firms acting together to limit output, raise price, and increase economic profit. When a duopoly charges the perfectly competitive price, each firm receives ____ (no; positive) economic profit. When a duopoly charges the monopoly price, economic profit is ____ (maximized; minimized).

True or false

1. Oligopoly is a market in which a small number of firms compete.
2. The aim of a cartel is to lower price, increase output, and increase economic profit.
3. In a duopoly, the highest price that the firms might set is the perfectly competitive price.
4. A duopoly is currently making the same economic profit as a monopoly. If one firm increases its output, the economic profit of the other firm will increase.

Multiple choice

1. An oligopoly is a market structure in which
   a. many firms each produce a slightly differentiated product.
   b. one firm produces a unique product.
   c. a small number of firms compete.
   d. many firms produce an identical product.

2. The problem for a firm in an oligopoly is that
   a. there are barriers to entry.
   b. one firm's profits are affected by other firms' actions.
   c. they can produce either identical or differentiated goods.
   d. there are too many of them for any one firm to influence price.

3. Collusion results when a group of firms
   a. act separately to limit output, lower prices, and decrease economic profits.
   b. act together to limit output, raise the price, and increase economic profit.
   c. in Canada legally fix prices.
   d. None of the above answers is correct.

4. A market with only two firms is called a
   a. duopoly.
   b. two-firm monopolistic competition.
   c. two-firm monopoly.
   d. cartel.

5. Cartel agreements are difficult to maintain because
   a. each member firm can increase its own profit by cutting its price and selling more.
   b. forming a cartel is legal but frowned upon throughout the world.
   c. supply will decrease because of the high cartel price.
   d. None of the above answers are correct.

6. The greatest amount of economic profit is earned by a cartel when the cartel produces the
   a. monopoly level of output.
   b. perfectly competitive level of output.
   c. output level that maximizes total revenue.
   d. output level that minimizes total cost.

Complete the graph

1. Anytown has two newspapers that have a duopoly in the local market. The table contains information on market demand and marginal revenue for newspapers. Marginal cost of a newspaper is 20 cents.

Quantity (thousands of newspapers per day)	Price (cents)	Marginal revenue (cents)
0	60	60
2	50	40
4	40	20
6	30	0
8	20	−20

    a. Graph the demand curve, marginal revenue curve, and marginal cost curve in Figure 14.3.

    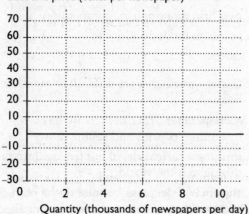

    ■ **FIGURE 14.3**
    Cost and price (cents per newspaper)

    b. What price and quantity represent the competitive outcome?
    c. What price and quantity represent the monopoly outcome?
    d. What price and quantity represent the duopoly outcome?

Short answer

1. In oligopoly, one firm's profit-maximizing actions might decrease its competitors' profits. Why is this fact a problem for firms in oligopoly?

2. What is a cartel? Why might a firm have the incentive to cheat on a collusive agreement to limit production and boost prices?

3. From the standpoint of efficiency, is it better to have firms successfully form a cartel or to have the cartel collapse and have the competitive outcome?

CHECKPOINT 14.4

■ Use game theory to explain how price and quantity are determined in oligopoly.

Practice Problem 14.4

Bud and Wise are the only two makers of aniseed beer, a new-age product designed to replace root beer. Bud and Wise are trying to figure out how much of this new beer to produce. They each know that if they both limit production to 10,000 litres a day, they will make the maximum attainable joint profit of $200,000 a day—$100,000 a day each. They also know that if either of them produces 20,000 litres a day while the other produces 10,000 a day, economic profit will be $150,000 for the one that produces 20,000 litres and an economic loss of $50,000 for the one that sticks with 10,000 litres. And they also know that if they both increase production to 20,000 litres a day, they will both earn zero economic profit.

a. Construct a payoff matrix for the game that Bud and Wise must play.
b. Find the Nash equilibrium.
c. What is the equilibrium if this game is played repeatedly?

Solution to Practice Problem 14.4

To find the Nash equilibrium of a game, place yourself in the position of the first player. Ask yourself "what if" your opponent takes one action: What will you do? Then ask "what if" the opponent takes the other action: now what will you do? This analysis allows you to determine the first player's action. Then place yourself in the position of the second player and repeat the "what if" analysis to determine the second player's action.

Quick Review

- *Game theory* The tool that economists use to analyze *strategic behaviour*—behaviour that recognizes mutual interdependence and takes account of the expected behaviour of others.
- *Nash equilibrium* An equilibrium in which each player takes the best possible action given the action of the other player.

a. **Construct a payoff matrix for the game that Bud and Wise must play.**

A payoff matrix is a table that shows payoffs for every possible action by each player given every possible action by the other

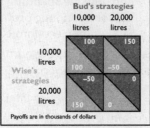

player. The payoff matrix is above. The number in each square is the economic profit in thousands of dollars.

b. **Find the Nash equilibrium.**

To find Wise's strategy, ask what Wise will do for each of Bud's choices. If Bud produces 10,000 litres (the first column of the payoff matrix), Wise produces 20,000 litres because that gives Wise a larger profit. If Bud produces 20,000 litres (the second column of the payoff matrix), Wise produces 20,000 litres because that gives him a larger profit. Regardless of Bud's action, Wise produces 20,000 litres. Similar reasoning shows that Bud also produces 20,000 litres. So the Nash equilibrium is for each to produce 20,000 litres and earn $0 economic profit.

c. **What is the equilibrium if this game is played repeatedly?**

In a repeated game, Bud and Wise produce the monopoly output of 10,000 litres a day each and earn the maximum economic profit. This outcome occurs if they use a tit-for-tat strategy.

Additional Practice Problem 14.4a

Bud and Wise from Practice Problem 14.4 are playing a repeated game and each is using a tit-for-tat strategy. Yesterday, both produced 10,000 litres but today Bud produces an additional 10,000 litres. What takes place today and in the future?

Solution to Additional Practice Problem 14.4a

Today, Bud earns an economic profit of $150,000 and Wise incurs an economic loss of $50,000. But on the second day Wise will produce 20,000 litres. Bud goes back to producing 10,000 litres to induce Wise to produce 10,000 on the third day. So on the second day, Wise earns an economic profit of $150,000 and Bud incurs an economic loss of $50,000. Over the two days, Wise earns an economic profit of $100,000 and Bud earns an economic profit of $100,000. If the two firms had both produced 10,000 litres a day, over two days each would have made an economic profit of $200,000. The tit-for-tat strategy will result in both firms producing 10,000 litres a day in the future and earning monopoly profit.

■ Self Test 14.4

Fill in the blanks

Game theory is the main tool that economists use to analyze _____ (rational; strategic) behaviour. Games feature _____, _____, and _____. The Nash equilibrium is _____ (always; not always) the best possible equilibrium for the players. Game theory shows that duopolists _____ (can; cannot) always reach the best possible equilibrium. In a _____ (repeated; single-play) game, a tit-for-tit strategy can be used. The _____ (larger; smaller) the number of firms, the harder it is for an oligopoly to maintain the monopoly output.

True or false

1. Game theory is used to analyze strategic behaviour.
2. A prisoners' dilemma has no equilibrium.

3. A Nash equilibrium is the best outcome for all players in a prisoners' dilemma game.

4. The monopoly outcome is more likely in a repeated game than in a one-play game.

Multiple choice

1. One of the main tools economists use to analyze strategic behaviour is
a. the Herfindahl-Hirschman Index.
b. game theory.
c. product differentiation.
d. collusion.

2. Game theory reveals
a. that the equilibrium might not be the best solution for the parties involved.
b. that oligopoly firms are interdependent.
c. that each player looks after his or her own self-interest.
d. All of the above answers are correct.

3. A Nash equilibrium occurs
a. when each player acts without considering the actions of the other player.
b. when each player takes the best possible action given the action of the other player.
c. only when players use the tit-for-tat strategy.
d. only when the game is played in Nashville.

4. The prisoners' dilemma game
a. shows that prisoners are better off if they cooperate.
b. shows it is easy to cooperate.
c. has an equilibrium in which both prisoners are made as well off as possible.
d. All of the above answers are correct.

5. Oligopolists can achieve an economic profit
a. always in the long run.
b. if the firms cooperate.
c. only if demand for their products is inelastic.
d. only if demand for their products is elastic.

6. When duopoly games are repeated over time and a tit-for-tat strategy is used,
a. the competitive outcome prevails.
b. the monopoly outcome prevails.
c. both firms begin to make economic losses.
d. one firm goes out of business.

Complete the graph

1. Intel and AMD undertake research and development. If each spends $2 billion, economic profit is zero. If each spends $1 billion, economic profit is $500 million each. If one spends $2 billion and the other spends $1 billion, the one spending $2 billion has a $1,500 million economic profit and the other has a $100 million economic loss.

a. Complete the payoff matrix below.
b. What is the Nash equilibrium of this game?

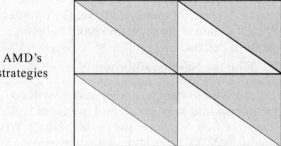

Intel's strategies

AMD's strategies

Short answer

1. What are strategies in game theory?

2. Why don't the players cooperate in a prisoners' dilemma? In a duopolists' dilemma?

3. How does the number of players in a game affect its outcome?

SELF TEST ANSWERS

■ CHECKPOINT 14.1

Fill in the blanks

In monopolistic competition there are a <u>large</u> number of firms producing <u>differentiated</u> products. The square of the percentage market share of each firm summed over the 50 largest firms is the <u>Herfindahl-Hirschman Index</u>. A firm in monopolistic competition produces the quantity where marginal revenue <u>equals</u> marginal cost. In the long run, a firm in monopolistic competition <u>cannot</u> earn an economic profit. A firm in monopolistic competition <u>has</u> excess capacity in the long run.

True or false

1. True; page 337
2. False; page 338
3. True; page 339
4. True; page 341

Multiple choice

1. a; page 336
2. d; page 336
3. b; page 338
4. d; page 339
5. a; page 340
6. b; page 341

Complete the graph

1. Figure 14.4 shows the average total cost curve and the marginal cost curve so that Seaside Pizza's output is 40 pizzas a day and economic profit is $160. The figure shows a short-run equilibrium because Seaside is earning an economic profit; page 339.

■ **FIGURE 14.4**
Price and cost (dollars per pizza)

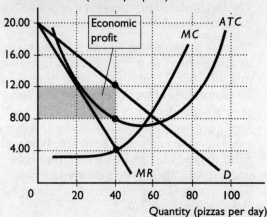

2. Figure 14.5 shows the average total cost curve and the marginal cost curve so that Surf Pizza's output is 20 pizzas a day and economic profit is zero. The figure shows a long-run equilibrium because Surf is earning zero economic profit; page 340.

■ **FIGURE 14.5**
Price and cost (dollars per pizza)

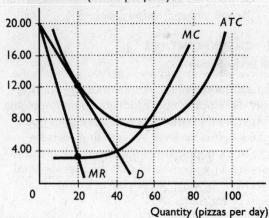

Short answer

1. Monopolistic competition occurs when a large number of firms compete, each firm produces a differentiated product, the firms compete on product quality, price, and marketing, and firms are free to enter and exit; page 336.

2a. The four-firm concentration ratios are the same for both industries, 60 percent; page 338.

b. The Herfindahl-Hirschman Index is 3,292 for Industry A and 940 for Industry B; page 338.

3. There is no restriction on entry in monopolistic competition, so if firms in an industry are making an economic profit, other firms have an incentive to enter the industry. The entry of new firms decreases the demand for each firm's product. The demand curve and marginal revenue curve shift leftward. When all firms in the industry are earning zero economic profit, there is no incentive for new firms to enter and the industry is in long-run equilibrium; page 340.

4. In monopolistic competition, price exceeds marginal revenue and marginal revenue equals marginal cost, so price exceeds marginal cost—a sign of inefficiency. But this inefficiency arises from product differentiation that consumers value and for which they are willing to pay. So the loss that arises because marginal benefit exceeds marginal cost must be weighed against the gain that arises from greater product variety; page 341.

■ CHECKPOINT 14.2
Fill in the blanks

Firms in monopolistic competition <u>are</u> continuously developing new products. In monopolistic competition, product improvement <u>does not</u> equal its efficient level. Advertising costs <u>are</u> large in monopolistic competition. Advertising costs are a <u>fixed</u> cost and shift the average total cost curve <u>upward</u>. Monopolistic competition <u>might be</u> efficient.

True or false

1. False; page 343
2. True; page 344
3. False; page 345
4. True; page 346

Multiple choice

1. c; page 343
2. b; page 343
3. c; page 343
4. b; page 345
5. c; page 345
6. b; page 346

Short answer

1. Firms innovate and develop new products to increase demand for their product and earn an economic profit; page 343.

2. Although advertising increases a firm's costs, it might also increase sales. If the quantity sold increases by a large enough amount, it can lower average total cost because the greater fixed cost is spread over a greater output; page 345.

3. The bottom line on the question of whether advertising and product differentiation are efficient is ambiguous. Advertising and product differentiation provide consumers with variety, which is a benefit. But this benefit needs to be weighed against the costs of advertising and product differentiation as well as the possibility that the actual differences between products may be very small; page 346.

■ CHECKPOINT 14.3
Fill in the blanks

In an oligopoly a <u>small</u> number of firms compete. A <u>cartel</u> is a group of firms acting together to limit output, raise price, and increase economic profit. When a duopoly charges the perfectly competitive price, each firm receives <u>no</u> economic profit. When a duopoly charges the monopoly price, economic profit is <u>maximized</u>.

True or false

1. True; page 348
2. False; page 348
3. False; page 350
4. False; pages 350-351

Multiple choice

1. c; page 348
2. b; page 348
3. b; page 348
4. a; page 348
5. a; pages 349-351
6. a; pages 349-351

Complete the graph

1. a. The curves are graphed in Figure 14.6.
   b. The competitive equilibrium is 8,000 newspapers a day and a price of 20¢ a newspaper; page 349.
   c. The monopoly equilibrium is 4,000 newspapers a day and a price of 40¢ a newspaper; page 349.

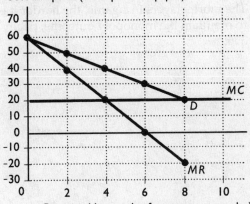

■ FIGURE 14.6

d. The exact price and quantity can't be predicted, but it will be somewhere between the competitive and monopoly outcomes. The price will be between 40¢ and 20¢ a newspaper and the output will be between 4,000 and 8,000 newspapers a day; page 350.

Short answer

1. The point that one firm's actions can decrease another firm's profits is what makes cooperation difficult in an oligopoly. While the firms might be better off cooperating, each firm trying to increase its profit takes actions that lead the profits of its competitors to decrease, so that all the firms wind up worse off; pages 350-351.

2. A cartel is a group of firms acting together to limit output, raise price, and increase economic profit. Every firm has the incentive to cheat on an output-limiting agreement because if it and it alone cheats by boosting its output and cutting its price, its economic profit will increase; pages 348, 351.

3. From the standpoint of efficiency, it is better off to have a cartel collapse and obtain the competitive outcome because the competitive outcome is efficient. If the cartel is successful, the monopoly outcome inflicts a deadweight loss on society; page 349.

■ **CHECKPOINT 14.4**

Fill in the blanks

Game theory is the main tool that economists use to analyze <u>strategic</u> behaviour. Games feature <u>rules</u>, <u>strategies</u>, and <u>payoffs</u>. The Nash equilibrium is <u>not always</u> the best possible equilibrium for the players. Game theory shows that duopolists <u>cannot</u> always reach the best possible equilibrium. In a <u>repeated</u> game, a tit-for-tit strategy can be used. The <u>larger</u> the number of firms, the harder it is for an oligopoly to maintain the monopoly output.

True or false

1. True; page 353
2. False; page 354
3. False; page 355
4. True; page 356

Multiple choice

1. b; page 353
2. d; page 354
3. b; page 354
4. a; page 355

5. b; page 356
6. b; page 356

Complete the graph

1. a. The completed payoff matrix is below. The payoffs are in millions of dollars; page 354.

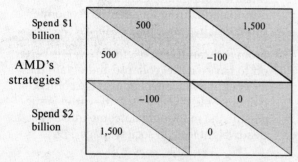

b. The Nash equilibrium is for both Intel and AMD to spend $2 billion on research and development and each earn zero economic profit; page 354.

Short answer

1. Strategies are all of the possible actions of each player. In the prisoner's dilemma, the two strategies are confess to the bank robbery and deny having committed the bank robbery; page 354.

2. In the prisoners' dilemma game, the players do not cooperate because they do not see cooperation as being in their best interest. Regardless of what the second player does, the first player is better off confessing. Similarly, regardless of what the first player does, the second player is better off confessing. Because it is in each players separate interest to confess rather than cooperate by denying, both players confess. In the duopolists' dilemma game, the players do not cooperate for precisely the same reason they do not cooperate in the prisoners' dilemma game; pages 354-356.

3. The more players in a game, the harder it is to maintain the monopoly outcome; page 356.

Chapter 15
Regulation and Competition Law

CHAPTER IN PERSPECTIVE

Chapter 15 studies government regulation of monopoly and oligopoly and Canada's competition laws. The chapter discusses the Competition Act and looks at some examples of how the Competition Act works.

- **Distinguish between the public interest and capture theories of regulation, and explain how regulation affects prices, outputs, profits, and the distribution of surpluses between consumers and producers.**

Regulation consists of rules administered by a government agency to influence economic activity by determining prices, product standards and types, and the conditions under which new firms can enter an industry. Two broad economic theories of regulation are public interest theory and capture theory. Public interest theory is the theory that regulation seeks an efficient use of resources. Capture theory is the theory that regulation helps producers to maximize economic profit. A natural monopoly is an industry in which one firm can supply the entire market at a lower price than can two or more firms. A marginal cost pricing rule, which sets price equal to marginal cost achieves an efficient use of resources in a regulated industry. A natural monopoly that is regulated to set price equal to marginal cost incurs an economic loss. A natural monopoly that is regulated with an average cost pricing rule, which sets price equal to average total cost covers its total cost. But the quantity is less than the efficient quantity and a deadweight loss arises. A regulation that sets the price at a level that enables a regulated firm to earn a specified target percent return on its capital is a rate of return regulation. This rate of return is part of the opportunity cost of the natural monopoly and is included in the firm's average total cost. So rate of return regulation is similar to average cost pricing.

- **Describe Canada's competition law and explain how it is applied in practice.**

Competition law is the body of law that regulates and prohibits certain kinds of market behaviour, such as monopoly and monopolistic practices. Canada's competition law dates from the Combines Investigation Act of 1889. Canada's competition law today is defined in the Competition Act of 1986. The Competition Act established a Competition Bureau and a Competition Tribunal. The Competition Act distinguishes between practices that are criminal—conspiracy to fix prices, bid-rigging, other anticompetitive price-fixing actions, and false advertising—and non-criminal—mergers, abuse of a dominant market position, refusal to deal, and other actions designed to limit competition such as exclusive dealing. In the case of a large merger that might reduce competition substantially, the firms most notify the Competition Bureau, which has the power to order the firms not to proceed with the proposed merger or to dissolve a merge that has been completed. The Competition Act also requires the Bureau to consider whether a proposed merger is likely to result in gains in efficiency that would benefit the economy as a whole.

EXPANDED CHAPTER CHECKLIST

When you have completed this chapter, you will be able to:

1 Distinguish between the public interest and capture theories of regulation, and explain how regulation affects prices, outputs, profits, and the distribution of surpluses between consumers and producers.

- Define regulation and discuss how regulation has changed during the past 20 years.
- Discuss the two economic theories of regulation.
- Explain the marginal-cost pricing rule and show that it achieves an efficient output in a regulated industry.
- Explain the average-cost pricing rule and show the deadweight loss that it creates.
- Describe how rate of return regulation can lead to manager of a firm exaggerating the firm's costs.
- Discuss regulation of an oligopoly, and describe how an oligopoly is regulated according to the public interest theory and the capture theory.

2 Describe Canada's competition law and explain how it is applied in practice.

- Define competition law.
- Discuss the Competition Act of 1986 and distinguish between practices that are criminal and non-criminal.
- Discuss the factors that the Competition Bureau examines when reviewing a merger proposal.
- Give examples to show how the Competition Act works.

KEY TERMS

- Capture theory (page 362)
- Competition law (page 372)
- Public interest theory (page 362)
- Rate of return regulation (page 367)
- Regulation (page 362)

CHECKPOINT 15.1

■ Distinguish between the public interest and capture theories of regulation, and explain how regulation affects prices, outputs, profits, and the distribution of surpluses between consumers and producers.

Practice Problem 15.1

An unregulated natural monopoly bottles Elixir, a unique health product that has no substitutes. The monopoly's total fixed cost is $150,000, and its marginal cost is 10 cents a bottle. The figure illustrates the demand for Elixir.

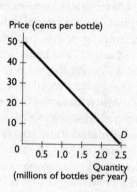

a. How many bottles of Elixir does the monopoly sell?
b. What is the price of a bottle of Elixir?
c. Is the monopoly's use of resources efficient?
d. How might government regulate the monopoly in the public interest?
e. If the government introduces a marginal cost pricing rule, what will be the price of a bottle of Elixir, the quantity of Elixir sold, and the monopoly's profit?

Solution to Practice Problem 15.1

This Practice Problem will help you to understand how regulation changes price and output in a natural monopoly. Remember that an unregulated monopoly produces the quantity where marginal revenue equals marginal cost and the price is determined by the demand curve.

Quick Review

- *Marginal cost pricing rule* A price rule for a natural monopoly that sets price equal to marginal cost.
- *Public interest theory* The theory that regulation seeks an efficient use of resources.

An unregulated natural monopoly bottles Elixir, a unique health product that has no substitutes. The monopoly's total fixed cost is $150,000, and its marginal cost is 10 cents a bottle.

a. **How many bottles of Elixir does the monopoly sell?**

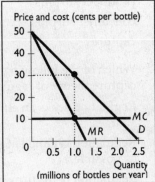

The monopoly produces the quantity at which marginal revenue equals marginal cost. In the figure, marginal revenue equals marginal cost when 1.0 million bottles a year are produced.

b. **What is the price of a bottle of Elixir?**

The price is 30 cents a bottle. The demand curve shows that 30 cents a bottle is the highest price at which the monopoly can sell the 1 million bottles.

c. **Is the monopoly's use of resources efficient?**

The monopoly's use of resources is inefficient. When resource use is efficient, the monopoly would produce the quantity at which price equals marginal cost. The efficient quantity is 2 million bottles a year.

d. **How might government regulate the monopoly in the public interest?**

The government can regulate the monopoly using a marginal cost pricing rule or an average cost pricing rule.

e. **If the government introduces a marginal cost pricing rule, what will be the price of a bottle of Elixir, the quantity of Elixir sold, and the monopoly's profit?**

If the monopoly is regulated using a marginal cost pricing rule, the price is set equal to marginal cost, which is 10 cents a bottle. When the price is 10 cents a bottle, the quantity demanded is 2.0 million bottles a year. The monopoly covers its total variable cost, but not its total fixed cost. So the monopoly incurs an economic loss of $150,000 a year.

Additional Practice Problem 15.1a

If the monopoly in Practice Problem 15.1 is regulated, which type of regulation would the owner of the monopoly prefer?

Solution to Practice Problem 15.1a

The owner of the monopoly would prefer a rate of return regulation. A rate of return regulation sets the price at a level that enables a regulated firm to earn a specified target percent return on its capital. So with a rate of return regulation, the monopoly does not incur an economic loss. A rate of return regulation, if based on a correct assessment of the producer's average total cost, results in a price that favours the consumer and does not enable the monopoly to maximize profit. But it may be possible for the managers of a firm to exaggerate the firm's cost and earn an economic profit.

Self Test 15.1

Fill in the blanks

The theory that regulation seeks an efficient use of resources is the _____ (capture; public interest) theory and the theory that regulation helps producers maximize economic profit is the _____ (capture; public interest) theory. Since the early 1980s, the government has _____ (increased; reduced) the amount of regulation in the Canadian economy. With _____ (an average; a marginal) cost pricing rule, a natural monopoly incurs an economic loss. Rate of return regulation makes price _____ (equal to; greater than; less than) average total cost. According to the capture theory, regulation of cartels _____ (maximizes; minimizes) economic profit.

True or false

1. Regulatory rules are administered by the regulated company.
2. Public interest theory assumes that the political process introduces regulation that eliminates deadweight loss.
3. The capture theory predicts that regulations benefit large interest groups.
4. In a regulated industry, firms are free to determine the price they charge but the regulating agency determines the production technology they must use.
5. A regulated natural monopoly produces the efficient quantity of output when it is regulated by a marginal cost pricing rule.
6. Rate of return regulation sets the price at a level that allows the regulated firm to earn a specified target percent return on its capital.
7. With rate of return regulation, the managers of a firm have an incentive to exaggerate the firm's costs.
8. According to public interest theory, oligopoly is regulated to ensure a competitive outcome.

Multiple choice

1. Regulation
   a. consists of rules administered by a government agency.
   b. is a theory that resources are used efficiently.
   c. consists of rules administered by private industry to avoid government interference.
   d. is a theory that firms maximize profits if government agencies assist.

2. Deregulation is the process of _____ restrictions on prices, product standards and types, and entry conditions.
   a. increasing
   b. not changing
   c. evaluating
   d. removing

3. The theory that regulation seeks an efficient use of resources is the _____ theory.
   a. public interest
   b. producer surplus
   c. consumer surplus
   d. capture

4. Which of the following best describes the capture theory of regulation?
   a. Regulation seeks an efficient use of resources.
   b. Regulation is aimed at keeping prices as low as possible.
   c. Regulation helps firms maximize economic profit.
   d. All of the above describe the capture theory.

5. The first regulation in Canada was the
   a. Canadian Wheat Act of 1883.
   b. War Measures Act of 1914.
   c. Railway Act of 1888.
   d. Conscription Act of 1917.

6. At a level of output where regulators force a natural monopoly to set a price that is equal to marginal cost, the firm will be
   a. earning a normal profit.
   b. earning an economic profit.
   c. incurring an economic loss.
   d. earning a normal profit.

7. If a natural monopoly is told to set price equal to average total cost, then the firm
   a. is not able to set marginal revenue equal to marginal cost.
   b. automatically also sets price equal to marginal cost.
   c. will earn a substantial economic profit.
   d. will incur an economic loss.

8. Rate of return regulation is designed to allow a natural monopoly to
   a. earn an economic profit.
   b. earn a normal profit.
   c. underestimate its average total cost.
   d. compete with any firm entering the market.

9. When a regulatory agency uses rate of return regulation, the
   a. agency is able to eliminate the deadweight loss.
   b. regulated firm has no incentive to cut costs.
   c. regulated firm's profit must be maximized for the market to be efficient.
   d. the regulated firm must receive a government subsidy.

10. According to the capture theory, regulation serves the interest of the
    a. consumer.
    b. government.
    c. producer.
    d. government and the producer.

11. Under a rate of return regulation, the managers of a firm try to make their apparent costs _____ the true costs.
    a. equal
    b. exceed
    c. less than
    d. less than or equal to

12. Why would members of a cartel be in favour of regulation by a government agency?
    a. Regulation follows the public interest theory.
    b. Industry output is controlled, which prevents members from cheating.
    c. Costs are reduced.
    d. Cartel members are never in favour of regulation.

Complete the graph

1. Figure 15.1 shows both the actual and exaggerated average total cost curves of a cable TV company that is a regulated monopoly. Also given are the demand curve and marginal revenue curve.

■ FIGURE 15.1
Price and cost (dollars per month)

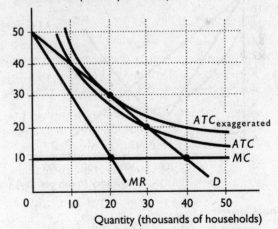

Quantity (thousands of households)

Answer questions (a) through (c) based on the assumption that regulators know the true costs of production.

a. What price would the regulator set using the marginal cost pricing rule?

b. What price would the regulator set using the average cost pricing rule?

c. What price would the firm set if it was unregulated?

d. Now assume that the monopoly successfully exaggerates its cost of production. What price would the regulator set using the average cost pricing rule?

2. A small town has only five restaurants. Figure 15.2 shows the demand curve, marginal revenue curve, and marginal cost curve for the restaurant market in this town.

a. What are the competitive price and quantity?

b. What price and quantity would result if the firms colluded and acted like a monopoly?

c. Suppose the restaurants are regulated. What price and quantity would prevail under the public interest theory?

d. If the restaurants are regulated, what price and quantity would prevail under the capture theory?

■ FIGURE 15.2

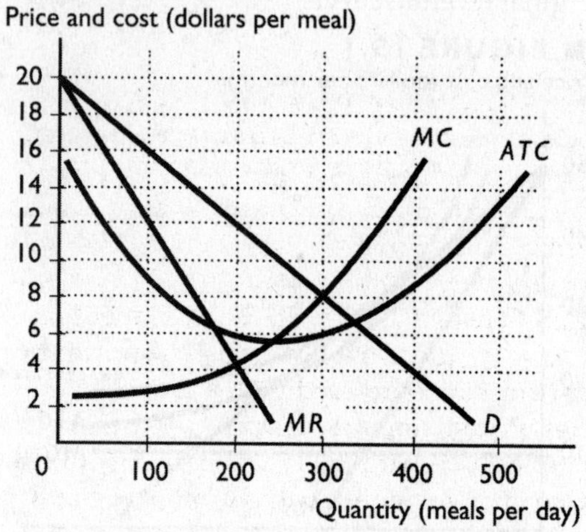

Price and cost (dollars per meal)

[Graph showing MC, ATC, MR, and D curves. Y-axis from 0 to 20 in increments of 2. X-axis Quantity (meals per day) from 0 to 500 in increments of 100.]

Short answer

1. Why doesn't the government regulate all industries?

2. What is the public interest theory of regulation? The capture theory?

3. What is the advantage of using a marginal cost pricing rule to regulate a natural monopoly? The disadvantage?

4. What is rate of return regulation? Does it attempt to set the regulated firm's price equal to its marginal cost or its average total cost? If a firm regulated using rate of return regulation exaggerates its costs, what occurs?

CHECKPOINT 15.2

■ Describe Canada's competition law and explain how it is applied in practice.

Practice Problems 15.2

1. The Competition Bureau allowed the merger of the Toronto-Dominion Bank and Canada Trust in 2000 only if the banks agreed to sell their branches in three local markets (Kitchener, Port Hope, and Brantford, Ontario). Why did the Competition Bureau require these branches to be sold and not others?

2. The Competition Bureau examines any merger in which the merged company ha a share of the Canadian market that exceeds 35 percent. The Competition Bureau is reviewing the proposed mergers of two drugstore chains that will give the merged company 39 percent of the Canadian market and of two furniture manufacturers that will give the merged company 50 percent of the Canadian market.

Explain why the Competition Bureau would be more concerned about the merger of the drugstore chains than the merger of the furniture firms.

Solution to Practice Problems 15.2

These Practice Problems will help you to understand many of the issues surrounding mergers. In reviewing a merger proposal, the Competition Bureau examines factors such as the degree of foreign competition; whether the firm (or one of the firms) is likely to fail if the merger is blocked;

the extent to which substitutes are available; whether barriers to entry exist; the extent to which effective competition would remain after the merger; whether the merger would eliminate another competitor; and any other factors that influence the degree of competition in the relevant market.

Quick Review

- *Competition law* The body of law that regulates and prohibits certain kinds of market behaviour, such as monopoly and monopolistic practices.

1. **The Competition Bureau allowed the merger of the Toronto-Dominion Bank and Canada Trust in 2000 only if the banks agreed to sell their branches in three local markets (Kitchener, Port Hope, and Brantford, Ontario). Why did the Competition Bureau require these branches to be sold and not others?**

The merger between Toronto-Dominion Bank and Canada Trust reduced competition significantly in Kitchener, Port Hope, and Brantford, Ontario. In all other market areas, consumers had an adequate choice even after the merger.

2. **The Competition Bureau examines any merger in which the merged company ha a share of the Canadian market that exceeds 35 percent. The Competition Bureau is reviewing the proposed mergers of two drugstore chains that will give the merged company 39 percent of the Canadian market and of two furniture manufacturers that will give the merged company 50 percent of the Canadian market.**

   Explain why the Competition Bureau would be more concerned about the merger of the drugstore chains than the merger of the furniture firms.

The market share of the merged furniture manufacturers, which is 50 percent of the Canadian market would be larger than the market share of the merged drugstore chains, which is 39 percent of the Canadian market. But foreign furniture manufacturers would still compete with Canadian producers. It is less likely that drugstores compete with foreign producers, so the merger of the drugstores would decrease competition in the Canadian drugstore market.

Additional Practice Problem 15.2a

Discuss the role of efficiency when the Competition Bureau approves a merger.

Solution to Additional Practice Problem 15.2a

The Competition Act requires the Bureau to consider whether a proposed merger is likely to result in gains in efficiency that would benefit the economy as a whole. If these gains in efficiency are likely to be large enough to outweigh the effects of any lessening of competition, the merger is to be allowed. This provision in the Competition Act is the "efficiency defence".

■ **Self Test 15.2**

Fill in the blanks

Canada's competition law dates from the _____ (Combines Investigation Act; Competition Act). Under the Competition Act conspiracy to fix prices and false advertising are _____ (criminal; non-criminal) offences and abuse of a dominant market position and refusal to deal are _____ (criminal; non-criminal) offences. In the case of a large merger that might reduce competition substantially, the firms must notify _____ (the Competition Bureau; Parliament). The Competition Bureau _____ (does not have; has) the power to order firms not to proceed with a proposed merger. Price-fixing practices are _____ (never; sometimes) international in scope. In April 1998, the Canadian Imperial Bank of Commerce and the Toronto-Dominion Bank announced their intention to merge, which was _____ (allowed; not allowed) to proceed.

True or false

1. Canada's competition law dates from the Competition Act of 1889.

2. The Competition Act distinguishes between practices that are criminal and non-criminal.

3. In the case of a large merger that might reduce competition substantially, the firms must notify the Department of Finance.

4. The Competition Bureau has the power to order firms not to proceed with a proposed merger.

5. The Competition Bureau does not allow a merger to proceed if there is a lessening of competition even if the merger results in gains in efficiency.

6. Following the merger of Air Canada with Canadian Airlines in April 2000, the Competition Bureau agreed to allow Air Canada to undercut the fares of small regional airlines.

7. It is not possible to recognize price-fixing practices that are international in scope.

8. The federal government has the final power to approve or reject bank mergers in Canada.

Multiple choice

1. Canada's competition law today is defined in the
   a. Tribunal Act of 1967.
   b. Competition Act of 1986.
   c. Combines Investigation Act of 1889.
   d. Canadian Charter.

2. Which of the following are criminal offences under the Competition Act?
   a. false advertising
   b. abuse of a dominant market position
   c. refusal to deal
   d. All of the above answers are correct.

3. The _____ sends alleged violations of a non-criminal nature to _____ for examination.
   a. Director of the Competition Bureau; Parliament
   b. Director of the Competition Bureau; Competition Tribunal
   c. Minister of Finance; Competition Tribunal
   d. Minister of Finance; a parliamentary committee

4. Which of the following are non-criminal offences under the Competition Act??
   a. abuse of a dominant market position
   b. exclusive dealing
   c. refusal to deal
   d. All of the above answers are correct.

5. The Competition Bureau and the Competition Tribunal were established by the
   a. Department of Finance.
   b. Combines Investigation Act.
   c. Competition Act.
   d. British North American Act.

6. In reviewing a merger proposal, the Competition Bureau examines factors such as
   a. whether one of the firms is likely to fail if the merger is blocked.
   b. the extent to which substitutes are available.
   c. whether the merger would eliminate another competitor.
   d. All of the above answers are correct.

7. If gains in efficiency that would benefit the economy as a whole are likely to be large enough to outweigh the effects of any lessening of competition,
   a. the merger is allowed.
   b. the merger is not allowed.
   c. the Bureau of Competition will negotiate changes to the proposed merger with the companies involved.
   d. None of the above answers is correct.

8. When NutraSweet tried to gain a monopoly, the Competition Tribunal ruled its action unduly limited competition. As a result, there was _____ in competition and a _____ in the price of aspartame in Canada.

   a. an increase; rise
   b. an increase; fall
   c. a decrease; rise
   d. a decrease; fall

9. Since Air Canada merged with Canadian airlines, the Competition Bureau has asked the Competition Tribunal to issue orders

   a. prohibiting Air Canada from competing in regional markets.
   b. prohibiting Air Canada from undercutting the fares of small regional airlines.
   c. that allow Air Canada to compete in regional markets.
   d. that allow Air Canada to purchase other small regional airlines.

10. Price-fixing practices

    a. are a non-criminal offence under the Competition Act.
    b. are the main reason why bank mergers in Canada in 1998 were disallowed.
    c. do not cross international borders.
    d. are international in scope.

11. In 1998, the federal government _____ allow the merger between the Royal Bank and Bank of Montreal and _____ allow the merger between the Canadian Imperial Bank of Commerce and the Toronto-Dominion Bank.

    a. did not; did not
    b. did not; did
    c. did; did not
    d. did; did

12. In Canada, the _____ has the final power to approve or reject bank mergers.

    a. Bank of Canada
    b. Competition Bureau
    c. federal government
    d. Competition Tribunal

Short answer

1. What is competition law?
2. The Competition Act distinguishes between two practices. Identify and describe each practice.
3. List the factors that the Competition Bureau examines when reviewing a merger proposal.
4. How does the Competition Bureau react when a proposed merger results in gains in efficiency?
5. What did the Competition Bureau conclude about the planned merger between the Royal Bank and the Bank of Montreal and between the Canadian Imperial Bank of Commerce and the Toronto-Dominion Bank in 1998?

SELF TEST ANSWERS

■ CHECKPOINT 15.1

Fill in the blanks

Fill in the blanks

The theory that regulation seeks an efficient use of resources is the <u>public interest</u> theory and the theory that regulation helps producers maximize economic profit is the <u>capture</u> theory. Since the early 1980s, the government has <u>reduced</u> the amount of regulation in the Canadian economy. With <u>a marginal</u> cost pricing rule, a natural monopoly incurs an economic loss. Rate of return regulation makes price <u>equal to</u> average total cost. According to the capture theory, regulation of cartels <u>maximizes</u> economic profit.

True or false

1. False; page 362
2. True; page 362
3. False; page 362
4. False; page 364
5. True; page 365
6. True; page 367
7. True; page 368
8. True; page 369

Multiple choice

1. a; page 362
2. d; page 362
3. a; page 362
4. c; page 362
5. c; page 362
6. c; page 365
7. a; page 366
8. b; page 367
9. b; page 368
10. c; page 367
11. b; page 368
12. b; page 370

Complete the graph

1a. Using marginal cost pricing, the regulator will set a price of $10 a month; page 365.
 b. Using average cost pricing, the regulator will set a price of $20 a month; page 366.
 c. The firm prefers the profit-maximizing price of $30 a month; page 367.
 d. If the firm successfully exaggerates its costs, the regulator will set a price of $30 a month; page 367.
2a. The competitive price is $8 a meal and the competitive quantity is 300 meals a day; page 369.
 b. The monopoly price is $12 a meal and the quantity is 200 meals a day; page 369.
 c. The price is $8 a meal and the quantity is 300 meals a day, the same as the competitive outcome; page 369.
 d. The price is $12 a meal and the quantity is 200 meals a day, the same as the monopoly outcome; page 369.

Short answer

1. The government does not regulate all industries because not all industries need to be regulated. Competitive industries do not need regulation because competition produces an efficient outcome. But a natural monopoly is not a competitive industry and so government regulation might help move the monopoly towards efficiency; pages 362, 364.

2. The public interest theory of regulation is the theory that regulation seeks an efficient use of resources. The capture theory of regulation is the theory that regulation helps producers to maximize economic profit; page 362.

3. The advantage of using a marginal cost pricing rule is that the firm produces the efficient quantity of output. The disadvantage is that the firm incurs an economic loss; page 365.

4. Rate of return regulation is a regulation that sets the price at a level that enables a regulated firm to earn a specified target percent return on its capital. The target rate of return is determined with reference to what is normal in competitive industries. This rate of return is part of the opportunity cost of the natural monopoly and is included in the firm's average total cost. So rate of return regulation attempts to set the price equal to average total cost. If the firm successfully exaggerates its costs, the regulators allow the firm to increase the price it charges so that it can cover all of its now higher, exaggerated costs; pages 367-368.

■ CHECKPOINT 15.2

Fill in the blanks

Canada's competition law dates from the <u>Combines Investigation Act</u>. Under the Competition Act, conspiracy to fix prices and false advertising are <u>criminal</u> offences and abuse of a dominant market position and refusal to deal are <u>non-criminal</u> offences. In the case of a large merger that might reduce competition substantially, the firms must notify <u>the Competition Bureau</u>. The Competition Bureau <u>has</u> the power to order firms not to proceed with a proposed merger. Price-fixing practices are <u>sometimes</u> international in scope. In April 1998, the Canadian Imperial Bank of Commerce and the Toronto-Dominion Bank announced their intention to merge, which was <u>not allowed</u> to proceed.

True or false

1. False; page 372
2. True; page 372
3. False; page 373
4. True; page 373
5. False; page 373
6. False; page 375
7. False; page 376
8. True; page 376

Multiple choice

1. b; page 372
2. a; page 372
3. b; page 372
4. d; page 372
5. c; page 372
6. d; page 373
7. a; page 373
8. b; page 374
9. b; page 375
10. d; page 376
11. a; page 376
12. c; page 376

Short answer

1. Competition law is the body of law that regulates and prohibits certain kinds of market behaviour, such as monopoly and monopolistic practices; page 372.

2. The Competition Act distinguishes between practices that are criminal and non-criminal. Conspiracy to fix prices, bid-rigging, other anti-competitive price-fixing actions, and false advertising are criminal offences. Mergers, abuse of a dominant market position, refusal to deal, and other actions designed to limit competition such as exclusive dealing are non-criminal offences; page 372.

3. In reviewing a merger proposal, the Bureau examines factors such as the degree of foreign competition; whether the firm (or one of the firms) is likely to fail if the merger is blocked; the extent to which substitutes are available; whether barriers to entry exist; the extent to which effective competition would remain after the merger; whether the merger would eliminate another competitor; and any other factors that influence the degree of competition in the relevant market; page 373.

4. The Competition Act requires the Competition Bureau to consider whether a proposed merger is likely to result in gains in efficiency that would benefit the economy as a whole. If these gains in efficiency are likely to be large enough to outweigh the effects of any lessening of competition, the merger is to be allowed; page 373.

5. The Competition Bureau reviewed the merger plans of the Royal Bank and the Bank of Montreal and the merger plans of the Canadian Imperial Bank of Commerce and the Toronto-Dominion Bank and found that they would likely lead to a substantial lessening of competition in some banking services; page 376.

Chapter 16
Demand and Supply in Factor Markets

CHAPTER IN PERSPECTIVE
This chapter studies demand, supply, and equilibrium in factor markets.

- **Describe the anatomy of the markets for labour, capital, and land.**

The four factors of production are labour, capital, land, and entrepreneurship. The wage rate is the price of labour, the interest rate is the price of capital, and rent is the price of land. A labour market is a collection of people and firms who are trading labour services. A financial market is a collection of people and firms who are lending and borrowing to finance the purchase of physical capital. A commodity market is a market in which raw materials are traded.

- **Explain how the value of marginal product determines the demand for a factor of production.**

The demand for a factor of production is derived from the demand for the goods and services it is used to produce. The value of marginal product is the value to a firm of hiring one more unit of a factor of production. To maximize profit, a firm hires labour up to the point at which the value of marginal product equals the wage rate. A firm's demand for labour curve is also its value of marginal product curve. The demand for labour depends on the price of the firm's output, the prices of other factors of production, and technology.

- **Explain how wage rates and employment are determined.**

An individual's labour supply curve can be backward bending at higher wage rates so that an increase in the wage rate decreases the quantity of labour supplied. The key factors that change the supply of labour are the adult population, preferences, and time in school and training. The labour market equilibrium determines the wage rate and employment.

- **Explain how interest rates, borrowing, and lending are determined.**

Other things remaining the same, the higher the interest rate, the smaller is the quantity of capital demanded. The quantity of financial capital supplied results from people's saving decisions. Other things remaining the same, the higher the interest rate, the greater is the quantity of saving supplied. Financial market equilibrium occurs at the interest rate where the quantity of capital demanded equals the quantity of capital supplied.

- **Explain how rents and natural resource prices are determined.**

Natural resources are either renewable or nonrenewable. The quantity of land is fixed, so the supply of each particular block of land is perfectly inelastic. Economic rent is the income received by *any* factor of production over and above the amount required to induce a given quantity of the factor to be supplied. The known quantity of a nonrenewable resource increases over time because advances in technology enable ever less accessible sources of the resource to be discovered.

EXPANDED CHAPTER CHECKLIST

When you have completed this chapter, you will be able to:

1 **Describe the anatomy of the markets for labour, capital, and land.**
- Identify the four factors of production.
- Describe labour markets, financial markets, and land markets.

2 **Explain how the value of marginal product determines the demand for a factor of production.**
- Explain why the demand for a factor of production is a derived demand.
- Calculate the value of marginal product.
- Explain how a firm decides the number of workers to hire.
- Explain the relationship between the value of marginal product curve and the demand for labour curve.
- State the factors that change the demand for labour.

3 **Explain how wage rates and employment are determined.**
- Describe an individual's labour supply curve.
- List the key factors that change the supply of labour.
- Illustrate labour market equilibrium.

4 **Explain how interest rates, borrowing, and lending are determined.**
- Explain the relationship between the interest rate and the quantity of capital demanded.
- Discuss the two main factors that change the demand for capital.
- Explain the relationship between the interest rate and the quantity of saving supplied.
- Discuss the main influences on the supply of saving.
- Use a graph to find the equilibrium interest rate and quantity of capital.

5 **Explain how rents and natural resource prices are determined.**
- Define the two categories of natural resources and give examples of each.
- Illustrate the market for land.
- Define economic rent and illustrate the components of a factor's income.

KEY TERMS

- Bond (page 385)
- Bond market (page 385)
- Commodity market (page 386)
- Derived demand (page 387)
- Economic rent (page 402)
- Factor price (page 384)
- Financial capital (page 385)
- Financial market (page 385)
- Job (page 384)
- Labour market (page 384)
- Nonrenewable natural resources (page 401)
- Renewable natural resources (page 401)
- Stock market (page 385)
- Value of marginal product (page 387)

CHECKPOINT 16.1

■ Describe the anatomy of the markets for labour, capital, and land.

Practice Problem 16.1

To stage the Sydney 2000 Olympic Games, the Sydney Organizing Committee:
a. Borrowed money and sold sponsorships.

b. Built the Olympic Village and venues on a disused industrial site.

c. Hired and trained 46,000 volunteers and 20,000 security guards.

d. Built water- and waste-recycling plants in the Olympic Park.

e. Set up an Internet site, which averaged 1 million hits a day.

f. Staged some events in the streets of Sydney.

Divide this list into land, labour, physical capital, human capital, financial capital, and entrepreneurship.

Solution to Practice Problem 16.1

To answer this Practice Problem, you need to know the definitions of the four factors of production.

Quick Review

- *Factors of production* The four factors of production are labour, capital, land, and entrepreneurship.

To stage the Sydney 2000 Olympic Games, the Sydney Organizing Committee:

a. Borrowed money and sold sponsorships.

Borrowing money and selling sponsorships is acquiring financial capital.

b. Built the Olympic Village and venues on a disused industrial site.

The Olympic Village and other venues are physical capital. The industrial site is land.

c. Hired and trained 46,000 volunteers and 20,000 security guards.

The volunteers and guards are labour and the skill they acquired is human capital.

d. Built water- and waste-recycling plants in the Olympic Park.

Water- and waste-recycling plants are physical capital.

e. Set up an Internet site, which averaged 1 million hits a day.

The Internet site exists on a server and so it, as well as the server, is physical capital.

f. Staged some events in the streets of Sydney.

The streets are physical capital and the people who worked at the events are labour. Overseeing all these activities was the Sydney Organizing Committee, which represents entrepreneurship.

Additional Practice Problem 16.1a

What is the difference between a stock and a bond?

Solution to Additional Practice Problem 16.1a

A share in the stock of a company is an entitlement to a share in the profits of the company. A bond is a promise to pay specified sums of money on specified dates.

■ Self Test 16.1

Fill in the blanks

The factors of production are ____, ____, ____, and ____. The funds that firms use to buy and operate physical capital are ____ (financial; stock) capital. The market in which raw materials are traded is the ____ (capital; commodity; labour) market.

True or false

1. The amount that an entrepreneur is paid is determined in a factor market.

2. Stocks and bonds are traded in a stock market.

3. As a factor of production, coal is considered to be land.

Multiple choice

1. The four factors of production that produce goods and services are

a. labour, capital, profits, and land.

b. money, labour, rent, and profit.

c. labour, capital, land, and entrepreneurship.

d. wages, interest, rent, and profit.

2. Individuals that create firms and hire labour, capital, and land in factor markets are called
   a. politicians.
   b. bureaucrats.
   c. exploiters.
   d. entrepreneurs.

3. The wage rate paid to labour is
   a. a factor output.
   b. a factor price.
   c. a factor input.
   d. an input of the workforce.

4. ____ capital consists of the funds that firms use to buy and operate capital.
   a. Human
   b. Physical
   c. Financial
   d. Logistical

5. Which of the following would be traded in the commodity market?
   a. 1,200 shares of Coca-Cola stock
   b. bonds issued by Cisco
   c. interest-bearing securities of the federal government
   d. petroleum

Short answer

1. For what are factors of production used?
2. What is the difference between capital and financial capital?
3. Petroleum is categorized as what type of factor of production?

CHECKPOINT 16.2

■ Explain how the value of marginal product determines the demand for a factor of production.

Practice Problem 16.2

Kaiser's Ice Cream Parlour hires workers to produce smoothies. The market for smoothies is perfectly competitive, and smoothies sell for $4.00 each. The labour market is competitive, and the wage rate is $40 a day. The table shows the workers' total product, *TP*:

Workers	Smoothies per day
1	7
2	21
3	33
4	43
5	51
6	55

a. Calculate the marginal product of hiring the fourth worker.
b. Calculate the value of the marginal product of the fourth worker.
c. How many workers will Kaiser's hire to maximize its profit?
d. How many smoothies a day will Kaiser's produce to maximize its profit?
e. If the price of a smoothie increases to $5, how many workers will Kaiser's now hire?
f. Kaiser's installs a new soda fountain that increases the productivity of workers by 50 percent. If the price remains at $4 a smoothie and the wage rate increases to $48 a day, how many workers does Kaiser's now hire?

Solution to Practice Problem 16.2

To answer this Practice Problem, remember that to maximize profit, a firm hires labour up to the point at which the value of marginal product equals the wage rate.

Quick Review

- *Value of marginal product* The value to a firm of hiring one more unit of a factor of production, which equals price of a unit of output multiplied by the marginal product of the factor of production.

a. **Calculate the marginal product of hiring the fourth worker.**

The marginal product of hiring the fourth worker equals the total product of hiring four workers, which is 43 smoothies minus the total product of hiring three workers, which is 33 smoothies. So the marginal product of hiring the fourth worker is 10 smoothies.

b. **Calculate the value of the marginal product of the fourth worker.**

To calculate the value of the marginal product, multiply the marginal product of the fourth worker by the price of a smoothie. The value of the marginal product of the fourth worker is 10 smoothies a day × $4.00, which is $40 a day.

c. **How many workers will Kaiser's hire to maximize its profit?**

To maximize its profit, Kaiser hires up to the point at which the value of marginal product equals the wage rate. The wage rate is $40 a day and the answer to part (b) shows that the value of the marginal product of the fourth worker is also $40 a day. So Kaiser's hires 4 workers.

d. **How many smoothies a day will Kaiser's produce to maximize its profit?**

To maximize its profit, Kaiser's hires 4 workers and the 4 workers produce 43 smoothies a day. So when Kaiser's produces 43 smoothies a day it maximizes its profit.

e. **If the price of a smoothie increases to $5, how many workers will Kaiser's now hire?**

The increase in the price of a smoothie increases the value of the marginal product. The value of the marginal product of the fourth worker is now 10 smoothies a day × $5.00, which is $50 a day. And the value of the marginal product of the fifth worker is 8 smoothies a day × $5.00, which is $40 a day. To maximize its profit, Kaiser hires up to the point at which the value of marginal product equals the wage rate. The wage rate is $40 a day, so when the price of a smoothie increases to $5, Kaiser's hires 5 workers.

f. **Kaiser's installs a new soda fountain that increases the productivity of workers by 50 percent. If the price remains at $4 a smoothie and the wage rate increases to $48 a day, how many workers does Kaiser's now hire?**

A worker's marginal product is now 50 percent higher than before. The marginal product of the 5th worker increases from 8 smoothies a day to 12 smoothies a day. The value of the marginal product of the fifth worker is 12 smoothies a day × $4.00, which is $48 a day. To maximize its profit, Kaiser hires up to the point at which the value of marginal product equals the wage rate. The wage rate is $48 a day, so when the productivity of workers increases by 50 percent, Kaiser's hires 5 workers.

Additional Practice Problem 16.2a

In Practice Problem 16.2, what is Kaiser's total revenue if it hires 3 workers,? What is Kaiser's total revenue if it hires 4 workers? If Kaiser's hires a fourth worker, what is the change in Kaiser's total revenue? How does the increase in Kaiser's total revenue compare to the value of marginal product?

Solution to Additional Practice Problem 16.2a

When Kaiser's hires 3 workers, Kaiser's produces 33 smoothies a day. Total revenue is 33 smoothies a day × $4.00, which is $132 a day. When Kaiser's hires 4 workers, Kaiser's produces 43 smoothies a day. Total revenue is 43 smoothies a day × $4.00, which is $172 a day. Kaiser's total revenue increases by $40 when Kaiser hires the fourth worker. The change in Kaiser's total revenue equals the value of marginal product of the fourth worker.

■ Self Test 16.2

Fill in the blanks

The value of marginal product equals the marginal product of the factor of production times the ____ (factor's price; price of a unit of output). The quantity of labour demanded by a firm is the quantity at which the value of the marginal product of labour equals the ____ (wage rate; price of a unit of output). When the price of the firm's output increases, the demand for labour ____ (decreases; increases).

True or false

1. The demand for labour is derived from the demand for the goods and services that the labour is hired to produce.

2. A firm's demand for labour curve is also its value of marginal product curve.

3. A rise in the wage rate decreases the quantity of labour demanded.

Multiple choice

1. The demand for a factor of production is derived from the
   a. supply of the factors.
   b. price of the factors.
   c. supply of the good the factor is used to produce.
   d. demand for the goods and services the factor is used to produce.

2. Which of the following is true?
   a. The value to a firm of hiring another worker is the worker's value of marginal product.
   b. A firm hires more workers if the wage rate is greater than the value of marginal product.
   c. The value of marginal product is the cost of hiring a worker.
   d. The value of marginal product increases as more workers are hired.

3. The value of the marginal product of labour is equal to the marginal product of the factor ____ the price of a unit of output.
   a. divided by
   b. multiplied by
   c. minus
   d. plus

4. The rule for maximizing profit is to hire labour up to the point at which the value of marginal product ____ the wage rate.
   a. equals
   b. is greater than
   c. is less than
   d. is a mirror image of

5. An increase in the price of a firm's output leads to a ____ the demand for labour curve.
   a. movement up along
   b. movement down along
   c. rightward shift of
   d. leftward shift of

Complete the graph

1. Gene's Lawn Service hires workers to mow lawns. The market for lawns is perfectly competitive and Gene charges $25 a lawn. The table shows the workers' marginal product schedule.

Quantity of labour (workers)	Marginal product (lawns per worker)	Value of marginal product 1 (dollars per day)	Value of marginal product 2 (dollars per day)
1	13	___	___
2	12	___	___
3	11	___	___
4	10	___	___
5	9	___	___

a. Calculate the value of marginal product for each quantity of workers and record your answers in the "Value of marginal product 1" column. In Figure 16.1, plot Gene's demand for labour curve and label it LD_1.

b. Suppose the price of mowing a lawn rises to $30 a lawn. Calculate the new value of marginal product and record your answers in the "Value of the marginal product 2" column. In Figure 16.1, plot Gene's new demand for labour curve and label it LD_2. How did the increase in the price of mowing a lawn change Gene's demand for labour curve?

FIGURE 16.1

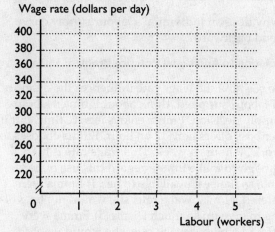

Short answer

1. Why does the value of the marginal product decrease as more workers are employed?
2. What is the relationship between the demand for labour curve and the value of marginal product curve?
3. What factors change the demand for labour and shift the demand for labour curve?

CHECKPOINT 16.3

■ **Explain how wage rates and employment are determined.**

Practice Problem 16.3

Fast-food outlets in Greenville hire both teenagers and retirees. In Greenville, the following events occur one at a time and other things remain the same. Explain the influence of each event on the market for fast-food workers.

a. A new theme park opens and hires teenagers to sell tickets for its rides.
b. The new theme park becomes the hottest tourist attraction in the province.
c. Retirees flock to Greenville and make it their home.
d. The demand for hamburgers and fries decreases and as a result the price of a hamburger and fries decreases.
e. New technology in the fast-food industry decreases the marginal product of fast-food workers.

Solution to Practice Problem 16.3

To answer this Practice Problem use a labour demand–labour supply diagram to determine the effect of each influence on the equilibrium wage rate and the level of employment.

Quick Review

- *Changes in the demand for labour* The demand for labour depends on the price of the firm's output, the prices of other factors of production, and technology.
- *Change in the supply of labour* The key factors that change the supply of labour are the adult population, preferences, and time in school and training.

a. **A new theme park opens and hires teenagers to sell tickets for its rides.**

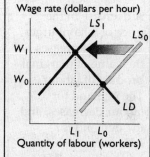

Some teenage workers prefer to work in the theme park, so the supply of fast-food labour decreases. In the figure, which shows the market for fast-food workers, the supply of labour curve shifts leftward from LS_0 to LS_1. The wage rate rises and the number of fast-food workers employed decreases.

b. **The new theme park becomes the hottest tourist attraction in the province.**

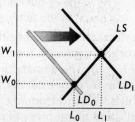

As the number of tourists increases, the demand for fast food increases and the demand for fast-food workers increases. In the figure, the demand for labour curve shifts rightward from LD_0 to LD_1. The wage rate rises and the number of fast-food workers employed increases.

c. **Retirees flock to Greenville and make it their home.**

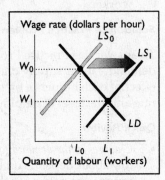

The influx of retirees increases the supply of labour. In the figure, the supply of labour curve shifts rightward from LS_0 to LS_1. The wage rate falls and the number of fast-food workers employed increases.

d. **The demand for hamburgers and fries decreases and as a result the price of a hamburger and fries decreases.**

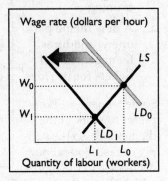

A decrease in the price of a hamburger and fries decreases the value of marginal product of labour. The demand for labour decreases, and the demand for labour curve shifts leftward from LD_0 to LD_1. The wage rate falls and the number of fast-food workers employed decreases.

e. **New technology in the fast-food industry decreases the marginal product of fast-food workers.**

A decrease in the marginal product of fast-food workers decreases the value of marginal product of labour. The demand for labour decreases. In the figure above the demand for labour curve shifts leftward from LD_0 to LD_1. The wage rate falls and the number of fast-food workers employed decreases.

Additional Practice Problem 16.3a

Why does an individual's labour supply curve bend backward?

Solution to Additional Practice Problem 16.3a

To see how the wage rate influences the quantity of labour supplied, think about Emma's labour supply decision. Emma enjoys leisure time, but if her boss offers her $12 an hour, Emma chooses to work 30 hours a week. This wage rate is high enough to make Emma regard this use of her time as the best available to her. If Emma were offered a lower wage rate, she would not be willing to give up so much leisure. If Emma were offered a higher wage rate, she would want to work even longer hours, but only up to a point. If Emma is offered $25 an hour, she would be willing to work a 40-hour week. But if the wage rate is increased above $25 an hour, Emma would cut back on her work hours and take more leisure. Emma's labour supply curve eventually bends backward.

■ Self Test 16.3

Fill in the blanks

An individual's ____ (demand; supply) of labour curve bends backward. An increase in the adult population ____ (decreases; increases) the supply of labour. If the wage rate exceeds the equilibrium wage rate, the quantity of labour supplied is ____ (greater; less) than the quantity of labour demanded.

True or false

1. An individual's supply of labour curve shows that the quantity of labour supplied always increases when the wage rate rises.

2. An increase in college enrolment decreases the supply of low-skilled labour.

3. If the wage rate is less than the equilibrium wage rate, the wage rate will rise to eliminate the surplus of labour.

Multiple choice

1. An individual's labour supply curve eventually bends backward because at a high enough wage rate,
   a. people are willing to work more hours.
   b. employers are willing to hire more workers.
   c. people desire more leisure time.
   d. very few workers are hired.

2. How does an increase in the adult population change the market supply of labour?
   a. It will become more inelastic.
   b. The supply of labour decreases.
   c. The supply of labour increases.
   d. None of the above answers is correct.

3. The supply of labour curve shifts leftward if
   a. the population increases.
   b. the demand for labour curve shifts leftward.
   c. the supply of labour increases.
   d. None of the above answers is correct.

4. If the wage rate is above the equilibrium wage rate, the quantity of labour demanded is ____ the quantity of labour supplied.
   a. greater than
   b. less than
   c. equal to
   d. the negative of

5. The more people who remain in school for full-time education and training, the _____ is the _____ low-skilled labour.
   a. smaller; demand for
   b. smaller; supply of
   c. larger; supply of
   d. larger; demand for

Complete the graph

1. Figure 16.2 shows Hank's supply of labour curve. At what wage rate does an increase in the wage rate decrease the quantity of labour Hank supplies?

■ FIGURE 16.2

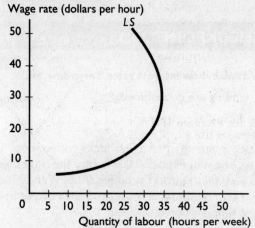

2. Figure 16.3 shows the labour market for webmasters. Suppose that more companies start conducting more business on the Internet. In Figure 16.3, illustrate the effect in the market for webmasters. What happens to the equilibrium wage rate and number of webmasters?

■ FIGURE 16.3

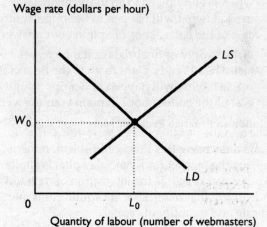

Short answer

1. How does an increase in the adult population change the supply of labour?

2. If more people decide to obtain an advanced education, after they graduate what is the ef-

fect on the supply of high-skilled labour? What is the effect on the equilibrium wage rate for high-skilled workers?

CHECKPOINT 16.4

■ **Explain how interest rates, borrowing, and lending are determined.**

Practice Problem 16.4

Wendy plans to open a Starbucks coffee shop. To do so, she will need $50,000 to buy the franchise and $20,000 to outfit the coffee shop. Wendy has $15,000 in her bank account, and the current interest rate is 5 percent a year.

a. What is Wendy's opportunity cost of opening the coffee shop?
b. What is the quantity of financial capital that Wendy plans to get from the financial market?
c. What is the quantity of financial capital that Wendy plans to provide herself?
d. If demand for financial capital increases just when Wendy plans to go to the financial market, what will happen to her opportunity cost of the coffee shop? Explain your answer.
e. If the supply of financial capital increases just when Wendy plans to go to the financial market, what will happen to her opportunity cost of the coffee shop? Explain your answer.

Solution to Practice Problem 16.4

When answering this Practice Problem, remember that the market for financial capital is similar to other markets. It is the interaction of demand and supply that determine the equilibrium interest rate and quantity of capital.

Quick Review

- *Factors that change the demand for capital* Two main factors that change the demand for capital are population growth and technological change.
- *Influences on the supply of saving* The main influences on the supply of saving are population, current income, and expected future income.

a. **What is Wendy's opportunity cost of opening the coffee shop?**

Wendy's opportunity cost is the interest she pays on the $55,000 she borrows plus the forgone interest on the $15,000 she provides. With an interest rate of 5 percent a year, her borrowing costs are ($55,000) × (0.05), which is $2,750 a year and the interest forgone equals ($15,000) × (0.05), which is $750. The total opportunity cost is $3,500 a year.

b. **What is the quantity of financial capital that Wendy plans to get from the financial market?**

Wendy needs $70,000 and she has $15,000. So the quantity of financial capital she plans to get from the financial market is the difference between $70,000 and $15,000, which is $55,000.

c. **What is the quantity of financial capital that Wendy plans to provide herself?**

Wendy plans to provide $15,000 herself.

d. **If demand for financial capital increases just when Wendy plans to go to the financial market, what will happen to her opportunity cost of the coffee shop? Explain your answer.**

If the demand for financial capital increases, the equilibrium interest rate rises. The interest rate that Wendy has to pay for her financial capital will exceed 5 percent a year and the opportunity cost of her coffee shop will increase.

e. **If the supply of financial capital increases just when Wendy plans to go to the financial market, what will happen to her opportunity cost of the coffee shop? Explain your answer.**

If the supply of financial capital increases, the equilibrium interest rate falls. The interest rate that Wendy has to pay for her financial capital will be less than 5 percent a year and the opportunity cost of her coffee shop will decrease.

Additional Practice Problem 16.4a

Describe the financial market equilibrium over time.

Solution to Additional Practice Problem 16.4a

Over time, the demand for capital and the supply of capital increase. Population growth increases the demand for capital. As the increased population earns a larger income, the supply of capital increases. Technological advances increase the demand for capital, and bring higher incomes. The supply of capital increases. The quantity of capital increases because the demand for capital and supply of capital increase, but the interest rate does not persistently increase or decrease.

■ **Self Test 16.4**

Fill in the blanks

The higher the interest rate, the ____ (greater; smaller) the quantity of capital demanded. The quantity of financial capital ____ (demanded; supplied) results from people's saving decisions. An increase in current income ____ (increases; decreases) the supply of capital. As the population grows, the demand for physical capital ____ (decreases; increases).

True or false

1. Technological change increases the demand for all types of capital.
2. A rise in the interest rate decreases the quantity of capital supplied.
3. If a household's current income is low and its expected future income is high, the household will have a low level of saving.

Multiple choice

1. The demand for financial capital stems from
   a. an individual's need to pay for benefits.
   b. a firm's requirement to pay for union wages.
   c. a firm's demand for physical capital.
   d. a firm's demand for labour.

2. When the interest rate falls, the ____ financial capital ____.
   a. demand for; increases
   b. demand for; decreases
   c. quantity demanded of; increases
   d. quantity demanded of; decreases

3. The quantity of financial capital supplied results from people's ____ decisions.
   a. saving
   b. spending
   c. investing
   d. employment

4. The higher the interest rate, the
   a. more incentive people have to consume.
   b. less incentive people have to save.
   c. higher the opportunity cost of current consumption.
   d. lower the opportunity cost of current consumption.

5. If a household's current income is ____ and its expected future income is low, it will have ____.
   a. zero; a high level of saving
   b. high; a negative level of saving
   c. high; no saving
   d. high; a high level of saving

Short answer

1. How does technological change affect the demand for capital?
2. What is the source of the supply of financial capital?

3. If people expect an increase in future income, what is the effect on the interest rate?

CHECKPOINT 16.5

■ Explain how rents and natural resource prices are determined.

Practice Problem 16.5

Which of the following items are nonrenewable natural resources, which are renewable natural resources, and which are not natural resources? Explain your answers.

a. Beaches on Prince Edward Island
b. The CN Tower
c. Diamond mines in northern Canada
d. The Great Lakes
e. National parks
f. Douglas fir forests in British Columbia
g. Oil reserves under the Atlantic Ocean off Newfoundland
h. The Lion's Gate Bridge in Vancouver

Solution to Practice Problem 16.5

To answer this Practice Problem, remember the distinction between renewable natural resources and nonrenewable natural resources.

Quick Review

- *Renewable natural resources* Natural resources that can be used repeatedly.
- *Nonrenewable natural resources* Natural resources that can be used only once and that cannot be replaced once they have been used.

a. **Beaches on Prince Edward Island**

The beaches are a gift of nature, which can be used repeatedly, so they are a renewable natural resource.

b. **The CN Tower**

The CN Tower is a national landmark, but it is not a national resource.

c. **Diamond mines in northern Canada**

The diamond mine is a gift of nature. Once the diamond is mined, it cannot be used repeatedly, so it is a nonrenewable natural resource.

d. **The Great Lakes**

The Great Lakes are a gift of nature. They can be used repeatedly, so they are a renewable natural resource.

e. **National parks**

The national parks are a gift of nature. They can be used repeatedly, so they are a renewable natural resource.

f. **Douglas fir forests in British Columbia**

The national parks are a gift of nature. They can be used repeatedly, so they are a renewable natural resource.

g. **Oil reserves under the Atlantic Ocean off Newfoundland**

The oil reserves are a gift of nature. They cannot be used repeatedly, so they are a nonrenewable natural resource.

h. **The Lion's Gate Bridge in Vancouver**

The Lion's Gate Bridge is a national landmark, but it is not a national resource.

Additional Practice Problem 16.5a

As a nonrenewable natural resource is used, what happens to the supply and its price?

Solution to Additional Practice Problem 16.5a

Using a natural resource decreases its supply, which causes its price to rise. But new technologies that lead to the discovery of previously unknown reserves increase supply, which causes the price to fall. Also, new technologies that enable a more efficient use of a nonrenewable natural resource decrease the demand for the resource, which causes its price to fall.

Self Test 16.5

Fill in the blanks

The supply of each particular block of land is perfectly ____ (elastic; inelastic). Economic rent can be earned by ____ (only land; any factor of production). Over time, advances in technology ____ (increase; decrease) the known quantity of a natural resource.

True or false

1. Forestland is a renewable natural resource.
2. The demand for land is perfectly elastic, and the supply of land is perfectly inelastic.
3. The price of a natural resource always rises over time.

Multiple choice

1. A natural resource is renewable if it
   a. never has to rest.
   b. can be used repeatedly.
   c. cannot be replaced once it has been used.
   d. is available at a price of zero.

2. Oil is an example of
   a. a nonrenewable natural resource.
   b. a renewable natural resource.
   c. physical capital.
   d. a resource for which the true value of the resource cannot be measured.

3. The supply of each particular block of land is
   a. perfectly elastic.
   b. unit elastic.
   c. elastic.
   d. perfectly inelastic.

4. Economic rent is the income over and above
   a. opportunity cost.
   b. average cost.
   c. factor income.
   d. marginal cost.

5. The income required to induce the supply of a given quantity of a factor of production is
   a. the value of marginal product.
   b. its marginal cost.
   c. its opportunity cost.
   d. its economic rent.

Complete the graph

1. The table shows the demand for land. The supply of land is 20,000 square hectares.

Rent (dollars per hectare per month)	Land (thousands of hectares)
400	10
350	20
300	30
250	40
200	50

   a. In Figure 16.4, label the axes and graph the market for land.
   b. Find the equilibrium rent and quantity and indicate the economic rent and opportunity cost.

   ■ FIGURE 16.4

   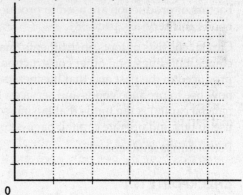
   Rent (dollars per hectare per month)

Short answer

1. Why is petroleum considered a nonrenewable natural resource?
2. John Travolta receives $18 million to act in a movie. Suppose Mr. Travolta would act in a movie as long as he received $100,000. What are his opportunity cost and economic rent?

SELF TEST ANSWERS

■ CHECKPOINT 16.1

Fill in the blanks

The factors of production are <u>labour</u>, <u>capital</u>, <u>land</u>, and <u>entrepreneurship</u>. The funds that firms use to buy and operate physical capital are <u>financial</u> capital. The market in which raw materials are traded is the <u>commodity</u> market.

True or false

1. False; page 384
2. False; page 385
3. True; page 386

Multiple choice

1. c; page 384
2. d; page 384
3. b; page 384
4. c; page 385
5. d; page 386

Short answer

1. Factors of production are used to produce goods and services; page 384.
2. Capital consists of tools, instruments, machines, buildings, and other constructions produced in the past and that businesses now use to produce goods and services. Financial capital is the funds that businesses use to buy and operate capital; page 385.
3. Petroleum is land; page 386.

■ CHECKPOINT 16.2

Fill in the blanks

The value of marginal product equals the marginal product of the factor of production times the <u>price of a unit of output</u>. The quantity of labour demanded by a firm is the quantity at which the value of the marginal product of labour equals the <u>wage rate</u>. When the price of the firm's output increases, the demand for labour <u>increases</u>.

True or false

1. True; page 387
2. True; page 389
3. True; page 390

Multiple choice

1. d; page 387
2. a; page 387
3. b; page 387
4. a; page 388
5. c; page 390

Complete the graph

1. a. The completed table is below. Figure 16.5 plots the demand for labour curve, LD_1.

Quantity of labour (workers)	Marginal product (lawns per worker)	Value of marginal product 1 (dollars per day)	Value of marginal product 2 (dollars per day)
1	13	<u>325</u>	<u>390</u>
2	12	<u>300</u>	<u>360</u>
3	11	<u>275</u>	<u>330</u>
4	10	<u>250</u>	<u>300</u>
5	9	<u>225</u>	<u>270</u>

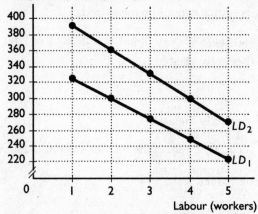

■ FIGURE 16.5

b. In Figure 16.5, the demand for labour curve shifts rightward; pages 388–390

Short answer

1. As more of the factor of production is employed, marginal product decreases, and value of marginal product, which equals the price of a unit of the output multiplied by the marginal product of the factor of production also decreases; page 387.

2. The demand for labour curve and the value of marginal product curve are the same; page 389.

3. Three factors change the demand for labour and shift the demand for labour curve: a change in the price of the firm's output, a change in the prices of other factors of production, and a change in technology; page 390.

■ CHECKPOINT 16.3

Fill in the blanks

An individual's <u>supply</u> of labour curve bends backward. An increase in the adult population <u>increases</u> the supply of labour. If the wage rate exceeds the equilibrium wage rate, the quantity of labour supplied is <u>greater than</u> the quantity of labour demanded.

True or false

    1. False; page 392

    2. True; page 394

    3. False; page 394

Multiple choice

    1. c; page 392

    2. c; page 394

    3. d; page 394

    4. b; page 394

    5. b; page 394

Complete the graph

1. Figure 16.6 shows that for wage rates exceeding $30 an hour, Hank decreases the quantity of labour he supplies as the wage rate rises; page 392.

■ FIGURE 16.6

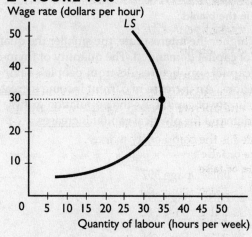

2. In Figure 16.7 the demand for Webmasters increases. The demand for labour curve shifts rightward from LD_0 to LD_1. The equilibrium wage rate rises and the quantity of webmasters employed increases; page 394.

■ FIGURE 16.7

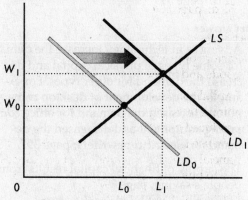

Short answer

1. An increase in the adult population increases the supply of labour; page 394.

2. As more people obtain advanced degrees the supply of high-skilled labour increases. The equilibrium wage rate for high-skilled labour falls; page 394.

CHECKPOINT 16.4

Fill in the blanks

The higher the interest rate, the <u>smaller</u> the quantity of capital demanded. The quantity of financial capital <u>supplied</u> results from people's saving decisions. An increase in current income <u>increases</u> the supply of capital. As the population grows, the demand for physical capital <u>increases</u>.

True or false

1. False; page 397
2. False; page 397
3. True; page 398

Multiple choice

1. c; page 397
2. c; page 397
3. a; page 397
4. c; page 397
5. d; page 399

Short answer

1. Advances in technology increase the demand for some types of physical capital and decrease the demand for other types. For example, the development of desktop computers increased the demand for office computing equipment and decreased the demand for electric typewriters; page 397.

2. The supply of financial capital results from people's saving; page 397.

3. If people expect an increase in future income, they save less now and the supply of capital decreases. The equilibrium interest rate rises; pages 398-399.

CHECKPOINT 16.5

Fill in the blanks

The supply of each particular block of land is perfectly <u>inelastic</u>. Economic rent can be earned by <u>any factor of production</u>. Over time, advances in technology <u>increase</u> the known quantity of a natural resource.

True or false

1. True; page 401
2. False; page 401
3. False; page 403

Multiple choice

1. b; page 401
2. a; page 401
3. d; page 401
4. a; page 402
5. c; page 402

Complete the graph

1. a. Figure 16.8 shows the completed figure; page 401.

■ FIGURE 16.8

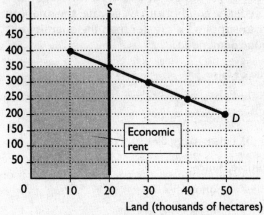

b. Equilibrium rent is $350 a hectare and the equilibrium quantity is 20,000 hectares. Figure 16.8 shows the economic rent. Opportunity cost is zero; page 402.

Short answer

1. Petroleum is a nonrenewable natural resource. It can be used only once; page 401.

2. Opportunity cost is $100,000 and economic rent is $17.9 million; page 402.

Chapter 17

Earnings Differences

CHAPTER IN PERSPECTIVE

This chapter explores the earnings differences between college graduates and high school graduates, between union and non-union workers, and between men and women.

■ **Explain why college graduates earn more, on the average, than high school graduates.**

Differences in skills lead to large differences in earnings. High-skilled labour has a higher value of marginal product than low-skilled labour, so at a given level of employment, firms are willing to pay a higher wage rate to a high-skilled worker than to a low-skilled worker. The vertical distance between the high-skilled worker's supply curve and the low-skilled worker's supply curve is the compensation for the cost of acquiring skill. The equilibrium wage rate of high-skilled labour is higher than that of low-skilled labour.

■ **Explain why union workers earn higher wage rates than non-union workers.**

A labour union is an organized group of workers whose purpose is to increase the wage rate and influence other job conditions for its members. A union strives to increase compensation, improve working conditions and expand job opportunities for its members. Because the labour demand curves slope downward, anything a union does that increases the wage rate or other employment costs decreases the quantity of labour demanded. Many unions control supply by organizing on-the-job training and limiting the number of workers who receive training. Some of the methods used by the unions to change the demand for the labour of its members are to: increase the marginal product of union members; encourage import restrictions; support minimum wage laws; support immigration restrictions; and increase demand for the good produced. Union wage rates are, on the average, about 30 percent higher than non-union wage rates. A monopsony is a market in which there is a single buyer. A union is like a monopoly. If the union (a monopoly seller) faces a monopsony buyer, the situation is one of bilateral monopoly.

■**Discuss reasons why men earn more than women and predict the effects of a pay equity law.**

Four possible explanations for earnings differences between men and women are job types, discrimination, differences in human capital, and differences in the degree of specialization. Some of the wage differences between the sexes arise because men and women do different jobs and the jobs that men do are better paid. But women earn less on the average than men even when they do the same job. Discrimination is hard to measure objectively. Historically, men have had more human capital than women, but this is changing. Women's careers have traditionally been interrupted more frequently than those of men. In most households, men have been more specialized in market activity than have woman. A pay equity law is a law that requires an employer to pay the same wage rate to workers who do different jobs that are judged comparable.

EXPANDED CHAPTER CHECKLIST

When you have completed this chapter, you will be able to:

1 **Explain why college graduates earn more, on the average, than high school graduates.**

- Discuss the demand for high-skilled labour and low-skilled labour.
- Discuss the supply of high-skilled labour and low-skilled labour.
- Illustrate the market for high-skilled labour and the market for low-skilled labour.

2 **Explain why union workers earn higher wage rates than non-union workers.**

- Define labour union.
- Explain a union's objectives and constraints.
- Discuss how and why unions attempt to change the supply of labour and the demand for labour.
- Define monopsony.
- Use a graph to show that compared with a competitive labour market, a monopsony decreases the wage rate and the level of employment.
- Describe the bargaining process between a union and a monopsony.
- Describe the effects of a minimum wage law in a monopsony labour market.

3 **Discuss reasons why men earn more than women and predict the effects of a pay equity law.**

- Describe the effect of job types on the wage differences between the sexes.
- Discuss the effect of discrimination in the labour market.
- Describe the relationship between human capital and the wage rate received and why this factor may be a source of lower wages, on the average, for women.
- Explain the role of specialization on wage differences between the sexes.
- Define pay equity law and use a supply and demand figure to illustrate how a pay equity law works.

KEY TERMS

- Bilateral monopoly (page 418)
- Collective bargaining (page 413)
- Labour union (page 412)
- Monopsony (page 416)
- Pay equity law (page 424)
- Rand Formula (page 413)

CHECKPOINT 17.1

■ **Explain why college graduates earn more, on the average, than high school graduates.**

Practice Problem 17.1

In Canada in April 2001, 83,000 people had full-time managerial and professional jobs that paid an average of $840 a week. At the same time, 125,000 people had full-time sales positions that paid an average of $340 a week.

a. Explain why managers and professionals are paid more than salespeople.

b. Explain why, despite the higher weekly wage, fewer people are employed as managers and professionals than as salespeople.

c. If Internet shopping becomes very popular and the range of goods and services available on the Internet expands rapidly, what changes do you expect will occur in the market for salespeople?

Solution to Practice Problem 17.1

This Practice Problem studies the relationship between skill differentials and the wage rate. Remember that high-skilled labour has a higher value of marginal product than low-skilled labour and that skills are costly to acquire.

Quick Review

- *Demand for high-skilled labour and low-skilled labour* The vertical distance between the demand curve for low-skilled labour and the demand curve for high-skilled labour is equal to the value of marginal product of skill.
- *Supply of high-skilled labour and low-skilled labour* The vertical distance between the supply curve of low-skilled labour and the supply curve of high-skilled labour is equal to the compensation that high-skilled workers require for the cost of acquiring the skill.

a. **Explain why managers and professionals are paid more than salespeople.**

The typical manager or professional has incurred a higher cost of education and on-the-job training than the typical salesperson. In the figure, the supply curve of managers and professionals, S_H, lies above the supply curve of salespeople, S_L, and the vertical distance between the two curves is the compensation for the cost of acquiring skill. The better education and more on-the-job training result in managers and professionals having more human capital and a higher value of marginal product than salespeople. So the demand curve for managers and professionals, D_H, lies above the demand curve for salespeople, D_L, and the vertical distance between the two curves is equal to the value of marginal product of skill.

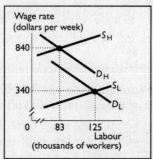

The demand for and supply of each type of workers determine the wage rate. In the figure, managers and professionals receive a higher wage rate than salespeople.

b. **Explain why, despite the higher weekly wage, fewer people are employed as managers and professionals than as salespeople.**

The figure shows that the combination of demand and supply leads to fewer managers and professionals than salespeople.

c. **If Internet shopping becomes very popular and the range of goods and services available on the Internet expands rapidly, what changes do you expect will occur in the market for salespeople?**

The demand for salespeople will decrease, the demand curve for salespeople will shift leftward, and fewer people will work in sales. The equilibrium wage rate will depend on what happens to the supply of salespeople.

Additional Practice Problem 17.1a

What is the opportunity cost of acquiring a skill?

Solution to Additional Practice Problem 17.1a

The opportunity cost of acquiring a skill includes actual expenditures on tuition and books and costs in the form of lost or reduced earnings while the skill is being acquired. When a person goes to school full time, that cost is the total earnings forgone. When a person receives on-the-job training, he is paid a lower wage than one who is doing a comparable job but not undergoing training. In this case, the opportunity cost of acquiring the skill is equal to the wage paid to a person not being trained minus the wage paid to a person being trained.

■ Self Test 17.1

Fill in the blanks

The demand curve for high-skilled labour lies ____ (above; below) the demand curve for low-skilled labour and the supply curve of high-skilled labour lies ____ (above; below) the supply curve of low-skilled labour. The wage rate paid high-skilled workers is ____ (greater; less) than the wage rate paid low-skilled workers.

True or false

1. At a given wage rate, the quantity of high-skilled labour demanded exceeds the quantity of low-skilled labour demanded.
2. The horizontal distance between the demand curve for high-skilled labour and the demand curve for low-skilled labour measures the marginal product of skill.
3. The greater the cost of acquiring a skill, the greater is the vertical distance between the supply curve of high-skilled labour and the supply curve of low-skilled labour.
4. The equilibrium wage rate paid high-skilled workers exceeds that paid low-skilled workers.
5. On the average, a person with a bachelor's degree earns a greater income than a person with a high school diploma.

Multiple choice

1. Differences in skills
   a. arise partly from differences in education and partly from differences in on-the-job training.
   b. can lead to large differences in earnings.
   c. result in different demand curves for high-skilled and low-skilled labour.
   d. All of the above answers are correct.

2. Other things being equal, the value of marginal product curve for low-skilled labour ____ the value of marginal product curve for high-skilled labour.
   a. lies below
   b. lies above
   c. is the same as
   d. is not comparable to

3. The cost of acquiring a skill explains why the
   a. demand for high-skilled workers is different than the demand for low-skilled workers.
   b. supply of high-skilled workers is different than the supply of low-skilled workers.
   c. demand for high-skilled workers is different than the supply of high-skilled workers.
   d. None of the above answers is correct.

4. The vertical distance between the supply curve of neurosurgeons and the supply curve of plumbers represents the
   a. difference in the demand for these two occupations.
   b. compensation that neurosurgeons require for the cost of acquiring their skill.
   c. difference in the value of the marginal product of the two professions.
   d. difference in on-the-job training.

5. The more costly it is to acquire a skill, the
   a. more people will go to school to learn the skill.
   b. less employers are willing to pay for the skill.
   c. greater the wage differential between high-skilled and low-skilled workers.
   d. smaller the wage differential between high-skilled and low-skilled workers.

6. A firm will pay a higher wage rate to a worker
   a. if the firm's demand for labour curve has a positive slope.
   b. the greater her value of marginal product.
   c. if the marginal product of the worker is decreasing.
   d. if the supply of workers is large.

7. The higher the value of the marginal product of a skill, the

a. greater the difference in the wage rate between high-skilled and low-skilled labour.
b. smaller the vertical difference between the demand curves for high-skilled and low-skilled labour.
c. greater the vertical distance between the supply curves of high-skilled and low-skilled labour.
d. All of the above answers are correct.

8. The wage differential between high-skilled labour and low-skilled labour depends on

a. the value of marginal product of skill.
b. the cost of acquiring skill.
c. the value of marginal cost of skill.
d. Both a and b are correct.

Complete the graph

1. Figure 17.1 show the demand curves for high-skilled and low-skilled labour and the supply curves of high-skilled and low-skilled labour.

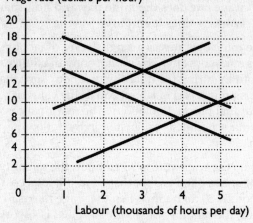

■ **FIGURE 17.1**

a. Label the demand curve for the high-skilled workers D_H and demand curve for low-skilled workers D_L. Label the supply curve of high-skilled workers S_H and the supply curve of low-skilled workers S_L.

b. What is the value of marginal product of skill?
c. What is compensation required for the cost of acquiring the skill?
d. What is the equilibrium wage rate for high-skilled workers and low-skilled workers?

Short answer

1. How does the value of marginal product of high-skilled workers compare with the value of marginal product of low-skilled workers?

2a. How does the demand for high-skilled workers compare to the demand for low-skilled workers? How does the supply of high-skilled workers compare to the supply of low-skilled workers?

b. How does the wage rate of high-skilled workers compare to the wage rate of low-skilled workers?

c. How does the quantity of high-skilled workers employed compare to the quantity of low-skilled workers employed?

CHECKPOINT 17.2

■ **Explain why union workers earn higher wage rates than non-union workers.**

Practice Problems 17.2

1. In Canada in 2001, 10,000 people worked as flight attendants and earned an average of about $20.00 an hour. Most flight attendants are members of a union, the Canadian Union of Public Employees. To be a flight attendant, a person must be a high school graduate, and formal training is provided by the airlines. The air transportation industry is competitive.

a. If flight attendants were not members of a union, how might the wage rate and number of flight attendants be different?

b. Currently, the Canadian Aviation Administration (CAA) requires one attendant for every 50 seats. If the union lobbies for a change in the rule and the CAA responds by requiring one attendant for every 25 seats, how might the wage rate and number of flight attendants change?

c. If the union provided the formal training of flight attendants, how might the wage rate and number of flight attendants change?

2. The table gives the demand and supply schedules of labour in a remote mining town. The mine is the only employer. What wage rate does the mine pay and how many workers does it employ?

Wage rate (dollars per hour)	Quantity of labour supplied (workers)	Quantity of labour demanded (workers)
2	2	10
3	3	9
4	4	8
5	5	7
6	6	6
7	7	5
8	8	4

Solution to Practice Problems 17.2

The first Practice Problem studies the effects of a union in the labour market. The second Practice Problem looks at a monopsony. A monopsony recognizes that by hiring less labour, it can pay a lower wage rate, so its marginal cost of labour exceeds the wage rate. To find the profit-maximizing quantity of labour, the monopsony firm sets the marginal cost of labour equal to the value of the marginal product of labour. The wage rate the monopsony pays is the lowest wage for which that labour will work, which comes from the supply of labour curve.

Quick Review

- *Monopsony* A market in which there is a single buyer.

1a. If flight attendants were not members of a union, how might the wage rate and number of flight attendants be different?

In this particular market, the union does not appear to be very effective. If the flight attendants were not members of a union, supply would not change because any high school graduate can apply to the airlines for training. And demand would not change because the airlines provide the training. The wage rate and number of flight attendants would not change significantly.

1b. Currently, the Canadian Aviation Administration (CAA) requires one attendant for every 50 seats. If the union lobbies for a change in the rule and the CAA responds by requiring one attendant for every 25 seats, how might the wage rate and number of flight attendants change?

If the union is successful in lobbying, the demand for flight attendants will increase. The wage rate rises and the number of flight attendants increases.

1c. If the union provided the formal training of flight attendants, how might the wage rate and number of flight attendants change?

If the union provides the formal training, then the union might be able to restrict the number of people who receive the training. The supply of flight attendants would decrease. The wage rate rises and the number of flight attendants decreases.

2. The table gives the demand and supply schedules of labour in a remote mining town. The mine is the only employer. What wage rate does the mine pay and how many workers does it employ?

The mine operates as a single buyer of labour so it is a monopsony. The monopsony maximizes profit by hiring the quantity of labour such that the marginal cost of labour equals the value of marginal product of labour. The marginal cost of labour schedule is calculated in the following table.

When the wage rate is $3 an hour, the quantity of labour supplied is 3 workers and the total cost of labour is $9 an hour. When the wage rate is $4 an hour, the quantity of labour supplied is 4 workers and the total cost of labour is $16 an hour. So the marginal cost of increasing the quantity of labour from 3 workers to 4 workers is $16 − $9, which is $7. When the wage rate is $5 an hour, the quantity of labour supplied is 5 workers and the total cost of labour is $25 an hour. So the marginal cost of increasing the quantity of labour from 4 workers to 5 workers is $25 − $16, which is $9 an hour.

The marginal cost of labour for the 4th worker is $8 (the average of the marginal cost of increasing labour from 3 to 4 workers, $7, and the marginal cost of increasing labour from 4 to 5 workers, $9). The demand schedule of labour, which is the monopsony's value of marginal product schedule, shows that the value of marginal product of the 4th worker is $8. So the mine hires 4 workers. From the supply schedule, when the mine hires 4 workers, the wage rate is $4 an hour.

Wage rate (dollars per hour)	Quantity of labour supplied (workers)	Total cost of labour (dollars per hour)	Marginal cost of labour (dollars per worker)
2	2	4	
			5
3	3	9	
			7
4	4	16	
			9
5	5	25	
			11
6	6	36	
			13
7	7	49	
			15
8	8	64	

Additional Practice Problem 17.2a

Suppose the miners in the Practice Problem decide to form a union.

a. What tactic can they use to boost their wages?
b. Is the outcome of bargaining entirely predictable?

Solution to Additional Practice Problem 17.2a

a. **What tactic can they use to boost their wages?**

The tactic that the miners can use is the threat of a strike. A strike is a group decision of the workers to refuse to work under prevailing conditions.

b. **Is the outcome of bargaining entirely predictable?**

The actual outcome of bargaining depends on the costs that each party can inflict on the other as a result of a failure to agree on the wage rate. The firm can shut down the mine and lock out its workers, and the workers can call a strike and shut down the mine. Each party knows the other's strength and knows what it will lose if it does not agree to the other's demands. If the two parties are equally strong and they realize it, they will split the difference. If one party is stronger than the other—and both parties know that—the agreed wage will favour the stronger party.

■ **Self Test 17.2**

Fill in the blanks

The requirement that all workers represented by a union pay dues to the union, whether they join the union or not is the ____ (Collective; Rand; Union) Formula. In a competitive labour market, a union ____ (faces; does not face) the tradeoff that a higher wage rate decreases employment. A union supports minimum wage laws and immigration restrictions to increase the ____ (demand for; supply of) the labour of its members. A monopsony is a market in which there is a single ____ (seller; buyer). For a monopsony, the marginal cost of labour (MCL) curve lies ____ (above; below) the supply of labour curve. In a monopsony labour market, it ____ (is; is not) possible for a minimum wage to increase the wage rate and employment.

True or false

1. The smaller the fraction of the work force controlled by a union, the more effective the union.

2. Unions try to make the demand for union labour less elastic.

3. A union tries to increase the demand for its labour and increase the supply of its labour.

4. A monopsony maximizes its profit by hiring the quantity of labour that makes the value of marginal product of labour equal to the market wage rate.

5. In a bilateral monopoly, the wage rate is equal to the competitive wage rate.

Multiple choice

1. A labour union is an organized group of workers whose purpose is to
a. increase the competition for a particular type of labour.
b. increase the supply of labour and decrease the wage rate.
c. restrict competition and decrease the wages of its members.
d. increase the wage rate of its members.

2. _____ is a process in which a third party—an arbitrator—determines the wage rate and other employment conditions on behalf of the negotiating parties.
a. Binding arbitration
b. Collective bargaining
c. Binding bargaining
d. Collective arbitration

3. In an open shop,
a. the firm is open only to union members.
b. a firm can hire non-union employees but they have to join the union after a specified time period.
c. both union and non-union employees can be hired.
d. the firm is organized in an open or outdoor space.

4. A firm's refusal to operate its plant and employ its workers is a
a. strike.
b. boycott.
c. lockout.
d. monopsony.

5. A union tries to shift the supply of labour curve of its members ____ and the demand for labour curve of its members ____.
a. rightward; rightward
b. rightward; leftward
c. leftward; rightward
d. leftward; leftward

6. A monopsony is a market in which there
a. is a single seller.
b. are many sellers.
c. is a single buyer.
d. are many buyers.

7. In a monopsony labour market, the wage rate is ____ and employment is ____ than in a competitive labour market.
a. higher; more
b. higher; less
c. lower; more
d. lower; less

8. In a bilateral monopoly, what determines the wage rate?
a. which bargaining party has the greater barriers to entry
b. the size of the firm's value of marginal product
c. which bargaining party pays the largest amount to the arbitrator
d. the costs that each party can inflict on the other if an agreement is not reached

Complete the graph

1. The table shows the supply schedule of nurses for Towne Hospital, the only employer of nurses in a small town.

   a. Complete the table.

Wage rate (dollars per day)	Quantity of labour demanded (nurses)	Quantity of labour supplied (nurses)	Marginal cost of labour (dollars per day)
20	10	2	
30	9	3	___
40	8	4	___
50	7	5	___
60	6	6	___
70	5	7	___
80	4	8	

   b. Plot the demand for labour curve, supply of labour curve, and the marginal cost of labour curve in Figure 17.2.

   c. How many nurses does Towne Hospital hire? What wage rate does Towne Hospital pay?

   d. Suppose there are many hospitals so that the market for nurses is perfectly competitive. How many nurses are hired and what wage rate are they paid?

   e. How does the wage rate that Towne Hospital pays when it is a monopsony compare with the wage rate paid if the market is perfectly competitive? How does the number of nurses hired compare in the two cases?

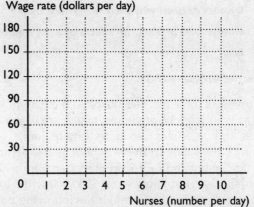

■ **FIGURE 17.2**

   f. Suppose a minimum wage law is passed that requires Towne Hospital to pay nurses $60 a day. How many nurses are hired and what wage rate are they paid?

Short answer

1. What is an open shop, a closed shop, and a union shop?

2. Why do unions attempt to increase demand for labour of their members?

3. Most members of labour unions earn wages above the minimum wage. Why, then, do unions support raising the legal minimum wage?

4. How does the wage rate paid by a monopsony compare to the wage rate in a competitive market?

5. How can a minimum wage affect the wage rate and level of employment in a monopsony labour market?

CHECKPOINT 17.3

■ **Discuss reasons why men earn more than women and predict the effects of a pay equity law.**

Practice Problem 17.3

Jenny is an attorney. Her husband, Pete, is an artist who works from home, takes care of the kids, and organizes the domestic help. Jodi, Jenny's classmate from law school, is also an attorney. Jenny and Jodi work the same number of hours a year, but Jenny earns $250,000 while Jodi earns only $175,000. Consider the following possible explanations for the income difference and explain why each might be correct or incorrect.

a. Jodi is less specialized than Jenny.
b. Jodi's employer is prejudiced against women lawyers and pays them less than he pays men.
c. Jenny's employer is prejudiced against men lawyers and makes a point of hiring women and paying them a high wage rate.
d. Jenny is a better lawyer than Jodi.

Solution to Practice Problem 17.3

This Practice Problem points out various reasons why people's incomes can differ. Remember that earnings differences can arise from reasons other than discrimination.

Quick Review

- *Earnings differences* Four possible explanations for earnings differences are job types, discrimination, differences in human capital, and differences in the degree of specialization.

a. Jodi is less specialized than Jenny.

When Pete specializes in handling domestic matters in the home, it allows Jenny to specialize in earning an income. It is possible that Jodi earns an income *and* works on home production jobs, which lowers her market income.

b. Jodi's employer is prejudiced against women lawyers and pays them less than he pays men.

Discrimination is a possibility. But it seems unlikely that Jodi's employer would pay women less than he pays men of comparable quality and skill. If he did, he would miss the opportunity to hire some excellent female lawyers.

c. Jenny's employer is prejudiced against men lawyers and makes a point of hiring women and paying them a high wage rate.

Discrimination is a possibility but discrimination can decrease the law firm's profit. Jenny's employer would make a larger profit by paying female lawyers the market rate.

d. Jenny is a better lawyer than Jodi.

It is possible that Jenny is a better lawyer than Jodi and that Jenny has a higher value of marginal product.

Additional Practice Problem 17.3a

Suppose the jobs performed by firefighters and dental assistants are judged comparable but firefighters are paid $30,000 a year and dental assistants are paid $20,000. According to pay equity advocates, what should be done? What problems arise?

Solution to Additional Practice Problem 17.3a

Because the jobs are comparable, according to pay equity proponents the salaries of the two jobs should be equal. Suppose the salary of dental assistants rises to $30,000. The quantity of dental assistants demanded decreases and the quantity of dental assistants supplied increases and unemployment occurs. Pay equity laws limit job opportunities and create unemployment among workers whose wage rate they raise.

■ **Self Test 17.3**

Fill in the blanks

Women earn ____ (less; more) on the average than men even when they do the same job. Discrimination is _____ (easy; hard) to measure objectively. Historically, men have had _____ (less; more) years of education than have women. The relative degree of specialization of women and men affects women's incomes _____ (adversely; positively). The available evidence suggests that, on the average, when never-married men and never-married women have the same amount of human capital, the wages of these two groups are _____ (not significantly; significantly) different. A pay equity law is a law that requires an employer to pay the same wage rate for _____ (different jobs that are judged comparable; the same job).

True or false

1. Women earn less on the average than men even when they do the same job.

2. In 1970, women comprised less than 20 percent of the students in university programs in professional fields and today they are 50 percent or more.

3. The more years of work and the fewer job interruptions a person has had, the higher is the person's wage, other things remaining the same.

4. The degree of specialization between working for a wage and working in the home has an effect on a person's market wage rate.

5. Pay equity laws increase job opportunities and decrease unemployment among workers whose wage rates they raise.

Multiple choice

1. Besides discrimination, what other factor can account for wage differentials between the sexes?
a. differences in the degree of specialization
b. different job types
c. differences in human capital
d. All of the above answers are correct.

2. Today women comprise _____ of the students in university programs in professional fields.
a. 20 percent
b. less than 40 percent
c. 50 percent or more
d. 10 percent

3. Some of the sex differences in wages arise because
a. males and females traditionally have had different jobs and the jobs held by males are better paid.
b. females are generally better educated than males.
c. males have more job interruptions than females.
d. All of the above answers are correct.

4. Because of its effect on wages, discrimination tends to ____ the cost of goods made with the favoured labour and ____ the cost of goods made with labour that is discriminated against.
a. increase; increase
b. increase; decrease
c. decrease; increase
d. decrease; decrease

5. A person's wage rate tends to be higher, other things remaining the same, if they have
a. more years of schooling.
b. more job interruptions.
c. fewer years of work experience.
d. None of these factors influence a person's wage.

6. _____ law is a law that requires an employer to pay the same wage rate for different jobs that are judged comparable.
   a. An efficient way
   b. A comparable worth
   c. A pay equity
   d. A comparable equity

7. Pay equity laws
   a. cannot eliminate wage differences.
   b. limit job opportunities and create unemployment.
   c. are an efficient method of correcting inequities in job markets.
   d. change wages, but have no effect on the amount of employment in a labour market.

8. An effective wage policy is one that emphasizes
   a. increased unionization of labour.
   b. higher minimum wages.
   c. pay equity laws.
   d. ongoing education and training.

Complete the graph

1. Figure 17.3 shows the value of marginal product curve and the supply curve of teachers. The competitive equilibrium wage rate is W_T. Show the unemployment that results if pay equity laws determine that teachers should be paid W_R, the wage rate of oil rig workers, which is higher than W_T.

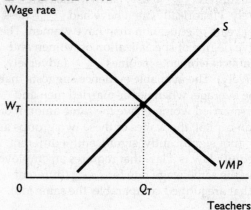

FIGURE 17.3

Short answer

1. To equalize wage rates, what would be possible policies if wage differences are the result of
   a. discrimination?
   b. differences in human capital?
   c. differences in the degree of specialization?

2. What role do years of schooling, years of work experience, and number of job interruptions play in affecting a person's wage rate?

3. Jason and Lisa form a household. They have decided that Lisa will specialize in earning an income and Jason will pursue activities both in the job market and in the household. If most households are like Jason's and Lisa's, what would be the result?

SELF TEST ANSWERS

■ CHECKPOINT 17.1

Fill in the blanks

The demand curve for high-skilled labour lies <u>above</u> the demand curve for low-skilled labour and the supply curve of high-skilled labour lies <u>above</u> the supply curve of low-skilled labour. The wage rate paid high-skilled workers is <u>greater</u> than the wage rate paid low-skilled workers.

True or false

1. True; page 408
2. False; page 408
3. True; pages 408-409
4. True; page 410
5. True; page 410

Multiple choice

1. d; page 408
2. a; page 408
3. b; page 408
4. b; page 409
5. c; page 410
6. b; page 410
7. a; page 410
8. d; page 410

Complete the graph

1a. Figure 17.4 labels the curves.

b. The value of marginal product of skill is $4 an hour because that is the vertical distance between the demand curve for high-skilled labour and the demand curve for low-skilled labour; page 408.

c. The compensation required for the cost of acquiring the skill is $8 an hour because that is the vertical distance between the supply curve of high-skilled labour and the supply curve of low-skilled labour; page 409.

d. The equilibrium wage rate for high-skilled workers is $14 an hour and the equilibrium wage rate for low-skilled workers is $8 an hour; page 409.

■ FIGURE 17.4

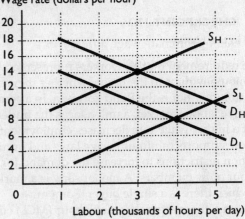

Short answer

1. The value of the marginal product of high-skilled workers exceeds that of low-skilled workers. High-skilled workers can perform a variety of tasks that low-skilled workers would perform badly or perhaps could not perform at all; page 408.

2a. The value of marginal product of high-skilled workers exceeds that of low-skilled workers, so the demand for high-skilled labour is greater than the demand for low-skilled labour. Skills are costly to attain, so the supply of high-skilled labour is less than the supply of low-skilled labour; page 408.

b. The demand for high-skilled labour is greater than the demand for low-skilled labour and the supply of high-skilled labour is less than the supply of low-skilled labour. So the wage rate of high-skilled workers is greater than the wage rate of low-skilled workers; page 410

c. The demand for high-skilled labour is greater than the demand for low-skilled labour and the supply of high-skilled labour is less than the supply of low-skilled labour. But we cannot answer this question unless we know how much greater is the demand for high-skilled labour than low-skilled labour and how much smaller is the supply of high-skilled labour than low-skilled labour; page 410.

■ **CHECKPOINT 17.2**

Fill in the blanks

The requirement that all workers represented by a union pay dues to the union, whether they join the union or not is the Rand Formula. In a competitive labour market, a union faces the tradeoff that a higher wage rate decreases employment. A union supports minimum wage laws and immigration restrictions to increase the demand for the labour of its members. A monopsony is a market in which there is a single buyer. For a monopsony, the marginal cost of labour (*MCL*) curve lies above the supply of labour curve. In a monopsony labour market, it is possible for a minimum wage to increase the wage rate and employment.

True or false

1. False; page 413
2. True; page 414
3. False; page 414
4. False; page 417
5. False; page 418

Multiple choice

1. d; page 412
2. a; page 413
3. c; page 413
4. c; page 413
5. c; page 414
6. c; page 416
7. d; page 417
8. d; page 418

Complete the graph

1a. The completed table is below; page 417.

Wage rate (dollars per day)	Quantity of labour demanded (nurses)	Quantity of labour supplied (nurses)	Marginal cost of labour (dollars per day)
20	10	2	
			50
30	9	3	
			70
40	8	4	
			90
50	7	5	
			110
60	6	6	
			130
70	5	7	
			150
80	4	8	

b. Figure 17.5 plots the three curves; page 417.

■ **FIGURE 17.5**

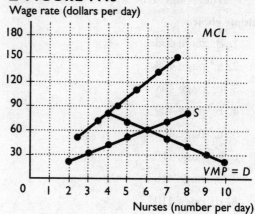

c. Towne hires 4 nurses because at this quantity the value of marginal product equals the marginal cost of labour. From the supply of labour curve, to hire 4 nurses a day, the wage rate is $40 a day; page 417.

d. If the market is competitive, 6 nurses are hired and the wage rate is $60 a day; page 417.

e. When Towne Hospital is a monopsony it pays a lower wage rate and hires fewer nurses; page 417.

f. Towne Hospital hires 6 nurses and the wage rate is $60 a day; page 419.

Short answer

1. An open shop is an arrangement in which no employee is required to join the union or pay union dues—there is no restriction on who can work in the "shop". A closed shop is an arrangement in which the firm can hire only union members. A union shop is an arrangement in which the firm can hire workers who are not union members, but new workers must join the union, usually at the end of their probationary period; page 413.

2. If a union can increase the demand for labour of its members, then the wage rate rises and employment of union members increases; page 414.

3. Unions support minimum wage laws to increase the cost of employing low-skilled labour. An increase in the wage rate of low-skilled labour leads to a decrease in the quantity demanded of low-skilled labour and to an increase in the demand for high-skilled union labour, a substitute for low-skilled labour; page 415.

4. Compared with a competitive labour market, a monopsony decreases both the wage rate and the level of employment; page 417.

5. A minimum wage can raise the wage rate and increase employment in a monopsony labour market as long as the minimum wage exceeds the initial wage rate paid by the monopsony. In this case, the minimum wage becomes the marginal cost of labour. Because the minimum wage is less than the initial marginal cost of labour, the monopsony hires more labour and pays them the minimum wage; page 419.

■ **CHECKPOINT 17.3**

Fill in the blanks

Women earn <u>less</u> on the average than men even when they do the same job. Discrimination is <u>hard</u> to measure objectively. Historically, men have had <u>more</u> years of education than have women. The relative degree of specialization of women and men affects women's incomes <u>adversely</u>. The available evidence suggests that, on the average, when never-married men and never-married women have the same amount of human capital, the wages of these two groups are <u>not significantly</u> different. A pay equity law is a law that requires an employer to pay the same wage rate for <u>different jobs that are judged comparable</u>.

True or false

1. True; page 421
2. True; page 421
3. True; page 423
4. True; page 423
5. False; page 424

Multiple choice

1. d; page 421
2. c; page 421
3. a; page 421
4. b; page 422
5. a; page 423
6. c; page 424
7. b; page 424
8. d; page 425

Complete the graph

1. Figure 17.6 shows the unemployment. Before the implementation of the pay equity law, the wage rate is W_T and the number of teachers employed is Q_T. When the wage rate rises to W_R, the quantity of teachers demanded decreases to D_T and the quantity of teachers supplied increases to S_T. Unemployment is equal to $S_T - D_T$; pages 424-425.

FIGURE 17.6

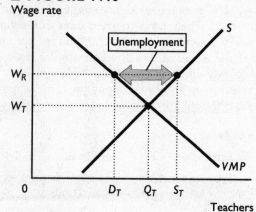

Short answer

1a. If discrimination is the reason wage rates differ, laws prohibiting discrimination are potential policy. Also if markets are competitive, then discriminating firms will have higher costs and lower profit; page 423

b. Human capital is affected by years of schooling, years of work experience, and number of job interruptions. To increase human capital, the government can implement policies that provide greater access to high-quality schools and on-the-job training; page 423.

c. If differences in the degree of specialization are the reason for wage differences, increased access to quality day-care facilities might have an impact; page 423.

2. The more years of schooling, the more years of work experience, and the fewer job interruptions a person has had, the higher is the person's wage, other things remaining the same; page 423.

3. If Lisa specializes in earning an income while Jason is diversified, Lisa's earning ability is likely to exceed Jason's because of the gains from her specialization. Lisa will become more productive than Jason and so Lisa's value of the marginal product will exceed Jason's. If most households followed this pattern of specialization, the income of women would exceed that of men; page 423.

Chapter 18

Inequality, Poverty, and Redistribution

CHAPTER IN PERSPECTIVE

Chapter 18 studies economic inequality—its extent, sources, and potential remedies. The chapter looks at taxes and government programs that redistribute incomes and studies their effect on economic equality in Canada.

■ **Describe the inequality in income and wealth in Canada and explain why wealth inequality is greater than income inequality.**

A Lorenz curve is a curve that graphs the cumulative percentage of income (or wealth) against the cumulative percentage of households. The farther the Lorenz curve is from a 45° line, the greater is the inequality. The wealthiest 20 percent of Canadians own 70 percent of the total wealth in the country. Throughout the 1980s and 1990s, income inequality increased. Statistics Canada measures the number of poor households by calculating the number of households that lie below a low-income cutoff—the income at or below which a household spends 20 percentage points more of its income on food, shelter, and clothing than does the average household. A low-income household is more likely to receive its income from government benefits, have a single female parent, be young, with little education, be out of work, and live in Quebec. Wealth is a stock, and income is the flow of earnings that results from that stock of wealth. Because the wealth distribution data excludes human capital, the income distribution is a more accurate measure of economic inequality than the wealth distribution. A typical household's income changes over time. It starts out low, grows to a peak when the household's workers reach retirement age, and then falls after retirement. So because different households are at different stages in the life cycle, the distribution of annual income exaggerates lifetime inequality.

■ **Explain how economic inequality arises.**

A household's income depends on resource prices, resource endowments, and choices. Wages are the biggest single source of income for most people. The skewed shape of the distribution of income results from the choices that people make. The quantity of labour supplied increases as the wage rate increases, so the distribution of income is more unequal than the distribution of hourly wages.

■ **Explain the effects of taxes, social security, and welfare programs on economic inequality.**

The three main ways in which governments in Canada redistribute income are income taxes, income maintenance programs, and subsidized services. Income taxes in Canada are progressive. The three major income maintenance programs are social security programs, unemployment compensation, and welfare programs. A household's market income is the income it earns in factor markets before tax and excluding transfers from the government. Money income is market income plus money benefits paid by the government. Taxes and government benefits reduce the degree of inequality that the market generates. The redistribution of income creates the big tradeoff between efficiency and fairness.

EXPANDED CHAPTER CHECKLIST

When you have completed this chapter, you will be able to:

1 Describe the inequality in income and wealth in Canada and explain why wealth inequality is greater than income inequality.

- Describe the distribution of income and wealth in Canada and discuss how these distributions have changed during the past two decades.
- Draw and interpret a Lorenz curve.
- Define low-income cutoff and describe the lowest-income household in Canada.
- Explain why income is a more accurate measure of economic inequality than wealth.

2 Explain how economic inequality arises.

- Discuss the role played by resource prices, resource endowments, and choices in determining a household's income.
- Explain why the distribution of income is skewed.
- Discuss the impact of saving and bequests on the distributions of income and wealth.

3 Explain the effects of taxes, social security, and welfare programs on economic inequality.

- Describe how income taxes, income maintenance programs, and subsidized services redistribute income.
- Define market income and money income.
- Explain how government actions change the distribution of income.
- Explain the big tradeoff and give two reasons why redistribution decreases the size of the economic pie.

KEY TERMS

- Lorenz curve (page 431)
- Low-income cutoff (page 433)
- Market income (page 443)
- Money income (page 444)

CHECKPOINT 18.1

■ Describe the inequality in income and wealth in Canada and explain why wealth inequality is greater than income inequality.

Practice Problem 18.1

Table 18.1 on page 430 of your textbook shows the distribution of income in Canada. The table below shows the distribution of income in Peru and in Sweden:

Peru		Sweden	
Households	Income (percentage)	Households	Income (percentage)
Lowest 20 percent	4.0	Lowest 20 percent	9.5
Second 20 percent	4.3	Second 20 percent	15.5
Third 20 percent	8.3	Third 20 percent	19.0
Fourth 20 percent	15.2	Fourth 20 percent	23.1
Highest 20 percent	68.2	Highest 20 percent	32.9

a. Draw the Lorenz curves for Canada, Peru, and Sweden.

b. Compare the distributions of income in Peru and Sweden with that in Canada. Which distribution is more unequal? Which is more equal?

Solution to Practice Problem 18.1

A Lorenz curve graphs the *cumulative* percentage of income (or wealth) against the *cumulative* percentage of households. To answer this Practice Problem, calculate the cumulative percentages.

Quick Review

- *Lorenz curve* A curve that graphs the cumulative percentage of income (or wealth) against the cumulative percentage of households. The farther the Lorenz curve is from a 45° line, the greater is the inequality.

a. **Draw the Lorenz curves for Canada, Peru, and Sweden.**

To draw the Lorenz curves, we first need to calculate the cumulative percentage of households and the cumulative percentage of income. The table below shows these calculations for Peru and Sweden.

Peru		Sweden	
Households (cumulative percentage)	Income (cumulative percentage)	Households (cumulative percentage)	Income (cumulative percentage)
20	4.0	20	9.5
40	8.3	40	25.0
60	16.6	60	44.0
80	31.8	80	67.1
100	100.0	100	100.0

The figure shows the Lorenz curves, which plot the cumulative percentage of income against the cumulative percentage of households for Canada, Peru, and Sweden.

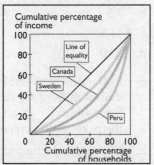

b. **Compare the distributions of income in Peru and Sweden with that in Canada. Which distribution is more unequal? Which is more equal?**

The closer the Lorenz curve is to the line of equality, the more equally is income distributed. Peru's Lorenz curve lies further from the line of equality than does Canada's so the distribution of income in Canada is more equal than that in Peru. Sweden's Lorenz curve lies closer to the line of equality than does Canada's, so the distribution of income in Canada is less equal than that in Sweden.

Additional Practice Problem 18.1a

The figure shows the Lorenz curves for three nations, A, B, and C. In which nation is income distribution most unequal? The most equal? In which nation is average income the highest?

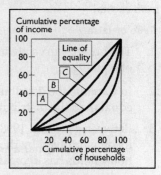

Solution to Additional Practice Problem 18.1a

The closer the Lorenz curve is to the line of equality, the more equally is income distributed. Nation A's Lorenz curve lies furthest from the line of equality so the distribution of income in nation A is most unequal. Nation C's Lorenz curve lies closest to the line of equality so the distribution of income in nation C is most equal. The Lorenz curve does not give information about average income, so it is impossible to know in which nation average income is the highest.

■ Self Test 18.1

Fill in the blanks

In Canada in 1999, the median household income was approximately ____ ($20,000; $40,000; $80,000). The poorest 20 percent of households received about ____ (4; 12) percent of total income and the richest 20 percent received about ____ (26; 46) percent of total income. A Lorenz curve for income graphs the ____ (percentage; cumulative percentage) of income against the cumulative percentage of households. During the past two decades, the distributions of income and wealth in Canada have become ____ (less; more) unequal. The income at or below which a household spends 20 percentage points more of its income on food, shelter, and clothing than does the average household is the ____ (low-income cutoff; poverty level). Wealth distribution is a ____ (less; more) accurate measure of economic inequality than income distribution because wealth distribution data _____ (excludes; includes) human capital.

True or false

1. The Lorenz curve always lies above the line of equality.

2. In Canada, the distribution of income is more equal than the distribution of wealth.

3. Between 1980 and 1998, the share of the total income received by the richest 20 percent of households has decreased.

4. The highest-income household in Canada is likely to be a married couple with two full-time jobs, between 45 and 54 years old, college-educated, and living in Ontario.

5. Inequality of annual income overstates the degree of lifetime inequality.

Multiple choice

1. The median income is the income that
a. is equal to the average income.
b. is most often observed.
c. is in the middle so that 50 percent of households have incomes above the median and 50 percent have incomes below the median.
d. defines the low-income cutoff.

2. The median household income in Canada in 1998 was approximately
a. $55,000.
b. $40,000.
c. $92,000.
d. $22,000.

3. Which of the following is correct about Canada?
a. Income is equally distributed.
b. Wealth is equally distributed.
c. Income is equally distributed but wealth is unequally distributed because of inheritances.
d. Both wealth and income are unequally distributed.

4. If income distribution is more unequal than wealth distribution, the
a. Lorenz curve for income is farther away from the 45° line than the Lorenz curve for wealth.
b. government has imposed a higher tax rate on income.
c. Lorenz curve for wealth is farther away from the 45° line than the Lorenz curve for income.
d. None of the above answers is correct.

5. In Canada between 1980 and 1998, the share of total income received by the richest 20 percent of households increased by ____ percentage points.
a. 1.0
b. 7.5
c. 11.5
d. 25.0

6. In Canada between 1984 and 1999, the median wealth of the richest 20 percent of households _____ and the median wealth of the poorest 40 percent of households _____.
a. increased; decreased
b. did not change; did not change
c. did not change; increased
d. increased; had almost no change

7. If the average household spends 35 percent of its income on food, shelter, and clothing, the low-income cutoff is the income at which a household spends _____ percent of its income on these items.
a. 35
b. 25
c. 15
d. 55

8. The inequality of annual income
   a. overstates the degree of lifetime inequality.
   b. understates the degree of lifetime inequality.
   c. cannot change from one year to the next.
   d. None of the above answers is correct.

Complete the graph

1. The table has data for the nation of Beta. Complete the table. In Figure 18.1, plot the Lorenz curve for Beta.

Household percentage	Percentage of income	Cumulative percentage of income
Lowest 20 percent	5.0	___
Second 20 percent	9.0	___
Third 20 percent	20.0	___
Fourth 20 percent	26.0	___
Highest 20 percent	40.0	___

■ **FIGURE 18.1**

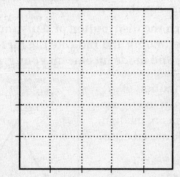

Short answer

1. Can a Lorenz curve for income ever lie above the line of equality? Why or why not?

2. What does the distance between a Lorenz curve for income and the line of equality tell about the distribution of income?

3. How has the distribution of income and wealth changed in Canada during the last two decades? Why have these distributions changed?

4. What is the low-income cutoff?

5. What is the relationship between income and wealth? Why does the Lorenz curve for income differ from that for wealth?

6. Is the distribution of annual or lifetime income more equal? Why?

CHECKPOINT 18.2

■ **Explain how economic inequality arises.**

Practice Problem 18.2

An economy consists of 10 people, each of whom has the labour supply schedule shown in the first table. The people differ in ability and earn different wage rates. The second table shows the distribution of wage rates that these people can earn. Calculate the:

Wage rate (dollars per hour)	Hours per day
10	5
20	6
30	7
40	8
50	10

Name	Wage rate (dollars per hour)
Alan	10
Bill	20
Carol	20
Denise	30
Ed	30
Frank	30
Gina	30
Hal	40
Ira	40
Jen	50

a. Mean (average) wage rate.
b. Ratio of the highest to the lowest wage rate.
c. Mean (average) daily income.
d. Ratio of the highest to the lowest daily income.
e. Median income.
f. Mode income.
g. Compare the mean, median, and mode incomes.
h. Sketch the distribution of daily income for this economy and indicate the mean, median, and mode income on your graph.

Solution to Practice Problem 18.2

A household's income depends on resource prices, resource endowments, and choices. Variations in wage rates account to some extent for the unequal distribution of income. This Practice Problem will show you that the choices people make exaggerate the differences among them, make the distribution of income more unequal, and make the distribution of income skewed.

Quick Review

- *Wages and the supply of labour* Because the quantity of labour supplied increases as the wage rate increases, the distribution of income is more unequal than the distribution of hourly wages.

a. **Mean (average) wage rate.**

To calculate the mean wage rate, take the sum of the wage rates in the second table, $300 an hour, and divide by the number of people, 10. The mean wage rate is $30 an hour.

b. **Ratio of the highest to the lowest wage rate.**

The highest wage is $50 an hour and the lowest wage rate is $10 an hour. The ratio of the highest to the lowest is 5 to 1.

c. **Mean (average) daily income.**

To find the mean daily income, the daily income of each person is calculated in the table below. To calculate the mean daily income, take the sum of the last column, $2,270, and divide by the number of people, 10. The mean daily income is $227.

Name	Wage rate (dollars per hour)	Hours per day	Income (dollars per day)
Alan	10	5	50
Bill	20	6	120
Carol	20	6	120
Denise	30	7	210
Ed	30	7	210
Frank	30	7	210
Gina	30	7	210
Hal	40	8	320
Ira	40	8	320
Jen	50	10	500

d. **Ratio of the highest to the lowest daily income.**

The highest daily income is $500 and the lowest daily income is $50. The ratio of the highest to the lowest is 10 to 1.

e. **Median income.**

The median income is the income that separates households into two groups of equal size. The median income is $210 a day.

f. **Mode income.**

The mode income is the most common income. The mode income is $210 a day.

g. **Compare the mean, median, and mode incomes.**

The mean income is $227 a day and the median income and mode income are $210 a day. The mean income exceeds the median income and the mode income. The mode income and the median income are equal.

h. **Sketch the distribution of daily income for this economy and indicate the mean, median, and mode income on your graph.**

The distribution of income is in the figure and the mean, median, and mode are labelled.

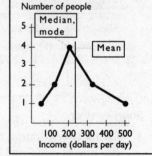

Additional Practice Problem 18.2a

In the Practice Problem, how does the ratio of highest to lowest wage rate compare to the ratio of the highest to lowest daily income? What accounts for the difference?

Solution to Additional Practice Problem 18.2a

The ratio of the highest to lowest wage rate is 5 to 1, and the ratio of highest to lowest daily income is 10 to 1. The difference occurs because of labour supply choices. Jen, who receives the highest wage rate, also works the most hours, and Alan, who receives the lowest wage rate, works the fewest hours. So Jen's income is higher than Alan's for two reasons: first, her wage rate is higher than Alan's, and second, she works more hours than Alan.

■ Self Test 18.2

Fill in the blanks

A household's income depends on three things: ____, ____, and ____. The labour market ____ (is; is not) the biggest single source of income for most people. Because the quantity of labour supplied increases as the wage rate increases, other things remaining the same, the distribution of income is ____ (more; less) unequal than the distribution of hourly wages. The tendency for people to marry within their own socio-economic class is called ____ (bequesting; assortative mating) and makes the distribution of wealth ____ (less; more) unequal.

True or false

1. People face the same wage rate but widely different interest rates.
2. The distribution of income has a normal, or bell-shaped, distribution.
3. Because people who are paid a higher wage rate tend to work more hours, the distribution of income is skewed.
4. Intergenerational transfers of wealth, such as bequests, increase economic equality.
5. Assortative mating makes the distribution of wealth more unequal.

Multiple choice

1. A household's income depends upon the
a. wage rate it receives.
b. household's endowments of capital and abilities.
c. choices it makes.
d. All of the above answers are correct.

2. Households have control over which of the following?
a. resource prices
b. resource endowments
c. choices
d. the distribution of income

3. Which market is the biggest single source of income for most people?
a. capital
b. land
c. labour
d. stock

4. Variations in wage rates account for ____ of the unequal distribution of income.
a. all
b. some
c. none
d. about 10 percent

5. In Canada the mean income is
a. equal to the median income.
b. less than the median income.
c. greater than the median income.
d. None of the above answers is correct.

6. The distribution of income is skewed because
a. of the distribution of individual abilities.
b. of monopoly power in the market place.
c. people have different personal poverty levels.
d. people make different choices.

7. The inequality in the distribution of income and wealth is increased by
a. the fact that debts cannot be bequeathed.
b. saving to redistribute an uneven income over the life cycle.
c. marrying outside one's own socio-economic class.
d. donating money to charities.

8. What is assortative mating?
   a. The right person for the job is always hired.
   b. Older men tend to marry younger women.
   c. Wealthy individuals marry wealthy partners.
   d. None of the above answers is correct.

Short answer

1. What three factors determine a household's income?
2. The distribution of individual abilities is bell-shaped but the distribution of income is skewed. What accounts for this difference?
3. What is assortative mating?

CHECKPOINT 18.3

■ Explain the effects of taxes, social security, and welfare programs on economic inequality.

Practice Problem 18.3

The first table shows the distribution of market income in an economy.

Households	Income (millions of dollars per year)
Lowest 20 percent	5
Second 20 percent	10
Third 20 percent	18
Fourth 20 percent	28
Highest 20 percent	39

The government redistributes income by collecting income taxes and paying benefits as shown in the following table.

Households	Income tax (percent)	Benefit (millions of dollars)
Lowest 20 percent	0	10
Second 20 percent	10	8
Third 20 percent	18	3
Fourth 20 percent	28	0
Highest 20 percent	39	0

a. Calculate the income shares of each 20 percent of households after tax and redistribution.
b. Draw the Lorenz curve for this economy before and after taxes and benefits.

Solution to Practice Problem 18.3

This problem emphasizes how the redistribution of income moves the Lorenz curve closer to the line of inequality.

Quick Review

- *Market income* The income a household earns in factor markets before tax and excluding transfers from government.
- *Money income* Market income plus money benefits paid by the government.

a. **Calculate the income shares of each 20 percent of households after tax and redistribution.**

To calculate the income shares, first multiply market income by the tax rate to find the taxes paid. The table below summarizes the calculations and shows the benefits received.

Households	Market income	Taxes paid	Benefits received
	(millions of dollars)		
Lowest 20 percent	5	0.0	10
Second 20 percent	10	1.0	8
Third 20 percent	18	3.2	3
Fourth 20 percent	28	7.8	0
Highest 20 percent	39	15.2	0

Then subtract the taxes paid and add the benefits received to the market income. Divide the result by total income, as shown in the following table.

Households	Income after taxes and benefits (millions of dollars)	Income (percentage of total income)
Lowest 20 percent	15.0	16.0
Second 20 percent	17.0	18.1
Third 20 percent	17.8	19.0
Fourth 20 percent	20.2	21.5
Highest 20 percent	23.8	25.4

b. **Draw the Lorenz curve for this economy before and after taxes and benefits.**

The table shows the cumulative percentage of income before taxes and benefits and after taxes and benefits.

Households	Cumulative percentage of income	
	before	after
Lowest 20 percent	5.0	16.0
Second 20 percent	15.0	34.1
Third 20 percent	33.0	53.1
Fourth 20 percent	61.0	74.6
Highest 20 percent	100.0	100.0

These cumulative percentages are plotted in the Lorenz curves in the figure.

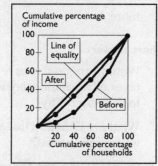

Additional Practice Problem 18.3a

Why does the economy in the Practice Problem have a smaller total income following the collection of income taxes and distribution of benefits?

Solution to Additional Practice Problem 18.3a

Prior to the collection of income taxes and distribution of benefits, total income is $100 million. Following the collection of income taxes and distribution of benefits, total income is $93.8 million. The redistribution of income creates the big tradeoff between efficiency and fairness. A dollar collected from a rich person does not translate into a dollar received by a poor person. Some of it gets used up in the process of redistribution.

■ Self Test 18.3

Fill in the blanks

A household's ____ (market; money) income is the income it earns in factor markets before tax and excluding transfers from the government. The distribution of income after taxes and benefits is ____ (more; less) equal than the distribution of market income. Redistribution of income creates the big tradeoff between ____ (fairness; tax revenue) and ____ (efficiency; redistribution). The long-term solution to the problem of single mothers on welfare in Canada is ____ (acquiring human capital; increasing welfare payments).

True or false

1. Canadian federal and provincial taxes are progressive.

2. Subsidized services from the government go to only households with below-average incomes.

3. The distribution of income after taxes and benefits is more equal than the market distribution of income.

4. The redistribution of income creates the big tradeoff between earning an income and losing welfare benefits.

5. A dollar collected from a rich person does not translate into a dollar received by a poor person.

Multiple choice

1. Which of the following is a way income is redistributed in Canada?
   a. subsidized services
   b. income taxes
   c. income maintenance programs
   d. All of the above.

2. A ____ tax is one that taxes income at an average rate that increases with the level of income.
   a. regressive
   b. progressive
   c. flat
   d. consumption

3. Of the following types of income tax systems, the one that can provide the greatest amount of redistribution from the rich to the poor is a
   a. progressive income tax.
   b. proportional income tax.
   c. regressive income tax.
   d. flat-rate income tax.

4. The three major types of income maintenance programs are
   a. social security programs, unemployment compensation, and welfare programs.
   b. minimum wage laws, unemployment compensation, and agricultural price supports.
   c. student loans, rent control, and welfare programs.
   d. welfare programs, minimum wage laws, and social security programs.

5. A household's income earned in factor markets before tax and excluding transfers from the government is
   a. money income.
   b. welfare.
   c. market income.
   d. exploitative income.

6. Which of the following measures shows the most equality?
   a. money income
   b. market income
   c. income after taxes and benefits
   d. wealth

7. When government redistributes income, one dollar collected from a rich person translates into ____ dollar received by a poor person.
   a. one
   b. less than one
   c. more than one
   d. Any of these is likely to occur.

8. Taxing people's income from their work and saving makes them work _____ and save _____.
   a. less; less
   b. less; more
   c. more; more
   d. more; less

Short answer

1. Would progressive or regressive income taxes redistribute more money from the rich to the poor? Why?

2. What are Canada's three major income maintenance programs?

3. Currently the government more heavily taxes high-income households and transfers money to low-income households. What are the likely reactions of the recipients of the money? Of the taxpayers? How do these reactions reflect the big tradeoff?

4. Discuss the major welfare challenge in Canada today.

SELF TEST ANSWERS

■ CHECKPOINT 18.1

Fill in the blanks

In Canada in 1999, the median household income was approximately $40,000. The poorest 20 percent of households received about 4 percent of total income and the richest 20 percent received about 46 percent of total income. A Lorenz curve for income graphs the cumulative percentage of income against the cumulative percentage of households. During the past two decades, the distributions of income and wealth in Canada have become more unequal. The income at or below which a household spends 20 percentage points more of its income on food, shelter, and clothing than does the average household is the low-income cutoff. Wealth distribution is a less accurate measure of economic inequality than income distribution because wealth distribution data excludes human capital.

True or false

1. False; page 431
2. True; page 431
3. False; page 432
4. True; page 433
5. True; page 436

Multiple choice

1. c; page 430
2. b; page 430
3. d; page 430
4. a; page 431
5. b; page 432
6. d; page 432
7. d; page 433
8. a; page 436

Complete the graph

1. The completed table and the Lorenz curve are in the next column; page 431.

Household percentage	Percentage of income	Cumulative percentage of income
Lowest 20 percent	5.0	5.0
Second 20 percent	9.0	14.0
Third 20 percent	20.0	34.0
Fourth 20 percent	26.0	60.0
Highest 20 percent	40.0	100.0

■ **FIGURE 18.2**

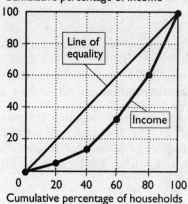

Short answer

1. A Lorenz curve for income can never lie above the line of equality. The Lorenz curve plots the cumulative percentage of income against the cumulative percentage of households. Because the households are arranged by order of income, the cumulative percentage of income is always less (except at 0 percent and 100 percent) than the cumulative percentage of households; page 431.

2. The farther away the Lorenz curve is from the line of equality, the less equal is the distribution of income; page 431.

3. Both the distribution of income and wealth have become less equal in Canada during the past two decades. The distribution of income changed because the better educated in the higher income groups have benefited more from recent rapid technological changes. The distribution of wealth changed because the wealthiest households have a larger propor-

tion of their wealth invested in stocks and they have benefited from the extraordinary performance of the stock market in the 1990s; pages 432-433.

4. The low-income cutoff is the income at or below which a household spends 20 percentage points more of its income on food, shelter, and clothing than does the average household; page 433.

5. Income is the flow of earnings that results from the stock of wealth. The Lorenz curves for income and wealth show that income is distributed more equally than wealth. The wealth distribution excludes human capital, so the income distribution is a more accurate measure of economic inequality than the wealth distribution; page 435.

6. The distribution of lifetime income is more equal than the distribution of annual income because in any given year, different households are at different stages in the life cycle; page 436.

■ CHECKPOINT 18.2
Fill in the blanks

A household's income depends on three things: <u>resource prices</u>, <u>resource endowments</u>, and <u>choices</u>. The labour market <u>is</u> the biggest single source of income for most people. Because the quantity of labour supplied increases as the wage rate increases, other things remaining the same, the distribution of income is <u>more</u> unequal than the distribution of hourly wages. The tendency for people to marry within their own socio-economic class is called <u>assortative mating</u> and makes the distribution of wealth <u>more</u> unequal.

True or false

1. False; page 438
2. False; page 438
3. True; page 439
4. False; page 440
5. True; page 440

Multiple choice

1. d; page 438
2. c; page 438
3. c; page 438
4. b; page 438
5. c; page 439
6. d; page 439
7. a; page 440
8. c; page 440

Short answer

1. The factors that determine a household's income are resource prices, resource endowments, and choices; page 438.

2. People's choices account for the difference between the bell-shaped distribution of abilities and the skewed distribution of income. People with high ability usually receive a higher wage rate and they tend to work longer hours. People with low ability usually receive a lower wage rate and they tend to work fewer hours. Because the quantity of labour supplied increases as the wage rate increases, the distribution of income is skewed; page 439.

3. Assortative mating is the tendency for people to marry within their own socio-economic class; page 440.

■ CHECKPOINT 18.3
Fill in the blanks

A household's <u>market</u> income is the income it earns in factor markets before tax- and excluding transfers from the government. The distribution of income after taxes and benefits is <u>more</u> equal than the distribution of market income. Redistribution of income creates the big tradeoff between <u>fairness</u> and <u>efficiency</u>. The long-term solution to the problem of single mothers on welfare in Canada is <u>acquiring human capital</u>.

Chapter 18 · Inequality, Poverty, and Redistribution

True or false
1. True; page 442
2. False; page 443
3. True; page 444
4. False; page 445
5. True; page 445

Multiple choice
1. d; page 442
2. b; page 442
3. a; page 442
4. a; page 422
5. c; page 443
6. c; page 444
7. b; page 445
8. a; page 445

Short answer
1. A progressive income tax will redistribute more income away from the rich to the poor. A progressive income tax has a higher average tax rate as income rises. As a result, the rich pay a greater amount of taxes than do the poor because the rich have more income and because the average tax rate on that income is higher; page 442.

2. The three types of income maintenance programs are social security programs, unemployment compensation, and welfare programs; page 442.

3. The recipients of the money payments likely will work less. If they were to work more, they might earn enough to move into a higher tax bracket and lose the money the government is giving to them. The taxpayers also will tend to work less. These effects illustrate the force of the big tradeoff: by making incomes more equal, the government program decreases people's incentives to work, decreases economic efficiency, and decreases the nation's income; page 445.

4. There are about 600,000 single mothers in Canada today, many of whom receive little or no support from their absent partners. The long-term solution to the problem of these women is education and job training—acquiring human capital. The short-term solution is welfare, to provide them with an income. But welfare must be designed to minimize the disincentive for these women to pursue the long-term goal of obtaining the education that will make them self-supporting; page 445.

Chapter 19

International Trade

CHAPTER IN PERSPECTIVE

Chapter 19 shows that all countries can benefit from international trade. The chapter also demonstrates the effects of trade barriers, and explains the arguments countries use to justify these trade barriers.

■ **Describe the patterns and trends in international trade.**

The goods and services that we buy from people in other countries are called imports. The goods and services that we sell to people in other countries are called exports. Total trade in goods accounts for 88 percent of Canadian exports and 85 percent of Canadian imports. The rest of Canada's international trade is in services. From 1960 to 2000 exports have grown from about 17 percent of Canada's GDP to 45 percent and imports have grown from 18 percent of GDP to more than 40 percent of GDP. The United States is Canada's biggest trading partner. In 2000, Canada had a trade surplus of $53 billion.

■ **Explain why nations engage in international trade and why trade benefits all nations.**

A nation has a comparative advantage in producing a good if it can produce that good at a lower opportunity cost than another country. To achieve the gains from trade, a nation specializes in the production of the goods and services in which it has a comparative advantage and then trades with other nations. By specializing and trading, a nation can consume at a point beyond its production possibilities frontier.

■ **Explain how trade barriers reduce international trade.**

A tariff is a tax on a good that is imposed by the importing country when an imported good crosses its international boundary. A tariff on a good reduces imports of that good, increases domestic production of the good, and reduces the gains from trade. An import quota is a specified maximum amount of a good that may be imported in a given period of time.

■ **Explain the arguments used to justify trade barriers and show why they are incorrect but also why some barriers are hard to remove.**

The three main arguments for protection and restricting international trade are the employment argument, the infant-industry argument, and the dumping argument. Other arguments for restricting international trade are that protection: maintains national security; allows us to compete with cheap foreign labour; brings diversity and stability; penalizes lax environmental standards; protects national culture; and prevents rich countries from exploiting developing countries. Each of these arguments is flawed. Tariffs are imposed in some nations to gain revenue for the government. The major reason why international trade is restricted is because of rent seeking.

EXPANDED CHAPTER CHECKLIST

When you have completed this chapter, you will be able to:

1 **Describe the patterns and trends in international trade.**

- Discuss Canadian international trade in goods and services and describe the trends in the volume of trade between 1960 and 2000.
- Discuss Canada's trading partners and the trading blocs in which Canada is a member.
- Define balance of trade.

2 **Explain why nations engage in international trade and why trade benefits all nations.**

- Discuss the relationship between comparative advantage and opportunity cost.
- Explain how to determine the goods in which Canada has a comparative advantage by comparing the Canadian supply curve and the world price line.
- Demonstrate how the production possibilities frontier can be used to determine the opportunity cost of producing a good.
- Use the production possibilities frontier to demonstrate the gains from trade.

3 **Explain how trade barriers reduce international trade.**

- Define tariff, nontariff barrier, and import quota.
- Explain the effects on domestic consumers, domestic producers, and the domestic government of a tariff and an import quota.

4 **Explain the arguments used to justify trade barriers and show why they are incorrect but also why some barriers are hard to remove.**

- Discuss the three main arguments for protection and explain why each is invalid.
- Discuss six other arguments for protection.
- Explain why governments and rent seekers are in favour of protection.

KEY TERMS

- Balance of trade (page 455)
- Dumping (page 470)
- Dynamic comparative advantage (page 462)
- Import quota (466)
- Infant-industry argument (page 469)
- Learning-by-doing (page 462)
- Nontariff barrier (page 464)
- Tariff (page 464)

CHECKPOINT 19.1

■ **Describe the patterns and trends in international trade.**

Practice Problem 19.1

Use the link on your Foundations Web site to answer the following questions:

a. In 1990, what percentage of Canadian production was exported to the United States and what percentage of total goods and services bought by Canadians was imported from the United States?

b. In 2000, what percentage of Canadian production was exported to the United States and what percentage of total goods and services bought by Canadians was imported from the United States?

Solution to Practice Problem 19.1

Canada participates more heavily in international trade than most nations. This Practice Problem emphasizes the role of the United States as Canada's biggest trading partner.

Quick Review

- *Imports* The goods and services that we buy from people in other countries are called imports.
- *Exports* The goods and services that we sell to people in other countries are called exports.

a. **In 1990, what percentage of Canadian production was exported to the United States and what percentage of total goods and services bought by Canadians was imported from the United States?**

In 1990, Canadian exports to the United States were 16.5 percent of total Canadian production and imports from the United States were 14.4 percent of the total goods and services bought by Canadians.

b. **In 2000, what percentage of Canadian production was exported to the United States and what percentage of total goods and services bought by Canadians was imported from the United States?**

In 2000, Canadian exports to the United States were 34.6 percent of total Canadian production and imports from the United States were 27 percent of the total goods and services bought by Canadians.

Additional Practice Problem 19.1a

The Bank of Montreal provides financial services to firms in the Bahamas. How do Canada and the Bahamas categorize these financial services?

Solution to Additional Practice Problem 19.1a

Canada considers the services rendered by the Bank of Montreal as exports from Canada to the Bahamas. The Bahamas considers the services as imports from Canada.

■ **Self Test 19.1**

Fill in the blanks

Manufactured goods account for more than ____ (one-half; two-thirds) of Canadian imports. ____ (Japan; Mexico; The United States) is Canada's biggest trading partner. Canada ____ (is; is not) a member of the Asia-Pacific Economic Cooperation. In Canada between 1960 and 2000, trade ____ (decreased; increased) as a fraction of GDP.

True or false

1. Canada exports more services than goods.
2. In 1960, Canadian exports were about 1 percent of Canada's GDP.
3. The United States, the European Union, Japan, China, and Mexico are Canada's biggest trading partners.
4. In 2000, Canada had a trade surplus.

Multiple choice

1. Goods and services that we buy from people in other countries are called
   a. imports.
   b. exports.
   c. inputs.
   d. raw materials.

2. The largest fraction of Canadian imports is ____ and the largest fraction of Canadian exports is ____.
   a. resource products; agricultural products
   b. resource products; manufactured goods
   c. manufactured goods; agricultural products
   d. manufactured goods; manufactured goods

3. Goods account for about ____ percent of Canadian exports and services account for about ____ percent of Canadian exports.

a. 50; 50
b. 88; 12
c. 12; 88
d. 100; 0

4. If a Canadian student vacations in Germany, the money spent in Germany are services

a. exported to Canada.
b. imported to Germany.
c. exported to Germany.
d. exported from Canada.

5. The largest Canadian trading partner is

a. the United States.
b. Mexico.
c. Japan.
d. the European Union.

6. The balance of trade equals the value of

a. imports minus the value of exports.
b. exports minus the value of imports.
c. imports.
d. exports.

Short answer

1. French cheese is flown to Canada aboard an Air Canada plane. Classify these transactions as exports or imports.

2. How has the amount of international trade changed in Canada between 1960 and 2000?

3. What is NAFTA and what is its goal?

CHECKPOINT 19.2

■ Explain why nations engage in international trade and why trade benefits all nations.

Practice Problem 19.2

During most of the Cold War, North America and Russia did not trade with each other. North America produced manufactured goods and farm produce. Russia produced manufactured goods and farm produce. Suppose that in the last year of the Cold War, North America could produce 100 million units of manufactured goods or 50 million units of farm produce and Russia could produce 30 million units of manufactured goods or 10 million units of farm produce.

a. What was the opportunity cost of 1 unit of farm produce in North America?

b. What was the opportunity cost of 1 unit of farm produce in Russia?

c. Which country had a comparative advantage in producing farm produce?

d. With the end of the Cold War and the opening up of trade between Russia and North America, which good did North America import from Russia?

e. Did North America gain from this trade? Explain why or why not.

f. Did Russia gain from this trade? Explain why or why not.

Solution to Practice Problem 19.2

This Practice Problem shows that when opportunity costs between countries diverge, comparative advantage enables countries to gain from international trade.

Quick Review

- *Comparative advantage* A nation has a comparative advantage in a good when its opportunity cost of producing the good is lower than another nation's opportunity cost of producing the good.

a. **What was the opportunity cost of 1 unit of farm produce in North America?**

In North America when 50 million units of farm produce are produced, 100 million units of manufactured goods are forgone. The opportunity cost of 1 unit of farm produce is (100 million units of manufactured goods) ÷ (50 million units of farm produce), which is 2 units of manufactured goods.

b. **What was the opportunity cost of 1 unit of farm produce in Russia?**

In Russia, when 10 million units of farm produce are produced, 30 million units of manufactured goods are forgone. The opportunity cost of 1 unit of farm produce is (30 million units of manufactured goods) ÷ (10 million units of farm produce), which is 3 units of manufactured goods.

c. **Which country had a comparative advantage in producing farm produce?**

The opportunity cost of producing farm produce was less in North America than in Russia, so North America had the comparative advantage in farm produce.

d. **With the end of the Cold War and the opening up of trade between Russia and North America, which good did North America import from Russia?**

Russia had the comparative advantage in producing manufactured goods. The opportunity cost of producing 1 unit of a manufactured good in Russia was 1/3 units of farm produce. The opportunity cost of producing 1 unit of a manufactured good in North America was ½ units of farm produce. So North America imported manufactured goods from Russia.

e. **Did North America gain from this trade? Explain why or why not.**

North America gained from this trade because it ended up with more of both goods. When countries specialize in the good in which they have a comparative advantage and then trade, both countries gain.

f. **Did Russia gain from this trade? Explain why or why not.**

Russia gained from this trade because it ended up with more of both goods. When countries specialize in the good in which they have a comparative advantage and then trade, both countries gain.

Additional Practice Problem 19.2a

In Practice Problem 19.2, suppose that new technology becomes available so that the production of manufactured goods doubles in North America and in Russia. Now which good does North America import from Russia?

Solution to Additional Practice Problem 19.2a

In North America when 200 million units of manufactured goods are produced, 50 million units of farm produce are forgone. The opportunity cost of 1 unit of manufactured goods is (50 million units of farm produce) ÷ (200 million units of manufactured goods), which is ¼ units of farm produce.

In Russia when 60 million units of manufactured goods are produced, 10 million units of farm produce are forgone. The opportunity cost of 1 unit of manufactured goods is (10 million units of farm produce) ÷ (60 million units of manufactured goods), which is 1/6 units of farm produce.

Russia still has the lower opportunity cost and the comparative advantage in manufactured goods. So North America continues to import manufactured goods from Russia.

■ Self Test 19.2

Fill in the blanks

A country has a comparative advantage in producing a good if it can produce the good at a _____ (higher; lower) opportunity cost than another country. If the world price of clothing is less than the price in Canada with no international trade and Canada imports clothing from Asia, Canadian buyers of clothing ____ (gain; lose) and Asian producers of clothing ____ (gain; lose). Trade ____ (allows; does not allow) a nation to produce at a point beyond its production possibilities frontier. Trade ____ (allows; does not allow) a nation to consume at a point beyond its production possibilities frontier.

True or false

1. Only the exporting country gains from free international trade because it has a comparative advantage.
2. Canada has a comparative advantage in the production of a good if the opportunity cost of producing that good is higher in Canada than in most other countries.
3. A country cannot reap any gains from international trade if it has an absolute advantage in producing all goods and services.
4. Hong Kong, South Korean, and Taiwan have become low opportunity cost producers in electronics and biotechnology industries through learning-by-doing.

Multiple choice

1. The fundamental force that drives trade between nations is
a. the government.
b. NAFTA.
c. absolute advantage
d. comparative advantage.

2. A nation will import a good if its
a. no-trade, domestic price is equal to the world price.
b. no-trade, domestic price is less than the world price
c. no-trade, domestic price is greater than the world price.
d. All of the above answers are correct.

3. When Italy buys GM locomotives produced in Canada, the price Italy pays is ____ than if they produced their own locomotives and the price GM receives is ____ than it could receive from an additional Canadian buyer.
a. lower; lower
b. higher; higher
c. lower; higher
d. higher; lower

4. When a good is imported, the domestic production ____ and the domestic consumption ____.
a. increases; increases
b. increases; decreases
c. decreases; increases
d. decreases; decreases

5. You can tell that specialization and trade make a country better off because then the country can consume at a point
a. outside its production possibilities frontier.
b. inside its production possibilities frontier.
c. on its production possibilities frontier.
d. on the trading partner's production possibilities frontier.

6. People can become more productive just by repeatedly producing a particular good or service. This is called
a. learning-by-doing.
b. learning-by-boredom.
c. absolute advantage.
d. dynamic absolute advantage.

Complete the graph

1. Figure 19.1 shows the Canadian demand and supply curves for apples.

■ **FIGURE 19.1**

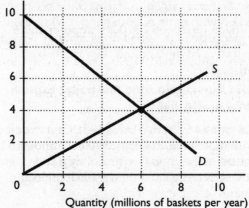

a. In the absence of international trade, what is the price of a basket of apples in Canada?

b. If the world price of a basket of apples is $6 a basket, will Canada import or export apples? Above what world price for apples will Canada export apples? Below what world price for apples will Canada import apples?

2. Figure 19.2 shows the Canadian and French PPFs.

■ FIGURE 19.2

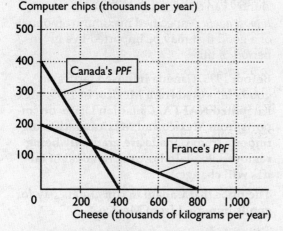

a. What is the opportunity cost of a computer chip in Canada? In France? Who has the comparative advantage in producing computer chips?

b. What is the opportunity cost of a kilogram of cheese in Canada? In France? Who has the comparative advantage in producing cheese?

c. When Canada and France trade, who exports chips and who exports cheese?

d. Canada produced 200,000 computer chips and 200,000 kilograms of cheese before trade. France produced 100,000 computer chips and 400,000 kilograms of cheese. Label as point A the point that shows the total chip and cheese production before trade.

e. Canada and France both specialize according to comparative advantage. Label as point B the point that shows the total chip and cheese production after trade. How does point B compare to point A?

Short answer

1. The table shows the Canadian demand and supply schedules for potatoes.

Price (dollars per tonne)	Quantity supplied (tonnes per year)	Quantity demanded (tonnes per year)
400	38	58
500	42	52
600	46	46
700	50	40
800	54	34
900	58	28

a. If there is no international trade, what is the equilibrium price and quantity?

b. If the world price of potatoes is $800 a tonne, what is the quantity supplied and the quantity demanded in Canada? Does Canada import or export potatoes? What quantity?

c. If the world price of potatoes rises to $900 a tonne, what is the quantity supplied and the quantity demanded in Canada? Does Canada import or export potatoes? What quantity?

d. Would Canada ever import potatoes?

2. Suppose Canada and France produce only ice cream and cheese. Canada can produce 50 tonnes of ice cream or 100 tonnes of cheese and France can produce 20 tonnes of ice cream or 120 tonnes of cheese.

a. What is the opportunity cost of a tonne of ice cream in France? In Canada? Which nation has the comparative advantage in producing ice cream?

b. What is the opportunity cost of a tonne of cheese in France? In Canada? Which nation has the comparative advantage in producing cheese?

c. If France and Canada trade, what does Canada import? What does it export?

d. Before trade Canada produced 25 tonnes of ice cream and 50 tonnes of cheese and France produced 10 tonnes of ice cream and 60 tonnes of cheese. What is the total production of ice cream? Of cheese?

e. After trade, France and Canada specialize according to comparative advantage. What is the total amount of ice cream produced? Of cheese?

f. Compare your answers to (d) and (e).

3. What are the gains from trade? How do countries obtain the gains from trade?

4. What is dynamic comparative advantage?

CHECKPOINT 19.3

■ **Explain how trade barriers reduce international trade.**

Practice Problems 19.3

1. Before 1995, Canada imposed tariffs on goods imported from Mexico. In 1995, Mexico joined NAFTA. Canadian tariffs on imports from Mexico and Mexican tariffs on imports from Canada are gradually being removed. Explain how the removal of tariffs will change:

a. The price that Canadian consumers pay for goods imported from Mexico.

b. The quantity of imports from Mexico into Canada.

c. The quantity of Canadian exports to Mexico.

d. The Canadian government's tariff revenue from trade with Mexico.

2. Almost all U.S. imports of potatoes come from Canada. In 1999-2000, the U.S. government banned potato imports from Prince Edward Island. Explain how this ban would have influenced:

a. The price that U.S. consumers paid for potatoes.

b. The quantity of potatoes consumed in the United States.

c. The price received by Canadian potato growers.

d. The U.S. and Canadian gains from trade.

Solution to Practice Problems 19.3

To solve these Practice Problems, think in terms of the supply and demand model. Imposing a tariff raises the domestic price, which changes the domestic quantity demanded and the domestic quantity supplied.

Quick Review

- *Tariff* A tax on a good that is imposed by the importing country when an imported good crosses its international boundary.

- *Import quota* A specified maximum amount of a good that may be imported in a given period of time.

1. **Before 1995, Canada imposed tariffs on goods imported from Mexico. In 1995, Mexico joined NAFTA. Canadian tariffs on imports from Mexico and Mexican tariffs on imports from Canada are gradually being removed. Explain how the removal of tariffs will change:**

a. **The price that Canadian consumers pay for goods imported from Mexico.**

When the tariff is removed Canadian consumers pay less for goods imported from Mexico.

b. **The quantity of imports from Mexico into Canada.**

As the price falls, the quantity of Mexican goods demanded by Canadian consumers increases. So the quantity of imports from Mexico into Canada increases.

c. **The quantity of Canadian exports to Mexico.**

As Mexican tariffs on imports from Canada are removed, the price of Canadian exports to Mexico falls and the quantity of Canadian goods demanded by Mexican consumers increases. So the quantity of Canadian exports to Mexico increases.

d. **The Canadian government's tariff revenue from trade with Mexico.**

When the tariff reaches zero, so that trade is totally free of tariffs, the Canadian government's tariff revenue is zero.

2. **Almost all U.S. imports of potatoes come from Canada. In 1999–2000, the U.S. government banned potato imports from Prince Edward Island. Explain how this ban would have influenced:**

a. **The price that U.S. consumers paid for potatoes.**

The ban decreases the supply of imported potatoes and raises the price paid by U.S. consumers.

b. **The quantity of potatoes consumed in the United States.**

As the price of potatoes rises, the quantity of potatoes consumed in the United States falls.

c. **The price received by Canadian potato growers.**

Because Canadian producers cannot export their potatoes to the United States, the supply of potatoes in Canada increases and the price of potatoes falls.

d. **The U.S. and Canadian gains from trade.**

The U.S. and Canadian gains from trade are decreased. Anything that limits international trade decreases the gains from trade.

Additional Practice Problem 19.3a

If Canada has an import quota on eggs entering Canada from the United States, what happens to the price of eggs for Canadian consumers? What is the difference between an import quota on eggs and a tariff?

Solution to Additional Practice Problem 19.3a

An import quota restricts imports. When an import quota is implemented, the domestic price of eggs rises. A tariff also increases the domestic price. But in the case of a tariff, the Canadian government collects tariff revenue. In the case of a quota, there is no tariff revenue and the difference between the world price and the Canadian price goes to the person who has the right to import the eggs under the import quota regulations.

■ Self Test 19.3

Fill in the blanks

A tax on a good that is imposed by the importing country when an imported good crosses its international boundary is ____ (an import quota; a tariff). A tariff ____ (raises; lowers) the price paid by domestic consumers and ____ (increases; decreases) the quantity produced by domestic producers. An import quota ____ (raises; lowers) the price paid by domestic consumers and ____ (increases; decreases) the quantity produced by domestic producers.

True or false

1. If Canada imposes a tariff on a good, the price paid by Canadian consumers for that good does not change.
2. If a country imposes a tariff on pasta imports, domestic production of pasta will increase and domestic consumption of pasta will decrease.
3. A tariff on imports decreases the gains from trade for the importing country but not for the exporting country.
4. An import quota specifies the minimum quantity of that good that can be imported in a given period.

Multiple choice

1. A tax that is imposed by the importing country when an imported good crosses its international boundary is known as
a. an import quota.
b. a nontariff barrier.
c. a tariff.
d. a sanction.

2. A nontariff barrier
   a. is used by the government to restrict international trade.
   b. is imposed by the exporting country.
   c. lowers the price of the imported good.
   d. is always a quantitative restriction.

3. Suppose the world price of a shirt is $10. If Canada imposes a tariff of $5 a shirt, then the price of a shirt in
   a. Canada falls to $5.
   b. Canada rises to $15 if $15 a shirt is less than the price in Canada without international trade.
   c. the world falls to $5.
   d. the world rises to $5.

4. When a tariff is imposed on a good, the _____ increases.
   a. domestic quantity purchased
   b. domestic quantity produced
   c. quantity imported
   d. quantity exported

5. When a tariff is imposed on a good, Canadian consumers _____ because they pay _____ then the opportunity cost of the good.
   a. win; less
   b. lose; more
   c. win; more
   d. lose; less

6. Which of the following parties benefits from an import quota but not from a tariff?
   a. the government
   b. domestic producers
   c. domestic consumers
   d. the person with the right to import the good

Complete the graph

1. Figure 19.3 shows the supply of and demand for sugar in Canada.

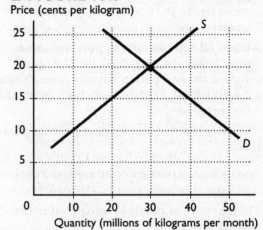

■ FIGURE 19.3

a. If the world price of sugar is 10¢ a kilogram, draw the world price line in the figure. What is the quantity consumed in Canada, the quantity produced in Canada, and the quantity imported?

b. Suppose the government imposes a 5¢ a kilogram tariff on sugar. Show the effect of the tariff in Figure 19.3 After the tariff, what is the quantity consumed in Canada, the quantity produced in Canada, and the quantity imported?

Short answer

1. Suppose the Canadian government imposes a tariff on steel. How does the tariff affect the price of steel, Canadian consumers, and Canadian steel producers?

2. Suppose the Canadian government imposes an import quota on steel. How does the import quota affect the price of steel, Canadian consumers, and Canadian steel producers?

3. Why do consumers lose from a tariff?

CHECKPOINT 19.4

■ **Explain the arguments used to justify trade barriers and show why they are incorrect but also why some barriers are hard to remove.**

Practice Problems 19.4

1. Japan sets quotas on imports of rice. California rice growers would like to export more rice to Japan. What are Japan's arguments for restricting imports of Californian rice? Are these arguments correct? Who loses from this restriction in trade?

2. In June 2001, Canada imposed tariffs as high as 45 percent on steel imports from nine countries that allegedly had been exporting steel to Canada at prices below their cost of production. What is the argument that Canada would use to justify this action? Who wins from this restriction? Who loses?

3. The United States maintains a quota on imports of textiles. What is the argument for this quota? Is this argument flawed? If so, explain why.

Solution to Practice Problem 19.4

Free trade promotes prosperity for all countries. Protection reduces the potential gains from trade. These Practice Problems discuss the arguments for protection.

Quick Review

- *Rent seeking* Lobbying and other political activity that seeks to capture the gains from trade.

1. **Japan sets quotas on imports of rice. California rice growers would like to export more rice to Japan. What are Japan's arguments for restricting imports of Californian rice? Are these arguments correct? Who loses from this restriction in trade?**

Japan has used number of arguments, but they are all incorrect. Japan has argued that Japanese rice is of a higher quality than U.S. rice, but if Japanese consumers detect a quality difference, they can purchase Japanese rice rather than U.S. rice. Japan has argued that rice is part of Japanese national heritage, but if Japanese consumers want to protect this part of their heritage, they can buy exclusively Japanese rice rather than U.S. rice. The major losers from the Japanese quota are Japanese consumers who must pay a higher price for rice.

2. **In June 2001, Canada imposed tariffs as high as 45 percent on steel imports from nine countries that allegedly had been exporting steel to Canada at prices below their cost of production. What is the argument that Canada would use to justify this action? Who wins from this restriction? Who loses?**

The argument for a tariff on steel imports is that foreign producers are dumping steel in Canada. By imposing a tariff on steel, Canadian steel producers face less competition from foreign firms. Canadian jobs are saved. The winners from the tariffs are the steel producers and steel workers. The losers are all Canadian steel consumers.

3. **The United States maintains a quota on imports of textiles. What is the argument for this quota? Is this argument flawed? If so, explain why.**

The argument for a quota on U.S. imports of textiles is the existence of cheap foreign labour in the textile industry in third world countries. This employment argument is flawed. The United States does not have a comparative advantage in textile production. Because of the quota the U.S. textile industry continues to produce. Without a quota, the U.S. textile industry would be smaller.

Additional Practice Problem 19.4a

In each of the three Practice Problems, identify who is rent seeking.

Solution to Additional Practice Problem 19.4a

In Practice Problem 1, the Japanese rice farmers are rent seeking. In Practice Problem 2, the Canadian steel producers and Canadian steel workers are rent seeking. And in Practice Problem 3,

U.S. textile producers and U.S. textile workers are rent seeking.

■ Self Test 19.4

Fill in the blanks

The assertion that it is necessary to protect a new industry to enable it to growth into a mature industry that can compete in world markets is the ____ (infant-industry; maturing-industry) argument. Protection ____ (is; is not) necessary to bring diversity and stability to our economy. Protection ____ (is; is not) necessary to prevent rich countries from exploiting developing countries. The major reason why international trade is restricted is because ____ (foreign countries protect their industries; of rent seeking).

True or false

1. The employment argument is the only valid argument for protection.
2. Dumping by a foreign producer is easy to detect.
3. Protection allows us to compete with cheap foreign labour.
4. International trade is an attractive base for tax collection in developing countries.

Multiple choice

1. The three main arguments for protection include all of the following except the
   a. employment argument.
   b. infant-industry argument.
   c. rent-seeking argument.
   d. dumping argument.

2. The argument that it is necessary to protect a new industry to enable it to grow into a mature industry that can compete in world markets is the
   a. national security argument.
   b. diversity argument.
   c. infant-industry argument.
   d. environmental protection argument.

3. ____ occurs when a foreign firm sells its exports at a lower price than the price in the foreign firm's domestic market.
   a. Dumping
   b. The trickle-down effect
   c. Rent seeking
   d. Tariff avoidance

4. Canada
   a. needs tariffs to allow us to compete with cheap foreign labour.
   b. does not need tariffs to allow us to compete with cheap foreign labour.
   d. should not trade with developing countries.
   d. does not benefit from trade with developing countries.

5. Why do governments in developing countries impose tariffs on imported goods and services?
   a. International trade is an attractive base for tax collection because transactions are well recorded and audited.
   b. Tariffs protect jobs.
   c. The nation's total income is increased.
   d. National security of the country is improved.

6. What is the major reason international trade is restricted?
   a. rent seeking
   b. to bring diversity and stability
   c. to save jobs
   d. to prevent dumping

Short answer

1. What is the dumping argument for protection? What is its flaw?
2. How do you respond to a speaker who says that we need to limit auto imports from Japan to save Canadian jobs?
3. Explain why trade with developing countries does not exploit workers in these countries.

SELF TEST ANSWERS

■ CHECKPOINT 19.1

Fill in the blanks

Manufactured goods account for more than <u>one-half</u> of Canadian imports. <u>The United States</u> is Canada's biggest trading partner. Canada <u>is</u> a member of the Asia-Pacific Economic Cooperation. In Canada between 1960 and 2000, trade <u>increased</u> as a fraction of GDP.

True or false

1. False; page 452
2. False; page 452
3. True; page 453
4. True; page 455

Multiple choice

1. a; page 452
2. d; page 452
3. b; page 452
4. a; page 452
5. a; page 453
6. b; page 455

Short answer

1. From the Canadian vantage, the cheese is an imported good and the air transportation is an exported service. From the French vantage, the cheese is an exported good and the air transportation is an imported service; page 452.

2. Between 1960 and 2000, international trade in Canada expanded. In 1960, Canadian exports were about 17 percent of Canada's GDP and imports were 18 percent of GDP. In 2000, exports were 45 percent of GDP and imports were more than 40 percent of GDP; page 452.

3. NAFTA is the North American Free Trade Agreement. It is an agreement between Canada, the United States, and Mexico to make trade among the three nations easier and freer; pages 453-454.

■ CHECKPOINT 19.2

Fill in the blanks

A country has a comparative advantage in producing a good if it can produce the good at a <u>lower</u> opportunity cost than another country. If the world price of clothing is less than the price in Canada with no international trade and Canada imports clothing from Asia, Canadian buyers of clothing <u>gain</u> and Asian producers of clothing <u>gain</u>. Trade <u>does not allow</u> a nation to produce at a point beyond its production possibilities frontier. Trade <u>allows</u> a nation to consume at a point beyond its production possibilities frontier.

True or false

1. False; page 461
2. False; page 457
3. False; pages 461-462
4. True; page 462

Multiple choice

1. d; page 456
2. c; page 457-458
3. c; page 456
4. c; page 459
5. a; pages 461-462
6. a; page 462

Complete the graph

1. a. In the absence of international trade, the equilibrium price of a basket of apples in Canada is $4; page 456.

   b. If the world price of a basket of apples is $6 a basket, Canada will export apples because the world price exceeds the no-trade price. If the price of apples exceeds $4 a basket, Canada will export apples. If the price of apples is less than $4 a basket, Canada will import apples; pages 457–459.

2. a. The opportunity cost of a computer chip in Canada is 1 kilogram of cheese. In France, the opportunity cost of a computer chip is 4 kilograms of cheese. Canada has the comparative advantage in chips; pages 459, 461.

b. The opportunity cost of a kilogram of cheese in Canada is 1 computer chip. In France, the opportunity cost of a kilogram of cheese is 1/4 of a computer chip. France has the comparative advantage in cheese; pages 459, 461.

c. Canada has the comparative advantage in chips, so it will specialize in producing chips and export chips to France. France will specialize in cheese and export cheese to Canada; page 461.

d. The point is point A in Figure 19.4; page 461.

■ **FIGURE 19.4**
Computer chips (thousands per year)

[Graph showing Canada's PPF from 400 chips to 400 cheese, and France's PPF from 200 chips to 800 cheese. Point A at (600, 300) and Point B at (800, 400).]

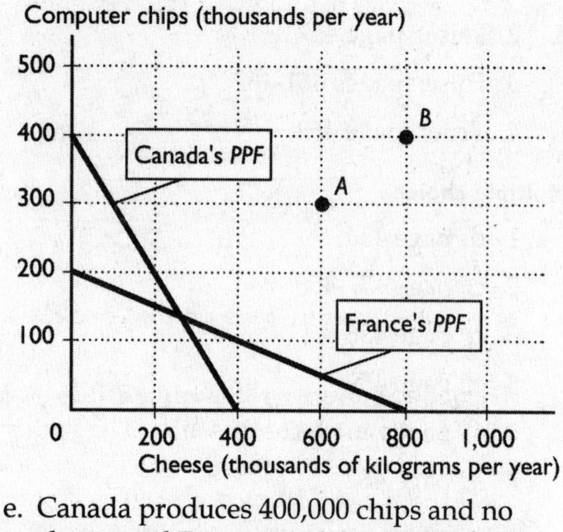

e. Canada produces 400,000 chips and no cheese and France produces 800,000 kilograms of cheese and no chips. Total production is 400,000 chips and 800,000 kilograms of cheese, labelled B in Figure 19.4. More chips *and* more cheese are produced at point B after trade than are produced at point A before trade; page 462.

Short answer

1. a. In the absence of international trade, the equilibrium price is $600 a tonne and the equilibrium quantity is 46 tonnes; page 456.

b. In Canada, the quantity supplied is 54 tonnes and the quantity demanded is 34 tonnes. Canada exports 20 tonnes of potatoes; page 456.

c. In Canada, the quantity supplied is 58 tonnes and the quantity demanded is 28 tonnes. Canada exports 30 tonnes of potatoes; page 456.

d. Canada imports potatoes if the world price is less than $600 a tonne; page 459.

2. a. In France, the opportunity cost of a tonne of ice cream is 6 tonnes of cheese; in Canada, the opportunity cost of a tonne of ice cream is 2 tonnes of cheese. Canada has the comparative advantage in producing ice cream; page 461.

b. In France, the opportunity cost of a tonne of cheese is 1/6 of a tonne of ice cream; in Canada, the opportunity cost of a tonne of cheese is 1/2 of a tonne of ice cream. France has the comparative advantage in producing cheese; page 461.

c. Canada imports cheese and exports ice cream; page 461.

d. 35 tonnes of ice cream are produced and 110 tonnes of cheese are produced; page 462.

e. 50 tonnes of ice cream are produced in Canada and 120 tonnes of cheese are produced in France; page 462.

f. The world production of ice cream *and* cheese increased, which demonstrates the gains from trade; page 462.

3. The gains from trade occur because after specialization and trade, a country can increase its consumption so that it can consume at a point beyond its production possibilities frontier. To obtain the gains from

trade a country must specialize and trade; page 462.

4. Dynamic comparative advantage is a comparative advantage that a person (or country) obtains by specializing in an activity, resulting from learning-by-doing; page 462.

■ CHECKPOINT 19.3

Fill in the blanks

A tax on a good that is imposed by the importing country when an imported good crosses its international boundary is called <u>a tariff</u>. A tariff <u>raises</u> the price paid by domestic consumers and <u>increases</u> the quantity produced by domestic producers. An import quota <u>raises</u> the price paid by domestic consumers and <u>increases</u> the quantity produced by domestic producers.

True or false

1. False; pages 465-466
2. True; pages 465-466
3. False; pages 465-466
4. False; page 466

Multiple choice

1. c; page 464
2. a; page 464
3. b; page 465
4. b; pages 465-466
5. b; pages 465-466
6. d; pages 466-467

Complete the graph

1. The world price line is shown in Figure 19.5.

■ **FIGURE 19.5**

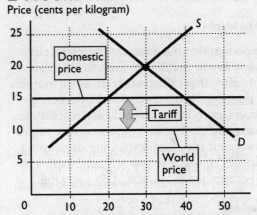

a. 50 million kilograms of sugar are consumed in Canada, 10 million kilograms are produced in Canada, and 40 million kilograms are imported into Canada; pages 464-466.

b. The tariff increases the domestic price as shown in Figure 19.5. The quantity consumed in Canada decreases to 40 million kilograms, the quantity produced in Canada increases to 20 million kilograms, and the amount imported decreases to 20 million kilograms; pages 464-465.

Short answer

1. The tariff raises the price of steel. Canadian steel consumers decrease the quantity they purchase and Canadian steel producers increase the quantity they produce; pages 464-465.

2. The import quota has the same effects as the tariff in the previous question. The import quota increases the price of steel. Canadian steel consumers decrease the quantity purchased and Canadian steel producers increase the quantity produced; pages 466-467.

3. Consumers lose from a tariff because the tariff raises the price they must pay and the quantity bought decreases. The tariff makes people pay more than the opportunity cost of the good; page 466.

■ CHECKPOINT 19.4

Fill in the blanks

The assertion that it is necessary to protect a new industry to enable it to growth into a mature industry that can compete in world markets is the <u>infant-industry</u> argument. Protection <u>is not</u> necessary to bring diversity and stability to our economy. Protection <u>is not</u> necessary to prevent rich countries from exploiting developing countries. The major reason why international trade is restricted is because <u>of rent seeking</u>.

True or false

1. False; page 469
2. False; page 470
3. False; page 471
4. True; page 474

Multiple choice

1. c; page 469
2. c; page 469
3. a; page 470
4. b; page 471
5. a; page 474
6. a; page 474

Short answer

1. Dumping occurs when a foreign firm sells its exports at a lower price than the price in the foreign firm's domestic market. The dumping argument is flawed for the following reasons. First, it is virtually impossible to detect dumping. Second, it is hard to think of a good that is produced by a natural global monopoly. Third, if a good or service were a truly global natural monopoly, the best way to deal with it would be by regulation; page 470.

2. Saving jobs is one of the oldest arguments in favour of protection. It is also incorrect. Protecting a particular industry likely will save jobs in that industry but will cost many other jobs in other industries. The cost to consumers of saving a job is many times the wage rate of the job saved; page 469.

3. Trade with developing countries does not exploit workers in these countries. Wage rates in some developing countries are very low. But by trading with developing countries, we increase the demand for the goods that these countries produce, and we increase the demand for their labour. When the demand for labour in developing countries increases, the wage rate also increases. So instead of exploiting people in developing countries, trade improves their opportunities and increases their income; page 473.

Chapter 20
Farms and Cities

CHAPTER IN PERSPECTIVE

Chapter 20 focuses on farms and cities. We study the issues of fluctuating farm incomes, urban sprawl, and road congestion.

■ **Explain why farm incomes fluctuate and why the prices of farm products are on a downward trend.**

The demand for farm products and the supply of farm products are inelastic. In an unfavourable growing season that results in a poor harvest, the price of wheat rises and farm total revenue increases. Farmers, whose crop is unaffected, earn an economic profit. In an unusually favourable growing season that results in a bumper harvest, the price of wheat falls and farm total revenue decreases. Farmers are incurring an economic loss. In normal conditions, farmers earn a normal profit. A small decrease in demand brings a large fall in price and farm total revenue. And a small increase in demand brings a large rise in price and farm total revenue. The prices of farm products have fallen and farm output has increased over the years because of an increase in demand and an even greater increase in supply. The two main sources of the increasing demand for farm products are population growth and rising incomes. The supply of farm products has increased at a rapid rate because of an incredible pace of technological change and productivity growth.

■ **Describe and evaluate the effects of government policies to stabilize farm incomes.**

An agricultural marketing board is an agency created by the federal government or a provincial government to buy and sell farm products, stabilize their prices, and provide farmers with an appropriate income. Agricultural marketing boards use two main tools: price support and quota. A price support is a price that exceeds the market equilibrium price at which an agricultural marketing board buys farm products. A price support boosts farm income, but it creates a surplus of output, increases taxes, raises price, might decrease the quantity of farm output consumed, and creates a deadweight loss. A quota is a limit on total production and the production of each farmer imposed by an agricultural marketing board. A quota can achieve an efficient farm output when used with a price support, and it can limit the size of the farm subsidy. But a quota can leave output at an inefficient level.

■ **Explain why cities grow, and evaluate tolls as a way of achieving an efficient use of roads.**

A city provides external production benefits and external consumption benefits. When natural barriers are absent, economic factors determine the size of an urban area. A model circular city has a central business district where the cost of land is highest. The value of land depends only on the distance from the centre. The equilibrium size of a city is the size at which the value of land in urban use equals its value in farm use. Roads become over-congested because road use creates an external cost but road users take into account the private cost only. A toll can create an efficient use of roads.

EXPANDED CHAPTER CHECKLIST

When you have completed this chapter, you will be able to:

1 **Explain why farm incomes fluctuate and why the prices of farm products are on a downward trend.**

- Explain the effect of output fluctuations in an agricultural market on the price and quantity of farm products and on farm total revenue.
- Discuss the elasticity of demand for farm products.
- Explain the effect of demand fluctuations in an agricultural market on the price and quantity of farm products and on farm total revenue
- Discuss the change in the prices of farm products and farm outputs between 1950 and 2000 and explain why these changes occurred.
- Illustrate the effects of technological change in farming.

2 **Describe and evaluate the effects of government policies to stabilize farm incomes.**

- Define agricultural marketing board.
- Describe how a marketing board uses a price support and illustrate the effects of a price support.
- Describe the inefficiency of a price support.
- Describe how a marketing board uses a quota.
- Explain why the world market is oversupplied with food.

3 **Explain why cities grow, and evaluate tolls as a way of achieving an efficient use of roads.**

- Describe the external production benefits and external consumption benefits of city living.
- Describe a Mills city.
- Describe the equilibrium size of a city.
- Explain why inefficient congestion arises on highways and city streets.
- Discuss the role of tolls in achieving efficient road use.

KEY TERMS

- Agricultural marketing board (page 490)
- Price support (page 490)
- Quota (page 490)

CHECKPOINT 20.1

■ **Explain why farm incomes fluctuate and why the prices of farm products are on a downward trend.**

Practice Problem 20.1

The table shows a demand schedule for oilseed in a normal year. The quantity of oilseed grown in a normal year is 50 million tonnes. In a boom year, the quantity demanded increases by 2 million tonnes at each price. In a slump year, the quantity demanded decreases by 2 million tonnes at each price. Calculate:

Price (dollars per tonne)	Quantity demanded (millions of tonnes per year)
7	47
6	48
5	49
4	50
3	51
2	52
1	53

a. Farm total revenue in a normal year.
b. Price and farm total revenue in a normal demand year but with a bumper crop of 52 million tonnes.
c. Price and farm total revenue in a normal demand year but with a poor crop of 48 million tonnes.
d. Price and farm total revenue in a normal supply year but with a boom in demand.

e. Price and farm total revenue in a normal supply year but with a slump in demand.

Solution to Practice Problem 20.1

This Practice Problem studies the effects of output fluctuations and demand fluctuations in the agricultural market and emphasizes the changes that occur in the price of a farm product and farm total revenue.

Quick Review

- *Total revenue* The total revenue from the sale of a good equals the price of the good multiplied by the quantity sold.

The quantity of oilseed grown in a normal year is 50 million tonnes. In a boom year, the quantity demanded increases by 2 million tonnes at each price. In a slump year, the quantity demanded decreases by 2 million tonnes at each price. Calculate:

a. **Farm total revenue in a normal year.**

In a normal year, the equilibrium quantity is 50 million tonnes. From the demand schedule, when the quantity demanded is 50 million tonnes a year, the price is $4 a tonne. Farm total revenue is ($4 a tonne) × (50 million tonnes), which is $200 million.

b. **Price and farm total revenue in a normal demand year but with a bumper crop of 52 million tonnes.**

With a bumper crop, the quantity demanded equals the quantity supplied, 52 million tonnes, when price is $2 a tonne. Total farm revenue is ($2 a tonne) × (52 million tonnes), which is $104 million.

c. **Price and farm total revenue in a normal demand year but with a poor crop of 48 million tonnes.**

With a poor crop, the quantity demanded equals the quantity supplied, 48 million tonnes, when price is $6 a tonne. Total farm revenue is ($6 a tonne) × (48 million tonnes), which is $288 million.

d. **Price and farm total revenue in a normal supply year but with a boom in demand.**

The table shows the demand schedule when there is a boom in demand. The quantity demanded equals the quantity supplied, 50 million tonnes, when the price is $6 a tonne. Total farm revenue equals ($6 a tonne) × (50 million tonnes), which is $300 million.

Price (dollars per tonne)	New quantity demanded (millions of tonnes per year)
7	49
6	50
5	51
4	52
3	53
2	54
1	55

e. **Price and farm total revenue in a normal supply year but with a slump in demand.**

The table shows the demand schedule when there is a slump in demand. The quantity demanded equals the quantity supplied, 50 million tonnes, when the price is $2 a tonne. Total farm revenue equals ($2 a tonne) × (50 million tonnes), which is $100 million.

Price (dollars per tonne)	New quantity demanded (millions of tonnes per year)
7	45
6	46
5	47
4	48
3	49
2	50
1	51

Additional Practice Problem 20.1a

In Practice Problem 20.1, assume you are a farmer who experiences a normal year. Would you rather the year be one in which the total crop is a bumper crop, a normal crop, or a poor crop? Why?

Solution to Additional Practice Problem 20.1a

With a poor crop, the price rises. Because you have a normal crop, your total revenue increases. You are better off when there is a poor crop.

■ Self Test 20.1

Fill in the blanks

Farmers with a normal harvest ____ (earn an economic profit; earn a normal profit; incur an economic loss) in a year in which the total harvest is normal. Farmers with a normal harvest ____ (earn an economic profit; earn a normal profit; incur an economic loss) in a year in which there is a poor harvest. Farmers with a normal harvest ____ (earn an economic profit; earn a normal profit; incur an economic loss) in a year in which there is a bumper harvest. The demand for farm products is ____ (elastic; inelastic) and the supply of farm products is ____ (elastic; inelastic). Between 1950 and 2000, the prices of farm products ____ (fell; rose), farm output ____ (decreased; increased), and the number of farms in Canada ____ (decreased; increased).

True or false

1. A poor harvest decreases farm total revenue.
2. A change in the demand for wheat brings a small change in the price of wheat.
3. After the crop has been harvested, demand is perfectly elastic.
4. The prices of farm products fell between 1950 and 2000 because the increase in the supply of farm products exceeded the increase in demand.
5. There are more farms operating in Canada in 2000 than in 1950.

Multiple choice

1. Once harvested, the supply of an agricultural product is ____ so the supply curve is ____.
   a. perfectly inelastic; vertical
   b. perfectly elastic; horizontal
   c. perfectly inelastic; horizontal
   d. perfectly elastic; vertical

2. In a normal year, a corn farmer
   a. earns a large economic profit.
   b. incurs a large economic loss.
   c. earns a normal profit.
   d. is able to set his own price.

3. Which of the following situations is most likely to result in an economic profit for some farmers?
   a. normal harvest
   b. poor harvest
   c. bumper harvest
   d. Farmers never make positive economic profits.

4. When the supply of coffee beans increases because of a bumper harvest, the price of coffee beans will ____ and total revenue for coffee bean producers will ____.
   a. rise; increase
   b. rise; decrease
   c. fall; increase
   d. fall; decrease

5. The major reason why the demand for food is ____ is because it is very ____ to find substitutes for food.
   a. inelastic; difficult
   b. elastic; difficult
   c. inelastic; easy
   d. elastic; easy

6. If the demand for agricultural products decreases, farm total revenue
   a. increases.
   b. decreases.
   c. remains the same.
   d. becomes negative.

7. The two major reasons why the demand for farm products increased between 1950 and 2000 are
   a. technology growth and population growth.
   b. rising incomes and population growth.
   c. rising incomes and technology growth.
   d. population growth and lower prices.

8. In Canada from 1950 to 2000, the number of farms ____ and total farm output ____.
   a. increased; increased
   b. increased; decreased
   c. decreased; increased
   d. decreased; decreased

Complete the graph

1. The table has the demand schedule for corn.

Price (dollars per basket of corn)	Quantity demanded (billions of baskets per year)
3	21
4	20
5	19
6	18

   a. Label the axes and plot the demand curve in Figure 20.1.

   ■ **FIGURE 20.1**

   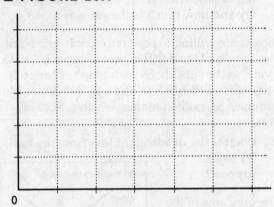

   b. A normal harvest of corn is 20 billion baskets of corn. Draw this supply curve in Figure 20.1 and label it S_0. What is the equilibrium price and quantity and what is the total revenue earned by corn farmers?

   c. A poor harvest of corn is 19 billion baskets of corn. Draw this supply curve in Figure 20.1 and label it S_1. What is the equilibrium price and quantity and what is the total revenue earned by corn farmers?

   d. A bumper harvest of corn is 21 billion baskets of corn. Draw this supply curve in Figure 20.1 and label it S_2. What is the equilibrium price and quantity and what is the total revenue earned by corn farmers?

   e. A corn farmer whose harvest was normal regardless of the overall harvest would prefer what type of overall harvest: poor, normal, or bumper? Why?

Short answer

1. Why is the demand for food products price inelastic?

2. Once harvested, the supply of farm products is perfectly inelastic. The demand for farm products is inelastic. How does a small decrease in demand affect the price and quantity of farm products?

3. Between 1950 and 2000, how have the prices and quantities of farm products changed? What factors brought about these changes?

4. How have technological advances affected farms' average total cost curves? What impact has this change had on the number of farmers?

CHECKPOINT 20.2

■ Describe and evaluate the effects of government policies to stabilize farm incomes.

Practice Problems 20.2

1. The table shows the demand schedule and supply schedule for barley. The barley marketing board decides to set a support price of $100 a tonne.

Price (dollars per tonne)	Quantity demanded (millions of tonnes per year)	Quantity supplied (millions of tonnes per year)
140	3.5	6.5
120	4.0	6.0
100	4.5	5.5
80	5.0	5.0
60	5.5	4.5
40	6.0	4.0
20	6.5	3.5

   a. What is the quantity of barley produced?

b. If the marketing board sells barley for $100 a tonne, how much barley does it stockpile and how much is the barley subsidy?

c. If the marketing board sells all the barley produced for the price that buyers are willing to pay, what is the market price of barley and how much is the subsidy?

d. What is the deadweight loss from the barley price support?

2. In the market described in the table, the marketing board imposes a quota at the efficient quantity.

   a. What is the quota?

   b. What is the marginal cost of producing the quota quantity?

   c. What is the barley subsidy?

Solution to Practice Problems 20.2

This Practice Problem studies the different effects of the two main tools used by agricultural marketing boards: price support and quota.

Quick Review

- *Price support* A price that exceeds the market equilibrium price at which an agricultural marketing board buys farm products.

- *Quota* A limit on total production and the production of each farmer imposed by an agricultural marketing board.

1. **The table shows the demand schedule and supply schedule for barley. The barley marketing board sets a price support at $100 a tonne.**

   a. **What is the quantity of barley produced?**

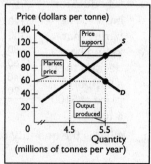

When the barley marketing board sets a price support at $100 a tonne, the board agrees to pay farmers $100 for every tonne of barley they produce. In the figure, farmers produce their profit-maximizing output where the supply curve, S, intersects the Price support line. The quantity of barley produced is 5.5 million tonnes a year.

   b. **If the marketing board sells barley for $100 a tonne, how much barley does it stockpile and how much is the barley subsidy?**

The quantity stockpiled is the difference between the quantity supplied at a price of $100 a tonne, which is 5.5 millions tonnes a year and the quantity demanded at a price of $100 a tonne, which is 4.5 million tonnes a year. So the stockpile is 1 million tonnes of barley. Barley farmers receive a subsidy of $100 a tonne on the 1 million tonnes held in storage, which is $100 million.

   c. **If the marketing board sells all the barley produced for the price that buyers are willing to pay, what is the market price of barley and how much is the subsidy?**

Buyers are willing to pay $60 a tonne for 5.5 million tonnes of barley. The price support is $100 a tonne, so the subsidy on each tonne of barley is $100 − $60, which is $40. The total subsidy is $40 a tonne × 5.5 million tonnes, which is $220 million.

   d. **What is the deadweight loss from the barley price support?**

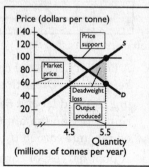

The grey area in the figure is the deadweight loss. The deadweight loss equals ½ × (5.5 million tonnes − 5.0 million tonnes) × ($100 − $60), which is $10 million.

2. **In the market described in the table, the marketing board imposes a quota at the efficient quantity.**

   a. **What is the quota?**

The efficient quota occurs at the quantity such that the quantity of barley supplied equals the quantity of barley demanded. The quota is 5 million tonnes a year.

b. **What is the marginal cost of producing the quota quantity?**

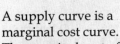

A supply curve is a marginal cost curve. The marginal cost of producing 5 million tonnes a year is $80 a tonne.

c. **What is the barley subsidy?**

With the quota, the quantity produced is 5 million tonnes. The marketing board buys the barley at a price of $100 a tonne and sells it for $80 a tonne. The figure shows the subsidy, which is equal to the quantity, 5.0 million tonnes a year multiplied by the subsidy, $20 a tonne. The total subsidy is $100 million.

Additional Practice Problem 20.2a

In the Practice Problem describe the effects in the barley market if the quota is not set at the efficient quantity.

Solution to Additional Practice Problem 20.2a

A quota set above the efficient quantity brings overproduction and deadweight loss. A quota set below the efficient quantity brings underproduction and deadweight loss.

■ Self Test 20.2

Fill in the blanks

_____ (An agricultural marketing board; A price support system) is an agency created by the federal government or a provincial government to buy and sell farm products, stabilize their prices, and provide farmers with an appropriate income. When a marketing board uses a _____ (price support; quota), it sets the price at which it buys farm products at a level that exceeds the market equilibrium price. When a marketing board uses a _____ (price support; quota), it sets a total production limit and a production limit for each farmer. A price support is _____ (efficient; inefficient). A quota _____ (is efficient; is inefficient; may be efficient or inefficient). Most countries _____ (do not subsidize; subsidize) their farms and as a result the world market is _____ (oversupplied; undersupplied) with food and world food prices are too _____ (high; low).

True or false

1. An agricultural marketing board uses two main tools, which are price ceilings and quotas.

2. A price support does not achieve its goal of increasing farm incomes.

3. A price support is efficient because it increases producer surplus and consumer surplus.

4. If a quota restricts farm production, then the supply curve becomes perfectly inelastic at the quota quantity.

5. Quotas and price supports on farm produce increase the amount of efficient international trade and raise the world price of farm products.

Multiple choice

1. When a marketing board uses a quota, it sets
a. the maximum price at which a farmer can sell his produce.
b. the minimum price at which a farmer can sell his produce.
c. a total production limit and a production limit for each farmer.
d. Both (b) and (c) and correct.

2. When a marketing board uses a price support,
a. it provides farmers with a larger income than they would otherwise have.
b. it provides farmers with a smaller income than they would otherwise have.
c. consumer-taxpayers lose less than farmers gain.
d. consumer-taxpayers gain because more farm produce is available.

3. With a price support and subsidy, farmers _____ and consumer-taxpayers _____.
a. gain; lose
b. gain; gain
c. lose; lose
d. lose; gain

4. A price support _____ producer surplus, _____ consumer surplus, and _____ deadweight loss.
a. increases; decreases; creates a
b. increases; increases; creates a
c. increases; decreases; eliminates
d. decreases; increases; eliminates

5. If a quota restricts farm production
a. supply curve becomes perfectly elastic.
b. supply curve becomes perfectly inelastic.
c. demand curve becomes perfectly elastic.
d. demand curve becomes perfectly inelastic.

6. A quota
a. may be efficient or inefficient.
b. is always efficient.
c. is always inefficient.
d. equals the competitive price.

7. Most countries
a. subsidize their farms.
b. encourage imports of food.
c. discourage exports of food.
d. All of the above answers are correct.

8. Increased domestic production of farm produce _____ in the rest of the world.
a. leads to an increase in supply
b. leads to a decrease in demand
c. leads to an increase in demand
d. does not change supply or demand

Complete the graph

1. The table has the demand and supply schedules for wheat.

Price (dollars per basket of wheat)	Quantity demanded (billions of baskets per year)	Quantity supplied (billions of baskets per year)
1	20	10
2	15	15
3	10	20
4	5	25

a. Label the axes and plot the demand curve and supply curve in Figure 20.2. What is the price and quantity of wheat?

■ **FIGURE 20.2**

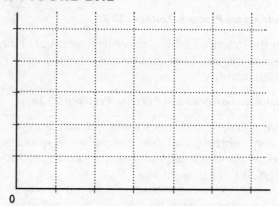

b. If the marketing board establishes a price support of $3 a basket, what is the quantity demanded and the quantity supplied? If the marketing board stockpiles the surplus, indicate the amount of the subsidy in Figure 20.2.

Short answer

1. Does a price support create a surplus or a shortage? What happens to the surplus or the shortage?

2. How does a price support affect a farmer's income? Is a price support efficient?
3. Most countries subsidize their farms. What is the effect of this subsidization on the global food market?

CHECKPOINT 20.3

■ Explain why cities grow, and evaluate tolls as a way of achieving an efficient use of roads.

Practice Problem 20.3

In the figure, the demand for urban land in Concentric City in 2000 was D_0. In 2010, the demand had increased to D_1. Farmland around the city was selling for $4,000 a hectare in 2000 and for $2,000 a hectare in 2010.

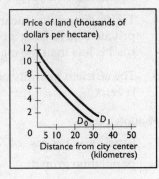

a. What was the size of Concentric City in 2000?
b. What was the size of Concentric City in 2010?
c. What was the price of a hectare of land at the centre of Concentric City in 2000?
d. What was the price of a hectare of land at the centre of Concentric City in 2010?
e. What was the price of a hectare of land 5 kilometres from the centre of Concentric City in 2000?
f. What was the price of a hectare of land 15 kilometres from the centre of Concentric City in 2010?

Solution to Practice Problem 20.3

To answer this Practice Problem remember that as we move down the demand curve and further away from the city centre, the price that someone is willing to pay for a hectare of land decreases.

Quick Review

- *Equilibrium size of the city* The equilibrium size of the city is the size at which the value of land in urban use equals its value in farm use.

a. What was the size of Concentric City in 2000?

In the figure, the demand for urban land in 2000 is D_0 and the supply of land for urban use rather than for farm use is S_0. The limits of Concentric City were 15 kilometres from the centre at the intersection of D_0 and S_0.

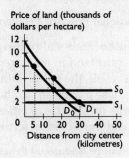

b. What was the size of Concentric City in 2010?

In the figure, the demand for urban land in 2010 is D_1 and the supply of land for urban use rather than for farm use is S_1. The limits of Concentric City were 30 kilometres from the centre at the intersection of D_1 and S_1.

c. What was the price of hectare of land at the centre of Concentric City in 2000?

A hectare of land at the centre of Concentric City in 2000 cost $10,000, at the point where the curve D_0 intersects the y-axis.

d. What was the price of a hectare of land at the centre of Concentric City in 2010?

A hectare of land at the centre of Concentric City in 2010 cost $12,000, at the point where the curve D_1 intersects the y-axis.

e. What was the price of a hectare of land 5 kilometres from the centre of Concentric City in 2000?

At each point along the x-axis, there is only one hectare of land available. The demand curve tells us the price that someone is willing to pay for that hectare. A hectare of land 5 kilometres from the centre of Concentric City in 2000 cost $8,000 (on curve D_0).

f. What was the price of a hectare of land 15 kilometres from the centre of Concentric City in 2010?

A hectare of land 15 kilometres from the centre of Concentric City in 2010 cost $6,000 (on curve D_1).

Additional Practice Problem 20.3a

Suppose large-scale climate changes occur that turn farmland in many regions into arid deserts. As a result, the value of the remaining farmland rises. Use a diagram to show the effect of this change on the size of cities that are surrounded by land that remains fertile.

Solution to Additional Practice Problem 20.3a

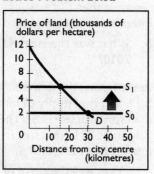

In the figure, the equilibrium size of the city initially is 30 kilometres, at the intersection of the D curve and the S_0 curve. Following the climate change, the supply curve of land for urban use rather than for farm use shifts upward from S_0 to S_1. The equilibrium size of the city decreases to 15 kilometres, at the intersection of the D curve and the S_1 curve.

■ Self Test 20.3

Fill in the blanks

As we move farther away from the city centre, the price that someone is willing to pay for a hectare of land _____ (decreases; increases). The _____ (demand curve determines; demand curve and supply curve determine) the price of land. Cities grow for one fundamental reason, which is _____ (an increase in population; technological change). Because of congestion, the marginal social cost of a trip is _____ (less; greater) than the marginal private cost. When tolls are used to achieve efficient road use, congestion _____ (decreases, but it might not be eliminated; is eliminated).

True or false

1. External consumption benefits are a benefit of living in a city.

2. The demand curve for urban land is upward sloping because buyers are willing to pay more for land farther from the city centre.

3. A decrease in the value of farmland surrounding a city leads to an increase in the equilibrium size of the city.

4. Traffic congestion means that the marginal private benefit from a trip on a congested road is less than the marginal social benefit.

5. The efficient quantity of congestion on a road is zero.

Multiple choice

1. Cities arise because of
   a. population growth.
   b. private production benefits and private consumption benefits.
   c. private production benefits and social consumption benefits.
   d. external production benefits and external consumption benefits.

2. Which of the following is an external consumption benefit of cities?
   a. a high cost of housing
   b. output from a group that exceeds the outputs of each individual working alone
   c. an increased number and quality of services and entertainment
   d. a lower crime rate

3. According to Mills, land values are highest
   a. in the suburbs.
   b. at the city centre.
   c. at the farthest point from the city centre.
   d. in the wealthiest suburban areas.

4. A main reason why the willingness to pay for land ____ as you move away from downtown Montreal is because transportation costs ____ as you get farther away.
   a. increases; increase
   b. increases; decrease
   c. decreases; decrease
   d. decreases; increase

5. The supply of urban land at a given distance from the city centre is
   a. perfectly elastic.
   b. perfectly inelastic.
   c. unit elastic.
   d. moderately elastic.

6. A city is at its equilibrium size when the value of land in urban use ____ its value in farm use.
   a. is greater than
   b. is less than
   c. equals
   d. A city's equilibrium size is unrelated to the value of land.

7. A main reason cities grow is
   a. technological change that lowers the value of land in farm use.
   b. the decreasing rural population.
   c. the falling cost of capital.
   d. the increase in the value of farmland.

8. If a toll is imposed on drivers who drive on congested roads, then
   a. road congestion is eliminated.
   b. the marginal social cost of using the road increases.
   c. the number of drivers increases because congestion is eliminated.
   d. the marginal private cost of using the road increases.

Complete the graph

1. Figure 20.3 shows the demand curve for urban land and the value of land in farming.

   ■ FIGURE 20.3

   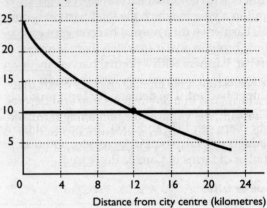

   a. Label the curves. What is the equilibrium size of the city?
   b. Suppose the value of land in farming falls to one half of its former value. Illustrate this change in the figure. What is the new equilibrium size of the city?

Short answer

1. In the model city, how does the value of urban land change as we move farther away from the city centre? Why?
2. Why does the marginal social cost of a trip on a congested road differ from the marginal private cost of a trip?
3. Why might a toll be necessary to eliminate inefficient congestion on roadways?

SELF TEST ANSWERS

■ CHECKPOINT 20.1

Fill in the blanks

Farmers with a normal harvest <u>earn a normal profit</u> in a year in which the total harvest is normal. Farmers with a normal harvest <u>earn an economic profit</u> in a year in which there is a poor harvest. Farmers with a normal harvest <u>incur an economic loss</u> in a year in which there is a bumper harvest. The demand for farm products is <u>inelastic</u> and the supply of farm products is <u>inelastic</u>. Between 1950 and 2000, the prices of farm products <u>fell</u>, farm output <u>increased</u>, and the number of farms in Canada <u>decreased</u>.

True or false

1. False; page 480
2. False; page 482
3. False; page 482
4. True; page 486
5. False; page 486

Multiple choice

1. a; page 480
2. c; page 480
3. b; page 480
4. d; page 481
5. a; page 482
6. b; page 482
7. b; page 484
8. c; page 487

Complete the graph

1a. The demand curve labelled D is in Figure 20.4; page 481.

b. The equilibrium price is $4 a basket and the equilibrium quantity is 20 billion baskets. Total revenue is $80 billion; page 481.

c. The equilibrium price is $5 a basket and the equilibrium quantity is 19 billion baskets. Total revenue is $95 billion; page 481.

d. The equilibrium price is $3 a basket and the equilibrium quantity is 21 billion baskets. Total revenue is $63 billion; page 481.

■ **FIGURE 20.4**

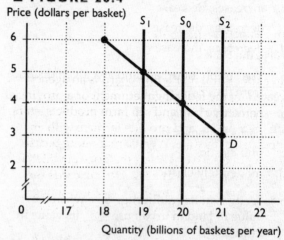

e. The corn farmer prefers an overall poor harvest because the price of corn is higher and he will earn an economic profit; page 480.

Short answer

1. The demand for food products is price inelastic because food products do not have good substitutes; page 482.

2. A change in the demand for a farm product has no effect on the quantity because the supply is perfectly inelastic. But the price changes by a large amount to restore the equilibrium quantity; pages 482-483.

3. By 2000, the price of farm products had fallen to 46 percent of their 1950 level and the quantity increased to 280 percent of the 1950 quantity. These changes occurred because the demand for and supply of farm products increased, but the increase in the supply was much larger than the increase in demand; page 486.

4. Technological advances have increased the capital intensity of farming. Average total cost has increased at low output levels (because average fixed cost has increased) and

decreased at high output levels. The average total cost curve has shifted downward. Each farm on average produces more in 2000 than in 1950, but the number of farms has decreased; page 487.

■ **CHECKPOINT 20.2**
Fill in the blanks

An agricultural marketing board is an agency created by the federal government or a provincial government to buy and sell farm products, stabilize their prices, and provide farmers with an appropriate income. When a marketing board uses a price support, it sets the price at which it buys farm products at a level that exceeds the market equilibrium price. When a marketing board uses a quota, it sets a total production limit and a production limit for each farmer. A price support is inefficient. A quota may be efficient or inefficient. Most countries subsidize their farms and as a result the world market is oversupplied with food and world food prices are too low.

True or false

1. False; page 490
2. False; page 491
3. False; page 492
4. True; page 493
5. False; page 494

Multiple choice

1. c; page 490
2. a; page 490
3. a; page 491
4. b; page 492
5. b; page 493
6. a; page 493
7. a; page 494
8. a; page 494

Complete the graph

1a. Figure 20.5 shows the demand curve and supply curve. The equilibrium price is $2 a basket and the equilibrium quantity is 15 billion baskets a year; pages 490-491.

b. If the marketing board sets a price support of $3 a basket, the quantity demanded is 10 billion baskets a year and the quantity supplied is 20 billion baskets a year. The marketing board buys the 20 billion baskets at $3 a basket and sells 10 billion baskets at $3 a basket. The rest of the wheat is stored and farmers receive a subsidy of $30 million ($3 a basket on the 10 billion baskets in storage), shown by the grey rectangle in Figure 20.5; page 491.

■ **FIGURE 20.5**
Price (dollars per basket)

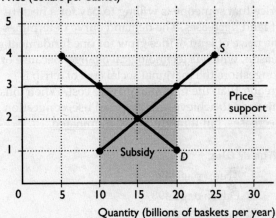

Short answer

1. A price support creates a surplus. The marketing board can keep the surplus in storage, sell the entire quantity supplied at the highest price the market will pay, or store some of the excess production and sell some of it; page 490.

2. A price support increases farm incomes, but it is inefficient. The price is above the market equilibrium price, so a farmer produces more than the efficient quantity; page 492.

3. To protect the high domestic food prices created by price supports and quotas, nations

often restrict imports of food, which decreases world demand for farm products and depresses the price in world markets.

Price supports create stockpiles. Governments try to dispose of unwanted stocks by promoting food exports. So increased domestic production leads to an increase in supply in the rest of the world, which lowers the price in the rest of the world and lowers farm incomes in other countries.

Because most countries engage in these practices, the world market is oversupplied with food, and world prices are too low; page 494.

■ CHECKPOINT 20.3
Fill in the blanks

As we move farther away from the city centre, the price that someone is willing to pay for a hectare of land <u>decreases</u>. The <u>demand curve determines</u> the price of land. Cities grow for one fundamental reason, which is <u>technological change</u>. Because of congestion, the marginal social cost of a trip is <u>greater</u> than the marginal private cost. When tolls are used to achieve efficient road use, congestion <u>decreases, but it might not be eliminated</u>.

True or false

1. True; page 496
2. False; page 498
3. True; page 499
4. False; page 500
5. False; page 501

Multiple choice

1. d; page 496
2. c; page 497
3. b; page 497
4. d; page 498
5. b; page 498
6. c; page 499
7. a; page 499
8. d; page 501

Complete the graph

1a. Figure 20.6 shows the curves. The demand for urban land curve is D and the value of land in farming is S_0. The limits of the city are 12 kilometres from the centre; page 498.

■ **FIGURE 20.6**

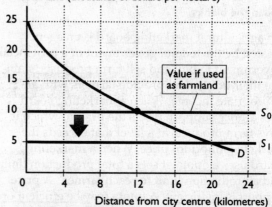

b. The value of land in farming decreases and the supply curve shifts downward from S_0 to S_1. The limits of the city are now 20 kilometres from the centre; page 498.

Short answer

1. As we move farther away from the city centre, the price that someone is wiling to pay for a hectare of land decreases because of the cost of transportation between the suburbs and the city centre. A longer commute makes people less willing to pay to live in a distant suburb; page 498.

2. One more vehicle on a road slows the trip for everyone and adds to everyone else's cost. So the marginal social cost exceeds the marginal private cost; page 500.

3. A toll can be introduced to find the new marginal private cost. The equilibrium number of vehicles decreases and the use of the road is efficient. Because marginal benefit changes throughout the day, to achieve an efficient outcome, tolls would need to vary by time of day; page 501

Chapter 21

International Financial Markets

CHAPTER IN PERSPECTIVE

Chapter 21 studies international accounts, what determines the balance of payments accounts, and how the value of the Canadian dollar is determined in the foreign exchange market.

■ **Describe a country's balance of payments accounts and explain what determines the amount of international borrowing and lending.**

The three balance of payments accounts are the current account, the capital account, and the official settlements account. The current account is a record of international receipts and payments—current account balance equals exports minus imports, plus net interest and transfers received from abroad. The capital account is a record of foreign investment in Canada minus Canadian investment abroad. The official settlements account is a record of the change in Canadian official reserves. The sum of the balances on the three accounts always equals zero. The rest of the world pays for its imports of Canadian goods and services in excess of Canada's imports from the rest of the world by borrowing from Canada. A net borrower is a country that is borrowing more from the rest of the world than it is lending to the rest of the world and a net lender is a country that is lending more to the rest of the world than it is borrowing from the rest of the world. A debtor nation is a country that during its entire history has borrowed more from the rest of the world than it has lent to it and a creditor nation is a country that during its entire history has invested more in the rest of the world than other countries have invested in it.

■ **Explain how the exchange rate is determined and why it fluctuates.**

Foreign currency is needed to buy goods or invest in another country. The foreign exchange rate is the price at which one currency exchanges for another and is determined by demand and supply in the foreign exchange market. The quantity of dollars demanded increases when the exchange rate falls. The demand for dollars changes and the demand curve for dollars shifts if the Canadian interest rate differential or the expected future exchange rate changes. The quantity of dollars supplied increases when the exchange rate rises. The supply of dollars changes and the supply curve of dollars shifts if the Canadian interest rate differential or the expected future exchange rate changes. At the equilibrium exchange rate, the quantity of dollars demanded equals the quantity of dollars supplied. The exchange is volatile because factors that change the demand also change the supply. Exchange rate expectations are influenced by purchasing power parity, a situation in which money buys the same amount of goods and services in different currencies, and interest rate parity, a situation in which the interest rate in one currency equals the interest rate in another currency when exchange rate changes are taken into account. The Bank of Canada can intervene directly in the foreign exchange market.

332 Part 7 · MICROECONOMIC POLICY ISSUES

EXPANDED CHAPTER CHECKLIST

When you have completed this chapter, you will be able to:

1 Describe a country's balance of payments accounts and explain what determines the amount of international borrowing and lending.

- Define the balance of payment accounts, the current account, the capital account, and the official settlements account.
- Define net borrower, net lender, creditor nation, and debtor nation.
- Discuss why Canada historically is a debtor nation and what Canada uses international borrowing for today.

2 Explain how the exchange rate is determined and why it fluctuates.

- Explain the role of the foreign exchange market.
- Define currency appreciation and currency depreciation.
- Discuss the relationship between the exchange rate and the quantity of dollars demanded.
- Explain how a change in the Canadian interest rate differential or in the expected future exchange rate change the demand for dollars.
- Discuss the relationship between the exchange rate and the quantity of dollars supplied.
- Explain how a change in the Canadian interest rate differential or in the expected future exchange rate change the supply of dollars.
- Illustrate equilibrium in the foreign exchange market and show how a change in the demand for dollars or supply of dollars changes the exchange rate.
- Explain how the Bank of Canada intervenes in the foreign exchange market.

KEY TERMS

- Balance of payments accounts (page 506)
- Canadian interest rate differential (page 514)
- Canadian official reserves (page 506)
- Capital account (page 506)
- Creditor nation (page 508)
- Currency appreciation (page 511)
- Currency depreciation (page 512)
- Current account (page 506)
- Debtor nation (page 508)
- Foreign exchange market (page 511)
- Foreign exchange rate (page 511)
- Interest rate parity (page 522)
- Net borrower (page 508)
- Net lender (page 508)
- Official settlements account (page 506)
- Purchasing power parity (page 520)

CHECKPOINT 21.1

■ Describe a country's balance of payments accounts and explain what determines the amount of international borrowing and lending.

Practice Problem 21.1

It is 2004 and the Canadian economy records the following transactions:

Imports of goods and services, $200 billion; interest paid to the rest of the world, $50 billion; interest received from the rest of the world, $40 billion; official settlements balance, $1 billion; net transfers, zero; capital account balance, $33 billion.

a. Calculate the current account balance and exports of goods and services.

b. Is Canada a debtor or a creditor nation in 2004?

c. If interest paid to the rest of the world increased by $10 billion, what happens to the current account balance?

Solution to Practice Problem 21.1

Problems such as this Practice Problem are straightforward to solve. Remember that the three balance of payments accounts are the current account, the capital account, and the official settlements account, and that the sum of the balances on these three accounts always equals zero.

Quick Review

- *Current account* The current account records receipts from the sale of goods and services to other countries (exports), minus payments for goods and services bought from other countries (imports), plus the net amount of interest and transfers (such as foreign aid payments) received from and paid to other countries.

  It is 2004 and the Canadian economy records the following transactions:

  Imports of goods and services, $200 billion; interest paid to the rest of the world, $50 billion; interest received from the rest of the world, $40 billion; official settlements balance, $1 billion; net transfers, zero; capital account balance, $33 billion.

a. Calculate the current account balance and exports of goods and services.

The current account balance, capital account balance, and official settlements balance sum to zero. So the current account balance is equal to the negative of the sum of the capital account balance and the official settlements balance. The current account balance equals –($33 billion + $1 billion), which is –$34 billion.

The current account balance equals exports minus imports plus net interest income plus net transfers. So exports equal the current account balance plus imports minus net interest income minus net transfers, which is –$34 billion + $200 billion – ($40 billion – $50 billion) + 0 = $176 billion.

b. **Is Canada a debtor or a creditor nation in 2004?**

Interest payments reflect the value of outstanding debts. Canada is a debtor nation because the value of interest payments received from the rest of the world is less than the value of interest payments made to the rest of the world.

c. **If interest paid to the rest of the world increased by $10 billion, what happens to the current account balance?**

If interest paid to the rest of the world increased by $10 billion, the current account balance decreases by $10 billion to –$44 billion.

Additional Practice Problem 21.1a

Suppose the official settlements account balance equals zero. In this case, what is the relationship between the current account and the capital account? Why does this relationship exist?

Solution to Additional Practice Problem 21.1a

If the official settlements account balance equals zero, then a deficit in the current account equals the surplus in the capital account or the surplus in the current account equals the deficit in the capital account. This relationship exists because the sum of the balances on the current account, the capital account, and the official settlements account equals zero. If the official settlements account equals zero, the current account balance equals the negative of the capital account balance.

■ Self Test 21.1

Fill in the blanks

The ____ (current; capital) account records payments for the imports of goods and services. The ____ (current; capital; official settlements) account records foreign investment in Canada minus Canadian investment abroad. The sum of the balances of the current account, capital account, and the official settlements account always equals ____ (1; real GDP; zero). Canada is a ____ (debtor; creditor) nation. Canada is borrowing for ____ (consumption; investment).

True or false

1. If foreign investment in Canada increases, and Canadian investment in the rest of the world decreases, the current account shows an increase in exports and a decrease in imports.
2. The official settlements account balance is positive if Canada's official reserves decrease.
3. In the year 2000, Canada had a current account surplus.
4. If Canada has a surplus in its capital account and a deficit in its current account, the balance in its official settlements account is zero.
5. In 2000, Canada was a net lender and a debtor nation.
6. If a country starts to run a current account surplus, which continues indefinitely, it would immediately become a net lender and would eventually become a creditor nation.
7. Canada is a debtor nation.
8. In 2000, Canadian borrowing from abroad financed investment.

Multiple choice

1. A country's balance of payments accounts records its
   a. tax receipts and expenditures.
   b. tariffs and nontariff revenue and government purchases.
   c. international trading, borrowing, and lending.
   d. international exports and imports and nothing else.

2. All the following are balance of payments accounts EXCEPT the
   a. capital account.
   b. labour account.
   c. official settlements account.
   d. current account.

3. Which balance of payments account records payments for imports and receipts for exports?
   a. current account
   b. capital account
   c. official settlements account
   d. reserves account

4. The current account balance is equal to
   a. imports − exports + net interest + net transfers.
   b. imports − exports + net interest − net transfers.
   c. exports − imports − net interest + net transfers.
   d. exports − imports + net interest + net transfers.

5. If an investment of $100 million from the United Kingdom is made Canada, the $100 million is listed as a ____ entry in the ____ account.
   a. positive; current
   b. negative; capital
   c. positive; capital
   d. negative; current

6. If Canada receives $20 billion of foreign investment and at the same time invests $16 billion abroad, then the Canadian
   a. capital account balance increases by $4 billion.
   b. current account must be in surplus.
   c. balance of payments must be negative.
   d. capital account balance decreases by $4 billion.

7. In the balance of payments accounts, changes in Canadian official reserves are recorded in the
   a. current account.
   b. capital account.
   c. official settlements account.
   d. international currency account.

8. If a country has a current account balance of $100 billion and the official settlements account balance equals zero, then the country's capital account balance must be
   a. equal to $100 billion.
   b. positive but not necessarily equal to $100 billion.
   c. equal to –$100 billion.
   d. negative but not necessarily equal to –$100 billion.

9. A country that is borrowing more from the rest of the world than it is lending to the rest of the world is called a
   a. net lender.
   b. net borrower.
   c. net debtor.
   d. net creditor.

10. A debtor nation is a country that
    a. borrows more from the rest of the world than it lends to it.
    b. lends more to the rest of the world than it borrows from it.
    c. during its entire history has invested more in the rest of the world than other countries have invested in it.
    d. during its entire history has borrowed more from the rest of the world than it has lent to it.

11. Borrowing and lending are _____, and debts are _____.
    a. flows; flows
    b. flows; stocks
    c. stocks; flows
    d. stocks; stocks

12. Canada's international borrowing is financing
    a. private and public investment.
    b. private consumption.
    c. government expenditure.
    d. private and public saving.

Short answer

1. What is recorded in Canada's current account? In its capital account? In its official settlements account?

2. If the official settlements account balance equals zero, what will a country's capital account balance equal if it has a $350 billion current account deficit?

3. The table has balance of payment data for Canada in 1998.

Item	(billions of dollars)
Canadian investment abroad	44
Exports of goods and services	368
Net transfers	1
Official settlements account balance	−7
Net interest	−29
Foreign investment in Canada	66

a. What is the capital account balance?
b. What is the current account balance?
c. What is the value of imports of goods and services?

4. What is a net borrower? A debtor nation? Is it possible for a nation to be net borrower and yet not be a debtor nation?

CHECKPOINT 21.2

■ **Explain how the exchange rate is determined and why it fluctuates.**

Practice Problem 21.2

Suppose that yesterday, the Canadian dollar was trading on the foreign exchange market at 68 U.S. cents per dollar. Today, the Canadian dollar is trading at 70 U.S. cents per dollar.

a. Which of the two currencies (the Canadian dollar or the U.S. dollar) has appreciated and which has depreciated today?
b. List the events that could have caused today's change in the value of the Canadian dollar on the foreign exchange market.
c. Did the events that you listed in part (b) change the demand for Canadian dollars, the supply of Canadian dollars, or both the demand for and supply of Canadian dollars?
d. If the Bank of Canada had tried to stabilize the value of the Canadian dollar at 68 U.S. cents per dollar, what action would it have taken?
e. In part (d), what effect would the Bank of Canada's actions have had on Canadian official reserves?

Solution to Practice Problem 21.2

To solve this Practice Problem, remember that the demand for and supply of Canadian dollars changes when the Canadian interest rate differential changes and when the expected future exchange rate changes.

Quick Review

- *Canadian interest rate differential* On the foreign exchange market, an increase in the Canadian interest rate differential, which is the Canadian interest rate minus the foreign interest rate increases the demand for Canadian dollars and decreases the supply of Canadian dollars.

- *Expected future exchange rate* On the foreign exchange market, a rise in the expected future exchange rate increases the demand for Canadian dollars and decreases the supply of Canadian dollars.

Suppose that yesterday, the Canadian dollar was trading on the foreign exchange market at 68 U.S. cents per dollar. Today, the Canadian dollar is trading at 70 U.S. cents per dollar.

a. **Which of the two currencies (the Canadian dollar or the U.S. dollar) has appreciated and which has depreciated today?**

The Canadian dollar has risen from 68 U.S. cents per dollar yesterday to 70 U.S. cents per dollar today. There has been a rise in the value of the Canadian dollar in terms of the U.S. dollar. The Canadian dollar has appreciated. The U.S. dollar has depreciated because it buys fewer Canadian dollars.

b. **List the events that could have caused today's change in the value of the Canadian dollar on the foreign exchange market.**

The factors that change the demand for and supply of Canadian dollars are the Canadian interest rate differential and the expected future exchange rate. Because the Canadian dollar rose in value, an increase in the Canadian interest rate differential, which could be the result of either a rise in the Canadian interest rate or a fall in the U.S. interest rate, or a rise in the expected future exchange rate could be the events that changed the value of the dollar.

c. **Did the events that you listed in part (b) change the demand for Canadian dollars, the supply of Canadian dollars, or both the demand for and supply of Canadian dollars?**

The events changed *both* the demand for Canadian dollars and the supply of Canadian dollars. Both events increased the demand for Canadian dollars and decreased the supply of Canadian dollars.

d. **If the Bank of Canada had tried to stabilize the value of the Canadian dollar at 68 U.S. cents per dollar, what action would it have taken?**

The Canadian dollar increased in value. To prevent the Canadian dollar from rising in value, the Bank of Canada would have sold dollars to increase the supply of dollars and keep the value at 68 U.S. cents per dollar.

e. **In part (d), what effect would the Bank of Canada's actions have had on Canadian official reserves?**

In part (d), when the Bank of Canada sells Canadian dollars it buys foreign currency. Canadian official reserves would have increased.

Additional Practice Problem 21.2a

How and why does an increase in the expected future exchange rate change the demand for Canadian dollars and the demand curve for dollars? How and why does an increase in the expected future exchange rate change the supply of Canadian dollars and the supply curve of dollars? What is the effect on the equilibrium exchange rate?

Solution to Additional Practice Problem 21.2a

An increase in the expected future exchange rate increases the demand for Canadian dollars and shifts the demand curve for dollars rightward.

The demand for dollars increases because at the current exchange rate people want to buy Canadian dollars now and sell them in the future at the higher expected exchange rate. An increase in the expected future exchange rate decreases the supply of Canadian dollars and shifts the supply curve of dollars leftward. The supply of dollars decreases because people prefer to keep Canadian dollars until they can sell them in the future at the higher expected exchange rate. Because the demand for dollars increases and the supply of dollars decreases, the equilibrium exchange rises.

■ Self Test 21.2

Fill in the blanks

The price at which one currency exchanges for another is called a foreign _____ (exchange; interest) rate. If the dollar falls in value against the Mexican peso, the dollar has _____ (appreciated; depreciated). An increase in the demand for dollars shifts the demand curve for dollars _____ (leftward; rightward) and an increase in the supply of dollars shifts the supply curve of dollars _____ (leftward; rightward). The exchange rate is volatile because supply and demand in the foreign exchange market _____ (are; are not) independent of each other. An increase in the expected future exchange rate _____ (raises; lowers) the equilibrium exchange rate. Purchasing power parity is equal value of _____ (interest rates; money). If the Bank of Canada buys dollars on the foreign exchange market, the exchange rate _____ (rises; falls).

True or false

1. The foreign exchange market is located in London, England.

2. If the exchange rate increases from 78 yen per Canadian dollar to 84 yen per Canadian dollar, the dollar has appreciated.

3. The larger the value of Canadian exports, the larger is the quantity of Canadian dollars demanded.

4. An increase in the Canadian exchange rate increases the supply of Canadian dollars and shifts the supply curve of dollars rightward.

5. A rise in the expected future exchange rate increases the demand for dollars and the supply of dollars and might raise or lower the exchange rate.

6. The equilibrium Canadian exchange rate is the exchange rate that sets the quantity of Canadian dollars demanded equal to the quantity of Canadian dollars supplied.

7. An increase in the Canadian interest rate differential raises the Canadian exchange rate.

8. To prevent the price of the euro from falling, the European Central Bank might sell euros on the foreign exchange market.

Multiple choice

1. The foreign exchange market is the market in which
a. all international transactions occur.
b. currencies are exchanged solely by governments.
c. goods are exchanged between governments.
d. the currency of one country is exchanged for the currency of another.

2. When E.D. Smith, a Canadian company, purchases Mexican strawberries, E.D. Smith pays for the strawberries with
a. Canadian dollars.
b. Mexican pesos.
c. gold.
d. Mexican goods and services.

3. If today the exchange rate is 64 U.S. cents per Canadian dollar and tomorrow the exchange rate is 63 U.S. cents per Canadian dollar, then the Canadian dollar ____ and the U.S. dollar ____.
a. appreciated; appreciated
b. appreciated; depreciated
c. depreciated; appreciated
d. depreciated; depreciated

4. In the foreign exchange market, as the Canadian exchange rate rises, other things remaining the same, the
a. quantity of Canadian dollars demanded increases.
b. demand curve for Canadian dollars shifts rightward.
c. demand curve for Canadian dollars shifts leftward.
d. quantity of Canadian dollars demanded decreases.

5. In the foreign exchange market, the demand curve for Canadian dollars shifts rightward if the
a. Canadian interest rate differential increases.
b. expected future exchange rate falls.
c. foreign interest rate rises.
d. Canadian interest rate falls.

6. As the exchange rate ____ the quantity supplied of Canadian dollars ____.
a. rises; increases
b. falls; increases
c. falls; remains the same
d. rises; decreases

7. In the foreign exchange market, the supply curve of dollars is
   a. upward sloping.
   b. downward sloping.
   c. vertical.
   d. horizontal.

8. In the foreign exchange market if the _____ the supply of Canadian dollars increases.
   a. U.S. interest rate rises.
   b. expected future exchange rate rises.
   c. Canadian interest rate rises.
   d. Canadian interest rate differential increases.

9. When there is a shortage of Canadian dollars in the foreign exchange market, the
   a. demand curve for Canadian dollars shifts leftward to restore the equilibrium.
   b. Canadian exchange rate will appreciate.
   c. Canadian exchange rate will depreciate.
   d. supply curve of Canadian dollars shifts leftward to restore the equilibrium.

10. In the foreign exchange market, when the Canadian interest rate rises, the supply of Canadian dollars _____ and the foreign exchange rate _____.
    a. increases; rises
    b. increases; falls
    c. decreases; rises
    d. decreases; falls

11. A situation in which money buys the same amount of goods and services in different currencies is called
    a. exchange rate equilibrium.
    b. purchasing power parity.
    c. exchange rate surplus.
    d. exchange rate balance.

12. Interest rate parity occurs when
    a. the interest rate in one currency equals the interest rate in another currency when exchange rate changes are taken into account.
    b. interest rate differentials are always maintained across nations.
    c. interest rates are equal across nations.
    d. prices are equal across nations when exchange rates are taken into account.

Complete the graph

1. Figure 21.1 shows the foreign exchange market for Canadian dollars.

■ **FIGURE 21.1**

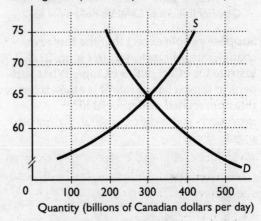

a. What is the equilibrium exchange rate?
b. The Canadian interest differential rises. In Figure 21.1, illustrate the effect of this change. What happens to the exchange rate?

2. Figure 21.2 shows the foreign exchange market for Canadian dollars.

FIGURE 21.2

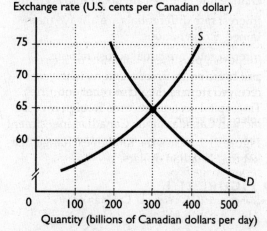

Suppose people expect that the future exchange rate will be lower. In Figure 21.2, illustrate the effect of this change. What happens to the exchange rate? Has the exchange rate appreciated or depreciated?

Short answer

1. If the exchange rate rises from 63 U.S. cents per Canadian dollar to 65 U.S. cents per Canadian dollar, has the Canadian dollar appreciated or depreciated? Has the U.S. dollar appreciated or depreciated?

2. What is the relationship between the value of Canadian exports and the quantity of Canadian dollars demanded? Why does this relationship exist?

3. What is the relationship between the value of Canadian imports and the quantity of Canadian dollars supplied? Why does this relationship exist?

4. How will a rise in the U.S. interest rate, everything else remaining the same, affect the demand for Canadian dollars, the supply of Canadian dollars, and the Canadian exchange rate?

5. If the Bank of Canada believes the exchange rate is too low and wants to raise it, what action does the Bank undertake in the foreign exchange market? What limits the extent to which the Bank can undertake this action?

SELF TEST ANSWERS

■ CHECKPOINT 21.1

Fill in the blanks

The <u>current</u> account records payments for the imports of goods and services. The <u>capital</u> account records foreign investment in Canada minus Canadian investment abroad. The sum of the balances of the current account, capital account, and the official settlements account always equals <u>zero</u>. Canada is a <u>debtor</u> nation. Canada is borrowing for <u>investment</u>.

True or false

1. False; page 506
2. True; page 506
3. True; page 506
4. False; page 506
5. True; page 508
6. True; page 508
7. True; page 509
8. True; page 509

Multiple choice

1. c; page 506
2. b; page 506
3. a; page 506
4. d; page 506
5. c; page 506
6. a; page 506
7. c; page 506
8. c; page 506
9. b; page 508
10. d; page 508
11. b; pages 508-509
12. a; page 509

Short answer

1. The current account records receipts from the sale of goods and services to other countries (exports), minus payments for goods and services bought from other countries (imports), plus the net amount of interest and transfers (such as foreign aid payments) received from and paid to other countries. The capital account records foreign investment in Canada minus Canadian investment abroad. The official settlements account records the change in Canada's official reserves; page 506.

2. The current account balance plus capital account balance plus the official settlements account balance sum to zero. So if the official settlements account balance equals zero, a $350 billion current account deficit means there is a $350 billion capital account surplus; page 506.

3. a. The capital account balance equals foreign investment in Canada, $66 billion, minus Canadian investment abroad, $44 billion, which is $22 billion; page 506.

   b. The sum of the current account balance, the capital account balance, and the official settlements account balance is zero. The capital account balance is $22 billion and the official settlements account balance is –$7 billion, so the current account balance is –$15 billion; page 506.

   c. The current account balance equals exports minus imports plus net interest and transfers received from abroad. Imports equal exports plus net interest plus transfers minus the current account balance, which is $368 billion –$29 billion +$1 billion + $15 billion = $355 billion; page 506.

4. A net borrower is a country that is borrowing more from the rest of the world than it is lending to the rest of the world. A debtor nation is a country that during its entire history has borrowed more from the rest of the

world than it has lent to it. It is possible for a nation to be a net borrower but not be a debtor nation. A country can be a creditor nation and a net borrower. This situation occurs if a creditor nation is, during a particular year, borrowing more from the rest of the world than it is lending to the rest of the world; page 508.

■ CHECKPOINT 21.2

Fill in the blanks

The price at which one currency exchanges for another is called a foreign <u>exchange</u> rate. If the dollar falls in value against the Mexican peso, the dollar has <u>depreciated</u>. An increase in the demand for dollars shifts the demand curve for dollars <u>rightward</u> and an increase in the supply of dollars shifts the supply curve of dollars <u>rightward</u>. The exchange rate is volatile because supply and demand in the foreign exchange market <u>are not</u> independent of each other. An increase in the expected future exchange rate <u>raises</u> the equilibrium exchange rate. Purchasing power parity is equal value of <u>money</u>. If the Bank of Canada buys dollars on the foreign exchange market, the exchange rate <u>rises</u>.

True or false

1. False; page 511
2. True; page 511
3. True; page 512
4. False; page 515
5. False; pages 513, 516
6. True; page 518
7. True; page 519
8. False; page 522

Multiple choice

1. d; page 511
2. b; page 511
3. c; pages 511-512
4. d; page 512
5. a; page 514
6. a; page 515
7. a; pages 515-516
8. a; page 517
9. b; page 518
10. c; pages 517-518
11. b; page 520
12. a; page 522

Complete the graph

1. a. In Figure 21.3 the equilibrium exchange rate is 65 U.S. cents per Canadian dollar at the intersection of the D_0 and S_0 curves; page 518.

   b. The increase in the Canadian interest rate differential increases the demand for Canadian dollars and decreases the supply of Canadian dollars. In Figure 21.3, the demand curve shifts rightward from D_0 to D_1 and the supply curve shifts leftward from S_0 to S_1. The exchange rate rises. In the figure, the exchange rate rises to 70 U.S. cents per Canadian dollar; page 519.

■ FIGURE 21.3
Exchange rate (U.S. cents per Canadian dollar)

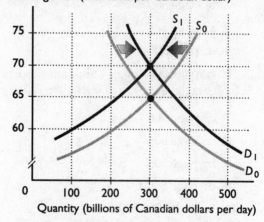

2. The fall in the expected future exchange rate decreases the demand for Canadian dollars and increases the supply of Cana-

dian dollars. In Figure 21.4 the demand curve shifts leftward from D_0 to D_1 and the supply curve shifts rightward from S_0 to S_1. The exchange rate falls from 65 U.S. cents per dollar to 60 U.S. cents per dollar. The exchange rate depreciates; page 519.

■ **FIGURE 21.4**

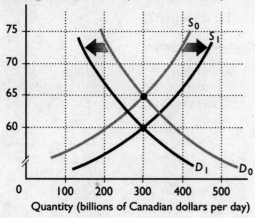

Short answer

1. When the exchange rate rises from 63 U.S. cents per Canadian dollar to 65 U.S. cents per Canadian dollar, the Canadian dollar appreciates because one Canadian dollar buys more U.S. dollars. The U.S. dollar depreciates because it now takes 65 U.S. cents to buy a Canadian dollar instead of 63 U.S. cents; pages 511-512.

2. The larger the value of Canadian exports, the larger is the quantity of Canadian dollars demanded. This relationship exists because Canadian firms want to be paid for their goods and services in Canadian dollars; page 512.

3. The larger the value of Canadian imports, the larger the quantity of Canadian dollars supplied. This relationship exists because Canadian consumers must pay for their imports in foreign currency. To obtain foreign currency, Canadian consumers supply Canadian dollars; page 513.

4. An increase in the U.S. interest rate decreases the Canadian interest rate differential. The smaller the Canadian interest rate differential, the smaller is the demand for Canadian assets and the smaller the demand for Canadian dollars.

   The smaller the Canadian interest rate differential, the greater is the demand for foreign assets and the greater is the supply of Canadian dollars.

   So when the U.S. interest rate rises, the demand for Canadian dollars decreases, the supply of Canadian dollars increases, and the equilibrium exchange rate falls; page 519.

5. If the Bank of Canada wants to raise the exchange rate, it will buy Canadian dollars to decrease supply. The Bank sells Canadian official reserves to buy Canadian dollars. The Bank is limited by its quantity of official reserves. If the Bank persists in this action, eventually it will run out of foreign currency; page 522.